CyberEthics

Terry Halbert, J.D.

Professor of Legal Studies

Temple University Fox School of Business & Management

Philadelphia, Pennsylvania

Elaine Ingulli, J.D., L.L.M.

Professor of Business

Richard Stockton College

Pomona, New Jersey

THOMSON

SOUTH-WESTERN

WEST

Australia · Canada · Mexico · Singapore · Spain · United Kingdom · United States

THOMSON

SOUTH-WESTERN

WEST

CyberEthics, 2e
Terry Halbert and Elaine Ingulli

VP/Editorial Director:
Jack W. Calhoun

VP/Editor-in-Chief:
George Werthman

Publisher:
Rob Dewey

Acquisitions Editor:
Steven Silverstein, Esq.

Developmental Editor:
Craig Avery

Marketing Manager:
Lisa Lysne

Production Editor:
Chris Sears

Technology Project Editor:
Christine Wittmer

Manufacturing Coordinator:
Rhonda Utley

Production House:
D&G Limited

Cover Designer:
Anne Marie Rekow

Cover Images:
© **Digital Vision**

Internal Designer:
Anne Marie Rekow

Printer:
Thomson-West
Eagan, MN

Contents

Chapter 1: Intellectual Property & Cyberspace

ETHICS CASE: NAPSTER 2

INTELLECTUAL PROPERTY LAW 3

U.S. Copyright Law Highlights 5

"Code" and Intellectual Property 4

The Law of the Horse: What Cyberlaw Might Teach, Lawrence Lessig 6

PERSPECTIVES ON NAPSTER 10

Industry 10

Address Before Members of the U.S. Congress, Michael Eisner, Chairman
& CEO, The Walt Disney Company 11

Musicians 15

Courtney Love Does the Math 16

Cybertarians 18

The Economy of Ideas: A Framework for Patents and Copyrights in the
Digital Age, John Perry Barlow 18

The Hacker Ethic & The Ten Commandments of Computer Ethics 23

ETHICAL ANALYSIS 24

Utilitarianism 24

Moral Rights and Duties 30

CYBERSPACE: NEW WORLD, NEW LAW? 35

Napster, Jefferson's Moose, and the Law of Cyberspace, David G. Post 35

CHAPTER PROBLEMS 38

Chapter 2: Privacy & Information Technology

ETHICS CASE: GENETIC TESTING IN 2007 44

SURVEILLANCE AT WORK 46

E-mail Interception 46

Michael A. Smyth v. The Pillsbury Company, United States District Court, 1996 46

Electronic Surveillance: The Debate 48

Electronic Surveillance: The Law 49

THE VALUE OF PRIVACY 50

The Functions of Privacy, Alan Westin 50

COUNTERTERRORISM: SECURITY VS. PRIVACY 54

Get Ready for PATRIOT II, Matt Welch 55

Terrorism Information Awareness, DARPA 57

A National Identity Card? 60

Spying for Fun and Profit, Kari Lydersen 61

PRIVACY & TRANSPARENCY 65

The Transparent Society, Interview with David Brin 66

Government Information Awareness, http://opengov.media.mit.edu 70

PRIVACY FOR ONLINE CONSUMERS 72

Privacy in the Digital Age: Work in Progress, Jerry Berman & Deidre Mulligan 72

Buyer Beware, Jonah Engle 75

What Cyberspace Knows About You 77

PRIVACY IN MEDICAL INFORMATION 78

The New Enemy of Privacy, Amitai Etzioni 78

CHAPTER PROBLEMS 82

Chapter 3: Cyberspeech

ETHICS CASE: BIG LIBEL 87

Freedom of Expression 90

From *Hit Man to Encyclopedia of Jihad:* How to Distinguish Freedom
of Speech from Terrorist Training, Rodney A. Smolla 92

CYBERSMEARING 95

Corporate Cybersmear, Margo E.K.Reder & Christine Neylon O'Brien 96

Cyberhoax: Word for Word/Tweaking the W.T.O., Barnaby Feder 99

ANONYMITY ONLINE 104

Internet Anonymity, David L. Sobel 104

A Right to Read Anonymously: A Closer Look at "Copyright Management" in
Cyberspace, Julie E. Cohen 105

BUILDING IN RESTRICTIONS: FILTERS, EDITORS AND NETIQUETTE 107

Symposium: Should Cyberspace be a Free Speech Zone? Filters,
"Family Friendliness," and the First Amendment 108

The Library Bill of Rights 114

Freedom of Speech in Cyberspace, Eugene Volokh 115

CYBERSPEAKING ABOUT RACE & GENDER 118

Contents v

Erasing Race? A Critical Race Feminist View of Internet Identity-shifting, Margaret Chon 118
HATE SPEECH, CYBER-HARASSMENT AND STALKING .121
Sexual Harassment in Cyberspace: Unwelcome E-mail, David K. McGraw 123
Romantic and Electronic Stalking in a College Context, Rebecca K. Lee 125
CYBERNORMS 130
Role Playing: Cyberharm Scenarios 130
Netiquette, April Mara Major 131
CHAPTER PROBLEMS 134

Chapter 4: E-Commerce

ETHICS CASE: ONLINE PILLS.COM 137
DIRECT-TO-CONSUMER SALES ONLINE 139
Online Pharmaceuticals 140
Statement of FDA Commissioner, Jane Henney, MD, U.S. Senate Committee of Health, Education, Labor and Pensions 141
TRUST IN CYBERSPACE 145
Securing Trust Online: Wisdom or Oxymoron, Helen Nissenbaum 145
Word of Mouse 152
From Word of Mouth to Word of Mouse, Business Wire .152
FIGHTING SPAM 153
Anti-Spam Legislation & the First Amendment 154
Anti-Spam Measures, Electronic Frontier Foundation 154
DOT-CONS & CYBERSWINDLES: FRAUD IN CYBERSPACE 157
FTC: Online Scams 157
ONLINE TOBACCO SALES 159
Tobacco Commerce on the Internet, Joanna E. Cohen, Vivian Sarabia, & Mary Jane Ashley 160
The Ad-Free Ad 164
CLICK WRAP LICENSES AND THE UCITA DEBATE 165
Why We Oppose UCITA, Americans for Fair Electronic Commerce Transactions 167
Why We Must Fight UCITA, Richard Stallman 169
Special Project: Re-Drafting UCITA 170
E-Mediation 171
Mediation in Cyberspace, Richard Birke & Louise Ellen Teitz 172
CHAPTER PROBLEMS 176

Chapter 5: E-Learning and The Business of Education

ETHICS CASE: SHARING OR CHEATING? 179
ACADEMIC HONESTY IN CYBERSPACE 181

But I Wasn't Cheating: Plagiarism and Cross-cultural
Mythology, Lise Buranen 182

Plagiarism, Norms and the Limits of Theft Law, Stuart P. Green 185

Collaborative Research, Rochelle Cooper Dreyfuss 190

Plagiarism, Copyright and Authorship 193

Stolen Content: Avoiding Trouble on the Internet, Jane C. Ginsburg 194

DISTANCE LEARNING 197

Perseus Unbound, Sven Birkerts 198

The Remaking of the American University, Arthur Levine 201

What the Research Shows 203

Breaching the Canyon Walls: Bringing the World to Isolated Reservations 204

THE DIGITAL DIVIDE 206

Just the Facts, National Commission on Web-Based Education 206

Diversity, Distance & the Delivery of Higher Education, Rachel Moran 208

Bridging the Divide: MIT Open Courseware Project 212

BUSINESS & EDUCATION IN CYBERSPACE: A HEALTHY PARTNERSHIP? 213

Partners Not Rivals, Martha Minow 215

ANOTHER GLANCE AT THE INTERNET: STUDENT USE OR ABUSE? 218

Role Playing: Guidelines for Internet Use 221

CHAPTER PROBLEMS 222

Chapter 6: Democracy, the Market and Cyberspace

ETHICS CASE: WHO'S IN CHARGE? HACKING AND CRACKING 225

OPEN SOURCE SOFTWARE 227

The Hacker's Ethic, Pekka Himanen 228

Microsoft: The Power of the Market 230

New Platforms for Communication: WiFi 232

GOVERNING IN CYBERSPACE 235

From Trademark to Domain Name 235

Internet Domain Names: Chronology of Control 236

Law and Borders—the Rise of Law in Cyberspace, David R. Johnson
& David Post 238

Governing the Internet, James Boyle 241

Impeach the Internet! Viktor Mayer-Schonberger 244

THE DIGITAL DIVIDE 246

The Dependence of Cyberspace, Amy Lynne Bomse 246

The Future of the Net, Reed Hundt 250

Western Frontier or Feudal Society? Alfred C. Yen 252

Contents   vii

DEMOCRACY AND THE INTERNET 256

Alienation 257

Massachusetts, Burma and the WTO: A Commentary on Blacklisting, Federalism,
and Internet Advocacy in the Global Trading Era, Peter L. Fitzgerald 259

Smart Mobs 264

The Dot.Com(munist) Revolution: Will the Internet Bring Democracy
to China, S. David Cooper 264

Cyber-Activism Assignment 268

Internet Campaign, Peter Overby Reporting 268

Privacy and Democracy in Cyberspace, Paul M. Schwartz 270

CHAPTER PROBLEMS 273

INDEX 277

Preface

Now more than ever—in education, business, and daily life—wherever we live in the global community, we make choices that have cyberethical consequences. Preparing students for independent thought and analysis in this new environment is what *CyberEthics* is all about.

Information technology is changing virtually everything: Not just the speed with which we communicate, but how we learn, how we create knowledge in our disciplines. Not just the variety of our cultural products, but the way we perceive them and the way we perceive ourselves. The tentacles of this transformation reach everywhere—how we behave as political beings, how we create economic value, how we get to know one another. It is the depth and breadth of this shifting reality we must face; we need to gather our wits, reflect on the values that we care about most, and find ways to respond to the Information Revolution.

One crucially important arena for such reflection is higher education. In the 1970s and 1980s, the Internet was pioneered by academics, scientists who were enthused about its potential for creating research communities beyond their original time-space boundaries. Academics are today in the front lines in this sense: while most of our students have grown up in a networked world, and can teach us a thing or two, they need our help in thinking critically about the moral shape of the world technology is creating. We may not know definitive answers—in fact, we probably can't have any. But what we can do is open the conversation, in our classrooms, to some of the major crunch-points, those places where we ask: Are these the changes we want? Is this what will allow human societies to flourish?

CROSS DISCIPLINARY APPROACH

This book is suitable for any course that deals with cyberspace and the way in which it is changing our culture. Currently, such courses are being generated from a variety of academic fields—business, economics, law, education, engineering, computer science, political science, sociology, philosophy, media studies and literature, for example. They tend to be cross-disciplinary, spanning traditional divisions between the humanities, social sciences and hard sciences. In fact, new courses that address cyber-culture are emerging every year throughout higher education, and for most of them *CyberEthics* would be an excellent choice. Below we explain why.

The readings in *CyberEthics* have been carefully culled from a wide range of sources. We have included nearly all of the most influential cyber-experts, such as intellectual property law scholars Lawrence Lessig and David Post, cybertarians John Perry Barlow and Richard Stallman, feminist scholars Helen Nissenbaum and Julie Cohen. But we have included too the voices of Disney CEO Michael Eisner, musician Courtney Love, and literary essayist Sven Birkerts. *CyberEthics* is pitched to bright, curious minds, and so broadly inclusive that, whatever the background of the instructors or students who use this book, it will be in some ways familiar.

INSPIRING CRITICAL THINKING

CyberEthics spans a broad range of political and philosophical viewpoints. In it, we hear from libertarians, communitarians, the ACLU, cyber-anarchists, federal regulators, social conservatives, feminists, e-executives, media editorialists, artists, and students. It's an exciting brew, a mix designed to prompt deep thinking and well-reasoned argument. Successful teaching is often based on lively debate, the kind that evolves once students have developed committed views that they wish to defend. We have written a book with the goal of fomenting such an atmosphere in every teaching moment.

CASE STUDY "CRUNCH-POINTS"

Each chapter of this book begins with a story—a case scenario that introduces one of the "crunch-points" where technology meets ethics. A music fan is using Napster at the start of chapter 1; chapter 2 opens with a biotech company requiring its employees to be genetically tested. There are many good cyberethics stories, and we have included a spectrum of the newest, most compelling examples, to stimulate student interest, and point them toward deeper inquiry.

- Chapter 1 takes Napster as its focus, and looks at intellectual property, and at the tension between traditional proprietary rights to artistic output, and cyber-culture, where sharing is free and instantaneous.
- Chapter 2 asks what has become of privacy in the information age, as it assesses the new surveillance capacity of corporations and government.
- Chapter 3 opens with cybersmearing of corporations, and then explores cyber-harassment and cyberstalking: How do we filter or limit expression online without chilling it?
- Chapter 4 addresses e-commerce: the way online marketing—of pharmaceuticals, of tobacco, of pornography—can be troubling. We look at Internet fraud, at click wrap licensing, and ask how we can create trust in e-business.

- Chapter 5 focuses on education issues: distance learning, and the digital divide.
- Chapter 6 begins with the problem of hacking, moves on to consider competition in the computer world (Open-source ware and WiFi), then widens its lens to look both at governance of the Internet and at how the Internet is affecting democracy itself.

CYBERETHICS: A UNIFYING THEME

To frame cyberethics as an overall theme, we gave it concentrated attention in chapter 1, bringing the reader through a detailed analysis of the Napster dilemma from a utilitarian and then a deontological perspective. Although there are limits to the usefulness of cleaving to traditional moral philosophy when your problems are the ever-moving targets of cyberethics, we do believe that, in this way, we launch students with a structure that they can reference repeatedly through the rest of the book. As they confront new cyberethics dilemmas, they will be able to refer to the basic theoretical models, and find their balance before moving into more open discussion. It couldn't hurt to have our students recognize that, for centuries, people have been struggling to find a path towards "doing the right thing," that it has never been easy to discover answers to questions like those raised in this book: What do we mean by creativity? Ownership? Identity? Privacy? Democracy? Education? Freedom? Equality? Fairness?

TEACHING TOOLKIT

This book is designed to teach skills: how to read and write critically, how to discuss, debate and persuade. We assume that every student can be motivated to chase down a good question, and have conceived our job as a matter of laying out good questions, of equipping students with enough information to sustain their curiosity without giving them so much that they feel there is nothing left to discover.

INTERNET ASSIGNMENTS

CyberEthics is sprinkled with dozens of tasks for students to complete online. Some include a suggested Web site address; others allow a variety of starting points for using the Internet effectively. For example, readers will be guided to Web sites that contain information about:

- government
- nonprofit organizations
- cyberlaw
- news
- cyber-terminology

Many of these assignments involve a multi-step process: students are asked to track down information to see where it leads, analyze it, or follow it to the point where they can interact with the information source.

INTERACTIVITY

We believe in hands-on, interactive learning, and have designed several assignments for students to work together, and experience the material directly. Examples:

- Students are asked to revise their school policy for monitoring e-mail
- Groups assess the degree of harm in cyberharassment and cyberstalking cases
- Role-players negotiate new contract rules for e-commerce
- Students search the Internet for personal information about themselves

SUPPLEMENTARY LEARNING AND WEB RESOURCES

The *CyberEthics* Web site at http://www.halbert.westbuslaw.com contains links for the Internet exercises and to other Internet addresses throughout the text. It also provides easy access to other West Legal Studies Web pages and links, such as updates for relevant legal cases.

THANKS

We thank Mary Ann Trail and Carolyn Gutierrez, Stockton College research librarians extraordinaire, inevitably creative and prompt in their responses to every plea for help.

We thank colleagues and friends who have helped us with feedback, insight and encouragement, especially Lucy Katz, Mike Olan, Linda Feeney and David Post. Once again we thank Gray McCord, computer professional—Elaine's brother in law— who helped unravel the mysteries of WiFi.

We thank the many bright, savvy students who pitched in so enthusiastically, especially the students in Stockton's seminar in Cyberethics/Cyberculture and Carrie Tolerico and Josh Olmstead of Temple.

At West Publishing, we thank Rob Dewey, Steve Silverstein, and Craig Avery for encouraging us to keep the faith through round two of this project. Craig, our developmental editor, was especially valuable not only as an overall guide but as a critical reader and writer. Also a delight at West was Chris Sears, who as our production editor amazed us by being consistently patient and upbeat, even under fire. We also wish to thank our designer, Anne Marie Rekow, for her sense of style and flair.

We thank our many anonymous e-survey respondents, whose judgment about prospective new topics, features, and our ongoing focus informed and energized the revision.

We thank Jeanne Calderon (New York University) for her enthusiastic and helpful comments that stimulated us to revise; Nick LaManna (New England Institute of Technology), for his detailed evaluation of the first edition; Lori Harris-Ransom (Caldwell College) for her perceptive comments; Nivea R. Castro Figueroa (University of Phoenix, Upper Iowa University, and Kaplan College) for her thoughts about teaching and using the text for online classes; and Maurice Tonissi (Quisigamond Community College) for his useful critique.

And once again, we thank each other. Let's hear it for the eros of work!

ACKNOWLEDGMENTS

We thank all of the authors and publishers who have generously allowed us to reprint their work with permission.

BOOKS

"Perseus Unbound," from *The Gutenberg Elegies: The Fate of Reading in The Electronic Age* by Sven Birkerts. Copyright © 1998. Reprinted by permission of Faber and Faber, Inc., an affiliate of Farrar, Straus and Giroux, LLC.

Lise Buranen, "But I Wasn't Cheating" is excerpted from a chapter in Lise Buranen and Alice M. Roy, editors: *Perspectives on Plagiarism and Intellectual Property in a Postmodern World* (Albany, N.Y.: State University Press 2001). Reprinted with permission.

Excerpts from *The Hacker Ethic* by Pekka Himanen, copyright © 2001 by Pekka Himanen. Used by permission of Random House, Inc.

"The Functions of Privacy" is reprinted with permission of Scribner, a division of Simon and Schuster Adult Publishing Group, from Privacy and Freedom by Alan F. Westin. © 1967 by the Association of the Bar of the City of New York.

ARTICLES

Amitai Etzioni, "The New Enemy of Privacy: Big Bucks," from *Challenge*, vol. 43, no. 3. (May-June 2000): 91-106. Copyright © 2000 M.E. Sharpe, Inc. Reprinted with permission.

Joan Bertin, Graham Cannon, Joe Diamond, Jason Heffner, Barry Steinhardt, "Panel II: Indirect/Industry Regulation of the Internet," originally published as part of "Symposium: Should Cyberspace be a Free Speech Zone?" in 15 *New York Law School Journal of Human Rights* 67 (1998). Reprinted with permission.

Jerry Berman and Deirdre Mulligan, "Privacy in the Digital Age: A Work in Progress," 23 Nova L.Rev. 551 (1999). Reprinted with permission.

Richard Birke and Louise Ellen Teitz, "Meditation in Cyberspace," 50 Am.J.Comp.L. 181, Fall 2002. Reprinted with permission.

Amy Lynn Bomse, "Note, The Dependence of Cyberspace," 50 Duke L.J. 1717 (2001). Reprinted with permission.

James Boyle, "A Nondelegation Doctrine for the Digital Age?" 50 Duke L.J.5 (2000). Reprinted with permission.

Business Wire, "From Word of Mouth to Word of Mouse", April 24, 2003. Reprinted with permission.

Margaret Chon, "Erasing Race? A Critical Race Feminist View of Internet Identity-Shifting," 3 J. Gender Race & Just. 439 (2000). Copyright 200 *Journal of Gender, Race & Justice*, Margaret Chon. Reprinted with permission.

Joanna E. Cohen, Mary Jane Ashley and Vivian Sarabia, "Tobacco Commerce on the Internet," 10:364-367 *Tobacco Control*, Winter 2001. Reprinted with permission from the BMJ Publishing Group.

Julie E. Cohen, "The Right to Read Anonymously," 28 Conn.L.Rev. 981 (1996). © 1996 Julie E. Cohen. Reprinted with permission.

S. David Cooper, "The Dot.Com(munist) Revolution: Will the Internet Bring Democracy to China?" 18 UCLA Pac.Basin L.J. 98 (2000). Reprinted with permission.

Rochelle Cooper Dreyfuss, "Collaborative Research: Conflicts in Authorship, Ownership and Accountability," 53 Vand.L.Rev. 161 (2000). Reprinted with permission.

Jonah Engle, "Buyer Beware: eBay Security Chief Turns Website Into Arm of the Law," July 7, 2003, *The Nation*. Reprinted with permission. For subscription information, call 1-800-333-8536. Portions of each week's Nation magazine can be accessed at http://www.thenation.com.

Barnaby Feder, "Word for Word/Tweaking the W.T.O., The Long and Winding Cyberhoax: Political Theatre on the Web," NYT, January

7, 2001. Copyright © (2001) The New York Times Co. Reprinted with permission.

Peter L. Fitzgerald, "Massachusetts, Burma and the WTO: A Commentary on Blacklisting, Federalism and Internet Advocacy in the Global Trading Era," 34 Cornell Int'l.LJ.1, 2001, Reprinted with permission of the author and the *Cornell International Law Journal*.

Jane C. Ginsburg, "Stolen Content: Avoiding Trouble on the Internet," Jan-Feb 2001 *ACADEME* 49. Reprinted with permission of the author.

Stuart P. Green, "Plagiarism, Norms, and the Limits of Theft Law: Some Observations on the use of Criminal Sanctions in Enforcing Intellectual Property Rights," © 2002 by University of California, Hastings College of the Law. Reprinted with permission from Hastings Law Journal, vol.54, no.1, 167 (November 2002).

Reed Hundt, Book Review, "The Future of the Net-Comments on Lawrence Lessig's Code and Other Laws of Cyberspace and The Future of Ideas," 68 Brook.L.Rev.289 (2002). Reprint with permission.

David R. Johnson and David Post, "Law and Borders—the Rise of Law in Cyberspace," reprinted from "Symposium: Surveying Law and Borders," 48 Stan. L. Rev. 1367 (1996). 1996 by the Board of Trustees of the Leland Stanford Junior University. Reprinted with permission of the author, the Stanford Law Review, and Fred B. Rothman & Co., the Publisher.

Rebecca Lee, "Romantic and Electronic Stalking in a College Context," 4 Wm. & Mary J. Women & L. 373 (1988). Reprinted with permission of the *William and Mary Journal of Women and the Law*.

Lawrence Lessig, "The Law of the Horse: What Cyberlaw Might Teach," 113 Harv.L.Rev. 501 (1999). Reprinted with permission.

April Mara Major, "Norm Origin and Development in Cyberspace: Models of Cybernorm Evolution," 78 Wash.U.L.Q. 59 (2000), Copyright Washington University, April Mara Major. Reprinted with permission.

David K. McGraw, "Note, Sexual Harassment in Cyberspace: The Problem of Unwelcome E-Mail," 21 Rutgers Comp. & Tech. L.J. 491. (1995). Reprinted with permission.

Martha Minow, "Partners, Not Rivals: Redrawing the Lines Between Public and Private, Non-Profit and Profit, Secular and Religious," 80 B.U.L.Rev. 1061 (2000). Reprinted with permission.

Rachel F. Moran, "Diversity, Distance and the Delivery of Higher Education," was originally published in 59 Ohio St. L. J. 775 (1998). Reprinted with permission of the author and Ohio State Law Journal.

Viktor Mayer-Schonberger, "Impeach the Internet!" 46 Loyola Law Review 569 (2000). Reprinted with permission.

Helen Nissenbaum, "Securing Trust Online: Wisdom or Oxymoron?" 81 B.U.L. Rev., 635, (June 2001). Reprinted with permission.

Peter Overby, "Analysis: Howard Dean Campaign's Sucessful Internet Exploitation," *All Things Considered*, NPR, July 28, 2003. Copyright © NPR® 2003. Reprinted with permission.

David G. Post, "Napster, Jefferson's Moose, and the Law of Cyberspace," January 2000. Reprinted with permission.

Margo E.K. Reder and Christine Neylon O'Brien, "Coporate Cybersmear: Emplyers file John Doe Defamation Lawsuits Seeking the Identity of Anonymous Employee Internet Posters," 8 Mich.Telecomm.Tech.L.Rev. 196 (2002). Reprinted with permission.

Paul M. Schwartz, "Privacy and Democracy in Cyberspace," 52 Vand. L. Rev.1609 (1999) Reprinted with permission.

Rodney A. Smolla, "From Hit Man to Encyclopedia of Jihad: How to Distinguish Freedom of Speech From Terrorist Training," 22 Loy.L.A.Ent.L.Rev 479 (2002). Reprinted with Permission.

David L. Sobel, "The Process that 'John Doe' is due: Addressing the Legal Challenge to Internet Anonymity," 5 Va. J.L.Tech. 3 (2000). © Virginia Journal of Law & Technology Association; David L. Sobel. Reprinted with permission.

Eugene Volokh, "Freedom of Speech in Cyberspace From the Listener's Perspective: Libel, State Action, Harassment and Sex," 1996 U.Chi.Legal F. 377 (1996). Copyright 1996, Eugene Volokh. Reprinted with permission.

Alfred C. Yen, "Western Frontier or Feudal Society? Metaphors and Perceptions of Cyberspace," 17 Berkeley Tech.L.J. 1207 (2002). Reprinted with permission.

ONLINE ARTICLES:

"Why We Oppose UCITA," Americans for Fair Electronic Commerce Transactions (AFFECT). http://www.ucita.com Reprinted with permission.

John Perry Barlow, "The Economy of Ideas: A Framework for Patents & Copyrights in the Digital Age," Wired Magazine, March 1994. Reprinted with permission. http://www.wired.com:80/wired/archive/2.03/economy.ideas_pr.html

David Brin, "The Transparent Society," Hotseat Interview with John McChesney, June 6, 1997. http//hotwired.lycos.com/packet/hotseat/97/22/transcript4a.html

Copyright © 2001 Wired Digital Inc., a Lycos Network site. All rights reserved. Reprinted with permission.

Electronic Frontier Foundation, "Public Interest Position on Junk Email: Protect Innocent Users—EFF Statement on Regarding Anti-Spam Measures," EFF October 16, 2001. http://www.eff.org/Spam_cybersquatting_abuse/Spam/position_on_junk_email.html. Reprinted with permission.

Arthur Levine, "The Remaking of the American University", Web-based Education Commission http://www.hpcnet.org/upload/attachments/The_Remaking_of_the_American_University_145442_000921083425.doc Reprinted with permission.

Kari Lyderson, "Spying for Fun and Profit," Alternet, May 28, 2003. http://www.alternet.org/story.html?StoryID=16009 Reprinted with permission.

Ryan McKinley, "Government Information Awareness," 2003, MIT Media Lab. http://opengov.media.mit.edu/ Reprinted with permission.

Richard Stallman, "Why We Must Fight UCITA," Linux Today, February 6, 2000. Copyright 2000 Richard Stallman. Verbatim copying, distribution and display of this entire article are permitted in any medium provided this notice is preserved. http://linuxtoday.com/stories/15948.html. Reprinted with permission.

Matt Welch, "Get Ready for PATRIOT II," Alternet, April 2, 2003. http://www.alternet.org/story.html?StoryID=15541. Reprinted with permission.

"Breaching the Canyon Walls: Bringing the World to Isolated Reservations," Web-based Education Commission. http://www.hpcnet.org/webcommission. Reprinted with permission.

CHAPTER 1

Intellectual Property and Cyberspace

Napster = FREE/If Napster decides not to = free any longer then I will switch to another freebie/There are many out there …/The Internet is a great place, you can get whatever you want on here. No matter what./Free Free Free.

—Anonymous

If seven million people are stealing, they aren't stealing.

—David Post, Professor of Law, Temple University

It is the nature of the idea to be communicated, written, spoken, done. The idea is like grass. It craves light, likes crowds, thrives on crossbreeding, grows better for being stepped on.

—Ursula LeGuin, The Dispossessed

No question the most insidious virus in our midst is the illegal downloading of music on the Net …. Many new, less-established artists, are in immediate danger of being marginalized out of our business. Ripping is stealing their livelihood one digital file at a time, leaving their musical dreams haplessly snared in this World Wide Web of theft and indifference.

—Michael Greene, President and CEO of the National Academy of Recording Arts & Sciences.

ETHICS CASE: NAPSTER

Let's say it is early in the year 2001, and you're up late one night, browsing e-zines for music reviews. You think you want to try out a group called Bats & Mice. The review says they sound like Radiohead, and Radiohead is your favorite band. So you go to the Napster site and look for Bats & Mice. Sure enough, it turns out several users have it, and one, Orlando Rodriguez in Madrid, is logged on right now. A click or two and a few minutes later and the new Bats & Mice CD is on your hard drive. You can listen to it as many times as you want. If you like it, you might send it to a dozen of your closest friends. All this you can do without moving out of your bedroom, without spending a cent.

Is this ethical?

Napster, as legend has it, is the nickname of a 19-year-old New Jersey college dropout named Shaun Fanning who, in January 1999, wrote a set of computer instructions—code—that allowed him and his friends to exchange their MP3 files. The code became a big hit because it allowed anyone, anywhere, to swap music, fast and free.

A few months later, Fanning dropped out of college, acquired venture capital and founded Napster, Inc. in July of 1999.

Napster operated on a peer-to-peer (P2P) computing model. Users who downloaded the free software from its site could then access the directory of available music and add tunes to their own files. Napster's server was an intermediary, allowing one user to reach the files of another.

It worked this way. First, you would download the Napster software from the Napster site. Then, when you ran the software, it scanned your hard drive for music files, compiling a directory of the songs there. The software would then relay that directory—not the actual music files, just the list—back to Napster, where it would be added to the main directory.

As a result, when you logged onto the Napster database looking for the Bats & Mice CD, you were effectively able to broadcast your request to the millions of other music lovers in the "Napster community." The technology allowed you to ask: Does anyone else have this CD on their hard drive? If so, are they online right now?

The Internet has been compared to a vast copying machine. Infused from its start with the sense that it is some sort of frontier, it combines blistering speed with awesome content availability. It is a place where "netizens" can get access—anyplace, anytime—to whatever is out there. And, in these early years of cyberspace, there seems to be no limit on what is or will be out there. As Edgar Bronfman Jr., head of Universal Corporation, the world's largest music company, recently put it: "A few clicks of your mouse will make it possible for you to summon every book ever written in any language, every movie ever made, every television show ever produced, and every piece of music ever recorded."

Is this a good thing or a bad thing?

For those who have the legal right to payment for these products—known as intellectual property—the news is disturbing. We are currently witnessing their use of the courts and legislatures to shore up their rights. Meanwhile, Internet users—from hackers to teachers to scholars to fans of obscure recordings—are pulling in the opposite direction, for open access to culture and to culture creation.

In this chapter we use Napster to discuss the ongoing upheaval over the way information technology is changing our understanding of intellectual property. First, we consider the law of copyright. Next, we compare the opinions that a number of experts and stakeholders have on these issues: the cybertarian vs. the media executive, for example, or the musician vs. the fan. The chapter then presents the question of values in a more formal sense by looking at Napster through the prisms of ethical theory. We close with a reading that invites us to think of cyberspace as a "new world," as strikingly different from the world that preceded it as the New World was to Europeans in the 18th century, and a place that allows us to think the unthinkable, to seriously reevaluate how we choose to live.

INTELLECTUAL PROPERTY LAW

Intellectual property is the work product of the human mind. Novels, poems, songs, and inventions are examples. It differs from ordinary physical property in one key way: If I own my house, you do not. If it's mine, I can keep you out. Intellectual property, though, can be shared without losing its value. I can listen to the Bats & Mice CD—and so can you, and so can any number of other people. We can all experience this bit of intellectual property without interfering with one another's experience.

Our legal system has developed protection for intellectual property, based on the understanding that if inventors and creative people are not rewarded for their efforts, they may not make them—to the detriment of science, the arts, and commercial progress. This is why the U.S. Constitution frames intellectual property protection in societal terms. Article 1, Section 8, empowers Congress to pass legislation "to promote the progress of science and (the) useful arts by securing for limited Times to authors and inventors the exclusive right to their respective Writings and Discoveries."

Congress responded by passing copyright, patent, and trademark laws. What is protected is the expression of an idea, not the idea itself. This follows from the high value we place on freedom of speech and expression. If ideas could be "owned," we would put at risk the free and open exchange of opinion that is key to a healthy democracy. The congressional report on the Copyright Act of 1909 articulates the tension underlying intellectual property protection in our legal system:

> In enacting copyright law Congress must consider...two questions: First, how
> much will the legislation stimulate the producer and so benefit the public,

and second, how much will the monopoly granted be detrimental to the public? The granting of such exclusive rights, under the proper terms and conditions, confers a benefit upon the public that outweighs the evils of the temporary monopoly.

Copyright law protects the tangible expression of an idea from being reproduced without the permission of the copyright holder. To qualify for a copyright, a work of art must be original and created independently by the artist. The law curbs this right, making it last only for a set time period. It also carves out the important exception of "fair use," permitting reproduction of portions of copyrighted work for limited purposes, such as criticism or classroom instruction.[1]

"Code" and Intellectual Property

In his pivotal writings about intellectual property and cyberspace, Stanford University Law Professor Lawrence Lessig has described four different mechanisms that can control how we behave: law, social norms, markets, and architecture—the physical infrastructure. In cyberspace, architecture is analogous to "code." By "code," Lessig means both hardware and software—both the computers themselves and the series of zeros and ones that program how they perform. He gives examples of these four "modalities of constraint" in cyberspace. The law of copyright shapes behavior there—or attempts to. Social or community norms affect behavior there also; if you are too talkative on a discussion list, "you are likely to wind up on a common bozo filter, blocking messages from you." Markets determine behavior in cyberspace as they do elsewhere, by price structures. Finally, architecture or code, "the software and hardware that make cyberspace the way it is," can determine radically different experiences online:

> In some places, one must enter a password before one gains access; in other places, one can enter whether identified or not. In some places, the transactions that one engages in produce traces, or 'mouse droppings,' that link the transactions back to the individual; in other places, this link is achieved only if the individual consents. In some places, one can elect to speak a language that only the recipient can understand (through encryption); in other places, encryption is not an option. Code sets these features; they are features selected by code writers; they constrain some behavior (for example, electronic eavesdropping) by making other behavior possible (encryption). They embed certain values, or they make the realization of certain values impossible.

---

[1] Title 17 of the U.S. Code (see chapter 5).

U.S. COPYRIGHT LAW HIGHLIGHTS

1790: The first copyright law is passed, giving holders a 14-year term with 14-year renewal possible; "maps, charts and books" are the only items covered, not music.

1831: Copyright law is expanded to protect musical compositions.

1909: The law defines "phonorecords," establishing a compulsory licensing scheme and a royalty rate.

1912: Motion pictures are covered by copyright.

1914: ASCAP is formed (American Society for Composers and Publishers).

1976: A major revision extends protection to radio and television broadcasts.

1980: Computer programs are protected as "literary works."

1984: Sony v. Betamax; Supreme Court allows use of VCRs by home viewers to "time-shift" television shows as a "fair use."

1992: Congress passes law permitting noncommercial home use of DAT ("digital audio tape") machines, allowing unlimited "first generation" copying, but blocking further copies.

1994: U.S. signs an international agreement, Trade-Related Aspects of Intellectual Property (TRIPS); Congress creates penalties for bootlegging audio recordings of performances and music videos.

1995: Digital Rights in Sound Recordings Act gives exclusive rights to holders of sound recordings to public play of digital versions.

1998: Digital Millennium Copyright Act (DMCA) extensively strengthens copyright for digitalized items.

1998: Copyright Term Extension Act (CTEA) extends the period protecting all copyrights by twenty years. Copyright now valid for author's life plus 70 years, longer if holder is a corporation.

2001: Napster is shut down as a federal court finds its system materially contributes to copyright infringement by its online users, violating the DMCA.

2001: A federal court upholds the constitutionality of the DMCA as applied to a computer hacker who disseminated a decoding algorithm for DVDs.

2003: The Supreme Court rejects a challenge to the CTEA as a violation of the First Amendment; Recording Industry Association of America launches lawsuits against individuals allegedly making numerous songs available for downloading.

Lessig writes that the different regulating factors may compete with one another, and in disturbing ways. In the excerpt that follows, he explains how code might affect copyright law, displacing important public values.

The Law of the Horse: What Cyberlaw Might Teach[2]

Lawrence Lessig

We have special laws to protect against the theft of autos, or boats. We do not have special laws to protect against the theft of skyscrapers. Skyscrapers take care of themselves. The architecture of real space, or more suggestively, its real-space code, protects skyscrapers much more effectively than law. Architecture is an ally of skyscrapers (making them impossible to move); it is an enemy of cars and boats (making them quite easy to move).

On this spectrum from cars to very big buildings, intellectual property is somewhat like cars, and quite unlike large buildings. Indeed, as the world is just now, intellectual property fares far worse than cars and boats. At least if someone takes my car, I know it; I can call the police, and they can try to find it. But if someone takes an illegal copy of my article (copying it without paying for it), then I do not necessarily know. Sales might go down, my reputation might go up (or down), but there is no way to trace the drop in sales to this individual theft, and no way to link the rise (or fall) in fame to this subsidized distribution.

When theorists of the Net first thought about intellectual property, they argued that things were about to get much worse. 'Everything [we know] about intellectual property,' we were told, 'is wrong.' Property could not be controlled on the Net; copyright made no sense. Authors would have to find new ways to make money in cyberspace, because the technology had destroyed the ability to make money by controlling copies.

The reasons were plain: the Net is a digital medium. Digital copies are perfect and free. One can copy a song from a CD into a format called MP3. The song can then be posted on USENET to millions of people for free. The nature of the Net, we were told, would make copyright controls impossible. Copyright was dead.

There was something odd about this argument, even at its inception. It betrayed a certain is-ism—'the way cyberspace is is the way it has to be.' Cyberspace was a place where 'infinite copies could be made for free.' But why exactly? Because of its code. Infinite copies could be made because the code permitted such copying. So why couldn't the code be changed? Why couldn't we imagine a different code, one that better protected intellectual property?…

Consider the proposals of Mark Stefik of Xerox PARC.…[He] describes what he calls 'trusted systems' for copyright management. [Using encryption, t]rusted systems enable owners of intellectual

---

property to control access to that property, and to meter usage of the property perfectly. This control would be coded into software that would distribute, and hence regulate access to, copyrighted material. This control would be extremely fine-grained and would enable the copyright holder an extraordinary control over copyrighted material....

[Stefik] offers an architecture for the network that would allow owners of copyrighted materials to sell access to those materials on terms that the owners set, and an architecture that would enforce those contracts.

A hierarchy of systems would develop; and copyrighted material would be traded only within that system that controlled access properly.

Stefik has turned airplanes into skyscrapers—he has described a way to change the code of cyberspace to make it possible to protect intellectual property in a far more effective way than is possible in real space.

Now imagine for a moment that a structure of trusted systems emerged. How would this change in code change the nature of copyright law?

Copyright law is an odd bird. It establishes a strange sort of property, at least in relation to other property. The Copyright Clause of the United States Constitution gives Congress the power to grant "Authors" an exclusive right over their "Writings" for "Limited Times." At the end of that time...the work enters the public domain. It is as if the ownership you have over your car were a lease, extending for four years, and then expiring, at which time your car is up for grabs.

The reasons for this limitation on copyright protection are many, though the reasons don't fully overlap. Some reasons are economic, and ultimately pragmatic. Property systems (costly and complex) are justified only if they produce some social good. In the case of tangible goods, the social good is obvious. The law protects my enjoyment of tangible property, such as my car. If you used it without my permission, I could not use it. If everyone could use it without my permission, there would be little reason for me to own it. By giving me the power to control its use, the law creates a benefit to my ownership, and therefore an incentive for me to seek ownership.

Intangible property is significantly different. Unlike your enjoyment of my car, your enjoyment of my poem will not interfere with my enjoying it at all. Intangible goods are non-rivalrous. When an idea is disseminated, its usefulness does not diminish. As Thomas Jefferson wrote: "[N]o one possesses the less, because every other possesses the whole of it. He who receives an idea from me, receives instruction himself without lessening mine; as he who lights his taper at mine, receives light without darkening me." Thus while the law needs to protect tangible property both so that there is an incentive to produce, and also so that the owner can enjoy it, the law needs to protect intangible property only in order to create the incentive to produce.

But economics is not the only justification for limiting the "property-like" protection for intellectual property. Constitutional law is another. Regulations of copyright are regulations of

Can we protect the "incentive to produce" without charging the recipient of intellectual property?

speech...in tension with the understanding that the law should leave speech free....As the Supreme Court said, the Framers intended copyright to serve as an 'engine of free expression.' It is justified only so long as it serves as such an engine.

Finally, and relatedly, the limits on intellectual property reflect a commitment to an intellectual commons....The limitations on the scope of intellectual property law serve to fuel this intellectual commons—to generate a resource upon which others can draw.

The essential nature of a commons is that each individual is free to use the commons without the permission of anyone else....I might have to pay a small fee to enter the park, but if I pay the fee, I have the right to enter. The park is a resource open to everyone. It is a space that individuals may occupy without asking the subjective permission of anyone else.

These three justifications for limits on intellectual property overlap, but they are not coextensive. They all, for example, would justify some form of "fair use"—a defense that the law of copyright gives users of copyrighted material.

From an economic perspective, fair use can be justified either because the use is small relative to transaction costs of charging for the use, or because certain uses tend to increase the demand for copyrighted work generally. The right to use excerpts in a book review benefits the class of book authors generally, since it enables reviews of books that in turn increase the total demand for books....

But from the perspective of the commons, what is important about fair use is not so much the value of fair use, or its relation to matters of public import....This is an autonomy conception. The right guaranteed is a right to use these resources without the approval of someone else.

"Fair use" thus balances the rights of an individual author against the rights of a user....But it is clear...that the development of trusted systems threatens to change the balance. From the economic perspective, it threatens to empower individual authors against the interests of the class; from the constitutional perspective, it threatens to bottle up speech regardless of its relation to matters of public import; and from the perspective of the commons, it fundamentally changes the nature of access. Within a structure of trusted systems, access is always and only with permission. The baseline is control, regardless of how far that control is exercised.

This is a problem particular to cyberspace. In real space, the law might guarantee me the right to fair use, or to make use of a work in the public domain. It guarantees me this right by giving me a defense if the owner of copyrighted work tries to sue me for taking her property. The law in effect then denies the owner any cause of action; the law withdraws its protection, and leaves the property within the commons.

But there is no similar guarantee with property protected by trusted systems. There is no reason to believe that the code that Stefik describes would be a code that guaranteed fair use....The code can be designed however the code writer wants....

Trusted systems, therefore,...are architectures of control that displace the architectures of control effected by public law. And to the extent that architectures of law are balanced between private and public values, we should worry if architectures of code become imbalanced. We should worry, that is, if they respect private values but displace public values.

CONCLUSION

We must make a choice about life in cyberspace—about whether the values embedded there will be the values we want. The code of cyberspace constitutes those values; it can be made to constitute values that resonate with our tradition, just as it can be made to reflect values inconsistent with our tradition.

As the Net grows, as its regulatory power increases, as its power as a source of values becomes established, the values of real-space sovereigns will at first lose out. In many cases, no doubt, that is a very good thing. But there...is nothing to guarantee that the regime of values constituted by code will be a liberal regime; and little reason to expect that an invisible hand of code writers will push it in that direction. Indeed, to the extent that code writers respond to the wishes of commerce, a power to control may well be the tilt that this code begins to take. Understanding this tilt will be a continuing project of the 'law of cyberspace.'

QUESTIONS

1. Think about Napster, both in its original free form and in its new incarnation as a paid music subscription service. Now think of Lessig's "modalities of constraint":

- Law
- Social Norms
- Market
- Code

How did each modality play a role in the history of Napster? What values do you think were embedded in each? Which modality "won"?

2. Elsewhere in this article, after explaining how trusted systems (code) can interfere with the legally-protected values of fair use, Lessig offers examples of the reverse—how law can interfere with code:

Anti-Circumvention: Trusted systems, as I have described them, are systems that enable control over the distribution of digital objects through encryption technologies that make unauthorized use difficult. These technologies, however, are not perfect; there is code that could crack them. Thus the threat of this code is a threat to these systems of control. Last year, Congress responded to this threat by enacting an anti-circumvention provision in the Digital Millennium Copyright Act. This provision makes it a felony to crack a protection regime, even if the use of the underlying material is not itself a copyright violation (i.e., is fair use).

What code is being displaced here? What values are in conflict in this scenario?

3. In the spring of 2001 a Princeton University computer science professor had planned to present a paper on cracking the music industry's antipiracy code for CDs, but he received a letter from the Recording Industry Association of America (RIAA) warning him that he would be violating the 1998 Digital Millennium Copyright Act if he went ahead. In June 2001, a group of computer scientists sued, asking a federal court to determine if the First Amendment protected discussion of such research, and asking it to declare the anti-circumvention provision of the DMCA unconstitutional. Go online to find out what happened. The lawsuit was financed by the Electronic Frontier Foundation.

PERSPECTIVES ON NAPSTER

Industry

In the following speech, Michael Eisner, CEO of The Walt Disney Company, addresses a congressional subcommittee, arguing for enforcement of copyright for digital media. Showing video footage to the legislators, he begins with an impressive review of the history of movie-making technology, concentrating on dinosaur films. While scenes from King Kong, Godzilla, and Jurassic Park run and then freeze-frame behind him, Eisner describes the technical wizardry that developed through the 20th century, allowing his audience to contemplate the increasing demands on human ingenuity, time, and investment that made all of this possible. He then switches gear and discusses the threat of online piracy to his industry.

Address Before Members of The United States Congress

Michael Eisner, Chairman & CEO, The Walt Disney Company
June 7, 2000

I'll resist the temptation to go on and on about the countless ingenious tricks that our animators and technicians devised to make this film, because my point isn't to promote the film. My point is that we have created a movie that took four years to make, during which 45 million megabytes were crunched—or enough data to fill 70,000 CD-ROMs—all to generate the necessary data for an 80-minute film—which, were it to get in the wrong hands, could be compressed onto a single DVD disk in a matter of minutes and instantaneously put on the Internet while the film is still in the theaters....

I'm not talking about the comical characters sailing the high seas...the Pirates of the Caribbean. Rather, I'm talking about an underground of secretive and sequestered Pirates of Encryption—the hackers who shamelessly assert that anything they can get their hands on is legally theirs.

You may be familiar with the recent controversy over a company called iCrave.com, which claimed the right to pluck television signals off the air and stream them on the Internet for all the world to see. You may also be aware of software programs like "Napster," "Wraptster," "Freenet" and "Gnutella," which allow college kids to build vast music collections on the hard drives of their lap top computers without ever buying a single CD.

These Internet programs enable the piracy of intellectual property. Their use is rapidly escalating, with a potential impact on our culture and our economy that is comparable to other Internet-related issues that many of you have expressed concerns about—such as cyber-security, credit card security and the safety of your children's Web surfing.

There is no question that the Internet is an exciting and dynamic new force in commerce and entertainment. But so were, in their time, radio and television. And they had to play by the same bor-

ing old rules involving copyright infringement.

Today's Internet pirates try to hide behind some contrived New Age arguments of cyberspace, but all they are really doing is trying to make a case for Age Old thievery. When they hack a DVD and then distribute it on the Web, it is no different than if someone puts a quarter in a newspaper machine and then takes out all the papers, which, of course, would be illegal and morally wrong.

The pirates will argue that this analogy is unfair, maintaining that all they're doing is cracking a digital code. But, by that standard, it would be justifiable to crack a bank code and transfer the funds from someone else's account into your own. There's just no way around it—theft is theft, whether it is enabled by a handgun or a computer keyboard....

The fact is that nobody signs up for the Internet because of the elegance of its routers. Nobody logs on because of the micro-chip inside. No, they use the Internet in ever-growing numbers because of the content. Right now, that content is largely information. But, increasingly, it will also be entertainment. The growth of bandwidth will increasingly make possible full video experiences. But, this expansion of Internet entertainment will stall if the creators of the content cannot enjoy the full rights of ownership of that content.

It does not take a CPA to figure out that a movie like "Dinosaur" does not come cheap. However, it is an investment worth making if there can be substantial reward in success. But, if this reward is allowed to be pirated away,

http://www.mpaa.org
http://www.riaa.com

then the creative risk-takers will put their energies elsewhere, and the Internet will become a wonderful delivery system with nothing wonderful to deliver.

One of the fallacies of the intellectual property debate is that it's really just a conflict between the pro-technology members of the "New Media" against the anti-technology members of the "Old Media." As I hope I made clear with the discussion of "Dinosaur," this characterization couldn't be more wrong. At Disney we embrace technology. And we always have.

Throughout his career, Walt Disney recognized new technology as the friend of the storyteller. He kept pushing the envelope with the first sound cartoon, the first color cartoon, the first use of the multi-plane camera, the first use of stereophonic sound, and the development of robotics for his theme parks. Walt was also almost alone among movie studio chiefs in the 1950s when he recognized television as a new opportunity and not a threat.

At Disney today, we are not only seizing the tremendous possibilities offered by technology in movies, as with "Dinosaur"—we are also active participants in the expansion of the Internet with our GO.com family of sites, such as Disney.com, ESPN.com, ABCNews.com, ABC.com and Family.com. And, we believe we are helping to pioneer the convergence of the Internet with television through the development of Enhanced TV, which allows viewers to become active participants in the programming, accessing stats during a football game, playing against the

contestants on "Millionaire" and guessing the winners on the Oscars.

We intend to continue to pour resources into the Internet—but not if this requires surrendering the rights to things we own.

Just as our society is beginning to address other security threats posed by the Internet, we must address the security of copyrights. With this in mind, our company is undertaking a wide-ranging strategy to make the Internet truly secure for intellectual property. This strategy consists of five main elements.

First of all, we are turning to our representatives in Washington....

[W]e ask you to begin to explore with us legislation that would assure the efficacy of technology solutions to copyright security. As we seek to develop measures such as watermarking, we need the assurance that the people who manufacture computers and the people who operate ISP's will cooperate by incorporating the technology to look for and respond to the watermarks. This same mandate could be part of the solution to a host of other Internet security issues as well.

The second element of our strategy to protect intellectual property is to work with governments around the world to respect our rights. We are actively involved in the Global Business Dialogue on E-Commerce, and our company is serving as chair of the Intellectual Property Work Group. The Internet is international. The issues involving it cannot be viewed with a myopic American eye....

The third element is education. Most people are honest and want to do the right thing. But they can't do the right thing if they don't know that they're doing a wrong thing. I am always amazed when I walk the streets of New York and stroll past an open fruit stand. Thousands of people go by each day respecting the fact that if they want an apple they need to pay for it, even though it would be incredibly easy to just take it. When it comes to the Internet, most people simply aren't aware that the same issues apply. According to a recent Newsweek cover story, college kids are simply oblivious to the legal and moral implications of downloading copyrighted material off the Internet. Working with Jack Valenti and the MPAA, we are advocating a more aggressive campaign to make people aware of intellectual property rights on the Internet, in much the same way as the FBI warning at the front of videotapes.

Fourth, we believe that the entertainment industry as a whole—and I mean all the companies with a stake in the e-future—should take meaningful technological measures. To an extent, piracy is a technical problem and must be addressed with technical solutions. The studios, broadcasters and record companies—working in cooperation with the technology companies—need to develop innovative and flexible watermarking or encryption systems that can stay one step ahead of the hackers.

The fifth and final of our initiatives is economic. History has shown that one of the best deterrents to pirated product is providing legitimate product at appropriate prices. In the music industry, we have already seen that most people will gladly pay fair prices for legally-produced product even when it can be easily reproduced and unlawful copies can be easily acquired. I am certain that the same person who pays a reasonable price for an apple at his local fruit stand will pay a reasonable price for a video on his local hard drive.

All we need is for this basic rule of society to be acknowledged and enforced in the cyber world as it is in the real world. If this can be achieved, then the possibilities of the Internet—for communication, for education, for entertainment and for commerce—will be as limitless as the lightspeed at which it has brought the world together.

QUESTIONS

1. Eisner was addressing Congress in this statement. Part of the multi-pronged strategy he was recommending was new legislation. His testimony was given in the year 2000. Look back at the Copyright Law Highlights (page 5). What laws have been passed since that year? Meanwhile, Lawrence Lessig, through the Stanford Center for Internet and Society, urges a very different legislative response to copyright in the 21st century. Find out what Lessig recommends. How would you compare recent legislative changes and Lessig's ideas?

2. Eisner mentions watermarking; the recording industry has been experimenting with several other technological means of protecting copyright. One process creates CDs that can be played only with CD players, not on computers. Another technique, "spoofing," involves spreading fake music files across networks like KaZaA and Morpheus. One woman sued the industry because the copy-protected CD she purchased was not compatible with her computer. And the day after Madonna had spoofed versions of songs from a new album released onto file-sharing networks, hackers broke into her Web site and made real copies of her entire album available there. What other counterpiracy technologies have the major labels employed or investigated? What reactions have they provoked?

3. During the month that Eisner spoke to Congress, the federal district court had issued a preliminary injunction against Napster. Eisner does not mention the Napster litigation. Nor does he mention litigation as one of the strategies that could be used to prevent piracy. Why do you think he did not mention it?

4. Although Napster was shut down, the copying of digital music showed no signs of abating. By April 2003 roughly half of all Americans accessing the Internet were also accessing free music. And college students were taking it a step further: Instead of relying on the slower Internet, they began using programs that allowed them to share music over the ultra-fast

networks that connect computers on their campuses. In the spring of 2003 the recording industry decided to file lawsuits against four college students, accusing them of enabling copyright infringement on a large scale and of having "taken a network created for higher learning and academic pursuits and convert[ing] it into an emporium of music piracy." The industry asked for billions in damages— $150,000 for each of the songs listed on the students' sites. These cases were settled, with the students agreeing to stop swapping files and to pay $12,000 to $17,500 each. But by mid-summer 2003, the industry had turned up the heat again, sending out hundreds of subpoenas to ISPs and universities to obtain the real identities of the music pirates they wanted to bring to justice, some of whom had allegedly stolen five songs. On September 8, 2003, the RIAA filed lawsuits against 261 individual file-sharers.

(a) Suppose you were an attorney representing one of the defendants. What would you argue in support of a file-sharer? See: **http://www. stopriaalawsuits.com/index1.html**

(b) Suppose you represented the industry. What arguments run against the file-sharers?

(c) What are the pros and cons of this litigation strategy, from the industry's perspective?

5. The way Eisner tells the story of copyright, there are good guys and bad guys. How does he characterize the bad guys?

His narrative suggests connections between the bad guys and a set of evil acts. What are they? What positive qualities does he suggest the good guys possess?

6. Eisner lists "education" as a strategy and mentions "an aggressive campaign to make people aware of intellectual property rights." In June 2003 the RIAA placed a full page announcement in the New York Times, with a huge headline: "Next time you or your kids 'share' music on the Internet, you may also want to download a list of attorneys." It took a threatening tone: "Stealing music over the Internet is no different than shoplifting CDs out of a record store. It's wrong, and it's against the law. It's also a very public activity—meaning that offenders can be easily identified." Locate this ad online. What do you think the industry hoped to gain from it? Do you think it is likely to have the desired effect?

"What's the Diff? A Guide to Digital Citizenship" was co-created by Warner Brothers and a business education organization called Junior Achievement. What do you think of this effort to bring the industry's education campaign into the public schools? See: **http://www.ja.org/ programs/programs_supplements_ citizenship.shtml**.

7. Have recent industry efforts to discourage file-sharing been effective? See: **http://www.pewinternet.org**.

Musicians

Courtney Love, lead singer of the rock group Hole, gave the following testimony to Congress on June 14, 2000.

Courtney Love Does the Math[3]

Today I want to talk about piracy and music. What is piracy? Piracy is the act of stealing an artist's work without any intention of paying for it. I'm not talking about Napster-type software.

I'm talking about major label recording contracts.

I want to start with a story about rock bands and record companies, and do some recording-contract math.

This story is about a bidding-war band that gets a huge deal with a 20 percent royalty rate and a million-dollar advance. (No bidding-war band ever got a 20 percent royalty, but whatever.) This is my "funny" math based on some reality and I just want to qualify it by saying I'm positive it's better math than what Edgar Bronfman Jr. [the president and CEO of Seagram, which owns Polygram] would provide.

---

[3] http://archive.salon.com/tech/feature/2000/06/14/love/

What happens to that million dollars?

They spend half a million to record their album. That leaves the band with $500,000. They pay $100,000 to their manager for 20 percent commission. They pay $25,000 each to their lawyer and business manager.

That leaves $350,000 for the four band members to split. After $170,000 in taxes, there's $180,000 left. That comes out to $45,000 per person.

That's $45,000 to live on for a year until the record gets released.

The record is a big hit and sells a million copies. (How a bidding-war band sells a million copies of its debut record is another rant entirely, but it's based on any basic civics-class knowledge that any of us have about cartels. Put simply, the antitrust laws in this country are basically a joke, protecting us just enough to not have to re-name our park service the Phillip Morris National Park Service.)

So, this band releases two singles and makes two videos. The two videos cost a million dollars to make and 50 percent of the video production costs are recouped out of the band's royalties.

The band gets $200,000 in tour support, which is 100 percent recoupable.

The record company spends $300,000 on independent radio promotion. You have to pay independent promotion to get your song on the radio; independent promotion is a system where the record companies use middlemen so they can pretend not to know that radio stations—the unified broadcast system—are getting paid to play their records.

All of those independent promotion costs are charged to the band.

Since the original million-dollar advance is also recoupable, the band owes $2 million to the record company.

If all of the million records are sold at full price with no discounts or record clubs, the band earns $2 million in royalties, since their 20 percent royalty works out to $2 a record.

Two million dollars in royalties minus $2 million in recoupable expenses equals... zero!

How much does the record company make?

They grossed $11 million. It costs $500,000 to manufacture the CDs and they advanced the band $1 million. Plus there were $1 million in video costs, $300,000 in radio promotion and $200,000 in tour support.

The company also paid $750,000 in music publishing royalties.

They spent $2.2 million on marketing. That's mostly retail advertising, but marketing also pays for those huge posters of Marilyn Manson in Times Square and the street scouts who drive around in vans handing out black Korn T-shirts and backwards baseball caps. Not to mention trips to Scores and cash for tips for all and sundry.

Add it up and the record company has spent about $4.4 million.

So their profit is $6.6 million; the band may as well be working at a 7-Eleven.

Of course, they had fun. Hearing yourself on the radio, selling records, getting new fans and being on TV is great, but now the band doesn't have enough money to pay the rent and nobody has any credit.

Worst of all, after all this, the band owns none of its work....

When you look at the legal line on a CD, it says copyright 1976 Atlantic Records or copyright 1996 RCA Records. When you look at a book, though, it'll say something like copyright 1999 Susan Faludi, or David Foster Wallace. Authors own their books and license them to publishers. When the contract runs out, writers gets their books back. But record companies own our copyrights forever....

Last November, a Congressional aide...with the support of the RIAA, added a "technical amendment" to a bill that defined recorded music as "works for hire" under the 1978 Copyright Act....

That subtle change in copyright law will add billions of dollars to record company bank accounts over the next few years— billions of dollars that rightfully should have been paid to artists. A "work for hire" is now owned in perpetuity by the record company....

QUESTIONS

1. How do you think Michael Eisner of Disney would respond to Courtney Love?

2. Lars Ulrich would no doubt be as aware as Courtney Love of the "math" involved in signing with a major recording company. Yet he and his band, Metallica, joined the RIAA in suing Napster. In what way might he respond to Love's argument?

Cybertarians

In the next reading, John Perry Barlow, co-founder and executive chair of the Electronic Frontier Foundation, grapples with the problem of digitalized property in cyberspace. He writes, "The enigma is this: If our property can be infinitely reproduced and instantaneously distributed all over the planet without cost, without our knowledge, without its even leaving our possession, how can we protect it? How are we going to get paid for the work we do with our minds? And, if we can't get paid, what will assure the continued creation and distribution of such work?"

The Economy of Ideas: A Framework for Patents and Copyrights in the Digital Age

John Perry Barlow

Throughout the history of copyrights and patents, the proprietary assertions of thinkers have been focused not on their ideas but on the expression of those ideas. The ideas themselves, as well as facts about the phenomena of the world, were considered to be the collective property of humanity. One could claim franchise, in the case of copyright, on the precise turn of phrase used to convey a particular idea or the order in which facts were presented.

The point at which this franchise was imposed was that moment when the "word became flesh" by departing the mind of its originator and entering some physical object, whether book or widget. The subsequent arrival of other commercial media besides books didn't alter the legal importance of this moment. Law protected expression and, with few (and recent) exceptions, to express was to make physical.

Protecting physical expression had the force of convenience on its side. Copyright worked well because, Gutenberg notwithstanding, it was hard to make a book. Furthermore, books froze their contents into a condition which was as challenging to alter as it was to reproduce. Counterfeiting and distributing counterfeit volumes were obvious and visible activities—it was easy enough to catch somebody in the act of doing. Finally, unlike unbounded words or images, books had material surfaces to which one could attach copyright notices, publisher's marques, and price tags.

Thus, the rights...authorship adhered to activities in the physical world. One didn't get paid for ideas, but for the ability to deliver them into reality.

In other words, the bottle was protected, not the wine.

Now, as information enters cyberspace, the native home of Mind, these bottles are vanishing. With the advent of digitization, it is now possible to replace all previous information storage forms with one metabottle: complex and highly liquid patterns of ones and zeros....

Some will...argue that we have been dealing with unbottled expression since the advent of radio, and they would be right. But for most of the history of broadcast, there was no convenient way to capture soft goods from the electromagnetic ether and reproduce them with the quality available in commercial packages.

Generally, the issue of consumer payment for broadcast products was irrelevant. The consumers themselves were the product. Broadcast media were supported either by the sale of the attention of their audience to advertisers, by government assessing payment through taxes, or by the whining mendicancy of annual donor drives.

All of the broadcast-support models are flawed. Support either by advertisers or government has almost invariably tainted the purity of the goods delivered....

Broadcast media gave us another payment method for a virtual product: the royalties that broadcasters pay songwriters through such organizations as ASCAP and BMI.[4] But, as a member of ASCAP, I can assure you this is not a model that we should emulate. The monitoring methods are wildly approximate. There is no parallel system of accounting in the revenue stream. It doesn't really work. Honest.

In any case, without our old methods, based on physically defining the expression of ideas, and in the absence of successful new models for nonphysical transaction, we simply don't know how to assure reliable payment for mental works. To make matters worse, this comes at a time when the human mind is replacing sunlight and mineral deposits as the principal source of new wealth.

Furthermore, the increasing difficulty of enforcing existing copyright and patent laws is already placing in peril the ultimate source of intellectual property—the free exchange of ideas....

[Barlow goes on to describe the characteristics of information: "Information is an activity./Information is a life form. /Information is a relationship."—arguing that the essential properties of information place it beyond the boundaries of the intellectual property "container." Finally, he describes how he imagines the future.]

GETTING PAID IN CYBERSPACE

[O]ne of the aspects of the electronic frontier which I have always found most appealing...is the degree to which it resembles the 19th-century American West in its natural preference for social devices that emerge from its conditions rather than those that are imposed from the outside.

Until the West was fully settled and "civilized" in this century, order was established according to an unwritten Code of the West, which had the fluidity of common law rather than the rigidity of statutes. Ethics were more important than rules. Understandings were preferred over laws, which were, in any event, largely unenforceable.

I believe that law, as we understand it, was developed to protect the interests which arose in the two economic "waves" which Alvin Toffler accurately identified in The Third Wave. The First Wave was agriculturally based and required law to order ownership of the principal source of production, land. In the Second Wave, manufacturing became the economic mainspring, and the structure of modern law grew around the centralized institutions that needed protection for their reserves of capital, labor, and hardware.

Both of these economic systems required stability. Their laws were designed to resist change and to assure some equability of distribution within a

Does information "want to be free"?

---

[4] Barlow refers to the monitoring of radio and other commercial broadcasters by these organizations. Fees for playing songs are collected by the copyright holders, some portion of which reverts to the songwriters.

fairly static social framework. The empty niches had to be constrained to preserve the predictability necessary to either land stewardship or capital formation.

In the Third Wave we have now entered, information to a large extent replaces land, capital, and hardware, and information is most at home in a much more fluid and adaptable environment. The Third Wave is likely to bring a fundamental shift in the purposes and methods of law which will affect far more than simply those statutes which govern intellectual property.

The "terrain" itself—the architecture of the Net—may come to serve many of the purposes which could only be maintained in the past by legal imposition. For example, it may be unnecessary to constitutionally assure freedom of expression in an environment which, in the words of my fellow EFF co-founder John Gilmore, "treats censorship as a malfunction" and reroutes proscribed ideas around it.

Similar natural balancing mechanisms may arise to smooth over the social discontinuities which previously required legal intercession to set right. On the Net, these differences are more likely to be spanned by a continuous spectrum that connects as much as it separates.

And...companies that trade in information are likely to find that [e]very litigation will become like a game of Russian roulette, depending on the depth of the presiding judge's clue-impairment....

RELATIONSHIP AND ITS TOOLS

I believe one idea is central to understanding liquid commerce: Information economics, in the absence of objects, will be based more on relationship than possession.

One existing model for the future conveyance of intellectual property is real-time performance, a medium currently used only in theater, music, lectures, stand-up comedy, and pedagogy. I believe the concept of performance will expand to include most of the information economy, from multicasted soap operas to stock analysis. In these instances, commercial exchange will be more like ticket sales to a continuous show....

The other existing model, of course, is service. The entire professional class—doctors, lawyers, consultants, architects, and so on—are already being paid directly for their intellectual property. Who needs copyright when you're on a retainer?...

We can already see the emergence of companies which base their existence on supporting and enhancing the soft property they create rather than selling it by the shrink-wrapped piece or embedding it in widgets....

CRYPTO BOTTLING

Cryptography...is the "material" from which the walls, boundaries—and bottles—of cyberspace will be fashioned.

Of course there are problems with cryptography or any other purely technical method of property protection. It has always appeared to me that the more security you hide your goods behind, the more likely you are to turn your sanctuary into a target. Having come from a place where people leave their keys in their cars and don't even have keys to their houses,

I remain convinced that the best obstacle to crime is a society with its ethics intact.

While I admit that this is not the kind of society most of us live in, I also believe that a social over-reliance on protection by barricades rather than conscience will eventually wither the latter by turning intrusion and theft into a sport, rather than a crime. This is already occurring in the digital domain as is evident in the activities of computer crackers.

Furthermore, I would argue that initial efforts to protect digital copyright by copy protection contributed to the current condition in which most otherwise ethical computer users seem morally untroubled by their possession of pirated software.

Instead of cultivating among the newly computerized a sense of respect for the work of their fellows, early reliance on copy protection led to the subliminal notion that cracking into a software package somehow "earned" one the right to use it. Limited not by conscience but by technical skill, many soon felt free to do whatever they could get away with. This will continue to be a potential liability of the encryption of digitized commerce....

AN ECONOMY OF VERBS

The future forms and protections of intellectual property are densely obscured at this entrance to the Virtual Age.

Nevertheless, I can make (or reiterate) a few flat statements that I earnestly believe won't look too silly in 50 years.

- In the absence of the old containers, almost everything we think we know about intellectual property is wrong. We're going to have to unlearn it. We're going to have to look at information as though we'd never seen the stuff before.

- The protections that we will develop will rely far more on ethics and technology than on law.

- Encryption will be the technical basis for most intellectual property protection. (And should, for many reasons, be made more widely available.)

- The economy of the future will be based on relationship rather than possession. It will be continuous rather than sequential.

- And finally, in the years to come, most human exchange will be virtual rather than physical, consisting not of stuff but the stuff of which dreams are made. Our future business will be conducted in a world made more of verbs than nouns.

QUESTIONS

1. John Perry Barlow is a "cybertarian," a form of libertarian. In other words, he believes in bottom-up, decentralized solutions to the dilemmas that arise in cyberspace. Of the four modalities named by Lessig—law, norms, markets, and architecture—which does Barlow believe is most potently shaping the future for digitalized intellectual property? Explain.

2. What do you think Barlow would say about the ethics of Napster?

3. Recall the points made by Michael Eisner of The Walt Disney Company. How well does Barlow address the problem of movie piracy?

4. Think of the time and effort involved in writing a novel. In our culture, a novelist is unlikely to earn much money from "performances" or readings. (As Charles C. Mann has written, "If novelists make their living from public performances, Thomas Pynchon and J.D. Salinger would be penniless, and Salman Rushdie would be dead.") And a novelist is also unlikely to find much recompense in the "service" model that Barlow argues will replace the traditional proprietary rights to ideas. A novelist's expertise will not sell the way a doctor's or a lawyer's will. So what is Barlow's solution for the novelist in the digital age? Is there anything left for such creative people but to, as he writes elsewhere, "renew their acquaintance with humility?"

5. Barlow once wrote lyrics for the Grateful Dead, a band that gave away tapes of its concerts, which only enhanced the group's popularity. In fact, The Grateful Dead is truly a legend; its fans, many too young to have ever heard the band perform live, call themselves "Dead Heads," and gather annually. And although Jerry Garcia is actually dead, the remaining band members are considering playing together again.

What can you discover about the values of those who describe themselves as Dead Heads? To what extent does the Dead Head ethos match John Perry Barlow's thinking as described above?

THE HACKER ETHIC [5]

1. Access to computers—and anything that might teach you something about how the world works—should be unlimited and total. Always yield to the Hands-on imperative!
2. All information should be free.
3. Mistrust authority—promote the decentralization.
4. Hackers should be judged by their hacking, not bogus criteria such as degrees, age, race, or position.
5. You can create art and beauty on a computer.

---

[5] Steve Levy, *Hackers: Heroes of the Computer Revolution* (Garden City, New York: Anchor Press, 1984).

The Ten Commandments of Computer Ethics

Computer Ethics Institute

1. Thou shalt not use a computer to harm other people.

2. Thou shalt not interfere with other people's computer work.

3. Thou shalt not snoop around in other people's computer files.

4. Thou shalt not use a computer to steal.

5. Thou shalt not use a computer to bear false witness.

6. Thou shalt not copy or use proprietary software for which you have not paid.

7. Thou shalt not use other people's computer resources without authorization or proper compensation.

8. Thou shalt not appropriate other people's intellectual output.

9. Thou shalt think about the social consequences of the program you are writing or the system you are designing.

10. Thou shalt always use a computer in ways that insure consideration and respect for your fellow humans.

QUESTIONS

1. Compare "Hacker Ethics" with these rules. Do they have anything in common? How do they differ?

2. Consider the significance of each rule for the Napster scenario. Ask yourself how a proponent of the hacker ethic vs. a member of the Computer Ethics Institute would view it.

3. Look up the Computer Ethics Institute. Can you tell anything about the likely position of this organization in the "copyright wars" based on its membership and activities?

4. In his essay above, John Perry Barlow mentions "computer crackers." What can you find about the way the words "hackers" and "crackers" are used? Is there an ethical distinction?

ETHICAL ANALYSIS

Utilitarianism

How might we look at the ethics of Napster? Through much of our history, the most influential ethical reference point was religious; the rules to be followed were "written in the heavens" and were guidelines for achieving immortality of the soul. It was a radical break with tradition, then, for 18th-century philosopher and social thinker Jeremy

Bentham to suggest an entirely new frame of reference. Ethical behavior, he argued, was not a matter of pleasing God, but of bringing about as much happiness as possible for the greatest number of people. According to Bentham, the definitive moral standard is that of "utility," requiring us to consider the consequences of an act (or a social policy) for all those affected by it. One of Bentham's followers, 19th-century philosopher John Stuart Mill, would become the best known proponent of this ethical approach, known as **utilitarianism.**

According to the principle of utilitarianism, the right way to behave in a given situation is to choose the alternative most likely to produce the greatest overall good. First, we need to identify who is most affected by the situation at hand. Then we attempt to assess how they are affected. Are they hurt or helped by the Napster arrangement? We stack up the "benefits" against the "harms," focusing on both short- and long-term consequences for those who are most involved. Sounds simple enough, but let's see what happens when we use this approach to analyze online MP3 file sharing through Napster.

First, who cares about this situation the most; who is most affected by it? While a broad range of individuals and groups might have interests at stake in the Napster scenario, perhaps the most concerned are:

- Music fans
- "Signed" musicians (those with recording contracts)
- The recording industry
- "Indie" (independent) musicians

MUSIC FANS

Uploading a CD can take a long time, and the copy may be of relatively poor quality, but consumers voted with their mouseclicks, strongly in favor of Napster. A point of comparison: The number one Web site in July 2000, AOL, attracted about 80 million visitors to its Web portal. In the same month, Napster—then only a year old, attracted about 5 million individual visitors and could claim more than 20 million unique users in that first year of operation.[6]

Utilitarianism leads us to give weight to those figures; the huge number of satisfied Napster users must be factored into our harms/benefits analysis.

How do we measure the quality of their happiness with Napster? Fans praised the site for making conveniently available to them the riches of what some have called "the Celestial Jukebox." There were the simple monetary savings: whatever they

---

[6] According to Hank Barry, then CEO of Napster, quoted in CNNMoney online July 19, 2000. See http://www.money.cnn.com/2000/07/19/technology/napster.

would have spent on CDs if Napster did not exist. More difficult is the task of weighing the benefit of listening to the music files. Here we sense one of the problems with utilitarian analysis: how can immeasurables be measured?

People could download audio files from Napster, and sometimes that is all they wanted. But some used Napster to buy CDs more intelligently because it allowed them to hear whole tracks and CDs before investing in them. Rob Walker explained this in the New York Times in April of 2001 as Napster was being shut down. He likened the MP3 file to a paperback book: "a second tier of consumption allow[ing] readers to trade some of the timeliness and physical durability of the original product for a lower price and lower risk." He added:

> So why not paperback music? Is it worth spending $18 or $15 or even $12 to find out whether the rest of the Wheatus album is as cool as "Teenage Dirtbag"?

Music fans also appreciated the way Napster allowed them to get to know the work of relatively unknown, independent musical artists—the vast majority of performers who may not have had big-label backing.

But utilitarianism weighs competing harmful effects against any pluses. What might they have been for the users of Napster? One major consideration relates to the public policy behind copyright law itself: music fans (and society-at-large) benefit from the creative output of musicians, and—extending our utilitarian vision to the bigger intellectual property picture—of artists, thinkers, and inventors. If we do not protect their rights to profit from their work, will they lose the incentive to produce at all? Will music, art, culture, and science be drained of excitement, of fresh ideas? Some argue that this kind of idea-generation will still flow, that it does not depend on rewards, that starving artists will still be artists.

There may have been a more immediate dark side of Napster for its users, as this e-message suggests:

> Sure, it seems innocent enough. Let me just download this one song that I HAVE to have. But soon that one song isn't enough, you've had a taste, and now you're hooked. You become jealous of your roommate's extensive collection, or a car drives by your dorm room blasting your soon to be favorite song. You spend hours downloading. Just when you think there isn't another song you could possibly want, at 3 am the [********] downstairs start blasting Nelly's Ride Wit Me (with the base turned up so high initially you thought your rustic AKA old and decrepit dorm was collapsing). So you spring out of bed chastising yourself for being so neglectful for having forgotten that classic (meanwhile the fact that you also forget to study for your psych test doesn't faze you). Then you stare at the window with the anticipation of a pothead watching his friend pack a bowl, watching songs download with the

speed of a one-legged hurdler. Then an hour and twenty minutes later, when you have 99% of the song there, instead of enjoying this song like you used to, you are filled with scorn because you don't have it safely tucked away on your hard drive. Then you go to write a paper (because that's what you swore to your parents the brand new computer was for) and you can't save the document [because] there is no more room. So you tearfully delete the theme song to Gilligan's Island (which has brought you hours of enjoyment) to make room for your History paper. You contemplated deleting your Billy Joel collection that you cut class for three days and it took you 72 hours to download. The aggravation of it all was probably not worth the $20 it would have cost to buy his greatest hits CD. Meanwhile the hundreds of dollars you spent on CDs in the past is wasted [because] you haven't listened to a CD since you moved in. So you swear that you've had enough of Napster and you hate it and you hope it gets crushed in court and you'll never use it again. But the NAPSTER icon is still there, lurking on your screen, waiting for you to have a relapse.[7]

Capturing MP3 files may waste time, yet millions of people have demonstrated that they thought it was well worth it.

"SIGNED" MUSICIANS

Lars Ulrich and his band Metallica were plaintiffs fighting Napster. They believed they lost royalty payments because of online music sharing. While there is some evidence that that might be true, such as decreased CD sales in areas near college campuses,[8] there seems to be some evidence that online music sharing coexists with stronger sales of CDs. If you have ever used Napster (or Napster-like systems), were you then less likely to buy music? What might be the advantages of a Metallica CD compared to having a Metallica MP3 file on your hard drive? Rob Walker describes a CD as a cultural product, superior to downloads for several reasons. Napster, dependent as it was on peers, could bring in uneven sound quality and mislabeled or incomplete versions of songs, while, as Walker notes, a brand new CD is guaranteed to be of consistent quality:

It's an official, completed object. It's satisfying.

Then there's its portability and convenience. A CD is light, pocketable; it can go with you anywhere.

---

[7] Anonymous e-mail provided by Carrie Tolerico, Temple University undergraduate.
[8] The Ninth Circuit Court of Appeals in the Napster decision gave credence to such evidence in agreeing with the District Court that an injunction should issue.

There is arguably something importantly tactile, possess-able, about a CD as opposed to the sound we can call forth from a computer. Suppose we widen our lens to ask an analogous question: Will digital text/electric books replace the hard copy, paper book? On one side William Mitchell, dean of Massachusetts Institute of Technology, has said that physical books will be interesting only to those "addicted to the look and feel of tree flakes encased in dead cow." Charles Mann counters, "Who will curl up with a computer in bed?"[9]

While "signed" musicians might argue that Napster's existence loomed over the creative process itself, ultimately destroying the artist's urge to imagine and produce new work, another way to understand online music is as an opportunity: It blasts through the distribution bottleneck of the established system and offers musicians a direct link with their uncounted fans. As Courtney Love put it, a napsterized world could appeal to musicians who would normally sign contracts heavily weighted in favor of the recording companies: "Now artists have options. We don't have to work with the major labels anymore because the digital economy is creating new ways to distribute and market music." She goes on:

> Major labels are freaking out because they have no control in this new world. Artists can sell CDs directly to fans. We can make direct deals with thousands of other Web sites and promote music to millions of people that old record companies never touch. We're about to have lots of new ways to sell our music: downloads, hardware bundles, memory sticks, live Webcasts, and lots of other things that aren't invented yet.[10]

Musiclink is a system that allows consumers to take MP3 files and invites them to leave a voluntary payment behind—a "tip." What other ideas have surfaced that provide payment for music files? Do you think established musicians would perceive them as adequate—so that they might consider breaking out of the present system? Start your search at: **http://www.fairtunes.com and http://www.paypal.com**.

RECORDING INDUSTRY

Recording companies, like the musicians they sign, claim that Napster and other free online music has severely cut into profits. It may not be easy to determine cause and effect, but we do know that CD sales have weakened in the napsterized world. While CD sales increased 6.5% in 2000, a year in which there were an estimated 6

If you have ever down-loaded music for free, were you then less likely to buy it?

---

[9] Charles C. Mann, "Who Will Own Your Next Good Idea?" *The Atlantic Monthly*, September, 1998. (http://www.theatlantic.com/)

[10] Testimony to Congress, June 14, 2000.

billion downloads, from 2001 to 2002, about 62 million fewer CDs were sold, according to Nielson Soundscan, a decline of 9%. The industry blames downloading for a 25% slide in revenue since Napster began in 1999. Too, the industry points out that its financials are poorly understood, that only about 15% of all releases are profitable, and those support the 85% that are not. Free music deeply undercuts the whole arrangement.

The entertainment industry does have reason to take a sour view of the future. A 15-year-old Norwegian boy, Jon Lech, wrote a program that enabled DVD film to be copied onto a computer so that movies could be downloaded. Suddenly a multi-million dollar product could be traded freely. This unscrambling of film encryption represented perhaps the ultimate disturbance for media content providers. Although they succeeded in prosecuting Lech under the DMCA, it seems clear that there is a certain cat-and-mouse game ongoing between copyright protectors and hackers that is not at all amusing for the cats, and in which the mice are the ones who appear to have multiple lives. If we consider—as we must, according to utilitarian analysis—long-term likelihoods, the costs seem severe. Each move to encrypt digital CDs and films instantly becomes, for those around the world eager to make sure that information remains free, an invitation to decode.

Napster was eliminated, but its imitators—which share music files directly, leaving no one to sue—are still around. Grokster and KaZaA are still out there, to say nothing of what the cyberpunks have in the pipeline. Case-by-case enforcement of copyright is slow and expensive and seems like a clunky strategy in an environment where millions of consumers are accustomed to free access. As of July 2003 more than 2.6 billion songs and movies were being copied every month, according to industry estimates. It may be impossible to put all the cats back in the bag.

Are recent lawsuits against individual downloaders discouraging music file sharing? Compare reports: http://www.pewinternet. org vs. http://www. bigchampagne.com

"INDIE" MUSICIANS

A handful of labels control virtually all of the music sold in the U.S., and the vast majority of musicians are not signed, not within the golden orbit of their promotion and distribution systems. As Courtney Love explained, 85% of the members of the American Music Federation do not work regularly.

That said, this independent majority of musicians experiences music file sharing as a mixed blessing. Depressingly, it represents the demise of the royalty system of payment. Yet, as peer-to-peer trading educates the music audience, it gives artists exposure, a chance to be heard, perhaps even the momentum they need to break into popular consciousness. In fact, many musicians have given permission for their works to be shared, free—on Napster and Napster-like systems, viewing the Internet as an alternative to the normal channels of marketing and distribution. Arguably, artists could make money beyond the Net—in recordings and performances—once the Net has given them to their fans. The same benefits that established musicians could enjoy by embracing this new model would also be available to unsigned artists, to be appreciated more intensely by those who never had a break. As hip-hop artist Chuck D puts it:

> File sharing and downloadable distribution is the new radio. It's a fantastic way for art to get exposed. This new realm can actually introduce artists into the marketplace and allow a global expansion of their art.

So, let's try to do the overall utilitarian calculation: Is free music online more harmful, or more beneficial, on balance, for the important stakeholders? In the assessment above, we tend to see more pros than cons. While the shareholders of the recording industry, those employed by the major labels, and those artists who are signed by them are at risk financially, it is not clear to what extent. Meanwhile, fans are eagerly suctioning the music, music culture is being rendered more diverse, and musicians previously locked out of the system are getting some exposure. The largest stakeholder group, the fans, seems mostly satisfied, while the smallest group, the major labels—bears the greatest loss. Meanwhile, musicians have an opportunity to ride the new technology and make an end-run around established industry practice. Roughly speaking, online music sharing seems to hold up under utilitarian ethical scrutiny.

Utilitarian thinking asks us to measure things that do not seem measurable: the happiness of hearing Bats & Mice, or the unhappiness of knowing your new song will be traded for free, for example. It asks us to compare apples and oranges: the loss of profits against the knowledge that your once-obscure music can reach a world-wide audience. It asks us to consider long-term consequences, and cyberspace is likely to have more than the usual amount of unknowns or immeasurables, particularly as we look to the future. Perhaps most troubling, the utilitarian model doesn't seem to address a primary ethical issue in the Napster situation: Is online MP3 sharing stealing?

http://www.
futureofmusic.org

Moral Rights and Duties

Another ethical approach may provide us with a more satisfying means of analyzing Napster.

Deontological[11] ethics is marked by steadfastness to universal principles—respect for persons and property, freedom of speech, fairness, honesty, for example—no matter what the consequential fallout. At the core of this approach to making ethical choices is the understanding that moral action should be guided by certain overriding rights and duties.

---

[11] From the Greek *deon,* or duty.

The most famous deontological thinker, 18th-century German philosopher Immanuel Kant, believed that human beings could reason their way to a set of absolute rules for morally correct behavior. A person should never lie, according to Kant, even when lying seems to produce a good result. Suppose someone running away from a murderer tells you where he is going to hide, and then the murderer rushes up to ask you where the runner went. Wouldn't this be a good time to lie? Kant would say there is never a good time, even in this example.

Technology allows us to do many new things. Because we can do them, does that make them right? Technology allows the government to read our license plates from satellites. Does that mean it is right for the government to learn every detail of our private lives? Technology allows Napster fans to get free music online. Does that mean they should take it? The deontological approach to ethics does not necessarily let us get away with behavior just because it is possible, even if that behavior serves many purposes, even if it makes many millions of people happy. What is moral must be justified as aligned with absolute rights and duties.

There are times, though, when a number of different rights and duties seem to be woven into the fabric of an ethical dilemma. What to do when they are in conflict? In the digitalized intellectual property context, we observe an intricate pattern in which claims to property ownership and claims to freedom of expression are in partnership and also at odds.

One right that surfaces in the Napster situation is the right to property. Late 17th-century political theorist John Locke articulated a justification of the natural right of each person, by dint of the labor he invested in it, to own property. Locke wrote:

> Though the earth, and all inferior creatures, be common to all men, yet every man has a property in his own person: this no body has any right to but himself. The labour of his body, and the work of his hands, we may say, are properly his. Whatsoever then he removes out of the state that nature hath provided, and left it in, he hath mixed his labour with, and joined to it something that is his own, and thereby makes it his property. It being by him removed from the common state nature hath placed it in, it hath by this labour something annexed to it, that excludes the common right of other men: for this labour being the unquestionable property of the labourer, no man but he can have a right to what that is once joined to, at least where there is enough, and as good, left in common for others.

Note that Locke reasons from the natural right each person has to bodily integrity ("property in his own person") to the right to own land upon which a person has physically worked—this some have called "sweat equity." Lockean thinking expresses belief in individual freedom, in the right of each person to choose how to live. It represents a break with the feudal world, where a social caste system preempted any such choice, and where the powerful could keep what superior physical force allowed them to take. By the 18th century, our legal tradition echoed Locke's ideas. William Blackstone's authoritative treatise on the common law described a "bundle" of property rights, including the right of an owner to use property as he saw fit, to keep other people out, and to derive income from the property or transfer it to someone else for value. Locke's philosophy underpins the modern liberal state, legitimating government as the arbiter of property division and exchange.

Locke was writing about land and other tangibles. Does his theory fit when we look at the output of the human mind, at intellectual property? Surely the novelist, artist, musician, and inventor are deserving of the fruits of their labor, much as the Lockean laborer? Yet there is a critical difference between intellectual and other forms of property, as Lessig and Barlow have pointed out: You steal my car and it's gone from me; you sing my song, and I still have it. Intellectual property is not a zero-sum game; it is "non-rivalrous." How might this impact our ethical analysis?

And does the right to intellectual property belong entirely to the creator of it? Recall the Constitutional language. It empowers Congress to pass laws "*to promote the progress of science and (the) useful arts* by securing for limited Times to authors and inventors the exclusive right to their respective Writings and Discoveries." [emphasis added] The language does not focus on rewards, but on rewards as a means to an end: to provide the public with the benefits of human intelligence. In other words, copyright was designed with a public purpose, to give creators the incentive to create for us all. In 1790, as George Washington asked Congress to enact copyright laws, he made the point that increasing the national stock of knowledge was in our fundamental interest as a society. Knowledge, he said, is "the surest basis of public happiness."

See the writings of Columbia law professor Jane Ginsburg on "author control."

So if writers and artists lose the copyright system and its incentives, will they no longer produce, and will the public right to intellectual property be compromised? One jazz student wonders:

> Will music of the future be written for purer, higher reasons by a group of truly starving musicians? Or can't one argue that even the greatest musical masterpieces ever written were commissioned or "patronized?" Even Bach, the greatest religious composer of all time, who wrote more than 200 cantatas for the Church, was a professional musician, paid for his time and for his artistry. Mozart's final unfinished mass requiem was supposedly written under the most dire financial circumstances, a sort of last hope at collecting.[12]

---

[12] Joshua Olmstead, Temple University student, e-message received July 12, 2000.

Many have noted the paradigm shift that has overtaken us in the postmodern age: Culture is less a matter of a series of discrete, utterly original achievements, each by a single brilliant individual; it is instead a stream of inventive consciousness, generated through multiple interactions and perspectives. As a society, we have the right to benefit from our collective genius, the argument goes, and there can be no better place for stimulating it than cyberspace. If knowledge is socially constructed, online content must be free.

What of the rights of the Napster user, or of any of us, to access and copy and re-use digitalized information? Some argue that the fundamental values of freedom of expression are at stake here—not of the original creators, but of "second generation" creators, who would receive, process, and reassemble creative product. Much of art and culture is derivative, is pastiche. This has always been so—Shakespeare based Anthony and Cleopatra on Plutarch—but in our postmodern world, it is even more so. Think of "sampling"—the practice of weaving snippets of songs within songs. In 1998, a CD plant refused to manufacture a new CD by an experimental group that had created an "audio-collage" by mixing sounds from different sources. Negativland's *Over the Edge, Volume 3: The Weatherman's Dumb Stupid Come-Out Line* never made it to our collective ears. And then there is the way the Internet is an interactive medium, allowing users to move around, selecting the way they receive data and images. Does this capability transform the passive listener into an agent, a creator? As Lawrence Lessig writes, "What is important is the right to use without permission," framing the right as "an autonomy conception."

Is cutting and pasting, taking and removing, a fundamental right of 21st-century expression? And if this is the way our culture is evolving, should law be used to stem that flow?

Kantian thinking leads us to wonder if all this is just a blurring of the simple truth that, when all is said and done, what is happening with online music sharing is *stealing*—and there is a fundamental duty not to steal. We can contextualize intellectual property rights and discuss competing claims to free speech—but isn't this just a case of greed, of taking what, under the present system, is not ours to take? Even here though, the ground shifts under us. Some would argue that the stealing that is going on is on the part of the industry. This is certainly Courtney Love's position, as she describes the unfair profits taken from "slave" musicians. Fans, too see the economic unfairness:

Today, if I want to purchase a song, old or new, the music industry forces me to buy a compact disc I don't want, in packaging I don't need, with photographs and artwork I couldn't care less about, and accompanied by 10 other songs I have not the slightest use for. For this service they charge me anywhere from $14 to $18. This is price gouging, plain and simple.[13]

Another fan put it even more succinctly: "It's OK to take money from the recording industry. They're the ones who inflate prices."[14]

In fact, there is some kind of disconnect here. Napster users seemed not to think of themselves as stealing when they took MP3 files. This may be a generational issue. One study found that most people 35 and older viewed using Napster as a violation of law, but most of those 18 to 24 saw it as acceptable.[15] One respondent said, "The only people who think it's wrong are just a lot of old people with a lot of money." Or it may be that people feel that, once they have purchased a CD, it is theirs. They feel free to play it for their friends; it is only a small step from there to sharing the music you've paid for with others who have done the same for you. While the industry puts file sharing on the same moral plane as walking out of a music store with a CD you haven't paid for, the 35 million adult Americans who, as of July 2003, admit they download music from the Internet,[16] seem to put this activity on a moral par with taping songs from the radio for a friend.

So, after we've explored the various and conflicting rights claims, where are we? Is there a "final answer" when we hold the deontological prism up to Napster? Perhaps not, unless we can reach some solid ground in terms of ranking different moral claims.

Central to deontology is Kant's view that each person has the right to be treated with respect as the equal of every other, and that each person has the corresponding duty to treat everyone else with respect as an equal. He arrived at this by means of his **categorical imperatives**. The first of these states that people should be willing to have the reasons for their actions become universal principles. That is, they should be willing to live in a world where the actions they chose to take are repeated whenever the same situations arise, even if they happen to be on the receiving end of such actions. Think of Napster. Assume music fans chose to download MP3 files because it is convenient, free, and serves their purposes as consumers and music lovers. If we apply Kant's first categorical imperative, the Napster user should ask: Would I want to live in a world where consumers of creative output could take it in digitalized form at no cost?

---

[13] Nick Straguzzi, letter to the editor, *Philadelphia Inquirer*, January 2001.

[14] Alex Roque. Chuck D claims that a CD costs 89 cents to produce.

[15] Institute for Online Commerce, a consumer behavior research organization.

[16] Pew Internet and American Life Project, July 2003.

Perhaps the question would have a sharper edge when the shoe is on the other foot. Kant also poses the question: What if you were the victim of the same behavior? Suppose it was your song that was freely available online? Or, to shift to the DVD context, suppose it was your film that was being flashed around the world for free? In Kantian terms, it appears that online sharing of intellectual property is unethical.

In another formulation of the categorical imperative, Kant states that we should have respect for the intrinsic value of other people, and not just use them as means to achieve our own purposes. Human beings are not tools or instruments to be manipulated, but must be respected as equal beings with the right to make fully informed choices for themselves. Again, this points to Napster as wrong, in that downloading free music from the Internet "uses" musical artists, disregarding whatever value they may wish to receive for their work.

REFLECTION AND EXPLORATION

Having mulled over Napster within the utilitarian and then the deontological frameworks, we have arrived at an uncertain place. The first approach seems to point one way, but the second leans in the opposite direction; we are left unsettled, shrugging. Still, this unresolved aftertaste may be exactly appropriate. Technology ethicist Jerden Van Den Hoven and many of his colleagues have concluded that we cannot expect to lay a utility or rights-based moral template down on Internet quandaries and reach a neat resolution as to what is right. These problems tend not to yield to traditional moral analysis, partly because the "pace of technological development and novelty" is constantly shifting the ground beneath us. What we can hope to do instead is allow our analysis to be fluid, to be a more "reflective, exploratory approach."

We could describe the questions and ambiguities we have considered so far to be just such a reflective process. We could say that we have been sharpening our awareness that they exist, that the kind of puzzling we are doing will continue, and will continue to be crucially important.

CYBERSPACE: NEW WORLD, NEW LAW?

Cyberlaw expert David Post reminds us of the stunning impact Napster had when it was new: "All of a sudden, thanks to a little string of (free) software, the whole world is your hard drive....Who would have thought that [the "celestial jukebox"] would come, not in the form of some gigantic machine housed in the basement of Time-Warner or Sony Music Corporation, but as a simple string of code written by a 19-year-old?" He describes cyberspace as a sort of paradise—"our newly-discovered little island." But there is trouble in paradise: "[I]t turns out that some people are "smuggling" things in across the border from real-space onto our island....And that makes...Metallica, many of the large music studios, [and] the Recording Industry Association of America...pretty unhappy, because they believe that copyright law protects them—or, at least, that it should protect them—from actions of this kind...." In this excerpt from his essay, Post invites us to look at the struggle over Napster and copyright in a fresh way, using a particular moment in U.S. history.

Napster, Jefferson's Moose, and the Law of Cyberspace

David G. Post

It seems that this place—"cyberspace"— is a place unlike any we have seen before; it's as if we've come across a hitherto undiscovered island—somewhere off the coast of Antarctica, say—that has some pretty strange features. We can travel to and from it in an instant; while we're there, we can move about completely unencumbered by geography, gravity, or the other inconveniences of the real, tangible world. We can engage in trade, form communities, and talk to one another there in new, sometimes bizarre, and occasionally unfathomable ways. It has strange new life forms—bots, web-crawlers, cookies, spiders, viruses....[T]he familiar lines on the map around which we organize so much of our lives don't seem to matter there at all. It is noplace, but somehow it seems to keep growing, and to have room for anyone and anything.

To find ways to think about this new place, I have...been spending considerable time recently with the writings of Thomas Jefferson. The American continent seemed as (or more) bizarre and unfathomable to Jefferson (and his contemporaries) as cyberspace does to us, and nobody thought as clearly, and as intelligently, about New Worlds, and

about how to think about New Worlds, as Jefferson did.

There's one scene I've come across that I can't seem to get out of my mind. The story goes like this. It is 1787, shortly after Jefferson had taken up his post as the American Minister to France. 1787 was, of course, a truly remarkable year in human history. On one side of the Atlantic, delegates were gathering in Philadelphia to begin deliberating over a new Constitution for the recently-formed United States of America. And on the other side, the French Revolution was just beginning; bread riots in the streets of Paris, and a beleaguered King's call for a gathering of the "Assembly of Notables" at Versailles, opened the first chapter in a complex and bloody chain of events that tore European society to pieces and fundamentally altered the course of the modern world.

In the midst of all of these earth-shaking events, Jefferson found the time to arrange for the display of the complete carcass of a moose, bones, skin and antlers attached and 7 feet tall at the shoulders, in the entrance hall of his residence, the elegant Hotel de Langeac in the center of Paris. This had been, as you might imagine, no small undertaking on his part; getting a moose from the American woods to Paris in 1787 was an almost unbelievably complicated business....Yet he spent his time and money on this, going so far as to call the moose carcass "an acquisition more precious than you can imagine" in a letter to a friend. What was going on?...

Jefferson brought the moose to Paris because there was a serious scientific debate raging in the 18th century about whether the New World was a degenerate place. The moose was a data point in this debate, ammunition in this intellectual war. The dominant scientific view at the time was that the native animals in the New World were smaller than those in the Old, that domestic animals actually got smaller if they were transported to the New World, and that the New World had smaller numbers of animal and plant species than the Old. They didn't know what it was—the New World was too humid?? too cold??—but there was something about the place that took away the Life Force.

So out comes the moose. The moose was part of Jefferson's campaign to show that this particular new world was not a degenerate place. Sometimes a picture— or, better yet, a carcass—is worth a thousand words. The moose is a big animal, larger by a considerable margin than its European counterparts (the reindeer and caribou). Its brooding presence in downtown Paris was intended to make observers think twice about the degeneracy theory. Degenerate animals in the New World? Just check out that moose!

The degeneracy theory of animals in America...was, in Jefferson's view, just one part of a general campaign in the Old World to discredit the New World's claims to self-government, and to discourage emigration....So the moose was a kind of advertisement for New World. It had, figuratively speaking, a sign hanging around its neck: "Come to America— see for yourself how degenerate life is there."

But...the moose was more than this, too. Jefferson used the moose to get his French friends to stand back, to gasp, and to say: There really is a new world out there, one that has things in it that we can hardly imagine. He wanted them to have an aha! moment in regard to that New World from out of which Jefferson (and his moose) had emerged, to share in his excitement about the possibilities inherent in this astounding new place. That the New World had these strange new beings was, to Jefferson, the good news, for it meant that it was a place where we could think the unthinkable, re-evaluate the Received Wisdom, and re-think the world in which we were to live.

Our first reaction to new things is often very different—fear. It was true then—lots of people, respectable and intelligent people, were genuinely fearful about what they'd find in the New World, and, once they were there, about what might lie in waiting on the other side of the Alleghenies. And it's true now....

But it was surely not Jefferson's reaction. The first thing he would ask, and the first thing we should ask, about Napster is not whether it constitutes an infringement of copyright under Section

Check out the Digital Media Project at http://www.cyber.law. harvard.edu

512 of the U.S. Copyright Act; instead, it is whether, and how, it opens up new possibilities and new horizons for the human species and how we might help it do so.

Napster can be our moose. It can and should tempt us to explore this new place, to try to understand the ways in which it is different than (and the ways in which it is the same as) more familiar terrain; it can show us that there are new and wonderfully exciting things out there. It can and should remind us that we don't know everything there is to know about how life can be lived and about how societies can be built, that we, too, can always rethink Received Wisdom. "Doubt," Jefferson wrote in connection with his moose escapade, "is wisdom." He was right. We need more doubt about law in cyberspace—fewer "answers" and more questions; fewer fences against, and more roads to, the lands lying on the other side of the Allegheny Mountains. We cannot seriously hope to govern wisely here without it.

CHAPTER PROBLEMS

1. In 2003, Walt Disney's copyright on Mickey Mouse was set to expire; its rights to Pluto, Donald Duck, and Goofy were due to end not long after. So, in the late 1990s, Disney, along with the other major players in the entertainment oligopoly, lobbied hard and contributed heavily to certain political campaigns. The result was a law Congress quietly passed, the so-called Sonny Bono Act, (the CTEA), which extended all copyrights by another twenty years. Professor Lawrence Lessig was deeply concerned by this. He thought the Bono Act was "not just another instance of fat cat favoritism but part of a disastrous trend toward what might be called property-right fundamentalism…threatening to destroy the Internet and plunge us into a cultural dark age."[17] Lessig organized *Eldred v. Ashcroft*, a lawsuit challenging the Bono Act as a violation of the First Amendment. Supporting briefs in the case were filed by dozens of sympathetic individuals and groups, including Intel Corporation, the National Writers Union, library associations, and economists. *Eldred v. Ashcroft* sparked a worldwide discussion of the future of the "public domain," those cultural artifacts that remain freely accessible to artists, scholars, musicians, and everyone else.

---

[17] James Surowieki, "Righting Copywrongs," *The New Yorker*, January 21, 2002.

(a) How did the Supreme Court rule in the 2003 case? What were the arguments on each side? (You can find out by reading the amicus briefs mentioned above.)

(b) A grassroots effort to support the "cultural commons" proposes legislation that would not burden copyright owners. Find out what you can about the Public Domain Enhancement Act.

2. In February 2001, as the federal appeals court paved the way for an injunction against Napster, the RIAA sent dozens of notices out to Internet Service Providers (ISPs) associated with Napster clones, warning them that their users were violating copyright laws. Such "cease and desist" letters operate as "notice" under the Digital Millennium Copyright Act, triggering the duty of the ISPs to "take down" the offending material.

One of those letters went out to Aimster. Like Napster, Aimster enables MP3 file sharing. It piggybacks on America Online, allowing the users of AOL's instant messaging service to exchange files. It was dubbed the "Pig Encoder" because the program automatically scrambles user names Pig Latin-style, moving first letters to the end of each word. In May 2001, Aimster filed suit against the RIAA, arguing the privacy of its members was at stake. Ironically, Aimster claimed that the Pig Encoder itself is copyrighted technology and any attempt to unscramble its encryption violates the DMCA's anti-circumvention provisions.

Is there a way to ethically distinguish Aimster from Napster? What can you find about the result of this legal wrangle?

3. The industry sued the online peer-to-peer music sharing services Grokster and StreamCast Networks for copyright infringement. The case was decided in 2003 by a federal judge in Los Angeles in April 2003. What was the ruling? What arguments did Judge Steven Wilson make in reaching it? Can you identify any ethical perspectives in Wilson's argument?

4. KaZaA is an online swapping program that enables its users to download copyrighted music, television shows, and movies. It was originally developed in Holland. It is distributed by Sharman Networks, a company incorporated in the South Pacific island nation of Vanatu. It is managed from Australia. It has servers in Denmark, and its source code was last tracked in Estonia. What happened when American recording and movie industry plaintiffs tried to bring KaZaA to justice in Los Angeles, again before Judge Steven Wilson? Does Wilson take the same ethical stance here that he took in the Grokster case?

5. Some scholars debunk the idea of single, original "romantic authorship," arguing that it has merely been conjured up by publishers who would profit from it. Rochelle Dreyfuss sets up the critique this way:

Nothing is genuinely creative and innovative; everyone just reworks the commons. The reason copyright law has so many problems (on determining originality, infringement, and the like) is that its conceptual categories are based on false assumptions; if there is no such thing as an original work of authorship, everything (or nothing) is infringement.

But she then explains how this argument misses the mark:

It fits so poorly with our intuitive sense of what goes into the creative process, matches so little with what those who innovate expect from their efforts, and accounts not at all for the attention that employers, funders, and audiences pay to resumes, publications, credits, and track records. More important, this view loses sight of the instrumental goals that intellectual property laws fulfill....[I]f grazing the common is not [so] hard...if "information products" are not as creative as intellectual property law assumes, then...[the] law is more necessary. An aim of law, after all, is to influence people to engage in socially valued activity, presumably including...the prosaic business of generating intellectual output. The heavy emphasis that [is placed] on authorship shows that there is also an instrumental role...in assuring quality, accuracy, and the accessibility of work product for further use.[18]

Analyze Dreyfuss' statement in ethical terms. Do you recognize any deontological or utilitarian elements here?

6. Eric Corley publishes *2600: The Hacker Quarterly* and runs an affiliated Web site. In 2001, Corley posted a story about DeCSS, the program devised by a Norwegian teenager that can crack the security code on DVDs so they can be copied, compressed, and distributed over the Internet. He detailed how the program was developed and the movie industry's efforts to shut down Web sites posting DeCSS. Corley included copies of the code because "in a journalistic world you have to show your evidence." Eight movie studios sued Eric Corley after he put DeCSS on his hacker site, arguing that his posting violated the anti-decryption provisions of the Digital Millennium Copyright Act. But Corley argued this part of the Act eliminates the "fair use" that now permits the replication of copyrighted material for scholarship, criticism, or parody. The lawyer for the studios countered that the Act is needed to prevent the "Napsterization of the movie industry."

---

[18] Rochelle Cooper Dreyfuss, Vand. L. Rev. 53:1161 (2000).

Find out what has happened in *Universal City Studios v. Reimerdes*. Using utilitarian analysis, determine whether or not Corley acted ethically. To explore a fascinating Web site on DeCSS de-encryption curated by Dr. David Touretzky of Carnegie Mellon University's Computer Information Sciences Department, visit: **http://www.cs.cmu.edu/~dst/DeCSS/Gallery/**.

7. If you can't fight 'em, join 'em: By late 2001, the five multinational companies that dominate the recording industry decided to introduce their own online music services. Two competing paid, licensed subscription services were launched: MusicNet (with songs from AOL Time Warner, BMG, and EMI) and Pressplay (with music from Sony and Universal). The major labels were not willing to license their full catalogs, however, and both services limited the number of songs that could be downloaded and what could be done with them. By April 2003 the Apple music service was unveiled, selling a bigger range of songs for 99 cents each, to immediate success. The price of online songs began to drop. Pressplay was sold to Roxio, which had also bought post-bankruptcy Napster's name and assets. Roxio then offered a subscription service under the Napster name—demonstrating that Napster remains the brand most closely associated with online music. What is the latest with online music fee-paying services? Are they popular? Are they profitable? Are they replacing music sharing? Do they solve the ethical problems raised by Napster?

8. Artist Mark Napier created a Web site that parodied the Barbie doll. With digital images and text, he commented on Barbie as a cultural icon. In an interactive section, visitors could share what Barbie meant to them as they were growing up. There was also an "Alternative Barbies" section, a behind-the-scenes look at the seamy underbelly of Barbie's world, including digitally-altered "Fat and Ugly Barbie" and "Mentally Challenged Barbie." Mattel, Inc., maker of Barbie and owner of the trademark, threatened to sue Napier. Access his Web site through **http://www.chillingeffects.org**. Find out what happened.

9. Scholar Debora Halbert foresaw, in a 1994 article, the struggle over copyright:

> Ultimately, given current trends, the power of the state will be used to continue to repress movements towards equal access to information. Those considered "subversive" will continue to be arrested, their property confiscated and they will be tried and sent to jail. Secrecy and ownership will continue to dominate our governmental relations to information even as challenges are made to these concepts. Change will probably only occur from the bottom up when individuals recognize that information and knowledge are power that they should have access to. This is begin-

ning to occur as grass roots organizations begin to talk about rights to information and communication.[19]

10. As this book goes to press, recent legal expansions of copyright which benefit content owners have distressed many activists. How are they responding? See **http://www.copyfight.org** and **http://www.creativecommons.org**. See also **http://www.mediatank.org**.

11. Music file swapping and the burning of downloaded music onto CDs is routine behavior outside of the United States, especially in Europe and in Asia. In China, for example, 90% of recordings are pirated. What, if anything, is the recording industry doing to staunch the flow of pirated music abroad? What can it do?

12. The Associated Press reported in June 2003 that "worldwide piracy of business software products like Microsoft Office declined slightly in 2002 because of better education and more aggressive tactics" to stop it. The main source of software piracy remains businesses buying one copy of software and then making copies to install on multiple computers. Compare the ethics of this practice to that of online music sharing.

13. Get together with a classmate, go online, and locate an ethical statement or code of ethics (other than those found in chapter 1 of this text). Talk it over. Decide whether you think it does a good job of addressing the issues raised in chapter 1.

---

[19] "Computer Technology and Legal Discourse," *Murdoch University Electronic Journal of Law* No. 2 (May 1994).

CHAPTER 2

Privacy & Information Technology

A wonderful fact to reflect upon, that every human creature is constituted to be that profound secret and mystery to every other. A solemn consideration, when I enter a great city by night, that every one of those darkly clustered houses encloses its own secret; that every room in every one of them encloses its own secret; that in every beating heart in the hundreds of thousands of breasts there is, in some of its imaginings, a secret to the heart nearest to it!

—Charles Dickens

You already have zero privacy—get over it.

—Scott McNealy, CEO, Sun Microsystems

Should the government be allowed to use complex software to find patterns of spending or patterns of activities to find out if someone has been committing illegal acts if there is no probable cause in the first place? Patriot I and Patriot II open the door to that, and that means everybody in the country is under suspicion.

—Ronald Kahn, professor of politics and law, Oberlin College

There is indeed a whole lot a scannin' goin' on. People surreptitiously intercept, record, and disclose the usual suspects for the usual reasons, in the perpetual parade of human perfidy. Popular motivations are love, sex, drugs, crime, politics, business, and employment. And if we reflect, we quickly see that none of us is perfect and that all of us are potential victims. Who among us does not sometime, somewhere, have something they would prefer to keep to themselves?

—Rodney A. Smolla, "Information as Contraband,"
96 *Nw. Univ. L. Rev.* 1099 (2002).

Human beings as individuals must experience a degree of privacy to thrive. Yet, as they act inside organizations, they frequently need information about one another—information that may be sensitive and confidential. Employers want to find out if their workers are productive and loyal. Corporations want to know the preferences of potential customers or the strategies of their competitors. Health insurers want access to patient medical histories and genetic profiles. Governments want to thwart terrorists. Tension between privacy and the need to know is heightened as computer technology revolutionizes information gathering. The process has never been so fast, so efficient, so omnipresent.

This chapter highlights the conflict between the sweeping power of technology to access and assemble information and ongoing concerns about privacy that we all share. It starts with electronic surveillance at work—with the interception of e-mail by employers. Shifting to the public sector, we explore how the war on terrorism appears to justify enhanced technologies for government surveillance and data collection. Next, we look at the area of consumer privacy, as we consider the collection of personal information in the online marketplace. The chapter closes with a reading about the problem of information technology in the health care context.

ETHICS CASE: GENETIC TESTING IN 2007

It is 2007, the year a Liberian terrorist group claimed responsibility for the explosion of a small nuclear device in Los Angeles. In this first major domestic terror incident since 9/11/01, Lily Kim lost an uncle and two college friends. She was still grieving the loss when something was announced at work that upset her in a new way.

A 33-year-old divorced mother of two boys, Lily works for a rapidly expanding biotechnology company called Greengenes. The company hired her because she had exactly the right training to do what it needed: research in the field of food irradiation. Treating food with small doses of radiation increases crop yields and nutritional value. Lily did Ph.D. research in this area. She started as head of one lab, but by 2006 she was supervising three labs. Lily has been enjoying her job at Greengenes and has been receiving excellent performance evaluations, raises, and bonuses. Last year she earned $250,000.

Not long after the Los Angeles debacle, Greengenes announced that it was cooperating with the government in compiling a DNA database of its employees. All the employees had to do was allow the insides of their mouths to be briefly and painlessly swabbed for sample tissue. At the same time, Greengenes decided to begin a genetic testing program of its own, using the DNA samples it was gathering for the government to run tests on all of its employees. With a few cells from a cheek-swab, the company could discover whether a person had the genetic tendency to develop serious disease in the future. Greengenes planned to create a computerized database of all test results.

This kind of information, Greengenes explained, would be valuable in a number of ways. First, the genetic test results would help control rapidly escalating health care expenses. In the U.S., such costs were increasingly falling on the shoulders of employ-ers. To compete effectively in the global marketplace, Greengenes believed it had the right to know if the people it hired and trained might become seriously ill and have their productive capacities cut short. Its genetic testing program, Greengenes pointed out, would simply give the company improved information as to how best to invest its resources.

Lily read all of this and was not impressed. She thought Greengenes was probably trying to protect itself from being sued, should anyone become ill from being exposed to too much radiation at work. In her view, if there was a dangerous level of radiation around, the company should install better protective gear. Instead it claimed to be doing this for the employees' own good: "Many of our employees are exposed to chemicals and radiation on the job. There is much we still don't know about these low-level exposures. Should an employee be susceptible to getting cancer, we would want to know, so we could move that person to some other location in the company." To Lily that sounded like fear of lawsuits, and a possible demotion for anyone who tested with a "susceptibility."

Lily was familiar with DNA tests. She knew people who had had themselves tested—especially those with family histories of inherited illness that could be prevented with some degree of warning. One friend had the markers for heart disease and had started taking blood thinners. In such situations—where someone chose to be tested and where there was a way to respond to bad news, Lily thought getting tested made sense. But producing on demand was another matter. When the demand originated from the government, at least that was supposed to make the country safer. But Lily resisted the idea of having to submit to genetic testing for her employer:

"As a scientist, I hate to admit it", she said, "but there are times when cutting-edge technology can be used clumsily, so that it does *not* benefit human existence. *I don't want to know* if I am likely to develop, say, cancer. That's the kind of news I would really rather *not* get. *I don't want to know* whether or not I have a predisposi-tion towards Alzheimer's disease! I want to live my life the best way I can, without try-ing to "play god" with my future. And I don't want anyone else to know my private health story, either. What gives Greengenes the right to read my future? What business is it of theirs? And what if I test "positive" for getting some awful disease someday? Greengenes might start claiming I am underperforming, and that would be the end of my wonderful job. Once Greengenes has my data, I don't see how I can be certain the whole world won't find out—or at least the world of biotech companies. This could mean I am unable to get another job—or health insurance. Imagine being unable to get insurance *because* you desperately need it?"

Would you be comfort-able with a national DNA databank as part of the war on terror? With being genetically tested by your employer?

SURVEILLANCE AT WORK

E-mail Interception

Ninety percent of all companies with more than 1,000 employees currently use e-mail, putting about 40 million workers on e-mail systems sending some 60 billion messages annually. Because they use passcodes, employees may believe their e-mail messages are private, but the reality is, they are not. Even deleted messages are stored in archives easily accessible to employers and others. In 1996, a district court in Philadelphia was faced with the following situation: A Pillsbury employee and his supervisor were sending e-mail messages to one another, including one which, referring to sales management, mentioned plans to "kill the back-stabbing bastards." Another message described a holiday party as the "Jim Jones Kool-Aid affair." These messages fell into their boss's hands, and both men were fired for sending "inappropriate and unprofessional comments" over Pillsbury's e-mail system. One of the employees sued, claiming he was "wrongfully discharged" when he lost his $62,500 per year job as a regional manager.

Michael A. Smyth v. The Pillsbury Company

United States District Court, 1996
914 F. Supp. 97
Weiner, District Judge.

Defendant [Pillsbury Company] maintained an electronic mail communication system ("e-mail") in order to promote internal corporate communications between its employees. Defendant repeatedly assured its employees, including plaintiff, that all e-mail communications would remain confidential and privileged. Defendant further assured its employees, including plaintiff, that e-mail communications could not be intercepted and used by defendant against its employees as grounds for termination or reprimand.

In October 1994, plaintiff [Michael Smyth] received certain e-mail communications from his supervisor over defendant's e-mail system on his computer at home. In reliance on defendant's assurances regarding defendant's e-mail system, plaintiff responded and exchanged e-mails with his supervisor. At some later date, contrary to the assurances of confidentiality made by defendant, defendant, acting through its agents, servants and employees, intercepted plaintiff's private e-mail messages made in October 1994. On January 17, 1995, defendant notified plaintiff that it was terminating his employment…for transmitting what it deemed to be inappropriate and unprofessional comments over defendant's e-mail system.…

[First, the judge sets out the definition of the tort of "intrusion:"]

"One who intentionally intrudes, physically or otherwise, upon the solitude or seclusion of another or his private affairs or concerns, is subject to liability to the other for invasion of his privacy, if the intrusion would be highly offensive to a reasonable person...."

[To determine if the facts of the case fit the definition above, the judge uses a "balancing test," weighing the employee's privacy interests against the employer's need to discover information.]

[W]e do not find a reasonable expectation of privacy in e-mail communications voluntarily made by an employee to his supervisor over the company e-mail system notwithstanding any assurances that such communications would not be intercepted by management. Once plaintiff communicated the alleged unprofessional comments to a second person (his supervisor) over an e-mail system which was apparently utilized by the entire company, any reasonable expectation of privacy was lost. Significantly, the defendant did not require plaintiff, as in the case of a urinal-

ysis or personal property search, to disclose any personal information about himself. Rather, plaintiff voluntarily communicated the alleged unprofessional comments over the company e-mail system. We find no privacy interests in such communications.

Secondly, even if we found that an employee had a reasonable expectation of privacy in the contents of his e-mail communications over the company e-mail system, we do not find that a reasonable person would consider the defendant's interception of these communications to be a substantial and highly offensive invasion of his privacy....[T]he company's interest in preventing inappropriate and unprofessional comments or even illegal activity over its e-mail system outweighs any privacy interest the employee may have in those comments.

In sum, we find that the defendant's actions did not tortuously invade the plaintiff's privacy and, therefore, did not violate public policy.

QUESTIONS

1. How does Judge Weiner explain why Michael Smyth lost any "reasonable expectation of privacy" in his e-mail comments? List as many reasons as you can find, and then try to rank them. Which seems most important to the final ruling here?

2. Is there any difference between a password-protected message sent on company e-mail and a memo, sealed in an envelope marked "private," sent through company mail? Consider the

judge's reasons for his ruling that you articulated above. Would they also apply to the memo?

3. How ethical were the actions of Smyth? Of Pillsbury? What appears to be the ethical framework underlying the judge's ruling?

4. Corporate culture varies, and with it, corporate surveillance policies. Some companies give notice to employees that their e-mail communications are not private.

Kmart's policy, for example, introduced at every employee orientation, states that "misuse of the e-mail system could result in denial of access to the Kmart computing environment or dismissal." Apple Computer, on the other hand, has an explicit policy of not monitoring employee e-mail. What might be the advantages and disadvantages of such policies from an employer's viewpoint? An employee's?

5. Suppose you were responsible for developing a surveillance policy where you worked. How would you go about setting its parameters? How would you implement it?

6. Judge Weiner points out that Smyth's e-mail messages were "voluntarily" placed on the Pillsbury system and that Pillsbury never forced the kind of disclosure that goes along with urine testing for drugs, for example. In a sense, the judge is saying that Smyth consented to the monitoring. Do you agree?

http://www.scip.org

7. Hi-tech surveillance is not solely directed by employers at workers. American businesses have always been interested in capturing confidential information and trade secrets from competitors. Today, thanks to computer technology, they are able to spy on one another with more sophisticated means than ever before. What are some of the latest developments in this area? How far can a company go in this direction without crossing the line? Visit the Web site of the Society of Competitive Intelligence Professionals.

8. Should educational institutions be free to randomly monitor student and faculty e-mail? What is your school's policy on e-mail privacy? Once you have found it, review it and discuss with others. Are there elements of the policy that you would change, in light of what you have read? Rewrite it.

Electronic Surveillance: The Debate

As of 2001, more than one-third of all U.S. employees using computers—some 14 million—were being monitored in one form or another, with employers watching them on closed-circuit TVs, taping and reviewing telephone and e-mail conversations, or using sophisticated software from the new field of "human resource forensics" to record everything from the Web sites employees browse to the length of their e-messages to the data they download.

Businesses justify electronic surveillance in a number of ways. It is a form of quality control, enabling supervisors to better correct, improve, and evaluate employee performance. It measures efficiency. It may encourage productivity. It can uncover employee disloyalty, which can take the form of stealing anything from office supplies to trade secrets. Racially or sexually harassing e-mail is of concern. And recent legislation, such as the federal Health Insurance Portability and Accounting Act of 1996 (HIPAA) and the

Sarbanes-Oxley corporate reform law of 2002, may require employers to record and investigate their workforce.

Countering all of this, employees claim that electronic monitoring puts them under dehumanizing pressure in which computers, instead of people, judge their output. Because computers measure quantity better than quality, for instance, employees who work fast may look better than those who work best. The "electronic sweatshop," they say, causes psychological stress and physical symptoms. Apart from the more measurable costs, employees emphasize their need to preserve at work what they expect to maintain elsewhere—a sense of dignity and self-respect.

Electronic Surveillance: The Law

The right of the people to be secure in their persons, houses, papers and effects, against unreasonable searches and seizures, shall not be violated.

—Fourth Amendment, U.S. Constitution

In the U.S., there is no comprehensive, uniform legal standard protecting privacy. The constitutional "right of the people" to be protected from "unreasonable searches" applies only when the *government* is conducting a search; there is no constitutional protection against searches or surveillance by businesses or individuals. And although electronic surveillance is a kind of search that government employees might argue violates the Fourth Amendment, their constitutional right is not an absolute one. It depends on a balancing test: judges must decide which counts more weightily, an employee's privacy interest or the need of the government (as employer) to search. Once government's concerns are placed on the scale, the legal result will typically favor the employer.

Private employees may claim that electronic monitoring amounts to "intrusion," a variation on the tort of invasion of privacy. As the *Smyth v. Pillsbury* case indicates, intrusion involves invading another person's solitude in a manner considered highly offensive. Courts consider (1) the obnoxiousness of the means used to intrude, i.e., whether it is a deviation from the normal, accepted means of discovering relevant information, and (2) the reason for intruding. Because electronic monitoring is now commonplace, it may be considered "normal," if not "accepted," and, as long as employers can point to a legitimate purpose for monitoring, it will be difficult for employees to win cases against them. The 1968 federal Wiretap Law, as amended by the Electronic Communications Privacy Act of 1986 (ECPA), would appear to protect workers from electronic eavesdropping. However, that law permits a business to listen in on communications made in the "ordinary course of business." In other words, if business interests such as efficiency or avoiding legal liability are at stake, the surveillance would be allowed.

THE VALUE OF PRIVACY

Privacy is much more than just a possible social technique for assuring this or that substantive interest...it is necessarily related to ends and relations of the most fundamental sort: respect, love, friendship and trust. Privacy is not merely a good technique for furthering these fundamental relations, rather without privacy they are simply inconceivable. They require a context of privacy or the possibility of privacy for their existence....To respect, love, trust, feel affection for others and to regard ourselves as the objects of love, trust and affection is at the heart of our notion of ourselves as persons among persons, and privacy is the necessary atmosphere for those attitudes and actions, as oxygen is for combustion.

—Charles Fried, "Privacy," 77 Yale L.J. 475 (1968).

The following excerpt describes how privacy serves a set of important human needs. The author, Columbia University professor emeritus Alan Westin, now a corporate consultant on privacy issues, has been in the forefront of research on the effects of technology on privacy in our society, particularly in the workplace.

The Functions of Privacy[1]

Alan Westin

[T]he functions privacy performs for individuals in democratic societies...can [be]...grouped conveniently under four headings—personal autonomy, emotional release, self-evaluation, and limited and protected communication....

PERSONAL AUTONOMY

In democratic societies there is a fundamental belief in the uniqueness of the individual, in his basic dignity and worth as a creature of God and a human being, and in the need to maintain social processes that safeguard his sacred individuality. Psychologists and sociologists have linked the development and maintenance of this sense of individuality to the human need for autonomy—the desire to avoid being manipulated or dominated wholly by others.

[Scholars describe a] "core self,"...pictured as an inner circle surrounded by a series of larger concentric circles. The inner circle shelters the individual's "ultimate secrets"—those hopes, fears, and prayers that are beyond sharing with anyone unless the individual comes under such stress that he must pour out these ultimate secrets to secure emotional relief....The next circle outward contains "intimate secrets," those that can be willingly shared with close relations, confessors, or strangers who pass by and cannot injure. The next circle is open to members of the individual's friendship group. The series continues until it reaches the outer circles of casual conversation and physical expression that are open to all observers.

---

[1] Westin, Alan. *Privacy and Freedom.* (New York: MacMillan, 1967).

The most serious threat to the individual's autonomy is the possibility that someone may penetrate the inner zone and learn his ultimate secrets, either by physical or psychological means.

Each person is aware of the gap between what he wants to be and what he actually is, between what the world sees of him and what he knows to be his much more complex reality. In addition, there are aspects of himself that the individual does not fully understand but is slowly exploring and shaping as he develops. Every individual lives behind a mask in this manner; indeed, the first etymological meaning of the word "person" was "mask"....

EMOTIONAL RELEASE

Life in society generates such tensions for the individual that both physical and psychological health demand periods of privacy for various types of emotional release. At one level, such relaxation is required from the pressure of playing social roles....On any given day a man may move through the roles of stern father, loving husband, car-pool comedian, skilled lathe operator, union steward, water-cooler flirt, and American Legion committee chairman—all psychologically different roles....[N]o individual can play indefinitely, without relief, the variety of roles that life demands. There have to be moments "off stage" when the individual can be "himself:" tender, angry, irritable, lustful, or dream-filled. Such moments may come in solitude; in the intimacy of family, peers or woman-to-woman and man-to-man relaxation; in the anonymity of

park or street; or in a state of reserve while in a group. Privacy in this aspect gives individuals, from factory workers to Presidents, a chance to lay their masks aside for rest....

Another form of emotional release is provided by the protection privacy gives to minor non-compliance with social norms....[A]lmost everyone does break some social or institutional norms—for example, violating traffic laws, breaking sexual mores, cheating on expense accounts, overstating income tax deductions, or smoking in restrooms when this is prohibited. Although society will usually punish the most flagrant abuses, it tolerates the great bulk of the violations as "permissible" deviations....[I]f all transgressions were known—most persons in society would be under organizational discipline or in jail, or could be manipulated by threats of such action. The firm expectation of having privacy for permissible deviations is a distinguishing characteristic of life in a free society. At a lesser but still important level, privacy also allows individuals to deviate temporarily from social etiquette when alone or among intimates, as by putting feet on desks, cursing, letting one's face go slack, or scratching wherever one itches.

Another aspect of release is the "safety valve" function afforded by privacy. Most persons need to give vent to their anger at "the system," "city hall," "the boss," and various others who exercise authority over them, and to do this in the intimacy of family or friendship circles, or in private papers, without fear of being held responsible for such comments. This is very different from freedom of speech or press, which involves publicly voiced criticism without fear of interference by government....

Still another aspect of release through privacy arises in the management of bodily and sexual functions....

SELF-EVALUATION

Every individual needs to integrate his experiences into a meaningful pattern and to exert his individuality on events. To carry on such self-evaluation, privacy is essential.

At the intellectual level, individuals need to process the information that is constantly bombarding them, information that cannot be processed while they are still "on the go...." This is particularly true of creative persons. Studies of creativity show that it is in reflective solitude and even "daydreaming" during moments of reserve that most creative "non-verbal" thought takes place. At such moments the individual runs ideas and impressions through his mind in a flow of associations; the active presence of others tends to inhibit this process....

The evaluative function of privacy also has a major moral dimension—the exercise of conscience by which the individual "repossesses himself." While people often consider the moral consequences of their acts during the course of daily affairs, it is primarily in periods of privacy that they take a moral inventory of ongoing conduct and measure current performance against personal ideals. For many persons this process is a religious exercise....Even for an individual who is not a religious believer, pri-

Is technology making privacy irrelevant?

vacy serves to bring the conscience into play, for, when alone, he must find a way to continue living with himself.

LIMITED AND PROTECTED COMMUNICATION

The greatest threat to civilized social life would be a situation in which each individual was utterly candid in his communications with others, saying exactly what he knew or felt at all times. The havoc done to interpersonal relations by children, saints, mental patients, and adult "innocents" is legendary.

In real life, among mature persons all communication is partial and limited.... Limited communication is particularly vital in urban life, with its heightened stimulation, crowded environment, and continuous physical and psychological confrontations between individuals who do not know one another in the extended, softening fashion of small-town life....

Privacy for limited and protected communication has two general aspects. First, it provides the individual with the opportunities he needs for sharing confidences and intimacies with those he trusts...."A friend," said Emerson, "is someone before...[whom] I can think aloud." In addition, the individual often wants to secure counsel from persons with whom he does not have to live daily after disclosing his confidences. He seeks professionally objective advice from persons whose status in society promises that they will not later use his distress to take advantage of him. To protect freedom of limited communication, such relationships—with doctors, lawyers, ministers, psychiatrists, psychologists, and others are given varying but important degrees of legal privilege against forced disclosure. In its second general aspect, privacy through limited communication serves to set necessary boundaries of mental distance in interpersonal situations ranging from the most intimate to the most formal and public. In marriage, for example, husbands and wives need to retain islands of privacy in the midst of their intimacy if they are to preserve a saving respect and mystery in the relation....In work situations, mental distance is necessary so that the relations of superior and subordinate do not slip into an intimacy which would create a lack of respect and an impediment to directions and correction....

Psychological distance is also used in crowded settings....[A] complex but well-understood etiquette of privacy is part of our social scenario....We learn to ignore people and to be ignored by them as a way of achieving privacy in subways, on streets, and in the "non-presence" of servants or children....

QUESTIONS

1. What are the functions of privacy as described by Westin? For each, can you think of examples from your own experience?

2. Jeffrey Rosen, Associate Professor at George Washington University Law School, has written *The Unwanted Gaze: The Destruction of Privacy in America*,[2] in which he offers this description of one of the primary values of privacy:

> Privacy protects us from being misdefined and judged out of context.... When intimate personal information circulates among a small group of people who know you well, its significance can be weighed against other aspects of your personality....(Monica Lewinsky didn't mind that her friends knew she had given the president a copy of Nicholson Baker's *Vox*, because her friends knew that she was much more than a person who would read a book about phone sex.) But when your browsing habits or e-mail messages are exposed to strangers, you may be reduced, in their eyes, to nothing more than the most salacious book you once read or the most vulgar joke you once told. And even if your Internet browsing isn't in any way embarrassing, you run the risk of being stereotyped as the kind of person who would read a particular book or listen to a particular song. Your public identity may be distorted by fragments of information that have little to do with how you define yourself. In a world where citizens are bombarded with information, people form impressions quickly, based on sound bites, and these brief impressions tend to oversimplify and misrepresent our complicated and often contradictory characters.

---

[2] New York: Random House, 2000.

Is this aspect of privacy a function of the "Information Age?" Does Westin come close to mentioning it?

3. Which functions of privacy may have been served by the e-mail messages that Michael Smyth sent while working for Pillsbury?

4. To what extent can we describe privacy as an ethical imperative? Think of the *Smyth v. Pillsbury* scenario. Who are the most affected stakeholders? Under the utilitarian approach to ethics, was intercepting the e-mail the right thing to do? Now consider the case from the deontological perspective. Again, was Pillsbury's action ethical?

5. In his 2002 book *What Just Happened*, journalist James Gleick wrote:

> Information is everywhere, at light speed, immersing us—is this what we want? We seem unsure. We are the species that defines itself in terms of information....We're knowledge connoisseurs....Then again, we didn't evolve in a world with so much data and buzz. Our sense organs tuned into one slow channel at a time. Now we can tune in and out. The dream of perfect ceaseless information flow can slip so easily into a nightmare of perfect perpetual distraction.

Can you see any connection between Gleick's observation and Westin's set of privacy functions?

COUNTERTERRORISM: SECURITY VS. PRIVACY

In the immediate aftermath of the attacks of September 11th, as American citizens were newly expected to remove their shoes for inspection at airports or to empty their purses on entry to museums and other public buildings, they seemed not to mind letting go of some old assumptions about their personal privacy. Most U.S. citizens trusted their government as it gave itself heightened ability to fight terrorism. In 2001, roughly one-third of those polled were "very confident" and more than half were "somewhat confident" that federal authorities were handling their enlarged powers properly. In early 2003 the citizen comfort-level remained about the same. Yet some privacy advocates were asking whether such complacency was appropriate.

Journalist Matt Welch argues that the Bush Administration used terrorism and war as cover for pushing through the USA PATRIOT Act legislation, which dramatically impacts privacy. He sees the same syndrome underway in the drafting of PATRIOT II.

Get Ready for PATRIOT II

Matt Welch, AlterNet
April 1, 2003

The "fog of war" obscures more than just news from the battlefield. It also provides cover for radical domestic legislation, especially ill-considered liberty-for-security swaps, which have been historically popular at the onset of major conflicts.

The last time allied bombs fell over a foreign capital, the Bush Administration rammed through the USA PATRIOT Act, a clever acronym for maximum with-us-or-against-us leverage (the full name is "Uniting and Strengthening America by Providing Appropriate Tools Required to Intercept and Obstruct Terrorism").

Remarkably, this 342-page law was written, passed (by a 98-1 vote in the U.S. Senate) and signed into law within seven weeks of the Sept. 11 terrorist attack. As a result, the government gained new power to wiretap phones, confiscate property of suspected terrorists, spy on its own citizens without judicial review, conduct secret searches, snoop on the reading habits of library users….On Jan. 10, 2003, [Ashcroft] sent around a draft of PATRIOT II; this time, called "The Domestic Security Enhancement Act of 2003." The more than 100 new provisions, Justice Department spokesperson Mark Corallo told the *Village Voice* recently, "will be filling in the holes" of PATRIOT I, "refining things that will enable us to do our job…"

…Constitutional watchdog Nat Hentoff has called it "the most radical government plan in our history to remove from Americans their liberties under the Bill of Rights." Some of [PATRIOT II's] more draconian provisions:

The government would be instructed to build a mammoth database of citizen DNA information, aimed at "detecting, investigating, prosecuting, preventing or responding to terrorist activities." Samples could be collected without a court order; one need only be suspected of wrongdoing by a law enforcement officer. Those refusing the cheek-swab could be fined $200,000 and jailed for a year. "Because no federal genetic privacy law regulates DNA databases, privacy advocates fear that the data they contain could be misused," *Wired News* reported March 31. "People with 'flawed' DNA have already suffered genetic discrimination at the hands of employers, insurance companies and the government."

Authorities could wiretap anybody for 15 days, and snoop on anyone's Internet usage (including chat and email), all without obtaining a warrant.

The government would be specifically instructed not to release any information about detainees held on suspicion of terrorist activities, until they are actually charged with a crime. Or, as Hentoff put it, "for the first time in U.S. history, secret arrests will be specifically permitted."

Businesses that rat on their customers to the Feds—even if the information violates privacy agreements, or is, in fact, dead wrong—would be granted immunity. "Such immunity," the ACLU contended, "could provide an incentive for neighbor to spy on neighbor and pose problems similar to those inherent in Attorney General Ashcroft's Operation TIPS."

Americans could have their citizenship revoked, if found to have contributed "material support" to organizations deemed by the government, even retroactively, to be "terrorist."

Police officers carrying out illegal searches would also be granted legal immunity if they were just carrying out orders.

Federal "consent decrees" limiting local law enforcement agencies' abilities to spy on citizens in their jurisdiction would be rolled back....

American citizens could be subject to secret surveillance by their own government on behalf of foreign countries, including dictatorships.

And many of PATRIOT I's "sunset provisions"—stipulating that the expanded new enforcement powers would be rescinded in 2005—would be erased from the books, cementing Ashcroft's rushed legislation in the law books....

I wouldn't be writing this article today had an alarmed Justice Department staffer not leaked the draft to the Center for Public Integrity in early February. Ashcroft, up to that point, had repeat-

Is terrorism making privacy dangerous?

edly refused to even discuss what his lawyers might be cooking up. But if 10,000 residents of Los Angeles had been vaporized by a "suitcase nuke" in late January, it is reasonable to assume that the then-secret proposal would have been speed-delivered for a congressional vote, even though Congress has not so far participated in drafting the legislation (which is, after all, its constitutional role).

As a result of the leak, and the ensuing bad press, opposition to the measure has had time to gather momentum before the first bomb was dropped on Saddam's bunker. Some of the criticism has originated from the right side of the political spectrum—a March 17 open letter to Congress was signed not only by the ACLU and People for the American Way, but the cultural-conservative think tank Free Congress Foundation, the Gun Owners of America, the American Conservative Union, and more....

Safeguarding civil liberties is an unpopular project in the most placid of times. Since Sept. 11th, the Bush Administration has shown that it will push the envelope on nearly every restriction it considers to be impeding its prosecution of the war on terrorism. This single-minded drive requires extreme vigilance, before the fog of war becomes toxic.

QUESTIONS

1. According to Welch, in 2003, while Attorney General Ashcroft repeatedly denied that the released draft of PATRIOT II was anything like a final proposal, Justice Department spokesperson Mark Corallo also stated, "such measures [are] coming soon." Has the Domestic Security Enhancement Act become law? If so, are the provisions Welch lists above part of it? Modified in some way? If there is now a PATRIOT II, what events preceded its passage (e.g., a new terrorist attack, war against a state "sponsor" of terrorism, some political event)?

2. Look back at the "Functions of Privacy" outlined by Alan Westin. Keeping them in mind, go down the list of provisions of the PATRIOT II. How might the draft provisions impact privacy as it is defined by Westin?

3. Welch mentions that PATRIOT legislation rankles conservatives as well as liberals. Check the web sites of the Free Congress Foundation, the Gun Owners of America, and the American Conservative Union. What problems do these groups have with the PATRIOT II proposal?

4. Recall what Smyth wrote to his supervisor on e-mail: "Let's kill the back stabbing bastards…" Suppose Pillsbury had decided to turn the e-message over to the government. Would Pillsbury be liable under the draft of PATRIOT II? Suppose the government arrested Smyth as a possible terrorist and kept him locked up for several months without letting anyone know he was being held. Would that be permitted under the draft law?

5. How might this law impact the way you use the Internet?

6. Welch notes: "Safeguarding civil liberties is an unpopular project in the most placid of times." What does he mean?

Terrorism Information Awareness (formerly called Total Information Awareness) is a program designed by the Department of Defense to combat terrorism domestically and abroad by monitoring e-mail, financial, and travel data. The government explains that TIA's goal is:

> to revolutionize the ability of the United States to detect, classify and identify foreign terrorists – and decipher their plans – and thereby enable the U.S. to take timely action to successfully preempt and defeat terrorist acts. To that end, the TIA program objective is to create a counter-terrorism information system that: (1) increases information coverage by an order of magnitude, and affords easy future scaling; (2) provides focused warnings within an hour after a triggering event occurs or an evidence threshold is passed; (3) can automatically queue analysts based on partial pattern matches and has patterns that cover 90% of all previously known foreign terrorist attacks; and, (4) supports collaboration, analytical reasoning and information sharing so that analysts can hypothesize, test and propose theories and mitigating strategies

about possible futures, so decision-makers can effectively evaluate the impact of current or future policies and prospective courses of action.

The following Q&A about TIA appeared on the Web site of DARPA (Defense Advanced Research Projects Agency—the agency that developed the model for the Internet itself) in the spring of 2003.

http://www.darpa.mil/
body/tia/terrorism_
info_aware.htm.

Terrorism Information Awareness

Q: Why did you change the name?

A: The name "Total Information Awareness" program created in some minds the impression that TIA was a system to be used for developing dossiers on U.S. citizens. That is not DoD's intent in pursuing this program. Rather, DoD's purpose in pursuing these efforts is to protect citizens by detecting and defeating foreign terrorist threats before an attack. To make this objective absolutely clear, DARPA has changed the program name to Terrorism Information Awareness.

Q: How is DoD ensuring that TIA does not violate privacy and civil liberties?

A: The Department of Defense, which is responsible for DARPA, has expressed its full commitment to planning, executing, and overseeing the TIA program in a manner that protects privacy and civil liberties. Safeguarding the privacy and the civil liberties of Americans is a bedrock principle. DoD intends to make it a central element in the Department of Defense's management and oversight of the TIA program.

The Department of Defense's TIA research and development efforts address both privacy and civil liberties in the following ways:

• The Department of Defense must fully comply with the laws and regulations governing intelligence activities and all other laws that protect the privacy and constitutional rights of U.S. persons.

• As an integral part of its research, the TIA program itself is seeking to develop new technologies that will safeguard the privacy of U.S. persons.

• TIA's research and testing activities are conducted using either real intelligence information that the federal government has already legally obtained, or artificial synthetic information that, ipso facto, does not implicate the privacy interests of U.S. persons.

• The Secretary of Defense will, as an integral part of oversight of TIA research and development, continue to assess emerging potential privacy and civil liberties impacts through an oversight board composed of senior representatives from DoD and the Intelligence Community, and chaired by the Under Secretary of Defense (Acquisition, Technology and Logistics). The Secretary of Defense will also receive advice on legal and policy issues, including privacy, posed by TIA research and development from a Federal Advisory Committee composed of outside experts....

Q: Provide some examples of how TIA has been used by operational agencies to date.

A:

- Analyzing data from detainees from Afghanistan and finding relationships among entities in that data and with additional relationships from all-source foreign intelligence information.

- Assessing various intelligence aspects including weapons of mass destruction in the Iraqi situation.

- Aggregating very large quantities of information based on patterns into a visual representation of very complex relationships, which enabled rapid discovery of previously unknown relationships of operational significance.

Q: Which organizations are participating in or interested in participating in the TIA experimental network?

A: U.S. Army Intelligence and Security Command; National Security Agency; Defense Intelligence Agency (DIA JITF-CT); Central Intelligence Agency; DoD's Counterintelligence Field Activity; U.S. Strategic Command; Special Operations Command; Joint Forces Command; Joint Warfare Analysis Center.

QUESTIONS

1. Is TIA operational?

2. In the aftermath of 9/11, Attorney General John Ashcroft proposed the TIPS initiative, which would collate information given to the government by U.S. citizens reporting suspicions they might have about one another. Update the TIPS program. What were the arguments for and against it? Is it operational?

3. In the summer of 2003, DARPA came up with another terrorism-related technology concept: the creation of an online futures market in terrorist events, a government-sponsored Web site where anonymous speculators could place bets on the occurrence of the next terrorist attack. The idea was the brainchild of Admiral John Poindexter. National security advisor under President Reagan, he had been convicted in the Iran-Contra scandal of lying to Congress, but his conviction was reversed on a technicality. Democrats in Congress reacted swiftly to the concept of government-sponsored gambling on terror, calling it morally repugnant and grotesque. What were the arguments in favor of the idea? Find out what happened—to the concept, and to Poindexter.

A National Identity Card?

In the wake of September 11th, fear of terrorism has heightened safety and security concerns to the point where they greatly overshadow any privacy norms we might formerly have shared. One week after the attacks, a majority (54%) of Americans told pollsters they favored enhanced government monitoring of cell phone and e-mail communication, and 63% favored law enforcement monitoring of Internet chat rooms. The strongest support however, was for two new methods of identifying citizens: the national identity card and the use of facial-recognition technology to scan for terrorists at airports and other checkpoints. Sixty-eight percent of Americans favored the use of a national ID, while 86% supported the biometric scanning idea.

With the public's desire for comfort and security at such a peak, why worry about the privacy downside of these plans? Libertarian pundit William Safire addressed that question in a *New York Times* editorial published in December 2001. In his view, the danger is that a national ID would become a tightly-focused information bank, a "single dossier…supposedly confidential but available to any imaginative hacker:"

> [I]n the dreams of Big Brother and his cousin, Big Marketing, nothing can compare to forcing every person in the United States—under penalty of law—to carry what the totalitarians used to call "papers." The plastic card would not merely show a photograph, signature and address, as driver's licenses do.…In time, and with exquisite refinements, the card would contain not only a fingerprint, description of DNA and the details of your eye's iris, but a host of other information about you. Hospitals would say: How about a chip providing a complete medical history in case of emergencies? Merchants would add a chip for credit rating, bank accounts and product preferences, while divorced spouses would lobby for a rundown of net assets and yearly expenditures. Politicians would like to know voting records and political affiliation. Cops, of course, would insist on a record of arrests, speeding tickets, E-Z pass auto movements and links to suspicious web sites and associates.

For Safire, the central problem with this system is that those who resist it on principle will become suspicious to the authorities.

> What about us libertarian misfits who take the trouble to try to "opt out?" We will not be able to travel or buy on credit.…Soon enough, police as well as employers will consider [us]…to be suspect. The universal use and likely abuse of the national ID—a discredit card—will trigger questions like: When did you begin to subscribe to these publications and why were you visiting that spicy or seditious Web site? Why are you paying cash? What do you have to hide?

QUESTIONS

1. William Safire speaks for many privacy advocates. Compare his concerns with those of the Communitarians. Find out what their position is on the national ID.

2. Analyze the national identity card concept from a utilitarian ethical perspective. Now look at it through the lens of deontology.

3. Oracle chairman and CEO Larry Ellison has offered to supply the government with the software it would need to create a national identity card system "absolutely free." He has said:

This privacy you're concerned about is largely an illusion....All you have to give up is your illusions, not your privacy. Right now you can go onto the Internet and get a credit report about your neighbor, and find out where your neighbor works, how much they earn, and if they had a late mortgage payment and loads of other information.

Does Ellison's comment effectively counter Safire's concerns? What do you think about the proposed national ID?

Kari Lydersen writes for the *Washington Post* and is an instructor for the Urban Youth International Journalism Program in Chicago. In this article she explains the intermeshing of the public and the private sector in the war on terror.

Spying for Fun and Profit

Kari Lydersen, AlterNet
May 27, 2003

New technology has become ubiquitous in the post-Sept. 11 world. Biometric devices record the facial bone structures, iris scans, voices and other physical attributes of every person who walks by in an airport, stadium or park. Electronic monitors track web page visits or bank transactions. Even good old-fashioned video surveillance cameras are being used more than ever in conjunction with facial recognition software.

All these technologies raise serious questions about invasions of privacy and violations of civil liberties. They also cost a lot of money. Taxpayers fund this massively beefed up security. Private corporations and even individuals are also paying large amounts to boost their own security procedures in light of the war on terrorism. Naturally, someone is also profiting off this boom.

Market analysts and corporate watchdog groups note that there have been a raft of upstart companies jumping into the security/surveillance market, and existing major security and defense companies have expanded their product lines and sales. "There's definitely more demand," noted Lee Tien, a staff attorney for the Electronic Frontier Foundation, which monitors electronic-related privacy and civil liberties issues. "For example you see this stuff popping up in airports, and then that creates secondary effects where all these vendors realize they have something to sell and start marketing it, and then legislation like aviation security helps. And then there's this ripple effect where people [and corporations] say, 'Well if the government's doing it, maybe we better be doing it too.'"

There are several main technologies driving the market: bomb and explosives detection devices used at airports and other high security areas; biometrics technology used all across the spectrum for screening and identifying people; smart card technology to combine data on an all-purpose ID card, as has been discussed with the standardized national driver's license; and electronic data-mining technology of the type that would be used to compile records for the Terrorism Information Awareness (formerly Total Information Awareness) program.

THE SPY-TECH BOOM

One of the first widespread security technologies to be discussed after the Sept. 11 attacks was face recognition software in airports. Almost immediately after the terrorist attacks, two providers of this software—Visionis and Viisage—started marketing their products as terror prevention solutions.

"Their publicity stunt worked," said Chris Hoofnagle of the Electronic Privacy Information Center (EPIC) in a Nov. 2001 interview with the Multinational Monitor. "Their stock prices doubled very quickly, and it appeared as though different public transportation centers would adopt the technology. In fact, Oakland International Airport has." Since then, various other airports including Dallas, Rhode Island and Boston and other tourist destinations including the Virginia Beach oceanfront and a Tampa nightlife district have purchased facial recognition systems. One of the main beneficiaries has been Pelco Inc., the world's largest maker of video security systems.

The growth in demand for software alone to comply with the PATRIOT Act has been huge—the act requires financial institutions, including banks, credit card companies and insurance carriers, to closely monitor customer activity. Cisco, Sybase, Sun Microsystems and Oracle are just a few of the various software companies ready to meet these demands, often by expanding their existing lines of anti-money laundering (or AML) software. "Compliance with the USA PATRIOT Act has never been easier, thanks to Sybase's PATRIOT compliance solution," says a promo on the company's web site.

There has been some small protest within the companies; in March 2003, Groove Networks Inc. board member Mitch Kapor quit in protest over Groove selling its software to the government for anti-terrorism surveillance. And one vendor refused to sell its software to the government. But, for the most part, companies have jumped at the chance of government contracts.

VENI, VIDI, VENDORS

In a report called "The USA PATRIOT Act: Impact on AML Vendors and the Market," financial services analyst Breffni McGuire wrote that, "although the law imposes new burdens on banks, it is proving to be a boon for vendors of AML and related products and technology." The report said software vendors had seen inquiries rise 200 to 300 percent in the months following Sept. 11th. Many are hesitant to question the necessity or efficiency of security-related expenditures, but the fact is this may be more a matter of companies capitalizing on opportunity to create a demand rather than developing products that genuinely offer a needed service. In reality, much of the now-popular security technology had been developed and marketed for other purposes before Sept. 11th.

For example for years Oracle had been pushing for a national ID system which would include a standardized driver's license or other card with a biometric identifier. In the Multinational Monitor interview Hoofnagle noted that Oracle offered to donate software to run the program to the government, in hopes of future profit. "Donating the software is a significant move, however Oracle would significantly profit from maintaining the database in the future," Hoofnagle said. "National ID is extremely expensive, and in other countries where it has been proposed, officials invariably underestimate the cost."

Likewise in 2002 the Food and Drug Administration approved the long-in-development sale of subdermal microchips which would allow someone's location to be tracked at any moment. While now these chips are mentioned as parts of a hazy plan to keep tabs on all residents at all times, in the past they were marketed to parents on the basis that they could help them find their children should they be kidnapped.

"Lots of these technologies have been in the works and looking for a justification for a long time," said Charlie Cray of the group Citizen Works. "Then some news event comes along and they find someone to push it. For example, every once in a while you see a national story about some kid getting kidnapped. Then someone says that's a reason why parents should get their kids registered in some kind of national database. Of course, what they don't tell you is the corporate motive behind this fear-mongering. That Oracle just happens to own the national ID database that would be used."

BIOMETRIC BUNGLES

A report released by the General Accounting Office (GAO) in spring of 2002 said that government agencies had spent more than $50 million in the past five years on camera surveillance technology, with a notable increase in spending proposals after Sept. 11. A big chunk of this money was funneled toward facial recognition programs, which made up 90 percent of government surveillance budgets since 1997 according to the GAO report. In the pre-terrorism era, significant surveillance funds were also designated for catching and fining red light runners. In nabbing red light runners, surveillance technology has been highly effective. But for catching would-be terrorists, it is a different story.

While biometrics is currently all the rage for everything from scanning for terrorists in crowds at public events to recording participants at demonstrations, the fact is the technology is highly error-prone and not well-suited for these functions. A study by the National Institute for Standards in Technology showed that face recognition biometric technology turned up false positives in matching scans with a database 43 percent of the time. "There are enormous operational problems here," said Tien. "It's one thing to use biometrics to control who enters an office building, but it's another to try to screen thousands of people at an airport or border crossing." He noted that the use of biometrics and other surveillance equipment at borders is really in vain, since it can only be used at official border checkpoints and other small specific areas of the huge borders. "If a terrorist really wants to get into the country they'll just hire a marijuana smuggler to get them in a boat into the swamps in Louisiana," he said.

DEFENSE CEOS' CASH CROP

David Martin, a researcher and media coordinator at the non-profit United for a Fair Economy, noted that as with surveillance technology, increased government spending as well as speculation is leading to major profiteering for defense companies—and even more so for their CEOs. A recent report Martin co-authored, called "More Bucks for the

Bang," found that the salaries of CEOs of the top 37 publicly traded defense companies have mushroomed way out of proportion to other CEOs and also out of proportion to the companies' actual profits. "They're pocketing a lot," Martin said of the CEOs. "We had an inkling that their pay was increasing but after we did the study we were shocked by the actual numbers we saw."

While these companies are primarily involved with manufacturing weapons, many of them, including Dell Computers, also develop electronic or other surveillance-related technologies. The defense company CEOs' pay increased an average of 79 percent from 2001 to 2002, compared to 6 percent for CEOs in general. The CEO of Lockheed Martin, the country's largest defense contractor, increased 400 percent.

The study also found that the amount of a company's campaign contributions are in direct correlation (statistically .90) with the size of the defense contracts they receive.

As with most of the legislation and political programs that have come to pass since Sept. 11th, the growing market for security and surveillance isn't likely to go away even if our country goes years without suffering a terrorist attack. Even before most people had ever heard of Al Qaeda, Americans were becoming more and more obsessed with both locking themselves in and finding ways to sneak peeks at others—witness the parallel growth in both gated communities and voyeuristic web cams and reality TV shows. "You can't totally differentiate between what's going on now and the natural trends

What is a "gated community"? Have they become more popular?

before Sept. 11th," Tien said, noting the long-time grassroots popularity of low-level surveillance gadgets. "People are very interested in security and watching each other—we're all watched by Big Brother, but we're also all little brothers watching each other." Now, with security as the excuse for all kinds of surveillance, there are a few companies who stand to make a large profit—and a lot of citizens who will lose something even more precious—their privacy.

Questions

1. What are the drivers of surveillance technology sales?

2. To what extent do you think enhanced surveillance technology will make our society safer?

3. The writer reports that many of the anti-terror surveillance technologies were already under development before 9/11. Give examples and tell how the use shifted pre- and post-9/11.

4. What are some of the ethical issues that arise in this article?

5. As Lydersen notes, a major problem with surveillance technology has been false positives. Even the most sophisti-cated systems have been problematic in this way, especially when operating out of doors, and especially when applied to younger people. The top three systems had a less than 65% accuracy rate with people between 18 and 27, for example. What can you find out about the accuracy rates of the latest surveillance technologies? Are they improving?

6. The article mentions the curious paradox that Americans seem to be "more and more obsessed with both locking themselves in and finding ways to sneak peeks at others." Do you think it's a coincidence? Or is there some relationship between these trends?

PRIVACY & TRANSPARENCY

Knowledge will forever govern ignorance, and a people who mean to be their own governors, must arm themselves with the power knowledge gives. A popular government without popular information or the means of acquiring it, is but a prologue to a farce or a tragedy or perhaps both.

—James Madison (Fourth President of the United States)

The right to privacy is the power to keep secrets.

—Dale Carpenter, "Keeping Secrets," 88 *Minn.L.Rev* 1097 (2002).

David Brin is an astrophysicist, a science fiction novelist, and a cyberpundit. In this next reading, he presents a contrarian perspective on the privacy issue. In June 1997 when Brin was interviewed by John McChesney, technology correspondent for National Public Radio, he was working on his first nonfiction book, *The Transparent Society*. As you read the transcript, keep in mind the cybertarian, utilitarian, and the deontological frameworks for ethical analysis from chapter 1. Are there echoes of any of those philosophies here?

The Transparent Society
Interview with David Brin

JOHN McCHESNEY: How would you define privacy?

DAVID BRIN: The important thing about privacy is to recognize that there's always a tradeoff between it and accountability. Accountability demands light, privacy demands shadow. And whenever people get a choice between privacy and accountability, they always seem to choose privacy for themselves and accountability for everyone else. Especially those they don't trust....

Various power centers will do what human beings naturally do, that is conspire with one another, rationalize to themselves, "Hey, we're good guys, we can be trusted with power," and conspire to close down the system and leave themselves in charge. It's happened in every system but our own, and it's almost happened several times in ours....

JM: In your writing you've described a vision of two cities of the future, in which you bring up the idea of a tiny camera that can be mounted on any lamppost or flown into a room. Actually, I read the other day they're working on a little remote-controlled aircraft about the size of a personal check.

DB: Yes, the military is working on that, and it will probably be the greatest thing that ever happened to an infantry platoon. Because they'll be able to see where the snipers are. It's a fantastic advance, but what are you going to do, are you going to ban these things from hobby shops later? Are you going to ban private model airplanes?

JM: Keep the windows shut.

DB: Yes...but your real defense against peeping Toms will be that you will have mini-radars to find the kid who is flying this little thing over your house, follow the electronic beam over his house, and phone his mother. That will be the fundamental defense against peeping Toms, because almost nothing that you and your wife are doing in your bedroom will be as shameful as being discovered in the act of being a peeping Tom.

JM: It seems to me that what you're saying is that in the future...privacy is just not going to be there, so the best solution to this is to have equal snooping rights. That is, everybody has the right to look at everybody else, so you kind of iron this out that nobody has superior access to information about someone else.

DB: I think that society will have a sliding scale. The more powerful you are, the more you seek power or seek public attention or influence, the less you have to complain about when people look at you. And of course that's already engraved in law when you're a public figure.

There are five or six power centers in the world that need to be watched, and it's just a matter of your personality which one you want to be watched. Republicans worry about accumulations of undue power and authority by faceless academics and bureaucrats. Democrats—they turn their attention to faceless corporations and conspiratorial aristocrats. Then there's the criminal elites, there's the new oncoming technological elite.

All of these groups, if not kept under some degree of scrutiny, could become dangerous to us all, and we get the willies thinking about them operating in the dark. If preventing them from operating in the dark means that I've got to give up a bit of my privacy, I'd rather have that than have one of these groups pull a coup someday.

JM: There are some laws governing disclosure in government and accountability in government.

DB: [N]o government has ever known more about its people than ours does and no people has ever been so free. So the cause-and-effect relationship that they say, about preventing government from knowing things about you means you'll be more free, is disprovable. But how did this work, because it's counterintuitive? It worked because, almost instinctively, every single time the government asked for more information

about us, we said, all right, I can see you need this, but in exchange you must strip another article of clothing, you must walk more naked. So we got the Freedom of Information Act, the open-meetings laws, etc., etc....Instead of defending ourselves against the government with shields and masks, we defended ourselves with the light saber.

JM: Let's talk some specifics. One of the things the Federal Trade Commission will be looking into a couple of weeks from now are so-called "lookup" organizations, companies that collect information from all sorts of databases about us, to sell to marketers, to sell to private investigators, to sell to lawyers, to sell to potential employers. Now most of that information is public information. It's not being gathered illegally. But there's an ability to concentrate it now because of electronic communication.

DB: Well, this is worrisome, and it's worth our attention. It is not the end of the world. Public opinion polls have shown that most people are fairly relaxed about others knowing harmless information about them. After all, we could be upset that we can look up what you paid for your house. Well, guess what—you can, and people live with it.

JM: And that's been true for a long time.

DB: The problem is that you start to get to things like, can an insurance company know about some test that was taken that shows you have a genetic proclivity for some disease. Can they discriminate against you?

Right now, all you hear today is, "Ooh, they shouldn't know that information, let's prevent them from knowing it, let's cut the information flow." Now, that may be necessary from time to time, but it's a bad habit to get into. Information flow is like the lifeblood of our body politic. Ideally speaking, we should let it go free. There may be times when we say a doctor shouldn't know something about his patient, but if we make that a habit, that's the road to hell.

What I'm recommending is that every time we discuss this thing we also discuss the transparency solution, mutual transparency. In other words if somebody's collecting database information about everyone in America, the top 100 officers of that company have to publish all of the same information about themselves on a Web page, including their home phone number.

JM: [O]ften the accumulated personal information in these databases is incorrect….

DB: If a person is listed in the database, that person should have access to the database. That's light, that's using light as the weapon. If insurance companies are discriminating against people because of their genetic proclivities, don't pass a law preventing doctors from knowing information about their clients. Instead, pass a law saying that the top 100 officers of an insurance company, if they want to use genetic information, must take all the same tests and publish the results. They're not going to be as discriminatory if everyone in their family has all their genetic laundry out on the line….

JM: One thing that's also going on is the gathering of information about you…on

the Internet; that is, the use of certain technologies like cookies….

DB: [W]e have two lives….[T]here's the life you want to keep away from other people, and there's the life that you could shrug and say, well, it's none of their damn business, but if they're going to look, enjoy. And you should limit the number of things about which you're paranoid to a small enough amount of your life that you can conveniently keep…off to one side.

When it comes to cookies…there are two solutions. One is to outlaw it, but these systems also provide a lot to you. If you're going out on the Web and you're doing a lot of searches, these systems notice patterns of what you're looking for and sometime might volunteer information that you're looking for. And people will get used to that convenience.

There is an alternative solution, and that is to require that every time they give you something, every time they do a little search, they file a little report on your machine about exactly what they did….

JM: One of the things that's interesting about the Internet is that many people will defend anonymity to the death….

DB: [O]ne of the reasons why people are fighting for anonymity is that people fear the effects of the old village. In the old village, there were good things and bad things. You could go anywhere without a lock on your door. People were polite, they would take care, you didn't hear about some old person dying in an apartment and being discovered six months later when their electric bill went due. People took care of each other.

And yet there are the things we all remember and dread from the village. The local gossips, the conformity, the persecution of the eccentric. And I find that all the privacy aficionados, all the people pushing encryption and all that, it all boils down to one thing: Like me, they know that in any other culture they would have been squashed flatter than a bug. But in our civilization, they instead make money for being cantankerous curmudgeons....

JM: It sounds to me like you might include, in the ways of shutting the flow down, financial and medical information.

DB: Yes, I would certainly be amenable to having certain kinds of things shut down. However, I prefer pseudonymity to anonymity. I think people should be able to say anything they want, but they should be required to register their real identity with their bank. So that they can say what they want, they can blow whistles on people if they want, but if they're performing a criminal act, a court order could then find out who they were.

JM: Where do you come down on the encryption issue?

DB: I'm all in favor of giving law enforcement all the tools they say they need and they say they want under one condition: The more they get, the more light shines into them. I would be in favor of drafting random groups of citizens, 12 at a time, juries, and giving them a pass that lets them walk through any door in FBI headquarters at any time and listen to any conversation they want. If the FBI wants to be able to listen to us, then we should have people who we trust, members who've married our kids, members of our civilization and not part of the old-boy network, who will go in and verify—who will watch the watchman? If they are being watched then we'll be free, and I don't give a darn what the FBI knows about me, if I know what brand of toothpaste the head of the FBI uses. That's the fundamental thing: Can we shine light on the mighty?

JM: Some privacy groups have suggested a privacy commission to sort of oversee this sort of thing.

DB: Oh, big government agencies become powers unto themselves. I prefer the ad hoc jury. I prefer that several hundred little ad hoc juries of Americans be cut loose with little red passes that let them walk through any door in our government and see anything. And before they get co-opted the pass expires, it only lasts for six months. And as much as possible, let us see. As I said in my City A and City B, the difference between those two cities is not the numbers of cameras. Cameras are coming. There's no avoiding it, there will be cameras outdoors everywhere we go. The question is, will we as a citizen be able to use them? That guy who almost knocked you off the freeway, who almost killed you the other day by running you off and then gave you the finger and laughed driving away. Wouldn't it be great if your car automatically recorded the episode and you dialed in and showed the scene to his mother?

JM: Or the Highway Patrol.

DB: If his mother said "so what?", then the Highway Patrol, but in most families she would be far more terrifying and far more capable of changing his behavior.

JM: David Brin, thanks a lot for being with us. You've been very helpful and very interesting.

DB: It's a joy to live in this age.

Questions

1. What is Brin's solution to the threats to consumer privacy? Do you agree with his ideas? Think of Lily Kim's problem with her employer, Greengenes, presented at the start of this chapter. Would Brin's proposal help her?

2. Brin says: "[N]o government has ever known more about its people than ours does and no people has ever been so free.

So the cause-and-effect relationship that they say, about preventing government from knowing things about you means you'll be more free, is disprovable." A rough paraphrase of this is, "we cannot claim that our freedom depends on preventing our government from snooping, because our government snoops like crazy and we are very free." Do you agree?

David Brin speaks of the "saber of light," a means of revealing about others what they would want to know about us. This might remind us of Kant's notion of universalizing: an action is ethical only if the decision maker would be willing to live in a world where his choice became the rule each time a similar choice had to be made; and of Kant's notion of reversibility: an action is ethical only if the decision maker would be willing to have it done to him. What would it take to actually equip citizens with those "light sabers," making Brin's vision of the "transparent society" real?

An attempt to shine the light of openness on the government was launched at MIT in 2003. They dubbed their project GIA (Government Information Awareness), after TIA. Their Web site portal explains their goals and why they believe the site was needed.

GOVERNMENT INFORMATION AWARENESS

Mission

To empower citizens by providing a single, comprehensive, easy-to-use repository of information on individuals, organizations, and corporations related to the government of the United States of America.

To allow citizens to submit intelligence about government-related issues, while maintaining their anonymity. To allow members of the government a chance to participate in the process.

Context

In the United States, there is a widening gap between a citizen's ability to monitor his or her government and the government's ability to monitor a citizen. Average citizens have limited access to important government records, while available information is often illegible. Meanwhile, the government's eagerness and means to oversee a citizen's personal activity is rapidly increasing.

As the government broadens internal surveillance, and collaborates with private institutions to access data on the public, it is crucial that we maintain a symmetry of accountability. If we believe the United States should be a government "of the people, by the people, and for the people" it is of central importance to provide citizens with the power to oversee their government. At least as much effort should be spent building tools to facilitate citizens supervising their government as tools to help the government monitor individuals.

Technology

The Open Government Information Awareness suite of software tools acts as a framework for US citizens to construct and analyze a comprehensive database on our government. Modeled on recent government programs designed to consolidate information on individuals into massive databases, our system does the opposite, allowing you to scrutinize those in government. Citizens are able to explore data, track events, find patterns, and build risk profiles, all in an effort to encourage and motivate action. We like to think of it as a Citizen's Intelligence Agency, giving people similar tools and technologies to those held by their government.

Central to GIA is its extensible model of data: Everything in its system is either an entity or a link—a thing or a relationship. This allows the system to grow in any direction, and accommodate as-yet unimagined institutions, organizations, or threats.

Getting Started

The best way to get started is simply by clicking around. Try looking for your elected representatives, judges in your area, or even your employer. You'll see some of the types of information available. Check back often, as the system grows quickly.

Check the progress on this site at http://opengov. media.mit.edu/.

PRIVACY FOR ONLINE CONSUMERS

The authors of the next reading believe that each of the various players—Internet users, businesses, government, and privacy advocates—realize it's in their own self-interest to want better privacy protection online.

Privacy in the Digital Age: Work in Progress

Jerry Berman & Deirdre Mulligan[3]

THE EXPECTATION OF ANONYMITY

[T]he Internet generates an elaborate trail of data detailing every stop a person makes on the Web. This data trail may be captured by the individual's employer if she logged on at work, and is captured by the Web sites the individual visits. Transactional data, click stream data, or "mouse-droppings," can provide a "profile" of an individual's online life.

Technologies such as "cookies," written directly onto your hard drive, enable Web sites to surreptitiously collect information about your online activities and store it for future use. Designed for the benign purpose of enabling Web sites to recognize a repeat visitor and respond accordingly, cookies were quickly adopted by Web sites to facilitate the tracking of specific individual's activities at Web sites for the purpose of customizing content and advertising....

Companies, such as Doubleclick, use this detailed transactional information to provide targeted online advertising. Others, such as Adfinity, combine these "mouse-droppings" or "click-stream data" with personal information collected from other sources into fully identifiable profiles of the individual's online and offline behavior.

The increased data collection enabled by the Internet and electronic commerce are part of a larger phenomena—the growing market in personal information....

An individual's choice of payment mechanism impacts on her privacy. The amount of personal information generated and collected varies from theoretically none in a cash transaction to identity, item or service purchased, merchant, and date and time in a credit transaction. Similarly, the list of parties who have access to personal data can range from the individual and the merchant in a cash transaction, to the merchant, affiliated issuer, transaction processor, credit card company, and individual in a credit card transaction. In general, cash provides the most privacy protection during financial transactions in the offline world. It is fungible, largely untraceable, and because its value is inherent and irrefutable, it requires no additional assurance of authenticity which often drives the collection of identity information.

---

[3] *Nova Law Review*, Volume 23, Number 2, Winter 1999.

In the online environment, the digital equivalent of cash has not yet achieved widespread use....

[C]onsider the differences between an auction/yard sale in the physical world and Ebay, the premiere auction/classified listing/yard sale on the World Wide Web. Attendees at a traditional auction while physically present do not reveal who they are prior to participation. At Ebay, prior to bidding individuals must provide a name, home address, phone number and e-mail address....

THE EXPECTATION OF FAIRNESS

When individuals provide information to a doctor, a merchant, or a bank, they expect that those professionals/companies will base the information collected on the service and use it for the sole purpose of providing the service requested. The doctor will use it to tend to their health, the merchant will use it to process the bill and ship the product, and the bank will use it to manage their account—end of story. Unfortunately, current practices, both offline and online, foil this expectation of privacy. Whether it is medical information, or a record of a book purchased at the bookstore, information generated in the course of a business transaction is routinely used for a variety of other purposes without the individual's knowledge or consent. Some entities go so far as to declare the information individuals provide them as company "property."

In recent years, a number of corporations, as well as government entities, have learned the hard way that consumers are prepared to protest against services that appear to infringe on their privacy. In 1996, public criticism forced Lexis-Nexis to withdraw a service known as P-Trak, which granted easy online access to a database of millions of individuals' Social Security numbers. Also in 1996, Yahoo faced a public outcry over its People Search service. The service, jointly run with a marketing list vendor, would have allowed Net searchers to put an instant finger on 175 million people, all culled from commercial mailing lists. After hearing the complaints, Yahoo decided to delete 85 million records containing unlisted home addresses. During August of 1997, America Online ("AOL") announced plans to disclose its subscribers' telephone numbers to business partners for telemarketing. AOL heard loud objections from subscribers and advocates opposed to this unilateral change in the "terms of service agreement" covering the use and disclosure of personal information. In response, AOL decided not to follow through with its proposal.

QUESTIONS

1. In September 2003, the low-fare, no-frills airline JetBlue saw its share value plummet at news that it had disclosed private information about more than 1 million of its customers—social security numbers and flight information, for example—to an antiterrorism consulting company working with the Pentagon. In doing this, the airline violated its own privacy protection policy. What are the ethical considerations in this situation?

2. Like industry, government has been known to profit from taking information for a stated purpose and releasing it for another—without notifying the people involved. In the early 1990s, states were earning millions of dollars annually selling drivers' license information to direct marketers, charities, and political campaigns. This practice caught the attention of the U.S. Congress after a particularly disturbing incident: A stalker murdered an actress after obtaining her unlisted address from California motor vehicle records. Are there reasons to make a policy distinction between government and industry in terms of regulating the use of personal data, or should the same rules apply to each? Congress passed a law banning state sales of drivers' licenses in 1994. In January 2000, the Supreme Court decided whether the ban was constitutional. What happened?

3. In June 1998, the Federal Trade Commission (FTC), the agency responsible for consumer protection, gave its report to Congress on Online Privacy, the culmination of three years of work in which the agency conducted hearings, requested comments from consumer and industry groups, and surfed hundreds of Web sites. It found that while 9 out of 10 sites collected personal data, only a small percentage (14%) gave notice of doing so. In the wake of this, it became clear that Congress might choose to regulate. To stave off the possibility, the industry made a collective effort to convince Congress and the public that it could regulate itself. In 1998 several major companies, including Hewlett Packard, IBM, AOL,[4] Microsoft and a few trade groups, such as the Direct Marketing Association, formed the Online Privacy Alliance (OPA). How many "Certified Merchants" are members of the OPA now? Check **http://www.privacyalliance.org**. What are the privacy principles it is promoting? What action has it taken lately? Are there any signs that consumer privacy has been better protected since the OPA was formed? Can you find other "enlightened" corporate privacy policies? Check **http://www.PrivacyExchange.org** under "Organizational Codes."

4. Do U.S. consumers care about privacy as they shop online? Find a recent poll.

5. Look up DigiCash.com. What can you find out about electronic money that could preserve anonymity of buyers?

---

[4] In 1998, America Online was successfully sued for revealing the screen name of one of its customers, a disclosure that led to retaliation on the part of his employer, the U.S. Navy. Although he had an unblemished 18-year record, the Navy tried to discharge this sailor without benefits once it learned that he had posted a message describing himself as "gay," using the e-mail address "boysrch."

Traditionally in Western democracies, the investigation and prosecution of criminal behavior is a function of government. But the next article explores a recent trend in the U.S. in which private companies are willing to participate in that process, becoming, as writer Jonah Engle puts it, "quasi-private law-enforcement agencies themselves."

Buyer Beware

Jonah Engle[5]

Speaking at a conference this winter on Internet crime, eBay.com's director of law enforcement and compliance, Joseph Sullivan, offered law-enforcement officials extensive access to personal customer information.

Founded in 1995 as a niche site for collectibles, eBay quickly grew into one of the Internet's largest websites, currently boasting 69 million daily visitors, who place an average of 7.7 million bids each day. The company, now valued at $29.6 billion, has become synonymous with online shopping, and is rapidly expanding overseas.

The talk, "Working with Law Enforcement," was delivered at the Cyber-Crime 2003 conference in Mashantucket, Connecticut. Sullivan, who left the Justice Department to become senior counsel for rules, trust and safety at eBay last year, told the audience of law-enforcement officials and industry executives that he didn't "know another website that has a privacy policy as flexible as eBay's," seemingly meaning that eBay acts particularly quickly to grant law enforcement extensive access to user information without regard to established legal procedures that protect individuals from civil rights abuses by the state.

Brags Sullivan, "If you are a law-enforcement officer, all you have to do is send us a fax with a request for information, and ask about the person behind the seller's identity number, and we will provide you with his name, address, sales history and other details—all without having to produce a court order." (eBay itself goes further than this, employing six investigators who are charged with tracking down "suspicious people" and "suspicious behavior.")

Seventy percent of eBay customers, as well as a significant portion of the rest of the online commercial world, make their purchases using (eBay-owned) Paypal, which provides clearing services for online financial transactions. Through Paypal, eBay has access to the financial records of tens of millions of customers. "If you contact me," said Sullivan to assembled law-enforcement authorities, "I will hook you up with the Paypal people. They will help you get the information you're looking for....In order to give you details about credit-card transactions, I have to see a court order. I suggest that you get one, if that's what you're looking for."

Sullivan even offered to conscript eBay's employees in virtual sting operations: "Tell

[5] *The Nation*, June 27, 2003

us what you want to ask the bad guys. We'll send them a form, signed by us, and ask them your questions. We will send their answers directly to your e-mail."

Sullivan's statements were first reported by Yuval Dror in the Tel Aviv-based daily *Ha'aretz*; surprisingly, they have received no coverage in the US media. And, while they may seem extreme, Sullivan's eBay policies seem to fit into a larger pattern of eroding online privacy.

In the fall of 2001 a Stanford-educated Pakistani scientist, a permanent resident of the United States, was visited at his home in the Bay Area by the FBI, who asked about several books he'd recently purchased on eBay. The man's lawyer said the FBI agent reported having been alerted by eBay. eBay denied having provided the information to the FBI, and the bureau refused to comment.

eBay avoids legal trouble with its customers by giving itself carte blanche to divulge any and all personal information. Its hard-to-find privacy policy says: "Due to the existing regulatory environment, we cannot ensure that all of your private communications and other personal information will never be disclosed in ways not otherwise described in this Privacy Policy."

Until recently, in the Internet world "cooperation with government was seen as a betrayal of the unwritten contract between the user and service provider," says Nimrod Kozlovski of the Information Society Project, a Yale-based center that studies democracy and freedom in the digital age. This understanding held that the "provider would protect the consumer from government snooping." Kozlovski believes that "September 11th changed things dramatically," much as it did for privacy and civil-liberties issues in other realms. He observes that eBay followed the trend by rebranding itself and changing its privacy and policy statements "to accommodate this new vision of the company as one which was [not only] cooperative with the government [but] actually a private law enforcement entity." eBay has also felt the sting of tough new laws: On March 28 its unit PayPal was charged by the Justice Department with violating the Patriot Act for providing money transfer services to gambling companies. eBay may be wary of turning down law-enforcement requests, and in this political climate, being pliant to law enforcement may be sound business in the sense that it can lead to better treatment from government and lower administrative costs associated with a company's security division. There is also the genuine anxiety surrounding the potential consequences of not following up on a perceived terrorist threat....

WHAT CYBERSPACE KNOWS ABOUT YOU

Notice what is available free and how cheaply much more data (and spying technology) can be obtained.

Information About You

(a) Go to **http://www.cdt.org** and take the Center for Democracy and Technology Privacy Quiz. Learn how much government and employers can discover about you.

(b) Go to **http://anywho.com**.

What information is on the Web about you?

Information About Other People

(a) Go to **http://www.aclu.org/privacy**.

Click on: Information About You

Click on: Ever wonder how much of your data is in the public domain?

Click on the link: "Commercial information brokers"

Of the items listed, what is the most intimate data you can access for less than $50?

- Criminal record
- Driving record
- Fax number
- Aliases
- E-mail address
- Medical records
- Credit history, including bank-ruptcies

- Social security records
- Alimony being paid
- Hidden assets
- Ownership of property
- Current employer
- Identity of neighbors, relatives

Spy Technology

Check out spytech retailers, such as:

http://www.intercept-spytech.com

http://www.eaglevision1.com

http://www.spybase.com

- What kinds of devices are available in your price range?
- Why do you think there is a market for them?

PRIVACY IN MEDICAL INFORMATION

> *Whatsoever things I see or hear concerning the life of men, in my attendance on the sick or even apart therefrom, which ought not to be noised about, I will keep silence thereon, counting such things to be as sacred secrets.*

—Hippocratic Oath

One of the most disturbing flashpoints where technology has outstripped privacy protection involves the health care industry. Profoundly confidential medical information is accessible to thousands of strangers as physicians, hospitals, HMOs, insurers, pharmacies, government agencies, pension funds, and employers find themselves generating and/or processing it.

Drawing on his book, *The Limits of Privacy*, Amitai Etzioni, a leading Communitarian, comments on what he believes to be an obvious but often ignored fact regarding privacy in the information age: that the main threat comes from the private sector, not government. In this excerpt, he focuses on the issue of privacy of medical information.

The New Enemy of Privacy[6]
Amitai Etzioni

Most violations of privacy of medical records are the result of legally sanctioned, or at least tolerated, unconcealed, systematic flows of medical information from the orbit of the physician-patient-health insurer and health management corporations to other, non-health care parties, including employers, marketers, and the press. I refer here not to the occasional slip-up or the work of a rogue employee, cases that often violate ethical codes or laws, but to the daily, continuous, and very numerous disclosures...that are legal but of highly questionable moral value,...acts that may be labeled authorized abuse.

One major problem area is the disclosure of information by some health insurance companies to employers, information which employers then use to the detriment of prospective or current employees. In 1996, 35 percent of the Fortune 500 companies acknowledged that they draw on personal health information in making employment decisions, in a survey conducted at the University of Illinois at Urbana-Champaign. These companies employ many millions of people.

Another example of authorized abuse is when corporations that self-insure (provide health insurance plans of their own to their workers) draw on their per-

---

[6] *Challenge*, Vol. 43, No. 2 (May/June 2000), pp. 91–106.

sonnel departments or medical claims divisions for privacy-violating data. According to recent figures from the General Accounting Office and the Employee Benefit Research Institute, as many as 48 million people are involved....

Another avenue of employer access to personal medical information is exemplified by the Southeastern Pennsylvania Transit Authority (SEPTA). SEPTA had contracted Rite-Aid pharmacy to provide prescription benefits to its workers. The contract included a requirement for the pharmacy to provide SEPTA with systematic access to employees' prescription records. In one case, the supervisor of an employee was told that the employee was taking AIDS medication. While it is unclear to what use the information was put in this case, one can imagine how such data could be abused.

While information about people's genetic predispositions is collected much less often than other medical information, its collection is on the rise. Two-hundred and six cases of genetic discrimination against asymptomatic individuals were documented in a 1996 study conducted by Harvard and Stanford universities. The individuals involved suffered loss of employment, loss of insurance coverage, or ineligibility for insurance based on the genetic potential for disease—not on any current maladies or symptoms....It is safe to assume that there are numerous other cases, unrecorded, of people unaware of the reasons they were not hired, were fired, and so on.

Regarding treatment, A. G. Breiten-stein, director of the Health Law Institute, an advocacy group based in Boston, said, "People are not going to feel comfortable going to the doctor, because now you are going to have a permanent record that will follow you around for the rest of your life that says you had syphilis, or depression, or an abortion or whatever else."

In addition to authorized abuse by employers, privacy merchants find that private medical information is a lucrative commodity. According to Kathleen A. Frawley, vice president of the American Health Information Management Association, "There is a whole market of people buying and selling medical information." One such marketing firm is IMS America of Totowa, New Jersey, which buys patient records—with personal identifying information attached—outright from state governments, medical clinics, and drug store chains.

The Medical Information Bureau (MIB) is a clearinghouse of personal medical information whose members include 680 life insurance companies and most major issuers of health and disability insurance in the U.S. and Canada. Member companies are required to submit any information about the individuals they insure or who have applied for insurance that pertains to their life expectancy. This includes medical information, encompassing conditions such as high blood pressure and obesity, and other information that may affect insurability, such as a reckless driving record or participation in hazardous activities. Whenever an individual applies for health, life, or disability insurance, the company obtains the record MIB has compiled on him or her.

Pharmaceutical companies have obtained medical records to discover which prescription drugs individuals are using and which physicians are prescribing them, so that these companies may solicit the physicians to prescribe their drugs. These companies also obtain patient lists and medical information from pharmacists in order to advertise prescription drugs directly to select patients. Metromail, known for its National Consumer Database profiling approximately 92 million American households, maintains a medical database, Patient Select, containing 15 million names. For about $.30 per name, large drug companies can pitch their products directly to angina sufferers, diabetics, or arthritics.

THE OPPOSITION TO REFORM

The opposition to measures to shore up privacy of personal medical information is led by major industry groups such as the Health Benefits Coalition, which has financed an advertising and lobbying campaign to stop the patient rights bill "dead in its tracks" and the Healthcare Leadership Council, comprising approximately 50 large pharmaceutical companies, trade groups, and managed care plans. The HLC, in fact, has hosted multiple meetings in the districts of Republican Members of Congress who support the patients rights bill to expose them to local leaders' complaints about the proposed legislation. The Health Insurance Association of America, along with the US Chamber of Commerce, the Blue Cross Blue Shield Association, and

others, pledged to oppose any effort to legislate patient rights. And the $1 billion-a-year data transaction industry, including companies such as IBM, MasterCard, and Electronic Data Systems fear that proposed new forms of data protection, included in the draft legislation, would complicate their work. As a result, like many other privacy-protecting acts before it, a proposed patients' bill of rights was not enacted in 1998.

Still, leading libertarians persist in their focus on the government as the great enemy to individual privacy.... Solveig Singleton stakes out this anachronistic position...starkly, in a Cato Institute report:

> We have no good reason to create new privacy rights. Most private-sector firms that collect information about consumers do so only in order to sell more merchandise. That hardly constitutes a sinister motive. There is little reason to fear the growth of private-sector databases. What we should fear is the growth of government databases.

[In what might be called the "privacy paradox," most civil libertarians and many other privacy advocates continue to point the finger at government as the enemy of privacy, despite massive evidence that privacy merchants are such a considerable threat right now, while at the same time these advocates have sought to stop massive and encompassing privacy violations by these profiteers by drawing on new legislation—that is, on the government.]

QUESTIONS

1. Locate a case in which the plaintiff was forced by an employer—as Lily Kim was in our hypothetical ethics case—to be genetically tested. What was the result?

2. Etzioni mentions the Cato Institute, a libertarian nonprofit. Look them up. What are their perspectives on some of the other privacy issues raised in this chapter? For instance, what do they think about e-mail monitoring at work? About recent government plans to collect data for counterterrorism?

3. This article was first published in 2000. In 2003 regulations went into effect protecting patient privacy. What do they mandate? Do you believe they are responsive to Etzioni's major concerns? Check **http://www.hhs.gov**.

4. On November 16, 2000, the *New York Times* reported on "prescriber profiling." Drug companies collate data about the prescribing patterns of physicians, their specialties and interests, and then use the information to court the doctors, to customize perks that will be offered to them. The companies buy data from pharmacies, the government, even from the American Medical Association. The AMA receives about $20 million a year by selling biographies of every doctor in America. Who are the stakeholders in this scenario? Is this ethical?

CHAPTER PROBLEMS

1. The Digital Millennium Copyright Act allows music companies to force Internet providers to reveal the identities of suspected violators with a unique subpoena that does not need a judge's oversight or signature. In 2003 Verizon Communications refused to turn over the names of two of its subscribers suspected by the recording industry of violating the DMCA. The industry then sued. Verizon argued it had to protect its subscribers' privacy and that a ruling forcing disclosure would "expose anyone who uses the Internet to a host of scam artists, crooks and stalkers." RIAA president Cary Sherman countered: "If users of pirate peer-to-peer sites don't want to be identified, they should not break the law by illegally distributing music." What happened in this case?

2. James Gleick in *What Just Happened*, writes this about privacy:

> In public opinion surveys, Americans' always favor privacy. Then they turn around and sell it cheaply. Most vehemently oppose any suggestion of a national identification system yet volunteer their telephone numbers and mothers' maiden names and even—grudgingly or not—their social security numbers to merchants bearing discounts or Web services offering "membership" privileges. For most, the abstract notion of privacy suggests a mystical, romantic cowboy-era set of freedoms. Yet in the real world it boils down to matters of small convenience...Certainly where other people's privacy is concerned, we seem willing to lower our standards. We have become a society with a cavernous appetite for news and gossip. Our era has replaced the tacit, eyes-averted civility of an earlier time with exhibitionism and prying. Even borderline public figures must get used to the nation's eyes in their bedrooms and pocketbooks. That's not Big Brother watching us. It's us.

Do you agree that Americans seem to be willing to sell their own privacy cheaply while simultaneously craving private information about one another? If so, what role do you think technology has played in all of this? Can you imagine technology being used in new and different ways that might affect these trends?

3. When should the right to privacy yield to public health concerns? In 1999, when San Francisco Department of Public Health officials were able to trace an outbreak of syphilis to an AOL chat room, they asked AOL how they could contact all the exposed sex partners and those who might have had contact with them. AOL responded that in the absence of a court order or a physical threat, its privacy policy prevented them from giving out names. Instead, AOL put the health department in touch with Planet Out, an online service for homosexuals based in San Francisco. Starting by e-mailing the infected men whose names were already known, Planet Out then posted instant messages to people who were in the chat rooms and sent trained volunteers to visit chat rooms, talk to people there, and post information. This method was successful, satisfying privacy advocates, advocates for homosexuals, and health officials, while allowing AOL to hold to its privacy rules.

Is this use of trusted intermediaries an "exportable" process? Can you think of other contexts in which it would produce best results?

4. In 1999, as Congress debated banking reform, President Clinton pushed for legislation requiring banks and other financial institutions to tell consumers when they plan to share or sell their personal financial information, and to give consumers the power to stop such transfers. He also wanted the law to restrict sharing of medical information within a financial conglomerate. "As banks and insurance firms merge, for example, consumers should not fear the results of a physical exam could be used to make a credit decision," said a White House statement.

Find out what became of the Financial Privacy and Consumer Protection Initiative.

5. "A company called DigitalAngel.net…[unveiled] its new product: a global tracking system that can be attached to a person. The device has a tiny antenna that captures not only one's location, but also such data as pulse and temperature and transmits it to an Internet ground station."[7] What might be some of the advantages of GPS? Disadvantages? Would you want to be implanted with a dime-sized GPS?

6. In June 1998 the FTC reported to Congress that 89% of 212 children's Web sites collected personal information about children without requiring some form of parental control over the process. According to a University of New Hampshire study, 20% of young people between the ages of 10 and 17 received unwanted sexual solicitations online in 2000, and only a quarter of them told their parents. Nancy Willard, a psychologist-attorney who directs Responsible Netizen, has this to say about the invasion of a child's online privacy:

> The emergence of an understanding of the appropriate boundaries of personal privacy is clearly a developmental process, tied to the child's emerging cognitive development. Technically proficient children are using the Internet before they have the cognitive ability to appreciate the possible consequences of disclosure of personal information. Dot.com companies can use this to their advantage in seeking to mold the children's perceptions about personal privacy. They are able to accomplish this largely outside of parental influence because most parents do not know about the actions and intentions of these companies.
>
>   Dot.com companies are asking children to disclose personal information and then using that information to develop a close relationship with the child for the purpose of influencing consumer behavior….Children raised in such an environment will likely fail to develop an understanding of the appropriate boundaries of personal privacy. They will be extremely vulnerable to all manner of manipulation and exploitation, not only from corporate marketers, but also from scam artists, cults, and sexual predators.[8]

---

[7] From an article about Global Positioning Systems: Michael Spector, "No Place to Hide," *The New Yorker* (November 27, 2000).

[8] "Capturing the 'Eyeballs' and 'E-wallets' of Captive Kids in School: Dot.com Invades Dot.edu," http://www.responsiblenetizen.org.

Do you agree that there are special concerns regarding privacy for children online? Has there been a legislative response to this problem? Check http://www.ftc.gov. What about a technological response? Find out about the "AOLSafety-Bot." Pros and cons?

7. Katy Johnson, a beauty queen who was twice named Miss Vermont, has her own Web site on which she promotes her "platform of character education." An ex-boyfriend, Tucker Max, also has a Web site. His includes, among other things, a scathing account of his relationship with Ms. Johnson. Johnson sued Max, claiming he had invaded her privacy by exposing intimate facts to the world. In June 2003, a judge ordered Max not to use the words "Katy," "Ms. Johnson," or "Miss Vermont" on his Website, to link to Ms. Johnson's website, or to disclose any intimate stories, facts, or information about her.

    Find out what happened in this lawsuit.

8. As of 2003, about five million Americans and 80 million Europeans and Asians were learning how to use the new technology of cellphone photography. What are the parameters of privacy in a public place? What are the ethics of cellphone cameras?

9. As Chapter 1 reveals, the recording industry has taken its battle against music file-sharers into the courts, filing suit against 261 individuals in 2003. But turning up the heat in this way, according to one expert,"is breeding antibiotic-resistant bacteria—"new systems that will allow people to continue to swap music files anonymously. For instance, Blubster, with a quarter million users, encrypts files and makes eavesdropping more difficult. Another response strategy has been to create so-called "darknets," small private, invitation-only networks for file-sharing that would be harder to detect than those used by millions. What is the right ethical balance between privacy protection and property protection?

10. While pointing to "the ascendancy of privacy as a dominant value" in modern American society, media scholars Gary Gumpert and Susan Drucker ask if much of that phenomenon doesn't actually amount to "cries for safety." As they see it,

    > [S]pontaneous and unprogrammed public life is perceived as risk laden. Public activity has moved into quasi-private physical public places such as shopping malls, gated communities, health clubs and play zones.

    This shift "from the uncontrollable exterior to the controllable interior" has been facilitated by media and information technology that brings so much of the public world into our private spaces and by sophisticated surveillance technology that we believe enhances safety in our society. But Gumpert and Drucker write that there is a "complex and often paradoxical relationship between privacy and surveillance." Surveillance technology is a two-way street: a person can be watched—but can also become the watcher. It is this capacity to observe the world secretly that concerns them:

> When observing public space within the cloak of privacy defines an individual's relationship to society we suggest that there are important implications for the survival of society.
>
> It has always been somewhat enticing to watch and listen to others while remaining hidden from those being watched and heard. It is difficult to single out the motive of surveillance, but eavesdropping...the eroticism of the voyeur, the surprises of the telephoto lens, the childhood adventures of discovering the other side of the keyhole, the anonymity of a disguise, the revelations of the accidental telephone connection—all respond to some unspoken need for secret observation which we share with others.
>
> The detached observer is a citizen without responsibility, disconnected from community, able to be mobile and free without the restraints and obligations of community, yet taking pleasure in a form of eavesdropping that in part recaptures the experience of human association—it is a form of closeness. It is exciting, but strangely upsetting, for it is a connection with others but without involvement. It is a private relationship to a public world.[9]

Do you agree that surveillance technology may represent, in this sense, a threat to civil society?

---

[9] "The Demise of Privacy in a Private World: From Front Porches to Chat Rooms," *Communication Theory* 8, no. 4 (November 1998), pp.408–25.

CHAPTER 3

Cyberspeech

The right to think is the beginning of freedom, and speech must be protected from the government because speech is the beginning of thought.

—U.S. Supreme Court, *Ashcroft v. Free Speech Coalition* (2002)

Censorship reflects a society's lack of confidence in itself. It is a hallmark of an authoritarian regime.

—Supreme Court Justice Potter Stewart, dissenting,
Ginzburg v. United States (1966)

It's not the censorship that you can see that you have to worry about. The censorship to look out for is the censorship that you can't see.

—Hassan Fattah, author and journalist (2003)

ETHICS CASE: BIG LIBEL

Anne and Bob have worked for Big Hamburger Company (BIG), a multinational corporation, since they were in high school. Recently, a left-wing environmental activist group has decided to take on BIG with hopes of starting a worldwide anti-BIG campaign. The group created a Web site, described below, called Anti-BIG. Among other things, they encourage activists who agree with them to print multiple copies of a "pamphlet" linked to the Web site and to distribute the pamphlet outside BIG fast-food restaurants around the world. Anne reads one of the pamphlets and decides to quit her job and join the picketers. Bob is thinking about doing the same. BIG is seriously concerned about its reputation and the possible snowball effect of both the Web site and the picketing.

VIRTUAL REALITY: THE WEB SITE

The anti-BIG homepage features a list of questions that link to other Web pages.

1. What is the connection between BIG and worldwide hunger?

This question links to a page explaining that First World countries and multinational corporations exploit the people of Third World countries. For example, this site claims that BIG—along with several other giant corporations—bought vast tracts of land in poor countries from dollar-hungry rulers (often military) and privileged elites. These greedy citizens evicted the small farmers who once grew food for their people. Millions of acres of the best farmland in poor countries are being used to grow tea, coffee, and tobacco for the First World while local people are starving. BIG is directly involved in this economic imperialism, which keeps most native people poor and hungry while others grow fat. Eating beef is a gross misuse of resources because cattle consume vegetable products that can feed many more people than can the beef that was ultimately produced. Staple crops are exported from Third World countries, where most children are undernourished, to countries where it will be used to fatten cattle to be turned into burgers in the First World.

2. Why is it wrong for BIG to destroy rainforests?

At this link, the reader learns that "BIG and its rival are two of the many U.S. corporations using lethal poisons to destroy vast areas of Central American rainforests to create grazing pastures for cattle. The cattle are sent back to the States as burgers and pet food."

3. How much recycled paper does BIG use?

The reader who clicks here is warned: "Don't be fooled by BIG's claim that they use recycled paper because in actuality, only a tiny percent of it is."

4. Why are BIG's products unhealthy for children or other living things?

From this question, the user is led to a page warning that there is a connection to heart disease and cancer, a danger of food poisoning, and negative health effects from the hormones, pesticides, and antibiotics used in the production of BIG's food products—despite BIG's claims that their food is nutritious. "BIG claims their food is a healthy part of children's diets, but what they don't make clear is that a diet high in fat, sugar, animal products, and salt...and low in fiber, vitamins, and minerals—an average BIG meal—is linked to cancers of the breast and bowel and to heart disease. This is accepted medical fact, not a crank theory. Antibiotics and growth hormones are routinely injected into animals used for meat. Those substances, together with pesticide residues in animal feed, build up in the animals' tissues, further damaging the health of people on a meat-based diet."

5. How does BIG exploit Third World workers?

Here the user finds out that the claim is made that even in First World countries, "Workers in the fast food business do badly in terms of pay and conditions. They work in the evenings and on weekends, doing long shifts in hot, smelly, noisy environments. Wages are low and chances of promotion, minimal. As there is no legally-enforced minimum wage even in Britain, BIG can pay what they like, helping to depress wage levels in the catering trade still further. Throughout the world, BIG exploits the most vulnerable workers (women, children, and men of color—those who have the fewest options)."

MATERIAL REALITY: THE FACTS

In fact, no evidence exists that BIG has purchased land in poor countries, although the company does buy beef from large landowners, some of whom have purchased their grazing lands from smaller farmers. There is evidence that cattle slaughtered to make BIG hamburgers in Europe have been fed, in part, with soy meal exported from Brazil, where soybeans are grown primarily for home use. BIG uses only "home grown" beef in the hamburgers it sells in the U.S. Tea and coffee products are purchased abroad—usually from large landowners who pay very low wages to the peasants who work the land.

In addition, BIG has never used lethal poisons to destroy any rain forest, for any reason. While the expansion of beef cattle production and other factors have led to the destruction of areas of rainforest in Costa Rica, Guatemala, and Brazil, there is no evidence that BIG or any of its partners have taken an active part in that destruction. Nor is there reason to think they urged anyone else to do so. Indeed, in 1989, BIG established a written policy not to purchase beef from ranches located in areas that had recently been part of a rainforest.

A small but nevertheless significant proportion of recycled fiber has been used in packaging for BIG restaurants in the U.K. and U.S. In addition, although many doctors and nutritionists believe that meals such as those sold by BIG can contribute to heart disease, the link to cancer is not so clear, and many experts challenge that such a link exists. Antibiotics are regularly included in feed for cattle in the U.S., both to prevent disease and to promote growth. Prior to the European ban on hormones, some U.K. chickens were regularly fed antibiotics for the same reasons and U.K. pigs were given prophylactic antibiotics when a pig in an "adjacent piggery" was ill. However, there is much dispute in the scientific community about the impact on humans of eating meat from hormone-fed animals. The U.S. is the only industrialized nation still allowing such hormone use.

Protected by the First Amendment to the U.S. Constitution, free speech is considered a fundamental freedom. The right to freedom of expression is the bedrock of American democracy, as it connects directly with the right of the people to criticize and influence their government. In principle, few Americans contest the importance of free speech—although the parameters of its legal protection have never been drawn clearly. Furthermore, what is legal may not necessarily be ethical. In this chapter, we explore the outer reaches of free speech in cyberspace, where it is relatively cheap to send a message around the world in a nanosecond.

We begin with a brief introduction to First Amendment law and to recurring themes in the debate about online freedom in the context of ongoing fear of terrorism.

Next, we look more specifically at cybersmearing (bad-mouthing a person or business over the Internet) and at cyberhoaxes as we consider the benefits and problems of online anonymity. We then explore a variety of views on filters, editing, and censorship before turning to cyberspeech that is both dangerous and potentially criminal, including hate speech, cyber-harassment, and online stalking. Throughout, we encourage readers to consider the overriding issues: To what degree should our culture be cleansed of material that is annoying, offensive, hateful, or likely to incite violence? In an open democratic society, shouldn't it be up to the people, according to their individual preferences and proclivities, to select or delete from the vast menu of choices as they will? To what extent is that possible?

FREEDOM OF EXPRESSION

> *Governments derive their just powers from the consent of the governed. You have neither solicited nor received ours. We did not invite you. You do not know us, nor do you know our world. Cyberspace does not lie within your borders. Do not think that you can build it, as though it were a public construction project. You cannot. It is an act of nature and it grows itself through our collective actions.*
>
> —John Perry Barlow
> A Declaration of the Independence of Cyberspace[1]

From the beginning of our nation's history, not every expressive act or statement has been sheltered by the Constitution. Obscenity, false advertising, and incitement to riot are examples of expression that can be outlawed by the government. While government is not allowed to ban speech outright, it can place limits on the time, place, or manner of its expression. For example, neo-Nazis who want to march through Skokie, Illinois, a community that includes many survivors of the Holocaust, cannot be prevented, but the hours and route of their march can be specified.

In the first decades of the 20th century, the U.S. Supreme Court decided a series of cases involving speeches and writings thought to be subversive to the government. In one instance, three anarchists were jailed for years after they distributed pamphlets in New York City that criticized President Wilson for his opposition to the Russian Revolution. Their convictions were upheld, but in his oft-cited dissent, Justice Oliver Wendell Holmes defended the right to criticize the government, even during wartime:

---

[1] John Perry Barlow, *A Declaration of the Independence of Cyberspace* (http://www.eff.org/ ~barlow/Declaration-Final.html).

*[W]hen men have realized that time has upset many fighting faiths, they may come to believe even more than they believe the very foundations of their own conduct that the ultimate good desired is better reached by free trade in ideas—that the best test of truth is the power of the thought to get itself accepted in the competition of the market, and that truth is the only ground upon which their wishes safely can be carried out....*Abrahms v. United States *250 U.S. 616 (1919).*

Gradually, Holmes' vision of democracy as a free marketplace of ideas gained acceptance, so that by the mid-1960s even subversive speech was not limited unless it was designed to—and likely to—cause imminent lawless action. Beginning in the mid-1990s, Congress seemed less worried about protecting the government from subversive speech than it was about protecting minors from indecent and offensive speech over the Internet. But the Communications Decency Act (CDA) and subsequent laws have been rejected by the Supreme Court. Adults have a constitutional right to see, speak, and hear offensive expression so long as it does not fall within the legal definition of obscenity. And, "regardless of the strength of the government's interest in protecting children from indecent and offensive speech over the Internet," the Court has insisted, "the level of discourse reaching a mailbox simply cannot be limited to that which would be suitable for a sandbox." In rejecting sections of this law because it "threatens to torch a large segment of the Internet community," Justice Stephens wrote:

Does government threaten cyberspeech? http://www.aclu.org and http://eff.org

The Government asserts that—in addition to its interest in protecting children—its "[e]qually significant" interest in fostering the growth of the Internet provides an independent basis for upholding the constitutionality of the CDA....[It] apparently assumes that the unregulated availability of "indecent" and "patently offensive" material on the Internet is driving countless citizens away from the medium because of the risk of exposing themselves or their children to harmful material.

We find this argument singularly unpersuasive. The dramatic expansion of this new marketplace of ideas contradicts the factual basis of this contention. The record demonstrates that the growth of the Internet has been and continues to be phenomenal. As a matter of constitutional tradition, in the absence of evidence to the contrary, we presume that governmental regulation of the content of speech is more likely to interfere with the free exchange of ideas than to encourage it. The interest in encouraging freedom of expression in a democratic society outweighs any theoretical but unproven benefit of censorship. Reno v. American Civil Liberties Union, *117 S. Ct. 2329 (1997).*

After September 11, terrorism took center stage in many of the debates about the appropriate limits on speech. Rodney A. Smolla, author of the first reading in this chapter, is a world-renowned constitutional law scholar and Dean at the University of Richmond School of Law. In the 1990s, Smolla represented the plaintiffs in a suit brought against the publisher of *Rex Feral, Hit Man: A Technical Manual for Independent Contractors* (1983). The plaintiffs were the survivors of a family murdered by a man who bought the book and followed its techniques. Known as a defender of the First Amendment, Smolla was criticized by some in the civil liberties community for attempting to stifle free speech. He defended himself in *Deliberate Intent: A Lawyer Tells the True Story of Murder by the Book* (1999). He draws on his experience with *Hit Man* as he discusses another how-to book: *The Encyclopedia of Jihad*.

From *Hit Man* to *Encyclopedia of Jihad*: How to Distinguish Freedom of Speech from Terrorist Training[2]

Rodney A. Smolla

Western intelligence and law enforcement agencies have in their possession a copy of a manuscript entitled the *Encyclopedia of Jihad*, a comprehensive training manual and religious/political manifesto for the worldwide Al-Qaeda terrorist network, the group held responsible for the September 11 attacks. The encyclopedia is eleven volumes long, and was reportedly obtained from a disgruntled Libyan fighter who claimed to have stolen the encyclopedia from the Kandahar, Afghanistan headquarters of Taliban fighters loyal to Osama Bin Laden. The manual first surfaced in the West during a police raid against a terrorist suspect in Manchester, England in 1998. I have seen excerpts from the *Encyclopedia of Jihad*, which I obtained by downloading segments released to the public by the U.S. Department of Justice. Based on what I have read, I am struck by the many similarities between the *Encyclopedia of Jihad* and a number of books published by various American publishers that also contain detailed training information regarding guerrilla warfare, sabotage, espionage, terrorism, and murder.

Most significantly, I am struck by the parallels in purpose, content, and tone between the *Encyclopedia of Jihad* and a book that was the subject of the most high-profile civil liability case to date involving training in violence, a book entitled *Hit Man: A Technical Manual for Independent Contractors,* which was the subject of a highly controversial federal court of appeals decision, *Rice v. Paladin Enterprises, Inc.* In that case, the court held that the murder instruction manual at issue might well not be protected by the First Amendment, and that a tort action seeking recovery for violence

---

[2] Rodney A. Smolla, "From *Hit Man* to *Encyclopedia of Jihad*: How to Distinguish Freedom of Speech From Terrorist Training," 22 *Loy. L.A. Ent. L. Rev.* 479 (2002).

allegedly aided by the manual could proceed to a jury trial....

The eleven volumes that comprise the *Encyclopedia of Jihad* include: detailed instruction on how to handle, manufacture, and detonate explosives (including Semtex, C4 explosives); methods of first aid, including the handling of psychological shock, the treatment of burns, and the handling of other medical needs; an illustrated guide to the handling of revolvers, specialized handguns, and other small arms; instruction on hand grenades, mines, and various bomb recipes; detailed instruction on military intelligence, sabotage, communications within Jihad, secret observation, assassination, brainwashing, protection of leaders, analyzing intelligence information, psychological warfare, use of poisoning, American military training procedures, and drive-by assassination using motorcycles; instruction in principles of war, including reconnaissance, infiltration, ambush, and incursion; information and diagrams regarding the tools and machines required to manufacture ammunition and silencers; biochemical warfare, sabotage, and bio-terrorism; instruction in tank warfare...hand-to-hand combat and self-defense....

The *Encyclopedia of Jihad* describes targets of opportunity in terms of both their symbolic and psychological importance and their practical destructive significance....

[Its] practical instruction in violence is presented under the rubric and imprimatur of religious obligation....

Within the United States, a society dedicated to freedom of speech and freedom of religion with a well-developed set of constitutional doctrines protecting both, what are we to make of the constitutional status of a work such as the *Encyclopedia of Jihad*? Is it constitutionally protected political and religious expression?...

What I eventually came to see...was that it was the combination of the technical training and the psychological suasion that made [*Hit Man*] so lethal. Neither the technical material alone nor the brainwashing rhetoric of violence alone would have been nearly as dangerous as the explosive cocktail produced when the two ingredients combined....

[T]o train a truly great assassin, a great terrorist, one must work on the killer's mind. The psychological training is the trick. Training the killer to believe in the righteousness of the cause, training the killer to carry forward his deadly task without flinching, without fear, without disabling remorse or guilt—that is the key. What made *Hit Man* so evil and so dangerous was not just that it taught the tricks of the trade; it was that it taught the tradesman to be so proud of them, to be so calm and composed during the execution. The *Encyclopedia of Jihad* is replete with this theme: teaching, for example, that the terrorist member "should have a calm personality that allows him to endure psychological traumas such as those involving bloodshed, murder, arrest, imprisonment, and reverse psychological traumas such as killing one or all of his Organization's comrades."...

[The Publisher] Paladin's astonishing stipulations, coupled with the extraordinary comprehensiveness, detail, and clarity of *Hit Man*'s instructions for criminal activity and murder in particular, the boldness of its palpable exhortation to murder, the alarming power and effectiveness of its peculiar form of instruction, the notable absence from its text of the kind of ideas for the protection of which the First Amendment exists, and the book's evident lack of any even arguably legitimate purpose beyond the promotion and teaching of murder, render this case unique in the law. In at least these circumstances, we are confident that the First Amendment does not erect the absolute bar to the imposition of civil liability....

Yet *Hit Man* pales in comparison to the *Encyclopedia of Jihad*. Osama bin Laden may be an unlikely defendant in a suit for money damages; however, there may be others trafficking in material such as the *Encyclopedia of Jihad*—and doing so with the purpose of aiding and abetting future acts of terrorism—who might well be meaningful targets in a civil action. The *Rice* case is a precedent that could be put to good use in such a suit. And I am proud of it.

QUESTIONS

1. What justification can you give for allowing the publication of the *Encyclopedia of Jihad*? For preventing it from being published? Given that much of the material contained in *Hit Man* was widely available from public sources, many of them online, do you think it was unethical for Paladin Press to publish the book? For the plaintiffs to try to remove it from bookstore shelves?

2. Is there any ethical distinction between publishing a book to be sold in bookstores and using the Internet to communicate the same information?

3. Perhaps even more troubling than books like *Hit Man* or the *Encyclopedia of Jihad* are what might be called "hate sites." One of the most infamous is a site which has become known as the Nuremberg Files. Run by radical anti-choice activists, the site accused various

abortion-providers of "crimes against humanity," listing their names and addresses in a manner that caused the doctors to fear for their lives. After a lawsuit filed by Planned Parenthood, the site was altered slightly. Find the anti-abortion site known as the Nuremberg Files. Do you see it as a "public presentation on a matter of current moral and political importance"—or a site that goes too far and poses a real threat to individuals? What can you find out about the context in which the site was developed? About the way the controversy evolved? Has it been resolved?

4. Since September 11, most of the struggles between civil libertarians and those more concerned with national security have revolved around the privacy issues discussed in chapter 2. But those are not the only issues, as free speech advocate

Floyd Abrams warned in a talk given at the University of Pennsylvania in September 2002. In it, Abrams mentions a 2002 court decision in which newspaper publishers sued to gain access to deportation hearings in "special interest" cases involving persons who might have connections to or knowledge of the September 11, 2001, terrorist attacks.

> One thing I am not prepared to even begin to compromise about is the First Amendment. In fact, as we give the government more power, it is all the more important that the press be utterly free to criticize the manner in which the government exercises that power and (more controversially) to be knowledgeable about what the government has done. If, for example, the government should abuse the new powers that are embodied in the anti-terrorist legislation (and some level of abuse is inevitable), only the press is likely to serve as a check upon that governmental conduct.

> That is why I believe the Court of Appeals for the Sixth Circuit was so correct in barring the government from effectively closing all immigration proceedings to public scrutiny, and why Judge Keith of that court was so eloquent in observing that "[d]emocracies die behind closed doors." That is why we must continue to resist every effort of the Administration to characterize dissent as treason...[and] oppose the ongoing and pervasive efforts of this Administration to prevent the public from learning just who is being detained, for how long, and for what reason, and otherwise to avoid public and congressional scrutiny.[3]

(a) What impact might the Internet have on the traditional role of print and mass media as government watchdogs? Does it mean we can rely less on non-electronic news? **(b)** Find out whether the Supreme Court agreed with Judge Keith about keeping the public out of some immigration hearings.

CYBERSMEARING

Neither judges nor legislators are allowed to stop one citizen from defaming another. Doing so would be a "prior restraint" on speech, prohibited by the First Amendment. But, once a person's words have hurt another's reputation, the speaker risks a civil suit for damages. To win a libel suit, an injured plaintiff must prove that the defendant "published" (communicated) to a third party an untrue statement that tends to lower the plaintiff in the eyes of the community. A defendant who can prove the "truth" of his statement will prevail. And in some instances, the law protects against libel suits

---

[3] Floyd Abrams, "The First Amendment and the War Against Terrorism," 5 *U.Pa.J.Const.L.* 1 (2002).

(e.g., statements made in litigation or on the floor of Congress). While defamation suits are notoriously difficult to win, they are relatively easy to initiate.

The BIG Libel case at the start of this chapter raises significant ethical questions. Bob and Anne have concerns about the environment and animal rights, but as employees, did they have a duty of loyalty to BIG? BIG itself has to protect its reputation and success as a business. One option available to BIG is to bring a lawsuit for defamation against those who created the damaging Web site. This is what happened in the actual case on which this material is based.[4]

As the following reading explains, the ease with which we can remain anonymous when we communicate in cyberspace makes it harder to use libel laws to protect one's reputation. As a result, companies have adopted new strategies to fight cybersmearing.

Corporate Cybersmear[5]

Margo E. K. Reder
Christine Neylon O'Brien

Consider the typical disgruntled employee's complaints: poor working conditions, bad management, long hours, low pay, limited opportunities for advancement, and so forth. Ten years ago, employee dissatisfaction was registered in limited ways—perhaps around the water cooler, out in the parking lot, or during meals, conferences, etc. Such dissatisfaction usually occurred against the backdrop of downward trending economic conditions or significantly changing industry patterns. Very infrequently would this dissatisfaction register in publications such as company or industry newsletters, or in local or national news and magazine publications. Such complaints would, in this era, reach an audience limited both in scope and geography. In any event, the identity of the employee was known, or at least easily discoverable, so it was possible for the employer to serve process and file a complaint for any allegedly defamatory remarks.

This is a dramatic contrast to today's legal environment. Communications systems are now wide open and fully accessible, with no limits in range, scope or geography. Targeted audiences are accessible with pinpoint accuracy. Messages reach millions of readers with one click. There is a chat room for everyone. Most importantly, there is no limit

---

[4] Marlene Arnold Nicholson, "McLibel: A Case Study in English Defamation Law," 18 *Wis.Int'l. L.J.* 1 (2000).

[5] Margo E. K. Reder & Christine Neylon O'Brien, "Corporate Cybersmear: Employers File John Doe Defamation Lawsuits Seeking the Identity of Anonymous Employee Internet Posters," 8 *Mich. Telecomm. Tech. L. Rev.* 196 (2002), available at http://www.mttlr.org/voleight/Reder.pdf. Copyright © 2002 University of Michigan Law School; Margo E. K. Reder; Christine Neylon O'Brien.

on content. Therefore, employees can register their dissatisfaction by posting a message in a chat room. Moreover, the identity of the posting employee is not easily discoverable due to anonymous and pseudonymous communications capabilities. The nature of these online messages is qualitatively different from real-world communications. By way of example, newspapers have a responsibility regarding the veracity of the content that they print. Sponsors of online bulletin board services do not bear the same level of responsibility. In cyberspace chatrooms, everyone is a publisher; there are no editors. Online messages reflect this, too. The culture of online communications is vastly different from traditional discourse, in that the former tolerates and even encourages the use of hyperbole, crudeness, acronyms, misspellings, and misuse of language. It is a fast and loose atmosphere, emphasizing speed rather than accuracy.

...Negative postings by employees also correlate to general economic conditions. During the current two year downturn in the financial markets, for example, there has been a tremendous increase in such postings. Employers have just begun to reply to these allegedly defamatory postings—in the form of John Doe lawsuits. Because it is difficult to discern who is speaking in cyberspace, plaintiffs often file a lawsuit listing "John Doe" as the defendant. Plaintiffs then invoke the power of a subpoena to compel the Internet Service Provider ("ISP") or Bulletin Board Service

("BBS") on which the posting was made to identify the poster, thereby unmasking these anonymous and pseudonymous individuals. It is worth noting that plaintiffs have an alternative course of action, in that they could investigate the postings and discover for themselves who is posting the messages. It is not clear whether any more effort or expense is involved in this strategy than immediately invoking the assistance—and the power—of the judicial system. But it is fair to say that involving the judicial system at this earliest stage is a coercive, and effective, strategy.

Armed with a subpoena—often issued even before a complaint has been filed—employers serve process on the posters' ISP/BBS directing them to divulge the identity of the poster. The vast majority of ISPs comply with such requests routinely and without challenge—and sometimes without the knowledge or consent of the posting subscriber.

...The fascinating aspect of pre-litigation subpoena cases is what happens next. Rather than continue with the lawsuit to test the merits of the contention that the postings were defamatory, a great number of companies that invoke the power of the judicial system to unmask the identities of the posters simply choose to fire the offending employee and drop the lawsuit. This naturally begs the question: what are the motives of the plaintiff companies—to be vindicated from the allegedly defamatory statements, or to silence their critics?

QUESTIONS

1. Is there a difference between online criticism and off-line criticism? Who has more leverage in each format, the speaker or the target?

2. Do you agree with the notion that speech on the Internet is, by its nature, the language of hyperbole? If so, why? Is there something about cyberspace that makes what we encounter there seem less real or less true than it would in traditional media: newspapers, magazines, radio, or television? Or would cyberspace make it seem more real?

3. It is difficult to win a libel suit. As one scholar explains, "[c]ommon law tradition has combined with constitutional principles to clothe the use of epithets, insults, name-calling, and hyperbole with virtually impenetrable legal armor."[6] For example, statements of opinion are generally not considered defamatory because they cannot be proven true or false. Jokes, parodies, and satire are not defamatory because they are understood to be humorous, not factual. If flaming and other outrageous forms of speech are the norm in cyberspace, should companies be forced to tolerate critical Web sites? Should it make any difference if the speaker is an employee or a customer?

4. Find out about the group once known as the John Does Anonymous Foun-

dation. What is its purpose? Compare it to other organizations concerned with free speech such as **Chillingeffects. org**.

5. Check out InternalMemos.com, claiming to be the world's largest collection of internal business correspondence from aggrieved employees of various companies. Who might benefit from a site like this? Who would be harmed? On balance, how ethical is it?

6. The authors describe the subpoena-unmasking strategy as "coercive." Which stakeholders are being coerced? Why?

7. Is it ethical for a corporation that has been cybersmeared to bring a lawsuit it does not realistically expect to win for the sole purpose of discouraging other critics? What alternative actions might the business pursue?

8. There are Web sites that criticize corporations generally, such as those run by Greenpeace or Public Citizen, and there are some that single out a particular business, such as **http://www.Microsoftsucks. com**. Locate one of these sites and evaluate it: Who are the critics? Is there any evidence given to support negative claims? How would you check the accuracy of such claims? Compare and contrast these sites to the imaginary BIG site mentioned at the start of this chapter.

---

[6] James J. Sack, *Libel, Slander & Other Related Problems*, Sect. 2.4.7 (3d ed. 2000).

Cyberhoax: Word for Word/Tweaking the W.T.O.[7]

Barnaby Feder

It's well known that some regions of cyberspace—Internet chat rooms, for instance—are rife with poseurs and imaginary characters. But the World Wide Web is also a breeding ground for more elaborate deceptions, as demonstrated by the following cautionary tale about gall and gullibility in the information age.

The story begins with www.gatt.org, which looks at first glance like an official Web site of the World Trade Organization, the five-year-old Switzerland-based successor to the organization that oversaw the General Agreement on Tariffs and Trade. Unfortunately for the organizers of an October legal seminar on international trade in Salzburg, Austria, a glance was all they gave it before clicking on the "contact" link and sending a speaking invitation to Mike Moore, the W.T.O.'s director-general.

Big mistake: it turns out the site is run by the "Yes Men", a loose-knit group of anti-free-trade activists that views hoaxes as a legitimate weapon of protest.

Excerpts of what transpired follow, culled from e-mail correspondence and faxes posted at **http://www.theyesmen.org/wto**.

It didn't take long for the Yes Men to accept the invitation in Mr. Moore's name, with a caveat:

Thank you for your kind invitation.

I may not be able to attend personally, but I would like very much to send a sub-stitute. Would this be possible? Please let me know and I will begin the search process.

Thank you,

Mike Moore

The director of the seminar's sponsor was happy to oblige....Charles Cushen, a computer programmer in Los Angeles who had been masquerading as Mr. Moore and "Alice Foley," Mr. Moore's secretary, created Andreas Bichlbauer (choosing the name at random from a Vienna phone book), and made travel arrangements for Dr. Bichlbauer and two "security agents," including a cameraman. Dr. Bichlbauer raised eyebrows with his speech, titled "Trade Regulation Relaxation and Concepts of Incremental Improvement: Governing Perspectives from 1970 to the Present." [The following e-mail came from Dennis Campbell, a conference participant.]

Dear Ms. Foley:

We were somewhat puzzled by Dr. Bichlbauer's participation in the conference....

The essential thrust of his speech appeared to be that Italians have a lesser work ethic than the Dutch, that Americans would be better off auctioning their votes in the presidential election to the highest bidder and that the primary role of the W. T. O. was to create a one-world culture. In the late afternoon, a cameraman (I think it was the same one

---

[7] Barnaby Feder, "The Long and Winding Cyberhoax: Political Theatre on the Web?" *New York Times,* Jan. 7, 2001, p. K-9.

who filmed Dr. Bichlbauer's speech) appeared at the hotel and sought to interview our delegates. He said Dr. Bichlbauer had been hit in the face with a pie outside the hotel and wanted to know if the delegates thought Dr. Bichlbauer's speech had provoked the attack....

Several of our delegates, including workethic-impaired Italians, approached me to express concern about the speech, the alleged pie incident, and the cameraman who sought interviews in the late afternoon.

Your clarification will be appreciated,

    Regards, Dennis Campbell

Alice Foley's/Cushen's immediate reply:

Indeed you are correct, Dr. Bichlbauer was in fact "pied" after speaking at the Salzburg C.I.I.S conference....This cameraman...seems to essentially have been an agent provocateur who planned the pieing from the start....

We hope you understand that this sort of incident reflects primarily the unfortunate circumstances under which the W. T. O. must accomplish its work, and that our security can never be entirely adequate to the situations we face....

After another message from Campbell in which he reiterated that some delegates found Dr. Bichlbauer's remarks offensive or flippant, Bichlbauer offered his side of the story:

I was disappointed to hear from Alice Foley that some people in the audience on Saturday disliked my lecture....Those who were upset by the lecture were

clearly unreceptive to any message departing from the simple W. T. O. "party line" as it is presented in larger arenas. At this conference we hoped to examine this "party line" through repackaging in a clearer and more carefully delineated fashion, for the sake of more lucid examination and a greater awareness of "issue extremes" for use in more politic descriptions—those intended for the consumption of larger blocs of the consuming public....

Two days later, hoping to elicit further response, Cushen slipped again into his Mr. Moore persona:

Dear Professor Campbell,

I was dismayed to learn of your unfortunate experience with our representative, Andreas Bichlbauer....I will recommend that Dr. Bichlbauer be required to attend a refresher course on public speaking, communication and policy before any further appearances on behalf of the W. T. O....

However, having examined the presentation exhaustively, I am forced to conclude that never in any particulars do Dr. Bichlbauer's statements...depart from the spirit—if not the precise letter—of our intentions and aims. That is, while we of course do not advocate vote-selling or siesta-banning at the present time, it is quite true that efficiency and the streamlining of culture and politics in the interests of economic liberalization is at the core of the W. T. O.'s programme, and such practices as described by Dr. Bichlbauer are useful in clarifying the long-range interests of global development as promoted by our organization and others.

Cyberhoax or unethical smear? Compare
http://www.wto.org
http://www.gatt.org

On Nov. 1, Alice Foley/Cushen had more bad news for Professor Campbell:

The situation has, I regret to say, somewhat deteriorated from an already unpleasant state of affairs: Dr. Bichlbauer has contracted a rather serious infection from the pie, which forensic analysis shows contained an active bacillus agent. It is not certain whether foul play was involved....I know that this question will sound harsh, but could any of the lawyers present have been angry enough at Dr. Bichlbauer's lecture to do this?...

On Nov. 6, using addresses collected in Salzburg, Alice Foley/Cushen e-mailed six conference participants with the message that Dr. Bichlbauer was near death from his infection and concluding:

Please, please let us know if anything at the conference struck you as strange....

A similar e-mail message sent two weeks later to 77 delegates elicited a range of responses, most indicating that the insult to Italian work habits had made the biggest impression. Dr. Bichlbauer's death was announced via e-mail on Nov. 27.

Postscript: A W. T. O. spokesman said last week that while his organization deplored the Yes Men's deceptive Web site and the hoax, it respects the nature of the Internet as a forum for free expression. Mr. Cushen said "Mr. Moore" had recently received an invitation to a textile conference in Finland and that his group was hoping to scrape together the money needed to send a successor to Dr. Bichlbauer. "We think the ethical thing to do is represent the W. T. O. more honestly than they represent themselves," he said.

QUESTIONS

1. Is cybersmearing ever justified? Under what circumstances?

2. Who was hurt by the hoax described above? How were they hurt? Were there any positive consequences? Was this a harmless prank or a deception that should be punished?

3. What sorts of obligations do the creators of Web sites have to government agencies or political groups? To international associations like the WTO? To the public?

4. What ethical obligation does an ISP like Yahoo!, Inc. have to its customers? Should Yahoo willingly release the identities of John Does who badmouth a company—or force the company to seek a subpoena? Find out what happened in the New Jersey lawsuit initiated by Dendrite International against four John Does who posted messages critical of Dendrite on a company bulletin board. Is your answer the same for the John Doe who criticizes an international group like the WTO?

5. The Yes Men—responsible for the WTO hoax—honored the thousands killed in a lethal gas spill at a Union Carbide plant in Bhopal India by sending fake e-mails on the anniversary of the disaster. Claiming to be from Dow Chemical (which now owns

Union Carbide), the e-mails purportedly explained why Dow refuses to help those in Bhopal still suffering the aftereffects of the disaster. Find out what else the Yes Men have been up to.

6. The Institute for Historical Review has a Web site that promotes the idea that the Nazis are innocent victims of a spiteful lie started by the Jews to "drum up world sympathy and political and financial support for Jewish causes, especially for the formation of the State of Israel." This site claims it is not anti-Semitic, but is presenting "facts." Is there any difference between this and the WTO hoax?

7. How does your ethical analysis change when it is an individual—rather than McDonald's or the WTO—who is smeared online? Evaluate the actions of each of the players in the following scenario from a recent lawsuit.

> In the summer of 1999, sometime-handyman Robert Smith was working for Ellen Batzel, an attorney licensed to practice in California and North Carolina, at Batzel's house in the North Carolina mountains. Smith recounted that while he was repairing Batzel's truck, Batzel told him that she was "the granddaughter of one of Adolf Hitler's right-hand men." Smith also maintained that as he was painting the walls of Batzel's sitting room he overheard Batzel tell her roommate that she was related to Nazi politician Heinrich Himmler. According to Smith, Batzel told him on another occasion that some of the paintings

hanging in her house were inherited. To Smith, these paintings looked old and European.

After assembling these clues, Smith used a computer to look for websites concerning stolen art work and was directed by a search engine to the Museum Security Network ("the Network") website. He thereupon sent the following e-mail message to the Network:

From: Bob Smith [e-mail address omitted]

To: securma@museum-security. org [the Network]

Subject: Stolen Art

Hi there,

I am a building contractor in Asheville, North Carolina, USA. A month ago, I did a remodeling job for a woman, Ellen L. Batzel who bragged to me about being the grand daughter [sic] of 'one of Adolph Hitler's right-hand men.' At the time, I was concentrating on performing my tasks, but upon reflection, I believe she said she was the descendant of Heinrich Himmler.

Ellen Batzel has hundreds of older European paintings on her walls, all with heavy carved wooden frames. She told me she inherited them.

I believe these paintings were looted during WWII and are the rightful legacy of the Jewish people. Her address is [omitted].

I also believe that the descendants of criminals should not be persecuted for the crimes of the [sic] fathers, nor should they benefit. I do not know who to contact about this, so I start with your organization. Please contact me via email [...] if you would like to discuss this matter.

Bob.

Ton Cremers, then-Director of Security at Amsterdam's famous Rijksmuseum and (in his spare time) sole operator of the Network received Smith's e-mail message. The nonprofit Network maintains both a website and an electronic e-mailed newsletter about museum security and stolen art. Cremers periodically puts together an electronic document containing: e-mails sent to him, primarily from Network subscribers; comments by himself as the moderator of an on-line discussion; and excerpts from news articles related to stolen works of art. [Cremers decides which e-mails and material to delete. The rest are posted on the Network web site and sent to subscribers via a listserv.]...The Network's website and listserv mailings are read by hundreds of museum security officials, insurance investigators, and law enforcement personnel around the world, who use the information in the Network posting to track down stolen art.

After receiving it, Cremers published Smith's e-mail message to the Network, with some minor wording changes, on the Network listserv... [and] on the Network's website, [and later]...posted a "moderator's message" stating that "the FBI has been informed of the contents of [Smith's] original message."

Batzel discovered the message several months after its initial posting and complained to Cremers about the message. Cremers then contacted Smith via e-mail to request additional information about Smith's allegations. Smith continued to insist on the truth of his statements. He also told Cremers that if he had thought his e-mail "message would be posted on an international message board [he] never would have sent it in the first place." *Batzel v. Smith,* 2003 WL 21453358, (9th Cir. 2003).

8. Ellen Batzel sued both Smith, the handyman who sent the e-mail, and the Network that hosted the website and the listserv. The court ruled that the Network was immune from suit, based on a law designed to encourage free use of the Internet without discouraging ISPs and others from screening out obscene or defamatory material. Do you think a small ISP like the Network has an ethical responsibility to prevent or discourage defamation? How about larger ISPs, like AOL or Juno?

ANONYMITY ONLINE

It is plain that anonymity has sometimes been assumed for the most constructive purposes.

—U.S. Supreme Court, *Talley v. California* (1960)

Just as anonymity might give you the strength to state an unpopular view, it can also shield you if you post an irresponsible view. Or a slanderous view. Or a hurtful view.

—Lawrence Lessig, *Code and Other Laws of Cyberspace*

The HIV-positive classical music buff should not lose his right to read information about HIV and AIDS anonymously simply because he has asked to be notified when new classical recordings are released.

—Julie E. Cohen, "A Right to Read Anonymously"

David L. Sobel, General Counsel, Electronic Privacy Information Center (EPIC), Washington, DC., has this to say about anonymity online:

Internet Anonymity[8]

David L. Sobel

In 1997 in [*Reno v. American Civil Liberties Union*] the Supreme Court reviewed the Communications Decency Act, the first federal statute seeking to regulate Internet content. In a landmark decision defining the scope of the online medium's First Amendment protection, the Court noted that the Internet

"provides relatively unlimited, low-cost capacity for communication of all kinds....[T]his dynamic, multifaceted category of communication includes not only traditional print and news services, but also audio, video, and still images, as well as interactive, real-time dialogue. Through the use of chat rooms, any person with a phone line can become a town crier with a voice that resonates farther than it could from any soapbox. Through the use of Web pages, mail exploders, and newsgroups, the same individual can become a pamphleteer."

What the Court described as "the vast democratic fora of the Internet" would be stifled if users were unable to preserve their anonymity online. The courts have long recognized that compelled identification can chill expression. [In a case striking down an Ohio statute prohibiting the anonymous distribution of campaign literature], the Court wrote:

The decision in favor of anonymity may be motivated by fear of economic or official retaliation, by concern about social ostracism, or merely by a

---

[8] Dazvid L. Sobel, "The Process that 'John Doe' is Due: Addressing the Legal Challenge to Internet Anonymity," 5 *Va. J.Law & Technology* 3 (2000).

desire to preserve as much of one's privacy as possible.

Anonymity is a shield from the tyranny of the majority....It thus exemplifies the purpose behind the Bill of Rights, and of the First Amendment in particular: to protect unpopular individuals from retaliation—and their ideas from suppression—at the hand of an intolerant society.

It is clear that anonymity often facilitates free expression, particularly where controversial or unpopular ideas are being voiced. Nondisclosure of identity is thus critical for websites, message boards and chat areas devoted to many topics, including corporate and governmental whistleblowing; labor organizing; dissident movements in repressive countries; gay and lesbian issues; and resources dealing with addiction, alcoholism, diseases and spousal abuse....

Electronic Privacy Information Center http://epic.org

A Right To Read Anonymously: A Closer Look at "Copyright Management" in Cyberspace[9]

Julie E. Cohen

...Communication may be oral or written, and participation in a given act of communication may be active or passive. It is a truism that both "active" modes of communication—speaking and writing—qualify as constitutional "speech." The relationship between the receipt of information and expression is less well-explored.

As a matter of both historical and current practice, the distinction between "active" expression and "passive" receipt is less clear than one might suppose. From a historical perspective, the strict demarcation between speaking and reading is a relatively recent one. For much of human history, everything from stories to important business matters was transmitted orally....We have come a long way from the days of medieval scribes and public readings of texts....However, with the advent of electronic networks and hyper-

text links, expression and receipt of information are blurring once again. Electronic text is dynamic; rather than following a single, linear progression, the reader is free to choose his or her own path through a network of linked material. Through this process, the reader participates in the construction of the author's message. While it may be premature to speak of the demise of the author, the creation of at least some "speech" in cyberspace thus reflects the combined efforts of both "authors" and "readers...."

Freedom of speech is an empty guarantee unless one has something—anything—to say. A central insight that both copyright and literary theory can lend to First Amendment jurisprudence is that the content of one's speech is shaped by one's response to all prior speech, both oral and written, to which one has been exposed....

---

[9] Julie E. Cohen, "The Right to Read Anonymously," 28 *Conn. L.Rev.* 981 (1996).

"Originality," as a prerequisite for copyright protection, is a term of art; it is well-understood that every "original" work of authorship is, in many respects, a distillation of the works that came before it. The same is true of any expression of an idea....Thoughts and opinions, which are the predicates to speech, cannot arise in a vacuum. Whatever their content, they are responses formed to things heard or read....

[In the next excerpt, Cohen links the right to read anonymously with freedom of association under the First Amendment.]

Last but not least, reading is an important dimension of the individual right of associational freedom....It has...been argued that a right of anonymity in one's interpersonal affiliations protects the individual's right to construct his or her identity without public scrutiny. Reading is intellectual association, pure and simple. As such, it is as profoundly constitutive of identity as direct interpersonal association. There are reasons for according even stronger protection to reading, moreover. Interpersonal association and group affiliation are, by definition, voluntary expressions of a common purpose or interest. Although disclosure of one's affiliations may chill protected conduct, the information revealed by such disclosure is, at least, accurate. In contrast, one may not wish to affiliate oneself with the authors of some materials one chooses to read; indeed, one may affirmatively wish otherwise. I may read *The Turner Diaries* or *The Fountainhead* for purely scholarly reasons, without any intent or desire to associate myself with the movements they have come to represent. To the extent that the dangers of being labeled by one's reading choices are greater than the dangers of being labeled by one's choice of associates, the case for First Amendment protection of association through reading is correspondingly stronger.

...Now that digital copyright management technology has made it possible to monitor reading habits, preferences regarding political commentary, artistic tastes—in short, to intrude to an unprecedented degree on private intellectual activity of all types—the doctrines that protect "speech" must be reshaped to ensure that the protection they afford is not diminished....

...It is technically feasible to design copyright management systems that protect the underlying works without compromising reader anonymity. For example, a digital work might contain embedded software that automatically frustrates second-generation copying without reporting the attempted duplication to the copyright owner. Alternatively, the system might collect fees via an anonymous payment system, or prevent the extraction of reader identifying data. Thus, it is difficult to avoid the conclusion that the anti-tampering provisions of the NIICPA are broader than necessary to protect copyright owners' legitimate interests.

QUESTIONS

1. What are the virtues of virtual anonymity? The vices?

2. What connections does the author draw between free speech and the right to read anonymously?

3. According to Cohen, "The new information age is turning out to be as much an age of information about readers as an age about information for readers." Is there potential for harm when a copyright owner generates—and keeps—precise and detailed records of a person's online reading habits? What benefits might flow from such activity? On balance, from a utilitarian perspective, how ethical would it be for a publisher to collect data on a particular reader that tracked what pages she opened, as well as how long and how often she looked at them?

4. Think back to the discussions of data-mining in chapter 2. In what ways might data-mining be altered by the added factor of knowing what a person has been reading? How might it uncover or distort or deepen knowledge of a person?

5. One provision of the USA PATRIOT Act allows the FBI to review certain business records of people under suspicion—interpreted to include buying or borrowing books and using the Internet at libraries, bookstores, and cafes. To protest, librarians in some parts of the country changed their practices to shred logs of people who sign up to use the library's computer stations. Other libraries have posted warning signs or handed patrons literature advising them of the new powers of the government. Which of those actions seem most ethical? Should bookstores adopt any of the same practices? Internet cafes?

6. Find out the status of a bill introduced in 2003, the "Freedom To Read Protection Act," which would prevent the government from accessing library and bookstore records without proper court approval. What arguments did the bill's sponsors and opponents make?

7. The Web site **http://www.PinStruck. com** allows customers to send an online curse ("a virtual voodoo doll") without revealing the identity of the priest or priestess who sent the hex. Is this a case where anonymity is ethically justified? Required?

BUILDING IN RESTRICTIONS: FILTERS, EDITORS, AND NETIQUETTE

One of the most controversial efforts to control Internet content is the introduction of "filters" that block out certain kinds of content—most often sex-related and pornographic. Their use by schools and public libraries, where the Internet is made available to less affluent adults and to children, has been particularly controversial. These and other methods of "indirect" regulation were explored in a panel discussion at a 1998 symposium.

Joan Bertin, Executive Director of the National Coalition Against Censorship, is the first panelist. As you read her remarks, ask yourself, "What arguments can I make against restrictions on Internet access?"

Symposium: Should Cyberspace be a Free Speech Zone? Filters, "Family Friendliness," and the First Amendment[10]

JOAN BERTIN: I always feel obliged, when I talk about this subject, to start by saying that I am the parent of two kids ages 12 and 15. I am as "family friendly" as the next person, but that does not mean that I embrace censorship or parental control over everything they see. In my own private life, I choose to protect my children from the world's dangers by helping them understand what those dangers are, how to recognize them, and how to protect themselves. Also, in the scheme of things that are unfriendly to children, harm to kids on the Internet is pretty far down on my list, and I think this is important to recognize as a contextual matter. Even though there is a lot of stuff on the Internet I don't particularly want to see and wouldn't particularly want to let my children to see, it does not rank with disease, war, malnutrition, bad education, bad health care, parental neglect and all of the other things many children face. Thus, I think we have to recognize that a lot of time and energy is directed to the Internet, when in point of fact the risks children face worldwide are much more impor-

tant. I wish more attention would be directed towards improving children's education and putting money into that, as opposed to figuring out how to keep kids from accessing particular sites and imagining what will happen if they happen to trip over those Web sites. I think that the notion of ratings and filters as a way to address concerns people have about Internet is insidious.

There is really no combination of letters or numbers that can distinguish good violence from bad violence. You can't tell the difference in a rating system between *Schindler's List* and the *Texas Chainsaw Massacre*. Nobody has devised a way to do that. So if you are going to have a blocking mechanism for violence, you will lose both *Schindler's List* and the *Texas Chainsaw Massacre* and a lot of history and other stuff, too. The same problem exists with sex, compounded by the difficulties of trying to distinguish between the maturity level of a six-year-old and a 16-year-old....

Moreover, if you block pornography, you also block the critics of pornography. If you block sex, you also block sex educa-

---

[10] Joan Bertin, Graham Cannon, Joe Diamond, Jason Heffner, Barry Steinhardt, "Panel II: Indirect/Industry Regulation of the Internet," 15 *N.Y.L.Sch. J. of Human Rts.* 67 (1998).

tion. If you block violence, you block information about the Holocaust. If you block hate sites, you also lose information about slavery issues. No one has come up with a solution to these problems.

[M]ost producers of blocking and filtering software refuse to disclose the list of sites that are blocked. Most claim this is proprietary information, and that even if it weren't they would refuse to disclose the list because that would be a "road map" for kids to use in finding all the "good stuff."...Thus, even though these tools are touted as enhancing parental control, they don't really give control, because they don't enable the user to make informed decisions. Finally, the sheer volume of material on the Internet makes it unrealistic to expect that any blocking system can keep up.

[T]he ability to use technology to implement personal values in the home often leads directly to a demand for the same thing in schools and libraries. The line between public and private decisions becomes blurred because the notion is that, if parents are entitled to control what their children see, they should be entitled to that kind of control wherever their children are. If we give parents the idea that their responsibility as parents means that they should only let their kids see pretty, "wholesome" content, then we have sacrificed the notion that both parents and teachers have a responsibility to help children negotiate the world as it is, with all its warts....We don't protect [children's] innocence by keeping them from accessing the unpleasant aspects of life, but surely they need our guidance in knowing how to deal with it.

[As you read comments from the next speaker, Graham Cannon, now an executive at **CameraPlanet.com**, ask yourself, why is he arguing against self-regulation?]

GRAHAM CANNON: Let me give you the perspective of a major media company that came to the Internet about four years ago and now delivers about 23 million page views a week....

[T]o major editorial providers, such as ourselves, *The Wall Street Journal* and the *New York Times*, there was increasing recognition of the dangers of self-regulation—in many ways even more dangerous than government regulation. At least with government regulation, there is due process. You can challenge it and be heard. What we realized was that under this kind of self-regulation we were asking editors to do something fundamentally insidious and dangerous to the practice of journalism—asking editors to make arbitrary ratings judgments about the content at their sites. What impact would that have on an editor, writer or photo journalist's conception of how their work would be presented to readers? It was an absurdity compounded by the realization that such an approach would constitute an incredible violation of the trust our readers place in us to report and cover the news as we see fit, relying on them to make the determination as to whether what we produce is appropriate and relevant for themselves or their families.

What added fuel to the fire was the notion that news organizations should be exempt from any kind of regulation. First we said, "That's great," but then we realized once you start doing that, you create a whole new dangerous standard. In effect, those regulating this new system would have the power to determine what is or isn't news—something we've always let readers decide. By any standard, magazines always considered themselves news, likewise with newspapers. The notion that you would create a form of protected speech for news which required a group of individuals to adjudicate who is in or out of that club was something we realized was very dangerous. Is Larry Flynt a member? How about an information site from the Kurdish Worker's Party?

The view that I believe is prevailing is that if outside organizations or individuals wish to rate our sites, that's fine. If an organization wants to create a page called Best News Sites, Worst News Sites, Most Sexually Explicit Sites, Least Sexually Explicit Sites, that's fine, and a user can freely decide whether and how to use the information as a guide for surfing the Internet.

As the online audience more and more becomes a reflection of the mainstream marketplace, users understand the conundrum. As a comparison, part of the price for enjoying New York's vast culture and sensibility is that it comes with a potentially dangerous underbelly—the alternative is Disneyland....

[The next speaker, Joe Diamond, calls himself an Internet activist. He described his involvement with a "crime advocacy organization" called "Take Back New York" that started a now-defunct Web site called Parole

Watch in 1997. Parole Watch posted notices on the Internet about violent felons coming up for parole. "We give you, the public, the chance to write letters, sign a petition or send e-mail to the parole board expressing your views about a particular person getting out early," said the Web site. At the time of this panel discussion, the New York State Department of Correctional Services was working with Parole Watch, providing them with a listing of more than 37,000 violent felons in state facilities. The organization hoped to expand to all 50 states, and provide "the single largest publicly accessible clearinghouse for information on violent criminals probably ever assembled, with the exception of the FBI." This was what Diamond said about regulation of the Internet:]

JOE DIAMOND: It is vital that society keeps control of the Internet....It is something too powerful; if ever put in the hands of the state, it could easily become authoritarian....The less government oversees the Internet, the more community involvement is necessary, especially from parents; that's mainly going to come with the use of filtering and blocking software.

...[T]he software industry—particularly the ones with the giant research and development budgets like Microsoft and Alta Vista Digital Equipment Corporation, which are very advanced as far as this type of stuff is concerned—should be striving to do two things. First, creating filtering software that gives maximum flexibility to the consumer, again, mainly parents so they can pick and choose according to their own values what they want their kids to see or not see.

The other attribute the software has to have is maximum accuracy, so if parents want to block out a sex site they are not throwing the baby out with the bath water....

[What concerns does the next speaker raise on behalf of the Gay and Lesbian Alliance Against Defamation (GLAAD)? What recommendations does he make?]

JASON HEFFNER: For over a decade, GLAAD has been promoting fair, accurate and inclusive representations based on sexual orientation and identity in all forms of media. As the Internet has become a mainstream reality, GLAAD has been a leader in ensuring equal access to it for gay men and lesbians.

In 1995, GLAAD became aware of a new technology that affected gay and lesbian presence on the Internet. Filtering software was being developed to help parents filter the Internet for indecent materials. Through keyword blocking, the use of descriptors to block sites, and outright censoring, we found gay and lesbian sites were being filtered off the Internet....The majority of software on the market, as well as the new products in development, places informational sites serving the gay, lesbian, bisexual and transgender community in the same category as sexually explicit sites. For example...a site which lists the contact information for groups of lesbians and gay men interested in square dancing is blocked by many of the filtering software makers, who are either unable or unwilling to consider that information about sexual orientation and identity has nothing to do with sexual behavior and everything to do with culture and identity. Among those most threatened by this software are gay, lesbian and bisexual and transgendered youth. The resources available on the Internet—again, the Web sites, the chat rooms and educational resources—are literally lifesaving to these young people, many of whom live in isolation, both geographically and emotionally.

GLAAD supports the need for children to have age appropriate images, and the need for organizations to provide sites with such images without interference from governmental regulation cannot be overstated....[R]ating systems may enforce invisibility as they become more widely used. Sites that refuse to rate themselves may be blocked from popular Web browsers such as Netscape or Explorer, or by the filtering software of companies afraid of lawsuits and backlash. These sites would then cease to exist in the eyes of the users whose software only allowed rated sites....

[Heffner describes GLAAD's criteria for selecting filtering software that is "fair, accurate and inclusive." A system is unfair if it treats lesbian, gay, bisexual, or transgender-related material differently from similar, but straight, material; allows specific tracking of lesbian, gay, bisexual, or transgender-related material; or encourages full tracking that might lead to "fishing expeditions." To be accurate, software must not be based on uninformed or outdated concepts, e.g., ratings, on the assumption that all gay sites "recruit gays" or "endorse a lifestyle."

[The final speaker, President and CEO of the Electronic Frontier Foundation, Barry

Steinhardt, explaining why he opposes the spread of filtering software.]

BARRY STEINHARDT: Let me start by talking about the so-called parental power of the filtering and blocking software. I think most advocates of free speech on the Internet would say they are not categorically opposed to the notion of parents or other end users being able to employ software on their own computers by their own choice which block and filter, but it is important to understand what that software does. This software largely blacklists. They are not rating systems for the entire World Wide Web or entire Internet, they are blacklists. They are sites which have been chosen to be blocked by a variety of criteria. Whether it is keywords or whether it is a third party examining the sites for their content and making a decision about whether they should be blocked, the industry that has promoted and provided software that has, to a large extent, misled consumers about the software.

[M]ost of those companies do not disclose either the blacklists or the criteria for the selection of the blacklists. [T]he products have largely been sold on the premise they are blocking out pornography and smut on the Internet. The truth is they...fail to block out a great deal of sexual material...[at the same time that] they are blocking non-sexual sites, as you have heard, including the American Association of University Women and the Quaker Web site....As a result, I don't think most of this software empowers parents. In fact, I think it disempowers

them. It blocks them from the richness of the Internet and it does so in ways they will never know and never be able to know.

[Steinhardt next points to what he considers a greater danger, the call for changes in the architecture of the Internet.]

But having said that, let me suggest that the attention that has been focused on this end-user-based software, the software you install, is misplaced. The larger issue are the proposals to change the very architecture of the Internet to facilitate a system of so-called self-regulation, so-called voluntary blocking and filtering of content on the Internet, and that change in the architecture of the Internet will be far more consequential than the individual programs that the end users may choose to use. Specifically what I am talking about is the growing and widespread acceptance of PICS. PICS was and is a labeling standard that was adopted by the World Wide Web Consortium, which is an industry standard setting body. The original concept behind PICS was it would be built into browsers, Microsoft's browser or Netscape's browser, and it would provide an empty vessel into which a multitude of third party rating systems would be poured. Usually the examples given are everything from the Christian Coalition to the ACLU. If you had a browser that was PICS compatible, you would be able to choose which of the rating systems best reflected your values. PICS is now built in, I should say, to the Microsoft browser and Netscape has agreed to build it into their next version.

It has morphed into a system of governmental blocking and governmental control. In the latest generation of PICS, PICS 1.1, PICS has been constructed so that entire domains, entire sections of the Internet can be blocked based on URLs. That means, for example, the Chinese government can block out everything in the domain '.gov', signifying it is the U.S. Government, or it can block out anything from Taiwan. It has also morphed into a system for blocking Internet access on the basis of keywords in URL so that words like "sex" or words like "political prisoner" can be blocked out.

PICS has become, in fact, an instrument for government control of the Internet...and we are beginning to see the proposals even here in the U.S. to use PICS and rating systems as instruments of government control. The vanguard of that, of course, has been in the libraries and in the schools, because it is sold to us as protecting children....

MS. BERTIN: [P]arents don't own children's minds....Certainly parents have both rights and responsibilities to guide their children through the early years, but that does not necessarily mean that parents should be in control of everything their children see, hear, and read....There has to be a gradual introduction into the realities of the world, because sooner or later children leave home. As parents, we hope that when they do, they are prepared to deal with what they find out there. So I am disturbed at the prospect of a library card that would allow parents to control what kids can access, what kids can read in the library. Frankly, as a parent, that is horrifying to me. You wouldn't leave your six-year-old alone in the adult section of a library without any guidance, but you would leave the 16-year-old....

MR. STEINHARDT: I think the widespread use of the blocking software is based on a false premise...that somehow the subjective elements about the value of speech can be quantified. We have heard a great deal about these products. Some people compared them to food labeling. They say it is like the label that's on a soup can.

The problem, I think, is very obvious. I am sure the scientists would tell us that the contents of a can of soup are relatively objective, quantifiable, and verifiable. How much sodium is in the soup is something you can measure. Whether or not something is violent, or whether or not something is impermissibly sexual, is not something that can be easily, I think, at all measured and I don't think that the software is going to get any better, Joe. I think that the manufacturers of the software face a conundrum. First of all, they are attempting to quantify something that is not quantifiable, and secondly, they have unlimited content to deal with on the Internet. It's never going to be possible even to use their subjective judgment to make decisions about the entire Internet.

THE LIBRARY BILL OF RIGHTS

- Books and other library resources should be provided for the interest, information, and enlightenment of all people of the community the library serves.
- Materials should not be excluded because of the origin, background, or views of those contributing to their creation.
- Libraries should provide materials and information presenting all points of view on current and historical issues.
- Materials should not be proscribed or removed because of partisan or doctrinal disapproval....

QUESTIONS

1. Should children be protected from offensive online speech? Should adults?

Who should do the protecting: Government? Schools? Public libraries?

2. Find a site that provides information on filtering systems. Who sponsors the site you visited? What position do they take on filtering in general? Do you agree?

3. Do you believe filters in public schools or libraries are justified? Are they a form of censorship? The Children's Internet Protection Act was passed by Congress to regulate pornographic material on the Internet. It requires all public and school libraries to install "technological protection measures" to block children from obscene materials on their computers. Find out how the Supreme Court ruled in 2003 when the filter-requirement was challenged as a violation of the First Amendment.

The Supreme Court has said that listeners have a right to decide what kind of speech they want to hear but that "no one has a right to press even 'good ideas' on an unwilling recipient." These statements led Eugene Volokh, Acting Professor, UCLA Law School, to explore free speech from the listener's perspective.

Freedom of Speech in Cyberspace[11]

Eugene Volokh

Speakers' desires are fairly simple: generally, they want more listeners. But listeners don't just want more speakers talking to them. Listeners want more control over their speech diet—a larger range of available speech coupled with greater ease of selecting the speech that's most useful or interesting to them.

The success of the new electronic media in the "marketplace of marketplaces" of ideas—where information providers compete for that scarcest of resources, the attention span of modern man—will turn on how well they can satisfy listeners' desires. The new media have one significant advantage: they can give listeners many more choices. But for listeners, that's not enough. For listeners, what the new media omit—time-wasting junk, insults, material that might be harmful to their children—is just as important as what they include. Listeners care about this outside the online world, and they care about it just as much online....

One of the most significant features of the new media is the interactive electronic conference—bulletin board, newsgroup, discussion list, or the like. People who listen in on these conferences (and most participants spend much more of their time listening than speaking) want speech that's relevant to their interests, readable, reliable, and not rude. Sometimes an open, unedited electronic conference can provide this, but often it can't. Often—as conference operators have been learning—editing is critical to making online speech worth listening to.

At the same time, editing is content control, the sort of thing that, if the government did it, would be called "censorship." It includes limitations on who may speak, removal of people who speak badly (in the editor's opinion), the deletion of inappropriate messages, and automatic screening of messages for profanities. Many have expressed concern about this sort of private speech restriction....

[C]onference users also want an emotionally congenial environment. It may be a pleasure to listen to people discuss an issue civilly, but a strain to listen to them yell at each other. Even if the intellectual content is the same, the tone of the speech can be a serious burden.

[As you read, ask: Are online conferences a unique form of human interaction?]

Few physical conferences, for instance, invite speakers who insult one another. Many newspapers refuse to print certain profanities. We don't go to clubs or parties where we know boors are likely to be declaiming; similar online conduct can make an electronic conference much less valuable for us. One bad apple on a discussion list can spoil many people's enjoyment. And as more people get online and begin to use online

---

[11] Eugene Volokh, "Freedom of Speech in Cyberspace From the Listener's Perspective: Private Speech Restrictions, Libel, State Action, Harassment and Sex," 1996 *U.Ch.Legal F.* 377 (1996).

resources, the risk of information overload and of the occasional rude participant escalates. Most electronic conferences try to keep both the signal-to-noise ratio and civility high by moral suasion. Each conference has an official topic; people generally know not to stray too far from it, and if they do, others might ask them to "take it off-list"—continue the discussion in personal e-mail rather than on the electronic conference. When people start getting rude, others might chime in to quiet everyone down. Most conferences have conference operators who are in charge of the technical details of conference administration; they often also take responsibility for informally keeping everyone in line.

But because these limitations are a matter of private decision, not of government rule, they are generally easier to avoid. If enough listeners want to hear a particular view and one conference doesn't carry it, others probably will. And if no conference is interested in carrying the view, then chances are that this is because too few listeners want to hear it. In that case, the only way that those who are interested can be satisfied is by imposing on the greater number who aren't interested.

We see this happening already. Among the big services, Prodigy advertises its editing, while CompuServe generally imposes no content controls. Counsel Connect provides lawyer-only discussions, while many conferences on the big services and on the Internet are open to everyone....

Of course, editing won't always be beneficial to listeners. To take one exam-

ple, Prodigy's notorious removal of messages critical of Prodigy's pricing policies was in no one's interests but Prodigy's own. One could defend this...as part of Prodigy's editorial control rights, but it's hard to justify it on listener autonomy grounds....

On the other hand, Prodigy's removal of anti-Semitic messages from some bulletin boards and its automatic editing of offensive words may be of significant value to many listeners. Just as I'm entitled to avoid magazines that print anti-Semitic propaganda, I have a legitimate interest in having magazine editors, acting as my agents, exclude the anti-Semitic material for me. Having Prodigy impose this editing policy gives me as listener a choice: be exposed to a restricted set of views on Prodigy, or to an unedited set on CompuServe or on the Internet. Barring Prodigy from editing would deprive me of that choice. On government property, we may have no choice but to suffer offensive speech, but there's no reason this has to apply to privately owned fora.

Naturally, by increasing listener choice, editing also increases listeners' ability to choose unwisely. Listeners who choose conferences that tolerate only their own viewpoint, or those that shut down passionate debate, or even those that exclude racist speech, might be sealing themselves off from important arguments, arguments they might find persuasive (or at least worth knowing) if they saw them. Some might see this danger as a justification for laws that would open up the conferences and make sure that listeners don't shut themselves off from balanced debate.

But though listeners may make the wrong decision, I believe it's better to leave these decisions to the listeners rather than to the government. It seems morally troubling for the government to force unwanted speech onto listeners; and I'm skeptical that even a well-motivated government can be good at determining what listeners really ought to hear and what they can legitimately seek to avoid.

Equally importantly, I doubt that any attempts to save listeners from their narrow-mindedness will really work....

[S]peech on electronic conferences should be protected even if it's offensive, insulting, profane, or bigoted, because restricting such speech would "permit majoritarian tastes...to preclude a protected message from [reaching] a receptive, unoffended minority." In this, electronic conferences are like billboards, demonstrations, and newspapers. The [Supreme] Court has made clear that restricting offensive speech in these media would impermissibly impoverish public discourse, and there's no reason the rule should be different online. The interests of the speaker and of the willing listeners must, I believe, prevail over those of the offended listener.

I can't deny that "hostile or abusive" speech can greatly diminish the value of an online conference—public or university—for those who are offended; but such speech, even racially, religiously, or sexually bigoted speech, is protected by the Free Speech Clause from government abridgment. It's protected on sidewalks, in private homes, in the pages of newspapers. Despite the recent spate of campus speech codes, courts have held that it's protected in universities. There's no reason it shouldn't be equally protected in Prodigy, Counsel Connect, and the like.

QUESTIONS

1. What might be the downside of leaving civility and netiquette up to private conference operators?

2. Did Prodigy's actions hurt consumers? Benefit them?

3. Volokh argues against government standard-setting in this realm as unconstitutional content control. What might be the value of government power to restrict online messages? Are there circumstances when government should get involved?

4. Since this article was first written, there has been an explosion of online, unedited blogs among students and others. Indeed, Volokh blogs at **http://volokh.com.** Take a look at it. To what extent is it of any interest? Would any of the things about it that enhance—or diminish—its value to you be better served if it were differently edited?

CYBERSPEAKING ABOUT RACE AND GENDER

Margaret Chon analyzes the Internet from what she calls a critical race feminist perspective. She assumes that racism is an ordinary and fundamental part of American society and that it makes a big difference in the distribution of material benefits. Justice will only be achieved, Chon believes, when we understand group oppression—of racial minorities, women, gays, and lesbians—including the racial meanings implicated in institutional power arrangements and social practices that are not necessarily explicitly marked as racial. One place where racism and sexism can be implicitly enacted, she explains, is cyberspace.

Erasing Race? A Critical Race Feminist View of Internet Identity-shifting[12]

Margaret Chon

When material identity markers such as physical appearance are erased from social dialogue, what takes their place are dominant cultural assumptions about what is normal. For U.S. Internet users, numerically dominated by White Americans who live and work in highly segregated environments, normal means White. At the cusp of the millennium, the default setting for virtual race is White. For those whose material race is non-White, racial formation on the Internet then can be viewed alternatively as a form of "passing," a type of assimilation, or an unstated racial assumption imposed by others upon the user. Regardless of one's material racial identity, participation on the Internet tends to encourage both voluntary and involuntary movement into a White virtual race.

[S]omeone can choose a White rather than Latino identity and continue to perform through language-based choices as White on the Internet. But the vaunted fluidity of identity on the Internet does not work equally in both directions. On the Internet, it is harder for this Latino to perform as Latino based on his identification with Latin American history, culture and norms, because non-textual markers such as dress, body movement, inflection and facial expression are absent in text-based interactions, which comprise the majority of Internet interactions. Even if we suppose that he is a light-skinned Latino with an Anglo surname, he may be able to perform his Latino identity in real space with many more tools than are available in virtual space....

Race is not only performed but is also imposed upon social actors...[in part by a] powerful ideological framework of race based on the concept of colorblindness, that is: race is a characteristic that should not be socially, politically, economically or legally significant....Virtual race is also coded as White because Internet users

[12] 3 J.Gender, Race & Justice 439 (2000).

respond to the technological...constraints that currently allow identities to be presented in textual form far more easily than in graphic representational form....

[W]hile people on the Internet may be exposed (perhaps for the first time in their lives) to women posing as men, they still treat virtual men as material men are treated in the real world....

The social activity of passing from one material identity to another almost invariably brings into question, sometimes violently, the prevailing social order and ways in which material identities are in fact critical sites of social control....

[T]he Internet has generated intense interest in the question of gender bending....

[Some] acknowledge that virtual identities have more "wiggle room" than material identities. Nonetheless, virtual identities are still captured by the same patterns that are used to organize social relations in material space. Even Sherry Turkle, who advocates a fluid line between real and virtual identities, concedes that:

> ...more men are willing to give virtual cross-dressing a try. But once they are online as female, they soon find that maintaining this fiction is difficult. To pass as a woman for any length of time requires understanding how gender inflects speech, manner, and the interpretation of experience. Women attempting to pass as men face the same kind of challenge. These cultural patterns, learned in material spaces, may overdetermine virtual responses

to gendered virtual identities and ultimately reinscribe gender hierarchy. In this context, when transgendering does occur it is collectively interpreted in terms of allowable fiction, deceit, [or] pathology. Virtual identity-shifting based on gender is not frictionless.

[T]he genealogy of the term passing in American history associates it with the discourse of racial difference and especially with the assumption of a fraudulent "white" identity by an individual culturally and legally defined as "Negro" or black by virtue of a percentage of African ancestry. As the term metaphorically implies, such an individual crossed or passed through a racial line or boundary—indeed trespassed—to assume a new identity, escaping the subordination and oppression accompanying one identity and accessing the privileges and status of the other. Trespass suggests a movement into identities that are off-limits because of their superior social status. Indeed, the examples of *Mulan* and *Shakespeare in Love* illustrate the incentives for passing from female to male identity. Passing connotes secrecy, fraud and the specter of violence upon discovery....

[A]rguably, passing on the Internet is not only more commonplace but also encompasses a wider variety of behavioral motivations than does passing in material space. Passing may be as temporary as a single chat room conversation....Women may pass as men with no particular benefit in mind, but simply to experience what it might be like to "be" male. Members of racial minority groups may pass involuntarily as White, without really intending to; passing may be

When people adopt an online persona they cross a boundary into highly charged territory.
—Sherry Turkle, "Who Am We?"

imposed upon them by the cultural assumptions of other users, in ways that would be impossible in material space abundant with physical signifiers. Whereas passing in the material world typically includes active deceit and/or desire to access privileges, passing on the Internet conceivably may not include either.

[Next, Chon contrasts passing and assimilation:]

In contrast to passing, assimilation connotes mutual consent or at least mutual accommodation (by both the one choosing to assimilate and the group into which the person assimilates) rather than disguise or fraud. The racial assimilationist strategies of some ethnic groups such as Irish Americans have been one way in which others such as Asian Americans have been "raced"—by reference to the latter's inherent unassimilability—into a negative non-White social standing....And although female bodies are visibly marked as different from male bodies, some women can assimilate culturally into male-dominated professions such as law by discarding female cultural markers and adopting male ones. An example of this, as explained by Professor Lani Guinier, might be the socialization of women law students into the combative verbal style of some male lawyers, despite the fact that many of these women feel that this style is alien to them.

When a virtual identity collides with material identity in a way that cannot be resolved easily in physical space, or in ways that are unfamiliar to other virtual users, then Internet social relations tend to revert to ones that are grounded in

material practices. Thus passing, assimilation, or other forms of movement across Internet identities, whether gender or race, always carry within them the potential of reversion into social relations that pre-figure the virtual self. This is often combined with Andrew Shapiro's concept of "oversteer," in which users control the type of information that construct their virtual environments (and may choose information that challenges their belief systems the least). [Predictably] virtual gender relations will resemble strongly the dominant social relations organizing material identities—and in fact may reinforce rather than disrupt the latter. I term this the "reversion effect." The so-called "digital divide" between White and Black (as well as White and Latino) widened dramatically—by over thirty percent—in the one year period between 1997 to 1998....

[O]ne's material racial status in the physical world predicts whether one is able to participate consistently in the digital dialogue. Thus material racial identities are linked to virtual racial identities, in ways that support and indeed maintain the silence surrounding the topic of race.

On a less apparent but just as significant level, the ideology of colorblindness ensures that many social activities are interpreted through a lens that demands the superficial erasure of a racialized other (either by coding that other as White, by casting the other out of the community as "deviant," or by imposing a distorting sameness on racial differences), rather than the recognition of the complex social responses elicited by materially racialized bodies. Whiteness is the predominant racial norm on the Internet, as it is heavily dominated by users in North America and Western Europe, as well as those who have English-language ability and whose socio-economic status is at the top of the world's population. Digital cultural norms also encourage textual choices such as the fluidity of "noms de 'net," which in turn tend to downplay racial identifiers such as appearances, accents or surnames. Another compelling reason for the dominance of a White virtual race is that it represents a higher status compared to other racial categories (material, virtual or otherwise)....

Questions

1. How does Chon describe the ways in which race factors into the virtual world?

2. How is passing or assimilation different in cyberspace than in the material world?

3. In a section of this writing not included here, Chon describes "a male therapist by the name of Sanford Lewin who signed onto a CompuServe chatline in the early 1980s under the name of Julie Graham." When Julie Graham's real identity was revealed to the women's discussion group in which Julie's virtual identity had operated, "some of the women did not bounce back with forgiveness. At least one said that she felt a deep emotional violation which, in her opinion, was tantamount to sexual assault." How would you feel if someone tricked you about his or her gender or race online? Is it ethical to hide your gender in cyberspace? Your race? To demand that users reveal their gender or racial identity?

Hate Speech, Cyber-Harassment, and Stalking

[It is] the 'realness' of the new porn which makes it so very different from anything that's been around before. As with every other type of interaction in cyberspace the viewer/user becomes a participant; a 'doer' of pornography rather than an observer of it.

—Dale Spender, *Nattering on the Net: Women, Power and Cyberspace*

Speech "may indeed best serve its high purpose when it induces a condition of unrest, creates dissatisfaction with conditions as they are, or even stirs people to anger."

—*Terminiello v. City of Chicago*, U.S. Supreme Court (1949)

Although hate speech is broadly condemned, its legal treatment varies enormously from country to country. Some nations, perhaps because of their relatively recent direct history with Nazism, are restrictive. German law strictly bans Nazi propaganda, the Hitler salute, and other symbols associated with the Nazi regime and prohibits any writing or broadcast that incites racial hatred or "describe[s] cruel or otherwise inhuman acts of violence against humans in a manner which glorifies or minimizes such acts." Canada and France ban the sale of Nazi paraphernalia.

In the U.S., the constitutional guarantee of freedom of speech and of the press generally forbids silencing speech because of its content. This means that even hate speech must be tolerated, according to the Supreme Court. Recently, for example, a federal appeals court knocked down an anti-harassment policy in a Pennsylvania school district because it was said to violate the free-speech rights of Christian students to speak out against homosexuality.[13]

In spring 2000, eBay decided to prohibit the sale of Nazi or Klan items that are less than 50 years old (considering older items of "historical value"). Yahoo, on the other hand, chose a lenient attitude; it would remove material that was inappropriate or violated its policies only when a user or watchdog group complained loudly enough. However, if they received no complaints, Yahoo did nothing.

As 2000 drew to a close, a French court ordered Yahoo to pay fines of $13,000 per day unless the company installed technology to shield French users from seeing Nazi-related memorabilia on Yahoo's auction sites. In December 2000, Yahoo auction sites still listed more than 1,000 items related to the Ku Klux Klan or Nazism, including knives, robes, and daggers. U.S. courts refused to enforce the French order, but by January 2001, Yahoo had installed a monitoring program that reviews information sellers want to post on the Web site and sends messages to sellers whose submissions appear in violation of company standards.

China—viewed as having the stiffest Internet censorship in the world—has extracted from Yahoo and others a voluntary Public Pledge of Self Discipline, under which companies agree to limit access to sites that reach China to online content that would not violate Chinese censorship laws.

Monitoring hate speech on Web sites or online auctions is one thing. But to what extent should e-mail be similarly scrutinized? The next reading explores some of the issues surrounding offensive e-mail. As you read it, ask yourself what are the costs and benefits of intruding on e-mail privacy.

---

[13] *Saxe v. State College Area School District* 2001 WL 123852 (3d Cir. 2001).

Sexual Harassment in Cyberspace: Unwelcome E-mail[14]

David K. McGraw

Stephanie Brazil, a freelance writer, made some remarks denouncing sexism during a computer discussion group. In response, she received a string of e-mail messages containing profanity-laced rape threats. At the University of Oregon, several male students obtained pictures of nude women from the Internet and sent them to five female students on the local network. When the women complained, the men printed the pictures and hung them on the walls of the computer lab. A number of companies with e-mail networks that permit anonymous e-mail messages have reported occurrences of sexually suggestive and obscene e-mail sent to female employees. At the National Science Foundation, a story depicting a rape in supposedly humorous terms was sent to every user on the computer system, drawing complaints from many female employees who argued that it was not only hostile and offensive, but exacerbated the gender-related tension in the predominantly male organization. Sexual harassment is not new, but the expansion of computer networks has seen a new form of communication develop that current law is ill-equipped to confront.

The actual or perceived anonymity of e-mail puts psychological distance between two communicators. The sender of an e-mail message is aware that it is unlikely he or she will ever have a personal contact with the recipient.

Accordingly, there is a sense that there will be no "real world" consequences of e-mail messages. The result is that e-mail often takes on a tone that does not resemble personal communication.

One phenomenon of this anonymity is gender hiding. Some users may create a user name that is gender neutral, while others adopt a false gender, either to avoid harassing e-mail, to be an insider on communication between members of the assumed gender, or for other reasons.

A common occurrence on the Internet is "flaming."…Flaming is, in one sense, a way of controlling behavior on the Internet—when one user steps across the line of acceptable behavior, flames are a form of punishment. For many, however, flaming is also considered a sport, a means of showing off one's ability to come up with a witty and biting response. Flaming is not always in good taste, but is generally accepted by most users as a normal part of life in cyberspace.

Proponents of restrictions on on-line communications are usually met with a chorus of disapproval from the regular users. A typical response is that any attempt to bring the Internet under the control of the legal system will not only be futile, but it will also be destructive, causing harm out of all proportion to the minuscule benefits that might follow. A cross-section of the cyberspace population seems to have a dislike of rules that

---

[14] David K. McGraw, Note, "Sexual Harassment in Cyberspace: The Problem of Unwelcome E-Mail," 21 *Rutgers Computer & Techn. L. J.* 491 (1995).

might restrict the free flow of information. One system administrator, Cliff Figallo echoed a common argument when he stated, "[t]he medium is too young, too immature to be frozen in place with rules." In his book *Hackers: Heroes of the Computer Revolution,* Steven Levy describes the hacker ethic as including the principles that access to computers should be unlimited, that all information should be free, that authority is to be mistrusted, and that all systems should be open and without boundaries. Specifically, he states, "[b]ureaucracies, whether corporate, government, or university, are flawed systems, dangerous in that they cannot accommodate the exploratory impulse of true hackers. Bureaucrats hide behind arbitrary rules...to consolidate power."

Many of the arguments claiming that [online sexual harassment poses] no problem are based on the assumption that it is acceptable that women not participate in using computer technology...that the sender of the harassing e-mail should be allowed to continue receiving access to the technological benefits of the Internet, whereas the aggrieved party should be required to give up that access. This reflects an attitude that "control" of the network should remain with the more aggressive parties to the detriment of those who can be subjugated by them....

QUESTIONS

1. To what does McGraw attribute the problem of e-harassment? Earlier, we read Volokh's argument that the workplace is fundamentally different from online conferences. Should there be different standards of tolerance for racially or sexually hostile speech in different spaces?

2. If Volokh is right, most people want a pleasant speech environment where they are not insulted—and don't have to hear other offensive speech. Should conference operators like CompuServe intervene when a member repeatedly posts slurs, sexually explicit statements, or racist jokes? Does your answer change depending on whether their reason is **(a)** they have a no-censorship-ever pol-

icy; **(b)** they disagree with the messages but believe they might provoke discussion; or **(c)** they agree with the messages? Would you apply the same rules to a university or business that operates its own Internet service?

3. U.S. law allows us to notify the Postmaster General if we want to stop receiving sexually suggestive advertisements. If the sender doesn't stop, he/she can be charged with a crime. Should the law treat e-mail the same way? Other annoying messages? Any messages at all, once warned that the receiver doesn't want any? So long as no such law exists, is there any ethical problem with continuing to send e-mail to a person who has told you it is unwanted?

4. Four freshmen at Cornell University sent an e-mail to 20 friends which was then forwarded to thousands of mailboxes. The e-mail contained a sexist diatribe against women entitled, "75 Reasons Why Women (Bitches) Should Not Have Free Speech" and included quotations such as, "If they can't speak, they can't cry rape." Should anyone do anything about this? Who? What should they do?

5. Many states outlaw various kinds of phone contact—threats, repeated or anonymous calls intended to annoy, and the use of indecent or obscene language. Should such laws extend to similar messages sent via e-mail? To electronic conferences? Posted on chat rooms? Is there any value to allowing such messages to groups?

Rebecca Lee, author of the next article, argues that cyberstalking—via e-mail, newsgroups, bulletin boards, and chatrooms—is a serious problem. Socio-cultural ideas about romance and electronic contact make it difficult for people to recognize a stalking situation. Yet "[t]he extensive and impersonal nature of the Internet offers increased accessibility and decreased accountability, making stalking easier than ever." In the following excerpt, Lee theorizes, on the basis of a review of popular literature, music, and courting manuals, that stalking is not deviant activity, but rather "socially-sanctioned behavior, instituted and encouraged by Western courtship mores and ideas of romance…enacted and even rationalized under the guise of romantic persistence."

Romantic and Electronic Stalking in a College Context[15]

Rebecca K. Lee

Stalking, like street harassment, is part of the spectrum of ways in which men may try to restrict women's citizenship, while forcing them to acknowledge man's presence and perceived power. Further, the incidence of stalking, especially on college campuses, may make women more skeptical of a man's romantic interest, and inhibit healthy and mutual expressions of love and sexuality.

It may be difficult to imagine what an individual who is being stalked, and knows it, must endure: always looking over one's shoulders, changing one's daily schedule, keeping one's window blinds closed, fear of answering one's phone or door, and (especially in the context of the Internet) even having to adopt a false or new identity. Nonetheless, this is the reality of many people

---

[15] Rebecca K. Lee, "Romantic and Electronic Stalking in a College Context," 4 *William & Mary Journal of Women & Law* 373 (1998).

in this country. Stalking is a violation of, and a threat to, one's privacy, safety, and personal space. It can lead to violation of the body. We need to understand, however, that stalking is insidious precisely because it affects the individual before and beyond this possibility of physical violation.

[While t]he typical stalker is portrayed as a deranged, socially ostracized individual who obsesses about his or her target,...we have to realize that this "typical profile" of a stalker is not accurate.... [S]tudies have shown [that] all stalkers do not have major mental conditions. There have been numerous cases in which the stalker does not exhibit any of the expected personality traits, but to all appearances is normal and perhaps even respected....[D]emographically, stalkers emerge from every segment of society and from various socio-economic backgrounds.

In order to explain how and why stalking has become so commonplace, I assert a socio-cultural hypothesis which states that stalking may be produced not primarily by mental disturbance but by popular Western romantic ideology, and in fact is implicated by common romantic norms. Specifically, I argue that stalking may be rooted in our "no means yes" culture, in which women are made to play the role of the resisting yet yielding target, and men the role of the romantic pursuer, relentless despite the woman's protests....

The "no means yes" ideology central to courtly persistence is rooted in Western romantic tradition, as love and courtship texts unmistakably invoke this belief. The history of stalking is tied to the history of courtship, and it is exactly this intimate and accepted association that makes stalking so dangerously common. The aspiring courtly lover quietly observed his love from a distance. Like many of his contemporary lovers, he would conceal himself in the bushes, waiting to steal sight of his love. By lurking and secretly following the object of his attention, the medieval lover engaged in stalking activity. But since this behavior was carried out under the rubric of romance, the lover was socially encouraged to pursue his object as proof of his affection, not of his obsession.

A modern version of a courtship handbook called *More Love Tactics,* ironically parallels its ancient predecessor in terms of language and advice, and tells the reader to be persistent and to disregard the other person's words or actions because they are irrelevant....This handbook also teaches the reader that love does not have to be mutual, at least not in the beginning stages. The book assures the reader, however, that love will not stay one-sided for long, for the love will inevitably be returned.

Popular music is an important conveyor of contemporary culture, and romantic ballads, complete with obsessive elements, comprise a good number of popular songs. These songs contribute to the way stalking is culturally facilitated, hiding its threat and harm under the facade of romance. For instance, the classic song by the British band The Police titled "Every Breath You Take" is highly romanticized and regarded as a champion of love songs. If we listen to and understand the significance of its lyrics, however, we see that they eerily revolve around the refrain of constant surveillance, which is inherent in stalking activity:

Every breath you take

Every move you make

Every bond you break

Every step you take I'll be watching you

Every single day

Every word you say

Every game you play

Every night you stay I'll be watching you....

Every move you make

Every vow you break

Every smile you fake

Every claim you stake I'll be watching you.

These lyrics repeat themselves in a haunting tone, while the singer accuses the subject of being unfaithful ("every vow you break"), insincere ("every smile you fake"), and self-interested ("every claim you stake"). All of these messages betray the singer's malicious obsession with the subject of the song. Despite its jealous and malevolent undertone, the song is romanticized because the singer's constant thoughts of the subject, and his passionate appeals, are seen as romantic longing and fidelity, not as an evil obsession. Hence, the song becomes a "love song."

In this information age, romantic pursuit and its stalking counterpart have found their way into another avenue—the Internet. Both men and women, but seemingly more men, are entering cyberspace in search of electronic courtship, more popularly referred to as "virtual love," as evidenced by the large number of on-line discussion forums devoted to meeting a mate. But on-line romance can be accompanied by or lead to on-line stalking. Indeed, the Internet is proving itself to be a hostile place for women, where female abuse can be found everywhere, including e-mail messages, chat rooms, and Usenet newsgroups. The atmosphere surrounding newsgroups (open electronic conferences) is charged with such high levels of sexual harassment and disrespect for women that many women are joining private mailing lists for cyberspace community and interaction. Technology has brought the emergence of electronic stalking, which differs from conventional stalking only in that the former is more sophisticated in its execution.

The term stalking seems to have a strange yet popular association with computer innovation, as one software company adopted as its name "Stalker Software Inc.," complete with a logo of yellow, preying, animal-like eyes and advertising for its website. Moreover, the term "lurk," which in real-life is one form of stalking activity, has entered standard computer vernacular to refer to what a computer user does when he or she observes, but does not participate in, a virtual chat room. One could argue that claiming such a word like "lurk" and "lurker" as computer jargon not only helps de-stigmatize the creepy meaning of the term, but also helps introduce the unsavory behavior associated with this term into a whole other realm, namely cyberspace.

Cyberangels.org calls itself the world's "oldest and largest Internet safety organization." Can they stop cyberstalking?

Cyberspace is mostly a male-beaten path, but women who do frequent the net find themselves the targets of cyber-stalking more often than men....It is a misconception that electronic stalking is less serious than conventional stalking. David Banisar of Electronic Privacy Information Center (EPIC) contends that "e-mail stalking...is a ridiculous con-cept," that it "trivializes" real or physical stalking. However, Banisar is confusing the act with the medium. Not only can a cyberstalker send e-mail to his target, threatening and informing her that she is being stalked, but he can also literally track down his victim through her e-mail activities, observing when and where she logs on, and accessing other personal information including her address and school or work affiliation. Banisar also fails to realize that electronic stalking often leads to, or is accompanied by, physical stalking, and explicitly or implicitly threatens physical stalking. In one case, a woman discovered that she was being watched from her home when her electronic stalker described her neighborhood in one of his messages. After receiving this message, she noticed that someone had cut the bushes outside her bedroom window....

Victims of cyberstalking have found the police neither responsive nor sympa-thetic, as officials do not perceive on-line stalking to present a real danger, and instead dismiss the complaint as a "triv-ial situation."...Law enforcement's inac-tion reflects the lack of legislation explicitly addressing electronic stalking. The vast majority of state laws neglect to acknowledge that stalking is now often perpetrated electronically....

As many have pointed out, the Internet is essentially a "decontextual-ized" medium in that people can send messages without revealing their hand-writing or other clues to their personal-ity, such as the type of stationary they opt to use. Cyberstalkers can easily dis-guise themselves by adopting several false names and forging e-mail messages. Compounding the fear behind the cyber-stalker's faceless threats is the amount of information electronically available on any given individual. A stalker can remain anonymous indefinitely and exert even greater control by gaining access to information regarding his tar-get. From an Internet connection alone, an electronic stalker can discover a per-son's full name, address, and phone number. Commercial on-line services like America Online (AOL) ask its users to voluntarily complete a "Personal Profile" in which users can reveal their name, age, marital status, and location, all of which are then accessible to AOL's four million subscribers.

QUESTIONS

1. The Stalker's Home Page is a Web site that lists resources available on the Internet and elsewhere to help find personal information, from a local street map to a person's residence, to a Social Security number. The site even tells users how to spy on other people. Its creator, Glen L. Roberts, issues the following caveat:

> Of course we don't encourage anyone to engage in stalking or other impolite behavior...but look at the resources! The information is there! It's available to ANYONE, who wants to ACCESS it for whatever his or her PURPOSE may be! Good or evil! The information is here, it is quick to access, it is free and from anywhere in the world you can learn about people anywhere in the USA!

Visit the Stalker's Home Page at **http://www.glr.com/stalk.html.** Give an ethical justification for posting this site. Give one for removing it.

2. Women are targeted for electronic stalking in three main areas of cyberspace: Internet Relay Chat (IRC) or Live Chat, Usenet newsgroups or other bulletin boards, and e-mail communication. Female Internet users, especially "newbies"—those obviously unfamiliar to the net—are usually first singled out for electronic stalking in real-time chat conversations. Cyberstalkers generally then contact their targets through their private e-mail accounts, leaving alarming messages and sending attached files. The danger and, as stalkers have mentioned, thrill, lie in the relative ease and anonymity by which someone can stalk another person via the electronic apparatus. Go online to see what sites you can find that offer advice or support for those who have been harassed or stalked. Evaluate their usefulness. (Hint: check out a feminist group like the National Organization for Women at **http://www.now.org** or use one of the standard search engines to find "women's groups" or "support groups.")

3. Not all victims of cyberstalking are women. Find out what happened to cyberpunk Jim Bell. Bell, a libertarian essayist, was charged with crossing state lines with the intent to stalk Jeff Gordon, a federal agent investigating Bell's activities.

4. What possible action can each of the following take to prevent cyberstalking: Employers? Universities? Victims? Police? Legislators? Internet Service Providers? What, if anything, do they have an ethical responsibility to do?

5. Some 100,000 online subscribers reportedly have joined the game "Sims Online." Its Terms of Service Contract tells players they cannot "harass, threaten, embarrass, or do anything else to another Member or guest that is unwarranted." Maxis, the owner, tries to enforce the terms by warning or suspending players, terminating threads in message boards, even banning some accounts. Still, there are reports that the game's virtual violence has spilled over into the real world in the form of people hacking into others' accounts, using instant messaging to spread false rumors about real people, and engaging in identity theft.[16] Is there anything anyone should—or can—do to prevent this problem?

CYBERNORMS

Role Playing: Cyberharm Scenarios

Role-play each of the following scenarios as a basis for evaluating the ethical choices available to each of the players.

- A creative writing teacher at Major University creates several newsgroups on Usenet, encouraging students in each group to try out their ideas. A male undergraduate posts a fantasy story about the rape, torture, and murder of a named female classmate on one of the newsgroups. The woman named in the story is in the class but is not a participant in that newsgroup.

- A male graduate student is expelled for stalking a former girlfriend, largely via e-mail. The university justifies the expulsion on the grounds that it does not differentiate e-mail from other types of communication and that offensive and unwanted contact is punishable under the school's harassment policy. Some members of the campus community question the appropriateness of the punishment, including the accused student's advisor. "[I]t's not clear to me that it's sexual harassment. It's e-mail."

- Archer, a 31-year-old graphic artist, meets Betty, a 29-year-old schoolteacher, through a video-dating service on America Online. After several months, Betty loses interest in their relationship, but Archer is smitten. Over the course of the next two months, he sends some 20 e-mail messages and several phone messages to Betty, trying to express his romantic interest through his persistence. One e-mail reads, "I stalked you for the first time today—you know I can't get you out of my mind," a statement he claims he made in jest. Betty goes to the police, who tell her there is nothing they can do or suggest for her to do. Alternatively, suppose the police warn Archer to end all communication with Betty. Archer continues to send some two dozen e-mail messages over the next two months. Finally, Betty e-mails back: "If you don't leave me alone, you are going to be sorry. You have been warned."

---

[16] Nick Wadhams, "Game Sparks Anti-Social Behavior Online." Associated Press, July 6, 2003.

- During the month of December 1997, Randi receives approximately 11 e-mails at work from an unknown source. The subject lines of these e-mails have vaguely suggestive topics and one has more explicit sexual content. Randi does not know who sent the e-mails, but when the supervisor was told, he responded, "Forget it."

As we have seen, there is currently little consensus as to the parameters of appropriate speech on the Internet. And the debates are not only about what kinds of speech—if any—should be curtailed. They are also about who should set limits, and how. The final reading in this chapter offers one possible solution.

April Mara Major, Assistant Dean for Academic Computing, Villanova University School of Law, looks to the creation of global cybernorms ("Netiquette") to govern communication over the Internet.

Netiquette[17]

April Mara Major

In the absence of legal rules or physical force, what causes someone to behave in a manner contrary to one's private desires? Why, for instance, does one tip a bellhop for carrying luggage to a hotel room? Legal rules do not mandate the tipping of bellhops, and bellhops typically do not threaten physical force. So why does one feel obligated to tip the bellhop and embarrassed when one does not? Tipping the bellhop is a social norm.

[C]ybernorms are practices that have developed through mutual user assent and in deference to the preferences of other users, rather than mere tendencies of user behavior. Checking one's e-mail when logging onto the Internet is a user tendency, not a cybernorm; responding to an e-mail message promptly is an obligation and thus invokes cybernorm concepts.

Most netiquette rules are cybernorms because Internet users adhere to these rules, even though they are not formally or legally enforced and may be contrary to users' private preferences....Including the word "long" in the subject header of an e-mail message to notify the recipient that the message consists of over one hundred lines and will take time to read and respond to is another example of a netiquette rule indicative of cybernorm behavior.

...Norms established by early users of e-mail, who commonly endorsed a

---

[17] Excerpted from an article by April Mara Major, "Norm Origin and Development in Cyberspace: Models of Cybernorm Evolution," 78 *Wash. U.L.Q.* 59 (2000).

relaxed attitude, greatly influenced the cybernorm of e-mail informality.

Norms also include rules deliberately formulated by private institutions such as churches, corporations, unions, and trade associations. While there are no formal mechanisms to enforce such rules, the obligation to follow them is just as strong, if not stronger, without them. The Internet Engineering Task Force (IETF) and the World Wide Web Consortium (W3C) are two Internet institutions that function as cyberspace counterparts to traditional private institutions…[whose] standards and protocols…[are] cybernorms.

…The Internet's core technology was developed in the 1960s. The United States was in the midst of the Cold War and the Department of Defense recognized a dire need for a communications network that could survive a nuclear attack. The RAND Corporation, a U.S. military think-tank, proposed the idea of a decentralized network…[consisting] of a series of interconnected communication nodes, each with the ability to originate, pass, and receive messages. The path that each message took was irrelevant, and if one of the nodes was destroyed, the message could take numerous other routes to reach its destination….

[In] the early 1980s…the National Science Foundation (NSF) funded the establishment of regional research and academic networks throughout the United States based on the same technology…[and] linked these regional networks into a single high-speed network….

Cyberspace began as a subculture of real world society, populated by techni-cally inclined academics, who were the primary users of the NSF-funded backbone in the late 1980's. [They] were generally an elite group of scientists, such as engineers, physicists, computer scientists, and mathematicians, who undoubtedly occupied a unique niche of society. They formed a culture that awarded respect based upon intellectual abilities rather than physical appearance. It was (and still is in many ways) a male-dominated culture dedicated to research, which had little time to fret over the details of social skills and encouraged casual attire. This culture permeated the roots of cyber-society and proceeded to mold a new set of norms.

Over the years, Internet use seeped into mainstream culture…eventually maturing into what is now a diverse, digital society….As more people started using the Internet, new norms emerged within the pre-existing set of cybernorms….

Certain social norms are entirely abandoned in cyberspace….Consider the social norm that imposes an obligation of personal constraint over revealing one's honest thoughts about a person or a situation in order not to offend the other person or embarrass oneself. For instance, while at a public lecture, perhaps one finds the speaker simple-minded and arrogant. Social norms dictate that one keep her opinion to herself, at least until the lecture is over. Even confrontation has socially imposed boundaries, depending on the environment….The element of non-confrontational discussion (meaning that the participants are not face-to-face) coupled with the asynchronistic communication style of these services, allows users a layer of anonymity not found in the non-digital world and leads to more honest and less civil interactions.

While cyberspace gave users a unique freedom from certain social norms, a number of completely original norms developed in cyberspace [such as the use of a] descriptive subject line [on e-mail messages]....

Digital data can travel an unprecedented distance, thus giving more people access to the relevant information and leading to a greater societal set of cybernorms. In other words, more people from remote corners of the world can subscribe to certain cybernorms simply because they know of them. In any event, the Internet offers potentially larger and more diverse groups. With the ability to exchange information so efficiently and quickly, perhaps the Internet has enabled the creation of global norms that have not been possible before.

QUESTIONS

1. Describe the culture of the 1980s Internet. How has it changed since then?

2. What is the difference between a norm and a law? How are norms created and reinforced? Is it always unethical to violate a norm?

3. What differences does the writer delineate between cybernorms and the norms of conventional life?

4. Locate information on "netiquette." Major describes it as if it exists more as a matter of tacit agreement than formality. Is she right? Can you find any attempts to formalize such norms?

To learn about cyber-norm development in a MUD read Julian Dibbell's "A Rape in Cyberspace" http://www.juliandibbell.com/texts/bungle

CHAPTER PROBLEMS

1. How ethical is each of the following:

   (a) Pseudonymous book reviews that pan books are posted on Amazon.com.

   (b) Negative comments appear on a Web site that invites citizens to anonymously post news and comments regarding events in their town.

   (c) A student-run Web site includes negative evaluations of teachers, some with bold, caustic comments on their physical appearance.

2. When Emulex stock soared in August 2000, one person was upset. MJS lost almost $100,000 on a bet that the stock would decline. Unhappy, he created a fake press release warning that the company's CEO had resigned and that earnings were over- stated. He e-mailed this to an Internet wire service. When the damaging release was sent on to news organizations and Web sites around the world, the company's stock prices dropped precipitously. Evaluate the conduct of MJS and the Internet Wire Service. Should either have to compensate shareholders?

3. In 2001, William Sheehan, a computer engineer, started a Web site on police cor- ruption in Washington State. There he collected news stories and public—but sometimes hard to get—court papers. There he also posted lists of police officers' home addresses, telephone numbers and Social Security numbers, and information gleaned from public records—voter registration, property, motor vehicles. Police throughout the state were furious, arguing that they already are forced to act in ways that make people angry and put their lives at risk. How ethical is Sheehan's site? Should court records that are available to the public at the courthouse be freely available on the Internet? Other kinds of public records? Find out what happened to the law passed by the Washington legislature to prohibit the dissemination of home addresses, telephone numbers, birth dates, and social security numbers of law enforcement personnel if done with the intent to harm or intimidate. What other reason might Sheehan have for his postings?

4. Students do not shed their constitutional rights to freedom of speech or expression at the schoolhouse gate, although teachers and other officials are clearly allowed to proscribe appropriate conduct. Indeed, since the Supreme Court issued its ruling in the 1988 *Hazelwood* case, school administrators have been free to censor student newspapers and yearbooks for educational reasons. Cyberspace, however, has opened a window of possibilities for the expressive rights of young people. More than 10,000 underground high school newspapers and Web pages are floating in cyberspace, according to a 2000 estimate of the Student Press Law Center in Arlington. Ranging in type and tone—occasionally gossipy or personal, often irrev- erent and satiric—sometimes these e-zines amount to serious journalism, where students expose problems at school or in the world. Many see them as an antidote to the censored and public relations fluff-pieces that pass for "newspapers" at many schools. Online weblogs ("blogs") are becoming even more popular. Is it ethical for educators to try to restrict off-campus Web activities of students? For them to ignore such activities?

5. Online voting systems have been controversial since they were first proposed. Diebold Election Systems became the center of the dispute in 2003, when concerns about possible flaws in its electronic voting machines began circulating over the Internet. Students began posting copies of the company documents discussing the problems, and Diebold went to court to stop them. What ethical arguments can you make in favor of such postings? Against them? Diebold sent one cease-and-desist letter to the Swarthmore Coalition for the Digital Commons. What can you find out about this campus group? What ethical theory best describes its approach?

6. The Child Pornography Prevention Act outlaws the transmission over the Internet of photographs depicting children engaged in sex. To circumvent the law, a child-porn-group has created computer-altered pictures that appear to show minors involved in sexual activity, for distribution to adults. In reality, no such activity occurs. Should virtual computer porn be outlawed? Is it unethical? Find out what the Supreme Court has said about the constitutionality of this law.

7. In a drug deal gone bad, a high school student killed three of his classmates. The student admitted that he had become involved in the drug trade and acquired his gun through an ex-con he met over the Internet. The two had communicated via the computer in the town library. Outraged parents flooded the most recent meeting of the library's board of directors, demanding that they take action to prevent young people from accessing chatrooms, conferences, or violent Web sites through the library's equipment. What, if anything, can the library do? What should it do? Why?

8. Since 2001, **http://www.whitehouse.org** has poked fun at members of the Bush administration. But in March 2003, Vice President Cheney caused an uproar when he requested that the site remove a satirical biography and pictures of his wife. Check out the website—and the official White House website at **http://www.whitehouse.gov**. Is there anything unethical about **http://whitehouse.org**? About the Vice President's letter? Since September 11, should there be more strict limits on speech that mocks our government?

9. How ethical is it for the U.S. government to make electronic foreign policy moves? Compare and contrast the following examples:

(a) To thwart Chinese government attempts to censor Internet access in China, in August 2001, U.S. agencies reportedly financed an American-based computer network that would make Chinese blocking less effective.

(b) In early 2003, before U.S. began to bomb Iraq, the military waged an e-mail assault at Iraq's leaders, urging them to break with Saddam Hussein's government.

10. We all know that the Internet is swamped with potentially dangerous and offensive Web sites. Think carefully about this assignment before you choose which option to do.

(a) Go online and locate a Web site that might be considered dangerous or offensive. Evaluate the site: Who runs it? Does the information on the site appear to be accurate? Is it serious—or a parody? Do you think the U.S. government would consider it to be dangerous? Why? Do you think it is actually dangerous? Is it unethical to sponsor the site?

(b) If this assignment worries you, think about why it worries you. Instead of locating an apparently "dangerous" or offensive site, write a brief (one page) essay explaining why you don't want to do the assignment. Relate your concerns to readings in this and/or other chapters in *CyberEthics*.

CHAPTER 4

E-Commerce

If companies want to continue putting their heads in the sand, they risk getting their heads cut off. The Internet is now the difference between getting in the game and sitting on the sidelines.

 —William Murphy, Director, Internet Marketing, Hewlett Packard

The problem with reducing online interaction to an exchange of bits, and the inter-active age to an information age, is that it allows cyberspace to be quantified, and ultimately commodified….The Internet was not something a person engaged with; it was a set of information that could be accessed. And anything that could be accessed could be given a price tag.

 —Douglas Rushkoff, media analyst

ETHICS CASE: ONLINEPILLS.COM

Ben Tweed woke up before his wife one morning, feeling more awake than he usually did at 5:00 AM, and turned on the family computer, almost without thinking why. But there was a reason, and he could tell himself, by the time the icon for Netscape had appeared on the monitor, that this might be his chance to get something done about that problem he'd been worrying about lately. There was the ad he'd seen on television recently—the one with the man about his age or younger—good-looking—shaving, smiling into the mirror as he tightened his tie, hustling out the front door and then appearing in a waiting room. "It's time," the ad had said, "time to ask your doctor about Viagra." But Ben knew he was never going to ask any doctors about Viagra. No way.

Once he was connected, he wrote in the URL of his favorite search engine, and in the box, he typed: viagra. Within seconds, a lengthy list appeared. The first address—**http://www.viagra.com**—carried the title "viagra/welcome." Ben was about to click on it when he noticed the title of the second: "cheap viagra online." A moment later and Ben was staring at the portal of **http://www.onlinepills.com**. There were a few icons at the top. He noticed the one for Claritin, the allergy med his wife took, and there was one for Viagra, with a picture of the blue pill beside it. Ben clicked.

The next page had a springtime photo of a man hugging a woman, and under that, just one paragraph: Ben read that he was not alone, that "approximately 52% of men 40–70 experience some degree of erectile dysfunction (ED)." This was comforting, but it was even better to read that it was not just the oldsters who had this: the screen told him 10% of men from 20 to 30 were in his same boat. The good news was that "almost all" cases were "treatable." Luckily, Ben didn't have to bother with anything "embarrassing" like the "vacuum devices, suppositories, or penile implants or other procedures" mentioned, and Ben felt a wave of genuine relief at this point. In fact, it was looking like Ben didn't even have to go through the embarrassment of showing up in person in a doctor's office like the guy in the TV ad. No—it looked like all he needed to do was click on for an "online consultation." Ben clicked.

The next page began by telling Ben that "an estimated 25,000 prescriptions for Viagra are filled each day." It also told him that he had to complete a four-step process: agree to the waiver, complete the questionnaire, select the strength and quality of the Viagra pills, and submit his questionnaire. In bold print the Web page promised Ben could have his Viagra shipped "discreetly" to his home "or office" within two days of approval. The price list followed. It looked like the cheapest deal was 10 50-mg. pills for $119.00. Not counting shipping and handling maybe, thought Ben. The prices per pill got lower the more you ordered. In red it said: "Best value when 100 mg. pills are split into (2) 50 mg. doses." Under that it explained that there was a $75 "consultation fee," but "there will be **no charge** if the physician determines that Viagra is not appropriate to your condition." Ben scrolled down the waiver of liability, warning him, among other things, that the Viagra might not "provide the results I seek," and that, if Ben didn't give them all the right information in the "consultation," they couldn't be held responsible. The waiver also said it was Ben's responsibility to have an annual physical exam and that the consultation "is not a substitute for my need to visit a local physician." Yeah yeah yeah, thought Ben, who had not been in a doctor's office since that time 5 years ago when he'd dislocated his shoulder playing touch football with the kids. Then he scrolled quickly through the side effects. "Facial flushing" he caught a glimpse of, and "visual changes to color sensitivity." "Mild headaches." Ben scrolled to the end. He saw that a "qualified licensed physician" was going to review whatever information he gave them. He clicked I AGREE, and the medical questionnaire appeared.

The origin of the Internet can be traced back to the 1960s. Although supported by resources from the Department of Defense, the university scientists who developed

Should there be any limits on what we can buy online?

computer networking were less concerned with its military application than with the idea of making it possible for scientists to communicate with one another easily to share knowledge and research results. From the beginning, the Internet was advanced by a network of hackers, talented university students who worked in collaborative fashion. There was no centralized control, and no significant corporate input. As one historian has put it, 'The Internet was designed informally, and with little fanfare, by a self-selected group of experts."[1]

Initially, the system was not open to commercial use. Then, in 1991, after a series of technological changes, the National Science Foundation lifted its ban on commercial traffic on the Internet. As the user-friendly graphical interface of the World Wide Web spread across the Internet, it became host to multiple uses, and a corporate and consumer presence took hold in the mid 1990s. By June 2001, just ten years after it was possible to do any e-business at all, market researcher Gartner Inc. forecasted that online commercial transactions would amount to about $6 billion over the next three years.

In this chapter we look at the flashpoints where e-commerce raises ethical concerns. We begin with the marketing of pharmaceutical drugs. When "Direct-to-Consumer" selling takes place online, consumers are potentially better informed, but they may also be more likely to take serious health risks. Next we look at what may be the prerequisite for healthy e-commerce—or for a vital Internet world generally—the development of online trust. We then consider spam, an expensive blight in cyberspace, and at "Dot-Cons," the varieties of fraud that have infiltrated e-commerce. We move from this to consider online sales of tobacco products. Next we explore the proposed uniform rules of contracting that would encompass click-wrap licenses. When contractual agreements are broken, litigation may not be the most efficient solution. This chapter ends with a reading on "e-mediation," alternative dispute resolution in cyberspace.

DIRECT-TO-CONSUMER SALES ONLINE

In the decade since the Internet was opened to e-commerce, advertising on the Internet has evolved rapidly. Many Web sites are themselves, of course, advertisements—shopping destinations. Marketers began placing "banner" ads—online billboards—on frequently visited sites: Yahoo's and AOL's user interfaces have long been decorated with banner ads for other sites. As collecting and collating data about customers and their

---

[1] Abbate, Janet, *Inventing the Internet* (Cambridge, Mass: MIT Press, 1999), p. 127.

preferences has become much more efficient—as we saw in chapter 2—e-businesses have been able to target sales efforts, contacting customers by e-mail.

Placing ads where consumers are likely to be, gathering information for customized mailings—all of this doesn't really represent a major departure from advertising practice in the bricks-and-mortar world, however. And as marketers discovered that consumers could click past online ads the way they could click away TV ads with remotes, they worked to develop selling techniques that would take better advantage of computer technology.

Online Pharmaceuticals

Twenty years ago, unless they had an expensive 2,000-page volume called the *Physicians' Desk Reference*, patients knew very little about what drugs were available, and even with a PDR, they had little sense of how to deal with their own health care choices. Today, according to one study, the Internet is consulted regularly by 52 million consumers for medical and health information.[2] There are more than 10,000 Internet sites devoted to health issues. Much of what people source online is beneficial: In health-oriented chat rooms or newsgroups, people from all over the world can share tips, research diseases, and help each other learn of new treatments or medications—to the point where they educate their own physicians. It is this new environment to which e-business had to adapt.

What is the American Medical Association's view? See: http://www.ama-assn.org

At its best, online direct-to-consumer (DTC) marketing both educates and interacts with consumers, helping them to take charge of their own health, while capitalizing on the distinctive features of cyberspace. Direct-to-consumer marketing, first used most profitably by the pharmaceutical industry in the more traditional venues of television and print media, has striking power on the Web. At **http://www.claritin.com**, for example, people can gain extensive knowledge about allergies, symptoms, and treatments. The site mentions other medications besides Claritin; it allows visitors to create their own allergy profile, to receive pollen counts and weather forecasts.

The Food and Drug Administration (FDA) is the federal agency responsible for regulating drug safety—for reviewing new drugs to determine which must be prescribed by a doctor and dispensed by a registered pharmacist. In the past few years, as online pharmaceutical promotions began to proliferate, the FDA has been investigating the e-drug business. It has scanned thousands of Web sites, evaluated some 400, and prosecuted many of those. In the following excerpt, Dr. Jane Henney, Commissioner of the FDA during the Clinton Administration, addresses a Senate committee on the pros and cons of e-drug marketing.

---

[2] 2000 Pew Internet & American Life study.

Statement of FDA Commissioner Jane Henney, MD

U.S. Senate Committee of Health, Education, Labor and Pensions
March 21, 2000

...The Internet is rapidly transforming the way we live, work, and shop in all sectors of the economy. In the health sector, tele-medicine allows people in remote areas to access the expertise of doctors in the nation's finest academic health centers. The Internet permits an increasing number of individuals to obtain a plethora of medical information that often helps them to understand health issues and treatment options. In fact, more than 22 million Americans used the Internet last year to find medical information, either in documentary resources or through online discussions with health professionals. According to Investor's Business Daily, 43 percent of web surfers access health care data online each year. Conducting research regarding their health concerns is the sixth most common reason that people use the Internet, and according to the market research firm, Cyber Dialogue Inc., this number is growing by 70 percent a year.

The increasing recognition of the Internet as a legitimate and important vehicle for drug sales is evidenced by the recent activity of major drugstore companies and Internet retailers in financing, supporting and sponsoring online pharmaceutical outlets. Last year, for example, CVS Corporation acquired the online pharmaceutical retailer Soma.com and merged the online retail sites of the two companies. We expect this expansion of the online drug sales industry to continue.

Prescription drug sales on the Internet can provide tremendous benefits to consumers. These benefits are many and include: access to drugs for the disabled or otherwise home-bound, for whom a trip to the pharmacy can be difficult; the convenience of shopping 24 hours a day; an almost unlimited number of products for customers; and privacy for those who don't want to discuss their medical condition in a public place. Hyperlinks and search programs provide online customers with written product information and references to other sources of information much more easily than in the traditional storefront. Finally, as the use of computer technology to transmit prescriptions from doctors to pharmacies expands, a reduction in prescription errors may be possible.

...[I]t must be noted that the traditional "brick and mortar" pharmacy offers benefits or services that are often not available through the Internet, such as immediate access to prescription drugs needed for immediate treatment. These pharmacies will undoubtedly remain an essential component in the delivery of effective health care.

The challenge for government at both the state and federal level is to pursue policies that will allow legitimate electronic commerce to flourish but provide that safety is assured. Consumers will have confidence in the quality of the medical prescription and in the medicine delivered because the protection for online consumers is equivalent to the safeguards of the traditional local pharmacy and the practice of medicine and pharmacy.

CONCERNS ABOUT ONLINE SALES

...[T]he Internet also creates a new marketplace for activity that is already illegal, such as the sale of unapproved new drugs, prescription drugs dispensed without a valid prescription, and products marketed with fraudulent health claims. As FDA considers the issues related to online drug sales, we recognize that there are various types of these websites. Many sites focus on selling prescription drugs and have been referred to by some as "Internet pharmacies." These sites offer for sale either FDA-approved prescription drug products, or in some cases, unapproved, illegal versions of prescription drugs. While the sales sites of legitimate, properly licensed pharmacies provide benefits to consumers, those that are unlicensed or otherwise engaged in the illegal dispensing of prescription drugs pose a serious threat to the health and safety of American citizens. Other drug sales sites do not sell prescription drugs, but may offer for sale unapproved drug products, products making fraudulent health claims, or drugs for recreational use. Examples of these sites are those that sell products containing gamma hydroxy butyrate (GHB), an unapproved drug used recreationally, for body building and for incapacitating the victims of sexual assaults, or sites that offer unproven cancer therapies....While the increase in "Internet pharmacy" sites engaged in illegal sales is seen by some as a particularly potent threat, FDA considers the non-pharmacy sites to be just as harmful, or in some cases more so, and we have moved aggressively against them....

USE OF THE INTERNET TO BYPASS THE REGULATORY SYSTEM

Patients who buy prescription drugs from an illegitimate site are at risk of suffering adverse events, some of which can be life-threatening. These risks include potential side effects from inappropriately prescribed medications, dangerous drug interactions or contaminated drugs, as well as the possible ill effects of impure or unknown ingredients found in drugs manufactured under substandard conditions. Further risk to patients is posed by their inability to know what they are really getting when they buy some of these drugs. Although some patients may be purchasing genuine product, some may unknowingly be buying counterfeit copies that contain inert ingredients, outdated legitimate drugs that have been diverted to illegitimate resellers, or dangerous sub-potent or super-potent versions that were improperly manufactured. Moreover, consumers who are desperate for a cure to a serious medical problem may be more susceptible to purchasing an unapproved product.

FDA is concerned about the proliferation of sites that substitute a simple online questionnaire for a face-to-face examination and patient supervision by a health care practitioner. According to the American Medical Association, a health care practitioner who offers a prescription for a patient they have never seen before, based solely on an online questionnaire, generally does not meet the appropriate medical standard of care.

Additionally, the use of such questionnaires may jeopardize the availability of legal protections for privacy of medical records.

The Agency is equally concerned that in some Internet transactions, there is an apparent absence of any health professional/patient relationship. This is a particular concern where the prescription involves a first-time use by a patient or where the patient may be taking other medications. FDA believes that the selection of prescription drug products or treatment regimens for a particular patient should be made with the advice of a licensed health care practitioner familiar with the patient's current health status and past medical history. In situations where a customary physician-patient relationship does not exist, the patient is essentially practicing self-diagnosis. Consequently, the risk of negative outcomes such as harmful drug interactions, contraindications, allergic reactions or improper dosing is greatly magnified.

JURISDICTIONAL ISSUES

In addition to magnifying existing problems by reaching potentially millions of consumers worldwide, online drug sales create unique issues for regulatory and law enforcement bodies at the state, federal and international level. Internet technology can obscure the source of the product as well as provide some degree of anonymity to persons responsible for making and shipping the product. The participants in a transaction can be widely dispersed geographically (in different States or countries) and they may never meet. Thus, the regulatory issues cross-traditional regulatory boundaries as well as federal and state jurisdictional lines. If one or more participants in the transaction are located outside of the United States, the task of regulating the activity is further complicated.

The sale of drugs to U.S. residents via foreign web sites is an extremely challenging area. Some medications sold on the Internet may be legal in foreign countries but not approved for use in the United States, and some products may include addictive and dangerous substances. Products not approved for sale in the United States often do not conform to the good manufacturing practice and quality assurance procedures required by U.S. laws and regulations, and it is illegal for a foreign pharmacy to ship such drugs into the United States....

QUESTIONS

1. In summer 2000, a 52-year old man died of a heart attack after taking Viagra and having sex three times with his girlfriend. He had purchased the drug without a prescription from a Web site that is now defunct. The man had heart disease; if he had gone to a doctor for the Viagra, his condition might have been a reason not to prescribe it. The most popular drugs sold online are called "lifestyle drugs," like Propecia for hair loss, Xenical for weight loss, and Viagra for sexual dysfunction. Why do you think these are bestsellers? What are the ethics of e-drug sales that are more about "lifestyle" than illness?

2. Online information can be both empowering and misleading. Patients, armed with what they believe is informed need, will sometimes pressure their doctors to prescribe what may not be required. Doctors can find themselves faced with the time-consuming task of trying to educate consumers. "If you have 15 minutes and you're spending each visit talking about the crazy things they're finding on the Internet, you can never deal with more substantive issues," says internist Barron H. Lerner. With managed care limits on their ability to deal with patients in depth, physicians may be tempted to prescribe useless drugs out of frustration. To the extent that many of these drugs are not available in generic form, and are not on HMO formularies, profits to the pharmaceutical industry mount, but so do health costs. In response to these concerns, the Council on Ethical and Judicial Affairs of the American Medical Association has declared:

> All physicians should make a concerted effort to respond to their patients' concerns. For example, when a patient comes to a physician with a request for a drug that he or she has seen advertised, the physi-

cian should initiate a dialogue that would assess and enhance the patient's understanding of what the treatment entails. This would confirm that the patient was informed properly and has given informed consent. In keeping with sound medical decision-making, physicians should make available to patients those drugs that would offer benefits to the patient. Although physicians should not be biased against drugs that are advertised, they should resist commercial pressure to prescribe such drugs when not indicated. This may involve denying requests for inappropriate prescriptions, educating the patient as to why certain advertised drugs are not suitable treatment options, and including, when appropriate, information on the cost effectiveness of prescription drug options.[3]

To what extent is this realistic advice? How is the Internet changing the doctor-patient relationship?

3. Commissioner Henney went on to mention the Clinton administration's plan for legislation that would treat online pharmacies like their "brick and mortar" counterparts, requiring them to post on their Web sites their ownership, state licensure, the name of pharmacist in charge, and his or her phone number. Update this initiative: What has the Bush administration done?

---

[3] "Direct-to-Consumer Advertisements of Prescription Drugs," 55 *Food & Drug L.J.* 119 (2000).

TRUST IN CYBERSPACE

In this essay, Helen Nissenbaum, scholar from Princeton University's Center for Human Values, explains that trust in cyberspace is essential: "Trust is a key to the promise the online world holds for great and diverse benefits to humanity—its potential to enhance community, enliven politics, hasten scientific discovery, energize commerce, and more." While she believes that improved trust online will invigorate cyberspace, and that insecurity will sap its energy, she argues that over-reliance on high-tech security is a misguided strategy.

Nissenbaum begins by describing why we value trust.

Securing Trust Online: Wisdom or Oxymoron?[4]

Helen Nissenbaum

[O]ne aspect of the value of trust for individuals [was] observed by Niklas Luhmann, a social theorist...Luhmann characterizes trust as a mechanism that reduces complexity and enables people to cope with the high levels of uncertainty and complexity of contemporary life. Trust makes uncertainty and complexity tolerable because it enables us to focus on only a few possible alternatives. Humans, if faced with a full range of alternatives, if forced to acknowledge and calculate all possible outcomes of all possible decision nodes, would freeze in uncertainty and indecision....According to this account, trust expands people's capacity to relate successfully to a world whose complexity, in reality, is far greater than we are capable of taking in.

Trust's rewards extend beyond the individual, leavening many important relationships. Some, like the relationships between friends, lovers, siblings, husbands and wives, parents and children, mentors and students, are predicated on trust. But even in impersonal and formal relationships, trust plays a critical role: for trade and commercial transactions, for relationships between professionals (caregivers, healers, lawyers, etc.) and their clients, between employers and employees, between constituents and their political representatives. The possibilities for action increase proportionately to the increase in trust....When such trust has been established, new ways of behaving become possible; jokes, unconventional initiatives, bluntness, verbal short cuts, well-timed silences, the choice of delicate subjects, etc. When trust is tested and proven in this way, it can be accumulated by way of capital....to induce cohesion and solidarity, to be there to tap in troubled times....

Trust among citizens may be the magic ingredient that helps undergird political and civil stability in multicultural societies....Trust by individuals of such institutionalized authority as

---

[4] 81 *B.U.L.Rev.*, 635, June 2001.

government may sustain a citizenry's engagement in a social system....

[W]e would expect that trust [in cyberspace] holds a key to similar good ends: improving the quality of personal experiences, relationships, and communal and civic life, and stabilizing governance. We can expect that more people and institutions will "buy in" to the online world, will engage with others online, if there is sufficient trust. If a climate of trust can be established on the Net, if attitudes of trust toward partners in electronically mediated transactions can be achieved, then the online world will thrive, it will attract information, it will be lively with interaction, transaction and association. This will attract further investment of all kinds, which in turn will fuel participation, and so on. Conversely, if people do not trust interactions mediated electronically, they will minimize them; they will be cautious and suspicious in their dealings, they will not place information and creative works on the web, they will not engage in E-commerce, they will not indulge in MUDS, MOOS, E-lists, B-boards, Listservs, chatrooms, buddy lists, electronic banking, and more. A great resource will be wasted.

[Nissenbaum then discusses how people are able to develop trust in one another. It is a process that involves knowing who people are, how they behave, whether we have anything in common with them. But, as Nissenbaum explains, this process is hampered in the online world, where people commonly hide their true identities. Anonymity online has its benefits, she acknowledges, but "it shrinks the range of cues that can act as triggers of trust."

Personal characteristics, too, are obscured online:]

We lack cues that may give evidence of similarity, familiarity, or shared value systems. We may not know the other's gender (male, female, or "other"), age, race, socioeconomic status, occupation, mode of dress, or geographic origins. We lack the bodily signals of face-to-face interaction. Are we communicating with a 14-year-old girl or a 57-year-old man posing as a 14-year-old girl? Are we selling a priceless painting to an adolescent boy or to a reputable art dealer? Are we sharing a virtual room with an intriguing avatar or a virtual rapist?...

[To Nissenbaum, the most "intriguing" factor affecting human willingness to trust involves the context within which trust develops. Is it a place where bad behavior can be made public? Where bad behavior is punished? Where norms exist that "condemn betrayal and celebrate fidelity?" Nissenbaum calls the online context "inscrutable."]

[A]t least for now, we cannot rely on traditional mechanisms for articulating and supporting social, professional and other roles. Even with roles that appear equivalent to offline counterparts, for example, "shopkeeper," we lack the explicit frameworks of assurances that support them. For the roles that have emerged in cyberspace (like "sysops," avatars, bulletin board moderators, and so on) that do not have obvious counterparts offline, their duties and responsibilities are even less defined and understood.

Just as roles are still relatively unformulated, so are such background constraints and social norms regarding qualities like fidelity, virtue, loyalty, guile, duplicity, and trickery. Are we sure that betrayal will be checked, that safety nets exist to limit the scope of hurts and harms, and so on? Although there is evidence of various groups—social groups, interest groups, cultural groups—vying for domination of their norms, the territory remains relatively uncharted, further compounded by the global nature of the medium....

[Next, Nissenbaum looks at how high-tech security systems attempt to engender trust by (a) controlling access, (b) making identity clear, and (c) surveillance.]

ACCESS CONTROL

...The old fears remain: namely, infiltration by unauthorized persons (hackers, crackers, etc.), damage to information and systems, disruptive software flowing across the Net, information "stolen" as it traverses the networks, terrorists and criminals invading the infrastructure and bringing down critical systems....

Working within the constraints of current network and system architectures, security experts have developed a toolkit of mechanisms to protect people and systems against unwanted and dangerous access. One reason why demands on such a toolkit are considerable is because the agents of unwanted access may be bits of code, like applets, and not only people. Standard techniques like passwords remain in use, fortified where needed by such mechanisms as "firewalls," which are software barriers built around systems in order to make them impermeable except to people or code that is "authorized." Cryptographic techniques are used to...protect against theft and manipulation as information travels across networks. Some protection is offered against treacherous applets—for example, one that might reformat a user's hard drive, or leak private information to the world—through security features built into JAVA that limit what applets can do. There are, however, regular announcements of flaws in this security. There is fundamentally no known technical means of differentiating "good" from "bad" applets. How could there be except in some possible future when computers would be able discern categories of human values?

TRANSPARENCY OF IDENTITY

The people and institutions of the online world have diverse tastes when it comes to identification. Some are happy to link themselves to their full-blown offline identities, while others prefer to maintain independent virtual selves....

The goal of security efforts in this category is to give more transparent access to online agents in order to stave off at least some of the threats and worries that follow from not knowing with whom one is dealing. Identifiability is considered particularly useful for recognizing malevolent or mischievous agents. And in general, it helps answer some of the questions that trust inspires us to ask: is there a recognizable and persistent identity to the institutions and individuals behind the myriad of websites one might visit? Can we count on agents online to keep their promises? For the sake of e-commerce, how do we prevent malicious agents from posing as legitimate customers or service providers, and conducting bogus transactions, tricking and defrauding legitimate participants? In other words, we strive to reintroduce identifying information, at least as much as is needed to create a history, establish a reputation, hold agents accountable, and so on....

Cryptographic techniques are deployed to authenticate users, computers, and sources of information by means of digital signatures and digital certificates working within a socially constructed system of Certification Authorities, trusted third parties who vouch for the binding of cryptographic keys to particular identities—persons and institutions....

Schemes of identification, even the attenuated forms, work hand-in-hand with access control, because controlling access almost never means preventing everyone from using a system or the information in a system....

Security experts seem always to be engaged in a Sisyphusian battle, warding off attack, repairing system flaws, closing up loopholes and "backdoors," and devising new layers of protection; a process that ends, temporarily at least, until the next attack occurs. Outspoken security experts accept that this is an inevitable consequence of the "open" architecture of the Internet...

SURVEILLANCE

A third layer overlaid upon the security offered through access control and transparency of identity is surveillance: we keep an eye on things both in order to prevent harms and also to apprehend perpetrators after harm has been done...

...Strong and smart walls, and limits on the flow of information and range of interactivity establish "safe" zones;

What does Nissenbaum mean by "a Sisyphusian battle"?

greater transparency of identity through authentication allows participants to steer clear of "suspicious" agents. By exposing identities or, at least, crucial dimensions of identities, agents—individuals, organizations, and computers—may more effectively make judgments about trustworthiness, and decide whether others are "safe bets." Mechanisms of non-repudiation restore accountability. This, then, is the compelling current generated by the proponents of security and e-commerce.

HIGH SECURITY VS. TRUST

[Nissenbaum believes it is a mistake to equate security with the richly textured, fundamentally social phenomenon of trust. Reliance on improved security both goes too far and does not go far enough, in her view.]

Trust...is an attitude. It is almost always a relational attitude involving at least a trustor and a trustee. In this relation of trust, those who trust accept their vulnerability to those in whom they place trust. They realize that those they trust may exercise their power to harm, disappoint, or betray....Trust, then, is a form of confidence in another....Adam Seligman holds trust to be "some sort of belief in the goodwill of the other, given the opaqueness of other's intentions and calculations." Francis Fukuyama adds a social dimension to his account, describing trust as the "expectation that arises within a community of regular, honest, and cooperative behavior, based on commonly shared norms, on the part of other members of that community."

Usually trust involves more than the trustor and trustee; there is almost always an object with respect to which the trustor trusts the trustee. For [philosopher] Annette Baier, this is demonstrated in her example of trusting the plumber to take care of the pipes in her home, but not to take care of her daughter; trusting a babysitter to take care of her daughter, but not to take care of the pipes in her home....In the online world, there is similar discretion over not only whom one is prepared to trust, but with what one is prepared to entrust them; for example, many consumers have learned that they can trust Amazon Books to deliver their orders, but not trust them with their personal information.

[A common] theme [is the] essential connection between trust and vulnerability. When people trust, they expose themselves to risk. Although trust may be based on something—past experience, the nature of one's relationships, etc.—it involves no guarantees....In trusting, we are acknowledging the other as a free agent, and this is part of the exhilaration both of trusting and being trusted. Where people are guaranteed safety, where they are protected from harm via assurances— if the other person acted under coercion, for example—trust is redundant; it is unnecessary. What we have is certainty, security, and safety—not trust. The evidence, the signs, the cues and clues that ground the formation, that give evidence of the reasonableness of trust must always fall short of certainty; trust is an attitude without guarantees, without a complete warranty. When we constrain variables in ways that make things certain—i.e. safe—

we are usurping trust's function. Trust is squeezed out of the picture.

...Online, we do not have the means at our disposal of assuring safety and certainty without paying this price: a streamlining and constraining of the scope and nature of online interactions, relationships, and community; a limiting of the range and nature of allowed activity and scope and nature of interaction; a need to make a priori judgments about with whom we will or will not interact; and an acceptance of greater transparency and surveillance. In general, then, we trade freedom and range of opportunity for this certainty and safety.

[Nissenbaum points to another flaw in the security strategy: it concerns itself more with the potential for "outsiders"—such as hackers and thieves—to wreak havoc online, while ignoring the more serious threat to trust that can be caused by "insiders."]

Far less systematic attention is paid to the threat of insiders, those agents— individuals and organizations—who, by degrees, have sanctioned access to our space. These agents, who count among the respectable, socially sanctioned, reputable members of online society, engage in actions that many citizens of the online world dislike, resent, or even consider harmful. They track our Web activities, they collect and use personal information without our permission, they plant "cookies" on our hard drives, they hijack our browsers while they download ads, they fill our mailboxes with spam, and they engage in relentless commercialism. Some of these insiders— perhaps not the "respectable" ones— "troll" our discussion groups, afflict us

Are there other important values that are linked to vulnerability?

with hateful, inflammatory, mean-spirited emails ("flame"), send us threatening chain mail, and even attack our virtual selves. In other words, even if the walls of security keep outsiders outside, they do not curtail the agents and activities that, behind the veil of respectability and legal sanction—sometime ambiguity—make online citizens skittish, cautious, and resentful....

Consider the more familiar case of physical safety. To protect ourselves from bodily harm, many of us go to great lengths: we stay clear of dangerous parts of town, we affix padlocks to our doors and install burglar alarms in our homes, and we support the use of Closed Circuit Television (CCTV) in public spaces. Homicide statistics, however, tell a curious story: when the relationship of the killer to victim is known, we find that only twenty-two percent of killers are strangers—the proverbial outsiders. Others are spouses, friends, and acquaintances. Betrayal comes from those who are allowed within our spheres of safety, within our safe zones....

In proportion to actual harm done to individuals online, too much attention is paid to the aberrant individual, the trickster, and the evil hackers lurking outside the borders of civilized society online. The media play up dramatic cases: the Melissa virus, spies who infiltrate systems and sell secrets to our enemies, or hackers who distribute unauthorized copies of intellectual works. These techniques do nothing against agents, acting behind the veil of respectability, who invade our privacy and offend us by turning Cyberspace to their own interests and not ours....

For the vast majority of Net users, it is the second group and not the first that is the significant danger; it is the second at least as much as the first, that affects our attitudes of trust online. Powerful security mechanisms may keep us safe from malicious outsiders at the cost of our online experience, but such mechanisms still leave us vulnerable to these agents....If we care about developing a climate of trust online—full-blown trust, not a thin substitute—we must address these conditions of imbalance between individuals and institutions. Evil hackers are not the only, nor are they the most important barriers to trust online. If we do not address the systemic problems, trust will erode and we will not easily recover from a sense of wholesale exploitation.

In holding fast to the progressive social vision of Cyberspace, my choice would be an insistence on preserving the degrees of freedom that trust needs, while continuing to support a path of technical development in which security would ideally aim both to construct pockets of high security and to maintain minimal protections—safety nets to prevent catastrophic harms—in the realms outside of these pockets. If we set these as our goals, then we will have set the stage for trust. But we will only have set the stage. The work of nourishing trust and trustworthiness remains and calls for a familiar range of complex responses, including the promulgation of norms, moral and character education, and comfort for the hurt.

QUESTIONS

1. What does Nissenbaum see as the value of trust?

2. Nissenbaum has no objection to high security for airplanes flights, military installations, nuclear power plants, banks, prisons, or national secrets. Yet she argues that, in cyberspace, "the pursuit of trust be decoupled from the pursuit of high security." What are Nissenbaum's

chief criticisms of the high tech security approach to protecting trust online?

3. What does Nissenbaum recommend instead? Do you think her prescriptions will work?

4. How is the problem of online trust handled at eBay, where every day, thousands of items are auctioned off among strangers? On your own Internet Service Provider?

Word of Mouse

In this article, MIT professor Chrysanthos Dellarocas discusses how the reputation of a business can be assessed globally and instantaneously online via consumer feedback mechanisms.

From Word of Mouth to Word of Mouse

Business Wire
April 24, 2003

The Internet has spawned such a powerful way of communicating opinion about products or services—call it word of mouse—that reputations are literally a click away from being made or broken, according to Professor of Management Dellarocas. What's needed now, he said, is the design of better systems to properly utilize the huge amount of on-line consumer feedback flowing hourly to Web-based sites.

"Word-of-mouth, which is one of the most ancient mechanisms in the history of human society, is given new significance by the unique properties of the Internet," said Dellarocas. "Feedback from consumers on the Web is global, instant, and persistent...."

"These systems are extremely powerful," he said. "Word of mouth has always had a big impact. But in pre-Internet societies, the impact of an individual's opinions was limited by geography and the extent of his social network, while the Internet has enabled anyone on this planet to make her personal thoughts and opinions accessible to the global community instantly and almost without cost."

This capability not only allows consumers to tap into the collective experience of the global community regarding the merits of a particular product or service, but it also enables each Internet user to influence the actions of millions of other consumers simply by posting personal experiences on the Web. Internet-based systems pose an important additional challenge, Dellarocas said. "In the real brick-and-mortar world, we usually know something about the source of a rumor, so it can be filtered or adjusted. But anyone can spread a rumor on the Internet. A bad review of a hotel posted three years ago is still there, even if the hotel has been totally changed."

"The growing popularity of these sites has implications for a wide range of business activities, from advertising and brand building to product development and quality control," said Dellarocas....

So the Norman Rockwell-like image of people freely exchanging product information over a cyber-clothes line can be shattered by abuse of the technology. As an example, Dellarocas cites the growing use of "promotional chat," by which companies hire people to post comments in chat rooms in order to influence the overall on-line rating of their product or service.

"Our response to such false chat should be to design more robust chat rooms," said Dellarocas. "It's like controlling for spam—if chat rooms become full of injected items, we have to deal with that." Dellarocas, a computer scientist by training, has become intrigued by the growing role of information technology in reshaping established social institutions and practices.

"People are only now beginning to look seriously at this issue of on-line reputation," he said. "As time goes by, vendors will learn how to properly measure online word-of-mouth and incorporate it into their marketing strategies. As a response to this, I anticipate that the current, low tech, anything goes chat rooms and feedback sites will be replaced by smarter, more mediated communities." That may mean systems where feedback is more carefully compiled, rather than just thrown out "raw," he said. Or perhaps systems where cleverly designed combinations of fees and rewards for submitting and accessing feedback will help prevent abuse.

"In pre-Internet societies word of mouth emerged naturally and evolved in ways that were difficult to control or model," Dellarocas said. "What is truly different today is that the Internet allows this powerful social force to be precisely measured and controlled through proper chat room engineering. It might well be that the ability to solicit, aggregate, and publish mass feedback will influence the organizational and social dynamics of the 21st century in a similarly powerful way as mass broadcast affected business and society in the 20th century."

QUESTIONS

1. In April 2003 the Sloan School at MIT hosted a conference on online reputation and word of mouse. Listen to the discussion at **http://www.si.umich.edu/ %7Epresnick/reputation/symposium/**.

2. Explore Web sites that collect consumer feedback: **http://www.epinions.com, http://www.PlanetFeedback.com.** Compare and contrast.

3. Does consumer feedback invite the kind of defamation and hoaxing discussed in chapter 3? Does that mean it is not a good idea?

4. What do you think Helen Nissenbaum would think of online consumer feedback? Would she support it as a means of enhancing trust online?

FIGHTING SPAM

In 2003, it was estimated that 40% of all e-mail was spam—unsolicited commercial e-mail—two thirds of which was false or misleading in some way. In 2003 the cost to business of spam was estimated at $10 billion annually. According to one Internet marketing researcher, some 206 billion spam items will be sent to American consumers by the year 2006—a figure which means every Internet user will receive 1,400 spam e-mails, twice as many as were received in 2003.

Spam-blocking technologies do exist, although they sometimes do such a good job they filter out *wanted* messages. Wharton legal studies professor Dan Hunter has likened escalating efforts to stop spam with filtering technology and the spammers' ingenuity at circumventing filtering technology to an "arms race."

Spam clogs ISP networks, undercuts the legitimacy of genuine online marketers, and burdens ordinary consumers with their staggering volume and their creepy content—typical spam entices the recipient to bank millions in Nigerian oil money for ex-dictators or offers magical sex cures.

Anti-Spam Legislation and The First Amendment

The Electronic Frontier Foundation, a nonprofit organization that advocates a range of policies affecting the Internet, is concerned that any federal law to prevent spam should not interfere with the ability of non-spam political messages to be communicated online. The following policy statement was posted by the EFF in October 2001.

Anti-Spam Measures[5]

Electronic Frontier Foundation

While members of the EFF staff and board find this unsolicited email to be as annoying as everyone else, we believe that the two most popular strategies for combatting it so far—legislation and anti-spam blacklists—have failed in their fundamental design. Anti-spam bills have been badly written, are unconstitutionally overbroad, and frequently wander into areas where legislators have no expertise, such as the establishment of Internet standards. And anti-spam blacklists, such as the MAPS RBL (Mail Abuse Prevention System Realtime Blackhole List, the most popular), result in a large number of Internet service providers (ISPs) surreptitiously blocking large amounts of non-spam from innocent people. This is because they block all email from entire IP address blocks— even from entire nations. This is done with no notice to the users, who do not even know that their mail is not being delivered.

The focus of efforts to stop spam should include protecting end users and should not only consider stopping spammers at all costs. Specifically, any measure for stopping spam must ensure that all non-spam messages reach their intended recipients. Proposed solutions that do not fulfill these minimal goals are themselves a form of Internet abuse and are a direct assault on the health, growth, openness and liberty of the Internet.

Email is protected speech. There is a fundamental free speech right to be able to send and receive messages, regardless of medium. Unless that right is being abused by a particular individual, that individual must not be restricted. It is unacceptable, then, for anti-spam policies to limit legitimate rights to send or receive email. To the extent that an anti-spam proposal, whether legal or technical, results in such casualties, that proposal is unacceptable.

THE TWO EXTREMES OF THE CURRENT EMAIL BATTLEFIELD

The legislative proposals that have dominated the anti-spam policy debate for the last several years have failed, and rightly so. The several existing state laws against spam are of questionable constitutionality, too hard to enforce even if they should be enforced, and have done nothing to stem the tide of spam. National legislation will not solve the problem either, while creating a morass of unintended consequences. Serious problems with the anti-spam legislation we have seen to date include:

- misdefinitions of key terms and concepts, including "commercial," list," and "spam" itself;
- technology-specific requirements that will be rapidly obsolete;
- a focus on punishing expression rather than protecting privacy;

---

[5] Archived at http://www.eff.org/spam_cybersquatting_abuse/spam/position_on_junk_email. html (last visited July 21, 2003).

- the giving of broad power or obligation to ISPs to control the private email of their customers;
- jurisdictional problems;
- unnecessary and excessive criminalization of private, civil disputes;
- requirements with which senders will find it impossible to comply;
- and a clear pattern of providing a defense for ISPs in the form of immunity from the simple realities and responsibilities of the marketplace, rather than one of enabling individuals to protect themselves....

The search for a nonexistent, and ultimately impossible, legislative or ISP-level blacklist "magic bullet" solution has actually distracted the Internet community for the last five years from the real solution: better voluntary user-end filtering and/or voluntary, informed and flexible ISP-level filtering. Only an end user-controlled solution will uphold the rights of the end users while serving to deter spam by removing most of the audience and making it unprofitable to continue junk emailing.

THE RIGHT WAY TO LOOK AT SPAM

Until we include the free speech rights of all end-users instead of trying to stop a few wrongdoers at the cost of innocent users, any solution for dealing with spam will be fundamentally flawed. End users, known as "customers" to ISPs, should

demand that none of their wanted email be censored in attempts to filter out unwanted messages. In addition, Netizens should express their dismay at spam by boycotting products advertised with spam.

On a larger scale, EFF supports combatting spam by providing end-users with adequate tools to filter unwanted messages on the receiving end. We also support the development of more robust and subtle technology for this purpose. Brightmail, for example, has created a system that does a good, if still imperfect, job....

From a technical standpoint, we would like to see the development of better filtration software on servers, something that could work interactively with the mail recipient in defining what he or she regards as spam using pattern recognition. That is, every time somebody gets a message of a sort he or she does not want, s/he could send it to the filter, thereby making that filter smarter over time, as well as giving it the ability to "learn" as spam techniques develop.

The rights of users to send and receive email must not be compromised for quick and dirty ways to limit unsolicited bulk email. Neither misguided and ignorant legislation, nor collusive, high pressure protection schemes, have a legitimate function or place in our online future. The Constitution, and the promise of a free, open Internet that exists for and is controlled by its participants, requires us to do better.

http://spam.abuse.net

QUESTIONS

1. Peter Fader, a marketing professor at the Wharton School, claims that people already have an excellent tool for dealing with spam: the delete key. Do you agree?

2. As this book was going to press, Congress was newly preoccupied with versions of legislation to curtail spam. Was a law passed? If so, would the EFF approve? Why/why not?

3. Consider the various stakeholders in the spam situation: spammers, legitimate online marketers, consumers, ISPs. Think of utilitarian ethical analysis. How do the harms and benefits fall among them?

4. ISPs Microsoft and AOL have sued spammers for flooding their users' e-mail services with billions of unwanted messages. Earthlink managed to have the "Buffalo Spammer" arrested on fraud charges. What can you find about the outcomes of any of those cases?

5. Does your state have any laws against spam? See **http://www.spamlaws. com**.

6. What can netizens do to fight spam? Research Junkbusters, Mail Abuse Prevention System (MAPS), or Coalition Against Unsolicited E-mail (CAUCE) to find out.

According to a 2003 study by the Pew Internet and American Life Project, spam is making many people's experience online miserable. Pornographic material was at the top of the list of annoying e-mail, with three quarters of Internet users, especially parents and women, complaining. For thirty percent of those with personal e-mail accounts, eighty percent of incoming messages were spam. See: **http://www.pewinternet.org**.

DOT-CONS AND CYBERSWINDLES: FRAUD IN CYBERSPACE

As in the bricks-and-mortar business world, in e-commerce there exist unscrupulous operators who will take advantage of the trust of others and cheat them. Their activities, ranging from credit card skimming to pyramid schemes to fake online auctions, have been of concern to legitimate e-business and to regulators. Without a pervasive understanding that people can trust one another, or can trust that the cheaters will be deterred or punished, any commercial environment will be poisoned. Just as the e-commerce pace began to accelerate in the mid-1990s, these Internet scams came to light, and the pressure was on to root them out. In 2003, Attorney General John Ashcroft announced 130 people had been arrested for Internet fraud. One California couple, for example, was charged with running a fraudulent Russian dating service, swindling 400 victims out of $600,000 over three years. A company called CD Direct sold pills to enlarge the penis for $60 a bottle. Containing pumpkin seed, sarsaparilla, and "oyster meat," they cost the retailer less than $3 per bottle.

FTC: Online Scams

The Federal Trade Commission (FTC) claims to be "on the cyber-case." While it cooperates with the FBI and other federal and state agencies to prosecute the offenders, it also sees itself in the role of public educator in the era of the "Dot-Con." Below is its October 2000 listing of the most prevalent online scams.

Internet Auctions

The Bait: Shop in a "virtual marketplace" that offers a huge selection of products at great deals.

The Catch: After sending their money, consumers say they've received an item that is less valuable than promised, or, worse yet, nothing at all.

The Safety Net: When bidding through an Internet auction, particularly for a valuable item, check out the seller and insist on paying with a credit card or using an escrow service.

Internet Access Services

The Bait: Free money, simply for cashing a check.

The Catch: Consumers say they've been "trapped" into long-term contracts for Internet access or another web service, with big penalties for cancellation or early termination.

The Safety Net: If a check arrives at your home or business, read both sides carefully and look inside the envelope to find the conditions you're agreeing to if you cash the check. Read your phone bill carefully for unexpected or unauthorized charges.

Credit Card Fraud

The Bait: Surf the Internet and view adult images online for free, just for sharing your credit card number to prove you're over 18.

The Catch: Consumers say that fraudulent promoters have used their credit card numbers to run up charges on their cards.

The Safety Net: Share credit card information only when buying from a company you trust. Dispute unauthorized charges on your credit card bill by complaining to the bank that issued the card. Federal law limits your liability to $50 in charges if your card is misused.

International Modem Dialing

The Bait: Get free access to adult material and pornography by downloading a "viewer" or "dialer" computer program.

The Catch: Consumers complained about exorbitant long-distance charges on their phone bill. Through the program, their modem is disconnected, then reconnected to the Internet through an international long-distance number.

The Safety Net: Don't download any program to access a so-called "free" service without reading all the disclosures carefully for cost information. Just as important, read your phone bill carefully and challenge any charges you didn't authorize or don't understand.

Web Cramming

The Bait: Get a free custom-designed website for a 30-day trial period, with no obligation to continue.

The Catch: Consumers say they've been charged on their telephone bills or received a separate invoice, even if they never accepted the offer or agreed to continue the service after the trial period.

The Safety Net: Review your telephone bills and challenge any charges you don't recognize.

QUESTIONS

1. Go to the FTC site **(http://www. ftc.gov)** and look for other common scams. Are any of them unique to cyberspace?

2. In early 2002 the FTC warned online marketers to stop making unproven claims about devices to protect against bioterrorism. Over 50 sites were found to be offering items such as oregano oil to treat anthrax and gas masks to withstand a nuclear attack. Visit the FTC site and check out the latest online scam warnings.

3. Check out **http://www.econsumer. gov** for an online consumer protection program jointly run by 17 governments to deal with multinational Internet fraud. What are the latest trends?

ONLINE TOBACCO SALES

The purchase of tobacco products by a minor under 18 years of age and the provision of tobacco products to a minor are prohibited by law. A minor unlawfully purchasing or using tobacco products is subject to criminal penalties.

—dirtcheapcig.com

According to the British Medical Association, 500 million people alive in the year 2003, half of them children, will eventually be killed by tobacco use. Smoking presently kills almost 5 million people per year. By 2030 the toll is expected to rise to 10 million, hitting hardest in the developing world, where—as of 2003—eight out of ten smokers live.

In recent decades, tobacco control advocates have been active on several fronts, struggling to strengthen legal restrictions, public education programs, and smoking cessation technologies.

The Internet poses a unique threat to these efforts. In the following article, three Canadian tobacco health researchers explore this threat. While the industry denies it markets on the web, it is well aware of the importance of this new tool and is already taking advantage of it. According to the authors, "Tobacco industry experts predict that within 10 years, at least one fifth of the $40 billion in annual US cigarette sales will occur over the Internet."

They begin by describing the difficulties that online marketing of tobacco products poses for tobacco control.

Tobacco Commerce on the Internet[6]

Joanna E. Cohen, Vivian Sarabia, Mary Jane Ashley

UNRESTRICTED SALES TO MINORS

The prevention of sales to minors is a key component of a comprehensive tobacco control strategy, but it is clear that there are few barriers to youth buying cigarettes online. A state investigation in Utah found that children aged 10–17 were able to obtain cigarettes with ease via the internet. In an Oregon undercover investigation, four internet based tobacco dealers were found to have sold cigarettes to children as young as 8 years old. A recent study also found that cigar sites on the internet have few barriers to purchases by minors. Further, filter software fails to protect children adequately from promotional tobacco content.

CHEAPER CIGARETTES THROUGH TAX AVOIDANCE AND SMUGGLING

Price controls are another key element in a comprehensive tobacco control strategy and young people are particularly price sensitive. However, internet tobacco sales offer an attractive route for many consumers seeking cheaper cigarettes, through the avoidance of tobacco taxes. Tax based tobacco control initiatives are often undermined and delayed by the argument that such measures will fuel smuggling and other criminal activity. Internet tobacco commerce can also fuel these problems, because it can be a source of legal tax-free cigarettes that are then resold illegally by intermediaries. For example, Seneca Indian reservations

---

[6] *Tobacco Control* 10:364–367, Winter 2001.

in New York State have over three dozen websites selling tax-free cigarettes. Recently, in Canada, a two year investigation found that 85% of all cigarettes sold tax-free by the Squamish Nation in British Columbia was diverted to buyers who then resold the product to non-natives for profit....

One popular internet cigarette site (www.discount-cigarettes.org) requires retailers listed on the site to fully disclose on their home page if they report customer names to state tax agencies. It also lists many sites that specifically indicate that they do not report names to state tax departments. This is despite the Jenkins Act, a US federal statute that requires anyone selling cigarettes in interstate commerce to report those sales to the tobacco tax administrator for that state into which the sales are made.

Unfettered Advertising, Marketing and Promotion

Comprehensive tobacco control programmes employ strategies to counter directly the advertising, marketing, and promotional activities of the tobacco industry. The internet is a powerful marketing tool for use by an industry with demonstrated prowess in sophisticated market manipulation...

Smoking sites glamourise tobacco use. The...site **http://smokingsection. com** even provides "A smoker's guide to the cool ways to smoke", and other tobacco sites include elements that appeal to youth. British American Tobacco (BAT) has sponsored a web site, "City Gorilla", that purportedly provides "independent" advice on night life; how-ever, the site features venues that promote and sell BAT cigarettes, and it collects information on smokers that could be used for marketing purposes.

Continued Normalisation of the Tobacco Industry

In Canada and the USA, denormalisation of the tobacco industry and its products is also regarded as a key strategy in a comprehensive approach to tobacco control. Tobacco sales on the internet offer a venue for the continued normalisation of these products by casting them as just another consumer item. Unrestricted cigarette sales to minors, cheap cigarettes, and unfettered cigarette advertising, marketing and promotion contribute to the normalisation of these products.

[The authors go on to outline several solutions to the challenge posed by online tobacco marketing.]

International Tobacco Control

The tobacco industry knows that e-commerce offers the industry "a chance not to be missed" as "it's difficult to imagine individual countries attempting to regulate cyber-space". The proposed World Health Organization Framework Convention on Tobacco Control (FCTC)...provides an opportunity to promote international cooperation and coordination of tobacco control efforts, particularly where the challenges are transboundary in nature. Potentially important areas that have been identified for protocol development include: tobacco smuggling; duty-free sales of tobacco; tobacco pricing and taxation;

and reporting of production, sales, imports, and exports of tobacco products. Because of the inherently global nature of the world wide web, it has the potential to impact upon and challenge all aspects of international tobacco control....

NATIONAL AND STATE REGULATION

Several bills are pending in the USA at state and national levels that would increase restrictions on the internet sale of tobacco. Measures include making it easier for states to prosecute out-of-state web sites that sell tobacco to minors, to prohibit on-line sales, and to mandate websites selling tobacco to display the surgeon general's warning. Following an investigation in Oregon, four internet based tobacco dealers signed an agreement not to sell their products to minors, or potentially face fines up to $25 000 for each occurrence.

New York State passed a law banning internet, mail, and telephone cigarette orders from being sent directly to consumers, which was scheduled to take effect on 1 January 2001. However, Brown & Williamson Tobacco challenged the law claiming that "The Constitution prohibits any one state from regulating avenues of national commerce such as the Internet . . .", and a federal judge ruled that the law did violate the commerce clause of the US Constitution. In Rhode Island, internet distributors can be fined if they sell cigarettes to a minor; distributors will have to obtain customer IDs, and an adult will have to sign on delivery. The attorneys general from 17 US states have joined in an effort to halt online sales of bidis (flavoured, hand rolled cigarettes) to children by sending letters asking the companies to stop selling to minors.

The advertising potential of the internet has not gone unnoticed and the US Department of Justice issued an opinion in 1998 affirming the Food and Drug Administration's authority, in the interest of comprehensive tobacco legislation, to extend prohibitions on tobacco advertising on television and radio to include the internet. In the UK, the proposed Tobacco Advertising and Promotions Bill would prohibit UK based internet service providers from selling space to cigarette advertisers. In China, the Law of Network Advertisement bans on-line advertisements for cigarettes and sexual products.

There are precedents for regulating the on-line sale of particular goods, in particular, alcohol...In the USA, widely disparate state laws have created conflicts around the sale of alcohol over the internet. In six states it is a felony to ship alcohol from out of state, and in other states it is a misdemeanour. Twenty three states ban shipment of alcohol by such carriers as Federal Express or United Parcel Service, and the states of Oregon and Maryland have bills pending that would make selling alcohol over the internet a felony....

LEGAL REMEDIES

...In Michigan, the attorney general recently announced the filing of 20 criminal complaints for selling tobacco and tobacco products to minors via the internet. California, Washington State, and

What are the ethics of marketing tobacco products online?

Alaska have attempted to recover unpaid taxes from sales made by the internet, mail order, and on American Indian reservations, although officials estimate that only 5% of online or mail order retailers report names and addresses of customers.

CONCLUSIONS

Of course, the internet provides many advantages for tobacco control, in addition to the challenges. For example, the communication and information networks available through the internet are tremendously important for the timely exchange of information between researchers, policymakers, programmers, health professionals, and advocates. The internet also has the potential of being a key source of information for the lay public regarding the health effects of tobacco use, smoking cessation aids, and the activities of the tobacco industry....

Although there are regulatory avenues that national and subnational jurisdictions can and should pursue, tobacco e-commerce may be best controlled, in the long run, through international agreements such as the FCTC. Collective action may not only be mutually beneficial, but may be required if our tobacco control strategies are to be effective in this era of globalisation....

We must also address the dearth of research in the area of internet tobacco sales, marketing, and promotion. We can begin with descriptive data on the epidemiology of on-line tobacco purchasers (for example, age, sex, location of residence, types and amounts of tobacco related on-line purchases, frequency of such purchases, and reasons for purchasing tobacco products on line). Changes in the profiles of these purchasers could be monitored over time. There is also a need for descriptive information on the number of web sites selling tobacco products, promoting tobacco products and their use, and sponsored by the tobacco industry; these sites could be described in terms of various characteristics, including their jurisdiction of origin and their apparent target audience....

Policy analysis research is also necessary. Working definitions of on-line tobacco advertising and promotion must be developed. The obstacles to policymaking in this area need to be ascertained, such as impediments related to the inter-jurisdictional reach of the internet....Options for addressing these obstacles should be analysed for their feasibility and potential impacts.

QUESTIONS

1. The Framework Convention on Tobacco Control (FCTC), sponsored by the UN's World Health Organization, includes severe restrictions and even bans on tobacco marketing. If ratified, it would be the first global treaty on public health. Has the FCTC been ratified? If so, find out how it deals with online marketing of tobacco.

2. Look for tobacco sales online. Do you notice sites or features of sites that might appeal to children?

3. The authors report that, in an effort to halt online sales to children of bidis—sweet-flavored, hand-rolled cigarettes popular in India—17 US attorneys general jointly wrote to the offending companies, asking them to stop. What can you find about the popularity of bidis among youth today?

4. Assume tobacco use is dangerous to human health; so are a number of legal activities, such as skydiving, excessive alcohol consumption, and overeating of refined sugar or fatty foods. Consider the arguments in favor of open discussion on the Internet in chapter 3. Is a ban on Internet sales of a deadly product like tobacco the most effective way to deal with them? The most ethical way? Might there be another response? Can tobacco use be distinguished from skydiving and the other behaviors named above?

5. Millions of Internet users have gambled online. Logging on to any of the 1,800 or so sites, which are often based in the Caribbean, they enjoy the convenience of the experience: "Wagering via modem means that they need not make their way to an Indian casino or a riverboat or to Las Vegas or Atlantic City. It means that they need not get dressed. Or tell a spouse. Or face the shame of losing large sums in public."[7] Online, they can win—or lose—very quickly. According to the investment bank Bear Stearns & Co., Inc., Internet users lost $1.4 billion worldwide in the year 2000; by 2003 the General Accounting Office estimates they will lose $4 billion. Online gamblers also run the risk of becoming addicted. As Cheryl G. put it after losing half of her income: "You just keep clicking and clicking and clicking the button. It's euphoria." Is gambling distinguishable from tobacco use? Should online gambling be banned?

CLICK-WRAP LICENSES AND THE UCITA DEBATE

The U.S. legal system is two-tiered; it encompasses both federal and state regulation. Under the Constitution, certain powers are given to the federal government, and the rest is a matter of state law. For example, while the Founding Fathers perceived the need for a centralized federal banking system, they left it to the states to set the legal rules for making contracts. Since there are fifty states, there is the potential for as many different contract rules to develop. As our economy became more complex, so did the variations in state law. Over time it became clear that, in order to make business across

[7] Matt Richtel, "The Casino on the Desktop," *New York Times*, March 29, 2001.

THE AD-FREE AD

Throughout her career as a journalist and a media commentator, Naomi Klein has tracked the rise of anti-corporate activism. In her recent book *No Logo,*[8] Klein focuses on the power of corporate marketing practices to "brand" our society. Here she discusses how, in cyberspace, brands are able to achieve a seamless blending of advertising into culture. She writes: "On the Web, marketing language reached its nirvana: the ad-free ad." In this example, she shows how companies are turning away from merely "bankrolling someone else's content," becoming "content providers" themselves.

> Absolut Vodka's 1997 Absolut Kelly Internet site provided an early preview of the direction in which branded media are headed. The distiller had long since solicited original, brand-centered creations from visual artists, fashion designers and novelists to use in its advertisements—but this was different. On Absolut Kelly, only the name of the site advertised the product; the rest was an illustrated excerpt from *Wired* magazine editor Kevin Kelly's book *Out of Control.* This, it seemed, was what the brand managers had aspired to all along: for their brands to become quietly integrated into the heart of the culture. Sure, manufacturers will launch noisy interruptions if they are locked on the wrong side of the commerce/culture divide, but what they really want is for their brand to earn the right to be accepted, not just as advertising art but simply as art. Off-line, Absolut is still a major advertiser in *Wired*, but on-line, it is Absolut that is the host, and a *Wired* editor the supporting act.

What is the ethical dimension to the way corporate marketers in cyberspace are becoming "content providers?" Isn't this just an intelligent way to sell in cyberspace? Isn't it useful to get advice and seemingly unrelated information from marketing Web sites?

---

[8] (*New York: Picador*, 1999).

state lines more efficient and predictable, the legal rules had to be simplified. Groups of legal scholars, judges, and attorneys began to confer over this, producing a system-atized version of contracts called the Uniform Commercial Code, which was eventually adopted by all the states.

By the late 20th century a similar project was under way to synthesize contract rules for computer information transactions. But the process became highly contentious. The resulting document, the **Uniform Computer Information Transactions Act (UCITA)**, remains highly controversial.

Critics fault UCITA primarily because it allows enforcement of so-called shrink-wrap or click-wrap software licensing agreements. A **shrink-wrap** license refers to retail software packages sealed in plastic (shrink-wrap), which state that tearing the shrink-wrap equals agreeing to the terms of the agreement inside. The license may be displayed and readable through the plastic, or—in the more sophisticated version—it may be inside the box. In any case, the concern is that contract terms have been imposed on the consumer after the purchase. The **click-wrap** license is agreed upon online. Supposedly, the consumer is made aware of all the terms of the agreement as she scrolls through the purchasing process, but some argue that, again, the effect is to impose terms upon the consumer after-the-fact. Matthew J. Smith has written about UCITA, arguing that it gives too much discretion to software vendors at the expense of licensees. Here he describes the problem with click-wrap:

> Think of the last time that you clicked on the "order now" button on your favorite internet shopping site, or the "I Agree" button when your browser flashed up the "Terms and Conditions" of some web site. Did you read all of the terms and conditions, or did you agree sight unseen? Did you print out the terms for later review?

The only recourse for a purchaser under UCITA is to return the goods before using them for a refund. But the right to a "cost-free return" is an empty right, critics complain, given that most people will use the software first and find out later what they did not read or absorb on those several pages or screens. As Matthew Smith points out:

> Every consumer is aware, on some level, that when they purchase com-puter software some additional terms and conditions upon the use of that program will be contained within the package. The same can be said for the consumer who purchases Tomb Raider, Quake, or Microsoft Office 2000 from a...web site....We, as consumers, know that we give up something to get something. The problem with this is that consumers are often unaware

of how much they are giving up. UCITA will make it easier for software manufacturers to force consumers to give up significant rights, while solidifying and protecting the manufacturer's rights. Proponents of UCITA state that the consumer has the greatest right of all, the right of return....But how much of a right is it when the consumer has purchased Microsoft Windows 98 to use as an operating system for their new computer?...[I]t is hard to imagine that the average consumer, with open box in hand somewhere in the middle of the installation process, will suddenly come to their senses, uninstall the product, and immediately send it back to the manufacturer for a full refund. The grant of an empty right is no grant at all.[9]

When scrolling down a lengthy online agreement, do you read it with care before clicking "I agree"?

From the software publishers' perspective, shrink-wrap and click-wrap licenses have the advantage of reducing transaction costs. If customers had to be walked though complex licensing terms step-by-step, those costs would be considerably higher and would likely be passed through to consumers, who would be charged more for the software. We can identify utilitarian benefits, then, for both licensor and licensee: Shrink-wrap and click-wrap agreements allow transfer of more software to more consumers at cheaper prices. But there are many—including consumer advocates, the Federal Trade Commission, and the attorneys general of 26 states—who believe there is a dark side to this efficiency. Shrink- or click-wrap contracting, they argue, becomes problematic when combined with UCITA's other features—allowing vendors to disclaim warranties or to shut down software remotely if they suspect license terms are being violated, for example.

Americans for Fair Electronic Commerce Transactions (AFFECT) is a nonprofit coalition established to oppose UCITA.

---

[9] "Comment: An Overview of UCITA," 25 *S.Ill.U.L.J.* 389 (Winter 2001).

Why We Oppose UCITA

Americans for Fair Electronic Commerce Transactions

UCITA would change software and informational purchases in the following ways:

THE SOFTWARE PURCHASED WOULD NO LONGER BELONG TO THE BUYER.

UCITA allows restrictions on use to be revealed after purchase.

UCITA allows software publishers to change the terms of the contract after purchase.

UCITA allows software vendors to prohibit the transfer of software from one person to another or from one company to another, even in the course of a merger or acquisition.

UCITA allows terms that may severely limit the use of the product.

UCITA allows restrictions that prohibit users from criticizing or publicly commenting on software they purchased.

UCITA WOULD PERMIT INVASIONS OF PRIVACY.

UCITA allows software publishers to legally track and collect confidential information about personal and business activities of licensees.

UCITA allows software and information products to contain "back door" entrances, potentially making users' systems vulnerable to infiltration by unauthorized hackers.

SOFTWARE COMPANIES COULD KNOWINGLY SHIP DEFECTIVE PRODUCTS.

UCITA allows software publishers to deny both large and small businesses many of the current warranty protections they have under present law.

UCITA allows software publishers to sell their products "as is" and to disclaim liability for product shortcomings. Imagine buying a refrigerator or stove where the producer does not guarantee that the product will work correctly.

If the consumer wants to sue over a defective product, UCITA allows the software publisher to restrict legal action to a specific jurisdiction—a particular county, state or even a different country.

UCITA WOULD ALLOW SOFTWARE TO BE DISABLED WITHOUT NOTIFICATION.

UCITA allows software publishers to shut down mission critical software *remotely* without court approval and without incurring liability for the foreseeable harm caused.

UCITA allows software publishers to modify the terms of contracts after the sale simply by sending an e-mail—regardless of whether the consumer receives the notification or not.

UCITA allows software publishers to remove their product, simply because usage fees arrive late.

How does UCITA impact on intellectual property? Privacy? Free speech?

UCITA puts consumers at the mercy of software publishers to "blackmail" users for more fees by their unhindered ability to disable or remove their product for unspecified "license violations."

UCITA WOULD THREATEN EXISTING PRIVILEGES GRANTED UNDER FEDERAL COPYRIGHT LAWS.

UCITA would permit an end-run around federal copyright law in mass-market licensing agreements that are used by virtually all consumers and that are the mainstay of most library and business operations.

UCITA threatens fair use privileges that allow for the provision of fundamental library services like inter-library loan, archiving and preservation.

UCITA threatens "first sale" privileges that permit donation, transfer or resale of a product.

QUESTIONS

1. Have any states adopted UCITA?

2. Locate the Web site for your state attorney general. Does she oppose UCITA? Why/why not? See **http://www. naag.org**.

3. AFFECT supports "bomb shelter" laws. What are they?

In the next reading, Richard Stallman, prominent in the "free software" movement, explains why he is an activist against UCITA.

Why We Must Fight UCITA

Richard Stallman

...UCITA says that by default a software developer or distributor is completely liable for flaws in a program; but it also allows a shrink-wrap license to override the default. Sophisticated software companies that make proprietary software will use shrink-wrap licenses to avoid liability entirely. But amateurs, and self-employed contractors who develop software for others, will be often be shafted because they didn't know about this problem. And we free software developers won't have any reliable way to avoid the problem.

What could we do about this? We could try to change our licenses to avoid it. But since we don't use shrink-wrap licenses, we cannot override the UCITA default. Perhaps we can prohibit distribution in the states that adopt UCITA. That might solve the problem—for the software we release in the future. But we can't do this retroactively for software we have already released. Those versions are already available, people are already licensed to distribute them in these states—and when they do so, under UCITA, they would make us liable. We are powerless to change this situation by changing our licenses now; we will have to make complex legal arguments that may or may not work.

UCITA has another indirect consequence that would hamstring free software development in the long term—it gives proprietary software developers the power to prohibit reverse engineering. This would make it easy for them to establish secret file formats and protocols, which there would be no lawful way for us to figure out.

That could be a disastrous obstacle for development of free software that can serve users' practical needs, because communicating with users of non-free software is one of those needs. Many users today feel that they must run Windows, simply so they can read and write files in Word format....

UCITA does not apply only to software. It applies to any sort of computer-readable information. Even if you use only free software, you are likely to read articles on your computer, and access databases. UCITA will allow the publishers to impose the most outrageous restrictions on you. They could change the license retroactively at any time, and force you to delete the material if you don't accept the change. They could even prohibit you from describing what you see as flaws in the material.

Some friends of free software have argued that UCITA would benefit our community, by making non-free software intolerably restrictive, and thus driving users to us. Realistically speaking, this is unlikely, because it assumes that proprietary software developers will act against their own interests....

Proprietary software developers intend to use the additional power UCITA would give them to increase their profits. Rather than using this power at full throttle all the time, they will make an effort to find the most profitable way to use it. Those applications of UCITA power that make users stop buying will be abandoned; those that most users tolerate will become the norm. UCITA will not help us.

This is too outrageous an injustice to wish on anyone, even if it would indirectly benefit a good cause. As ethical beings, we must not favor the infliction of hardship and injustice on others on the grounds that it will drive them to join our cause. We must not be Machiavellian. The point of free software is concern for each other.

Our only smart plan, our only ethical plan, is...to defeat UCITA!

QUESTIONS

1. Stallman argues against UCITA in part because it would inhibit reverse engineering. What is "reverse engineering?" Think of all the stakeholders in software development. Is reverse engineering ethical?

2. Read the shrink-wrap license on any software owned by you or a friend. What kind of agreement did the purchaser make? What terms or conditions appear to benefit the licensor? Find out what kinds of licensing agreements your school or employer has entered into for software. Again, what terms favor the licensor? Which favor the purchaser?

SPECIAL PROJECT: RE-DRAFTING UCITA

Preparation: Listed below are some of the groups lined up in opposition to UCITA, along with Web sites that explain their views. Students should divide into teams. Each team will represent one group and will use the links to begin researching why that group is against UCITA. Meanwhile, one team should represent the National Conference of Commissioners on Uniform State Law (NCCUSL, the lawyers who approved UCITA in July 2000), and research the arguments favoring it.

Information session: Each group against UCITA should explain its objections. Then, the NCCUSL representatives should explain the benefits of the draft law.

Negotiation session: In an open forum, team members should discuss how UCITA could be altered to satisfy the concerns of its critics. This process could begin in class and continue online as teams circulate ideas for compromise and work internally and then with others to reach a final agreement.

Association of Computing Machinery
http://www.acm.org
Open Source software community
http://www.linuxtoday.com
Institute of Electrical and Electronic Engineers
http://www.ieeeusa.org
Troubleshooters (grassroots activists)
http://www.TroubleShooter.com
academics
http://www.educause.edu
Digital Future Coalition
http://www.dfc.org

American Library Association
http://www.ala.org/washoff/ucita
National Writers Union
http://www.nwu.org
Computer Professionals for Social Responsibility
http://www.cpsr.org
Consumer Federation of America
http://www.consumerlaw.org
Federal Trade Commission
http://www.ftc.gov

E-MEDIATION

Helen Nissenbaum, author of the article about online trust at the start of this chapter, has described how the kind of environment within which trust will flourish develops. First, it must be a setting where "betrayal and fidelity are routinely publicized," where people cannot "effectively hide their deeds—especially their misdeeds." Nissenbaum goes on:

> The second is reward and punishment: settings in which rewards and sanctions follow trustworthiness and betrayal respectively, are likely to induce trustworthiness and trust. Thirdly, where reward and punishment for fidelity and betrayal are not systematically available, promulgation of norms through other means can effectively shape behaviors, and establish a climate of one sort or another. Finally, a society can nurture a trusting climate by setting in place, through public policy or other means, various forms of "trust insurance" to provide safety nets for those whose trust is betrayed.

Just as in bricks-and-mortar business, e-commerce transactions can end badly, with one or both parties to a deal feeling wronged. In the offline world, the legal system—in the U.S. the common law of contract—has for generations provided a system of rewards and punishment that is relatively clear and predictable. But cyberlaw is a work in progress, and the contracting parties in cyberspace are often not from the same nation, making resort to law uncertain.

The next article describes the appearance of a form of alternative dispute resolution—mediation—in e-commerce. "E-mediation"does not require much investment of time or money and may create the "trust insurance" to which Nissenbaum refers.

Mediation in Cyberspace

Richard Birke & Louise Ellen Teitz[10]

As consumer and business transactions ventured into cyberspace, it was natural that the mechanisms to resolve disputes would follow the source of disputes into the new medium. Online dispute resolution, or "ODR," its less appetizing acronym, is generally used to refer to various forms of alternative dispute resolution, ranging from traditional arbitration to mediation to consumer complaint systems. Currently, the majority of ODR providers offers some form of non-binding dispute resolution, usually mediation or a less-structured service that consists of some type of assisted negotiation....

[On-line generated disputes] result from transactions, such as purchases of goods or services, that have occurred in electronic commerce and may or may not be delivered on-line. These two categories, on-line handled and on-line generated, as a practical matter overlap at several places, especially when both the source of the dispute and the dispute resolution mechanism involve electronic commerce, such as disputes between buyers and sellers in internet auctions whose disputes are handled by on-line mediation. One example of this is the on-line auction service, eBay....

One way to differentiate ODR providers is by the level of automation, ranging from translating "traditional" forms of mediation into electronic form by internet to fully-automated platforms consisting of software that match demand/settlement responses without human intervention. In the high automation category there are several sites such as **clicknsettle.com**, **cybersettle.com**, **settlementonline.com**, and **ussettle.com** that are basically computer programs where there is no interaction between parties or with a human neutral or mediator. Software automatically compares settlement offers in what essentially amounts to a "bidding process." For example, in one site, clicknsettle, the plaintiff puts in three offers and the other side puts in three offers. If any of the offers are less than 30% apart, the dispute is automatically settled for a compromise figure. The sites vary with the degree of sophistication and differentiated standards for the basis of settling. All act without a neutral or decision-making human. These sites tend to be popular for settling insurance and financial claims and kinds of disputes where there is the expectation of settlement and all that is at issue is the final amount. It is not so clear what advantage this system offers the insured, as opposed to the insurance company. The bidding system, however, is predictable, in that both parties know the basic parameters and it provides a confidential means for the parties to exchange settlement offers. These amounts are not revealed to the other party even after the parties fail to settle. The system reflects the use of new technology applied to traditional issues of settlement. One critical

---

[10] 50 *Am.J.Comp.L.* 181, Fall 2002.

component of a successful dispute resolution system, however, is enforceability, which may be difficult, requiring resort to courts for enforcement of a "contract" made by a computer....

The SquareTrade [for-profit] on-line mediation services are illustrative of some of the crucial developments occurring in e-mediation and the symbiotic relationship between e-mediation and e-commerce, especially in connection with business to consumer, or B2C, transactions. SquareTrade offers a variety of services, ranging from assisted negotiation, to mediation, to arbitration. SquareTrade also has created a trustmark program, where it offers online sellers or e-tailers a trustmark. The trustmark includes an assurance of adequate dispute resolution services which are also generally provided on-line by SquareTrade. The need for on-line mechanisms for dispute resolution is a direct response to the uncertainty generated by a lack of uniformity in applying judicial and prescriptive jurisdiction to transactions occurring in cyberspace. This uncertainty, in turn, is creating an increasing barrier to transborder (both domestic and foreign) commerce. Parties must have confidence not only in the ability to surmount technological barriers, such as the need for authenticity and privacy, but also in the capacity to resolve subsequent disputes in an equitable and efficient manner, even if those disputes involve parties and occurrences 3000 miles away. Nowhere is this need more pronounced than in transactions involving consumers as purchasers. By assuring customers of an efficient process for dispute resolution

on-line, consumer confidence is increased. The trustmark, such as that offered by SquareTrade, encourages the buyer to trade the comforts of local (or national) courts for certain guarantees of conflict resolution, usually ODR mechanisms and usually including some form of e-mediation. One highly successful example of this is the e-tailer eBay, the on-line auction site. To increase consumer confidence in the virtual auction process, eBay hired SquareTrade to provide eBay customers with mediated ODR that would be an inexpensive and fast alternative to traditional litigation or off-line ADR. SquareTrade lists the five most important considerations to buyers as including "seller's commitment to mediation...."

THE PROMISE AND PITFALLS OF E-MEDIATION

The effectiveness of on-line mediation has been questioned. Mediation is often recommended and encouraged where parties have had an ongoing relationship and the mediator can draw on the parties' prior and continuing experience. That is missing in many ODR transactions where the parties are often consumers or buyers in one-shot deals and there is no past experience and not much interest in ensuring a future working relationship, but only an interest in resolving this one dispute. Most importantly perhaps, the medium itself creates a challenge for mediation, where interpersonal connection is often considered crucial. In ODR, written on-line communications often lose the tone of the participants. One is not able to judge how

What are the pros and cons of e-mediation?

flexible a party might really be and whether a party's feelings on a point are strong or weak. There are no visual cues to guide the mediator. Nor is there an opportunity for the parties to feel a sense of shared accomplishment and shared goals. The underlying question is whether physical distance means or creates psychological distance. Does loss of personal contact mean loss of personality, reputation and confidence, all important to mediation? The on-line medium for mediation also raises questions where there may be limited access to the new technology, especially in the consumer population in connection with on-line resolution of non-electronically generated disputes. Even among users of computers, there may be discomfort with using the medium for lengthy or detailed communications.

Indeed the actual mediators may not have technological competence. A final limitation of e-mediation is the perceived need for written procedures or rules when working in the written form and without verbal communication. Yet mediation often requires a level of flexibility and fluidity in process that does not lend itself to detailed procedures and rules....

The regulation of ODR as part of e-commerce has spawned extensive debates, both domestically and internationally, about self-regulation as opposed to governmental intervention, as well as about jurisdictional authority. Embroiled in the debate is the role of the "consumer." For example, in the area of consumer transactions, the approaches taken by different countries reflect underlying differences in philosophy and the role that government should play in controlling transactions in electronic commerce. The United States, although enforcing truthful advertising, has generally advocated a path of self-regulation, not government intervention. This philosophy has permeated not only the transactions but any mechanisms for dispute resolution such as e-mediation connected with these transactions in electronic commerce.

Unlike other forms of mediation where we may not want uniformity or standardization for fear of inhibiting the growth of robust dispute resolution to handle a diversity of interests and disputes, we may need to develop some standards and provide some oversight for e-mediation. E-mediation often slips between the cracks of regulators, both state and federal....[W]hat is missing in e-mediation is a means of ensuring quality and minimum standards, either by government regulation or co-regulation with industry. E-mediation services should meet minimum thresholds for disclosure (for example, of costs, training of mediators, selection and payment of neutrals). While there is a delicate balance between privacy and transparency, basic disclosure is necessary to protect users of e-mediation in cyberspace.

CHAPTER PROBLEMS

1. In 2000, the U.S. Department of Justice, collaborating with the FDA, DEA, and FBI, opened approximately 20 investigations of e-drug Web sites. Find out the facts that led to the investigation of one of these "rogue" online pharmacies. What were they doing? How was it unethical? See **http://www.fda.gov**.

2. Thirty years ago, the total retail value of the pornography industry in the U.S. was $5 to 10 million. What kept it small were the barriers between customers and product: a person would have to go to a seedy neighborhood to find hard-core books or films. But then came digital technology. Suddenly, people could simply rent a video. Or—even more conveniently—rent a film in their hotel room. (The hotel industry estimates that at least half of all guests rent adult movies.) Once the Internet was in place, all it took to view pornography was to sit in front of a PC—anywhere. Technology took the embarrassment out of the transaction, and today, business is booming. Selling sexual images is a $10 billion industry, and the online segment is growing fast. The number of people visiting porn sites doubled over the year 2000. Some of the more popular sites attracted in excess of 50 million hits. About one in a thousand visitors will subscribe, agreeing to fees averaging $20 month.[11] Is it ethical to maintain a Web site that offers porn?

3. Brian Lee, president of Los Angeles-based LegalZoom, here describes the recent spread of online divorce services that enable couples to legally end their marriages for $50–$300, far less than lawyers charge: "It's similar to the growth of online travel services and online stock trading. People are learning that they don't need a travel agent or a stockbroker or a lawyer—they can do it themselves."[12] Consider all the various stakeholders in a divorce situation. What are the ethics of offering divorce online?

4. For e-commerce to flourish, the consuming public must believe that, for the most part, their online transacting is safe. Customers need to believe that any information they reveal as they shop will be kept private and that their reasonable business expectations will be met. In April 2001, a consortium of e-tailers organized to set a global standard, a code of conduct to which companies can subscribe, and which they can then attach to their Web sites—a "seal of approval." Organizers of this effort to make the world safe for e-commerce include include European chambers of commerce and BBBOnLine, the Internet arm of the North American Better

---

[11] Flying Crocodile, Inc., which tracks and services the sex-content market.

[12] David Crary, "Web sites offer cheap divorces; objections rise," *The Philadelphia Inquirer*, May 29, 2003 (A6).

Business Bureau. Update these efforts. Are we closing in on international rules for doing business online? If so, could this serve as a model for other types of global agreements—on the environment, on human rights, for example? Why/why not? See **http://www.BBBOnLine.org**.

5. Three Dutch teenagers launched an e-mail virus that is programmed to trigger the default browser on an infected computer, automatically opening up a pornography Web site. The teens have no financial interest at stake; they claimed they wanted to introduce people to the "joys of being bad on the net." Imagine yourself interviewing the creators of this virus. What ethical perspective do you think would come closest to matching their values?

6. Back in the 1980s, marketers did not perceive children as a target audience for advertising. Apart from Saturday morning television, which was basically an excuse to show children ads for cereals and toys, children were not noticed by them. Then—big changes. Demographically, the traditional nuclear family model gave ground to the single-parent model, and old-style parenting faded into a baby-boomer philosophy which was more "laid back" about wielding authority. The result: "a much more influential kid," as Paul Kurnit, the president of a Madison Avenue ad agency puts it. In the late 20th century, our economy went through an extended period of growth, and the purchasing power of children increased enormously. At this point, children can influence their families' purchasing decisions—not just of breakfast cereals, but of "cars, vacations, computers." Today's children, according to Kurnit, are "getting older younger."

In "The Selling of the Clickerati,[13] reporter Bob Thompson tells this story about a 12-year-old, Tori Clifford.

> One day last spring…[s]he was looking through a magazine—she thinks it might have been Seventeen—and her eye was drawn to a blurb about a new Web site. It offered a way for kids like her, who are too young to have their own credit cards, to complete purchases online. "It was like, 'iCanBuy.com, your parents can give you an allowance and you can just go buy whatever you want.' And I said, 'Ooh, that sounds cool!'" She told her mother about it and they checked out the site together. Pretty soon she had an iCanBuy account with a $100 balance. Every time she signed on, she was greeted by a purple screen that proclaimed itself "Tori's Room" and reminded her how many days it was until her birthday. She began to compile an iCanBuy wish list, so people interested in buying gifts for her would know exactly what she wanted. On May 23, she made her first purchase: a purple-blue syn-

---

[13] *The Washington Post*, October 24, 1999.

thetic Vee Luv sweater from MXG with cranberry and gray stripes. It cost $32, plus $4.99 for shipping.

What are the ethical implications of "marketing in kidspace?"

7. Within its network of popular search engines, including Yahoo, Altavista, and AOL Time Warner, Overture.com provides paid listings for its more than 100,000 commerical customers worldwide. Firms pay to be included in keyword search results; the more a firm pays, the higher up it will appear on the search result list. Try the same search on two different search engines and compare results. Does the yield include sponsored sites? How high on the results list are they? What are the costs and benefits of the Overture concept?

8. The nonprofit Center for Democracy and Technology recommends anti-spam legislation but would want any such law to include "anti-spoofing" requirements, forcing unsolicited e-mail to contain accurate source and routing data, so that recipients (and filters) could recognize the real origins of any message. Others claim that such requirements would be unconstitutional, citing the free speech argument that it is more objectionable to force someone to speak what they would prefer not to say than to censor what they have chosen to say. Do you agree with that argument in the context of spam?

9. Free-market economists believe the most efficient marketplace, and the one most beneficial to consumers, is one of "perfect competition." This means a marketplace free of barriers that otherwise block companies from entering or leaving a particular business; one where many fully-informed buyers and sellers meet to exchange goods and services. In the ideal free market, every buyer would be matched by a supplier able to meet his needs; there would be no "transaction cost" attached to finding the right product or service.

Potentially, online consumers have more information, at lower cost, than ever before. "Shopbots," for example—like AuctionWatch.com—are search engines that use spiders to crawl the Web, make copies of Web sites, and amass product and pricing information that makes comparison shopping easy. In this way, we move toward a more perfect market.

Most businesses, however, are more concerned with their own profits than with the overall efficiency of the market. If they can, many dot.coms would choose to enhance their own market power to enable them to woo customers without having to lower prices. Some companies—especially those with high name recognition, like eBay and Ticketmaster—would rather consumers come to their sites directly. Technology and litigation have both been used to try to block shopbots from indexing information from some sites and limiting hyperlinks.

Do a utilitarian analysis of indexing Web sites by considering the costs and benefits to the various stakeholders: consumers, sellers, and the meta-indexers. Is interference with the potential of the Internet to deliver the "perfect market" unethical?

CHAPTER 5

E-Learning and the Business of Education

[T]rue reading is hard. Unless we are practiced, we do not just crack the covers and slip into an alternate world. We do not get swept up as readily as we might be by the big-screen excitements of the film. But if we do read perseveringly we make available to ourselves, in a most portable form, an ulterior existence. We hold in our hands a way to cut against the momentum of the times. We can resist the skimming tendency and delve; we can restore, if only for a time, the vanishing assumptions of coherence.

—Sven Birkerts, *The Gutenberg Elegies*

Intellectual Freedom implies a circle, and that circle is broken if either freedom of expression or access to ideas is stifled.

—American Library Association

The truly well-educated know that there are few straightforward paths to understanding the world and perfecting the self. There is no way to commodify the quest to reconcile conflicting images of a complex society and contradictory visions of a life well-lived.

—Rachel Moran (1998)

Knowledge will ever govern ignorance; and people who mean to be their own Governors must arm themselves with the power which knowledge gives.

—James Madison (1822)

ETHICS CASE: SHARING OR CHEATING?

Students in Twenty-First Century Communications, an upper-level general education class at Old City College, were assigned to teams of two for a final project on some topic related to their major.

Al and Andi, Art History majors, developed a Web site that provided an overview of art and architectural developments in the early 19th century, when Old City College was founded. They got the idea from a similar project put together by a friend of Al's at another university in another city. Their Web site included carefully labeled visuals downloaded from various art museum sites. Andi wrote the narrative, paraphrasing many of the 19th century documents originally distributed by the town and college, and rewrote descriptions of paintings that appeared in online museum tours.

Business students Bob and Beth developed a plan for marketing new restaurants in their city, where the downtown area was undergoing revitalization. They showed the class a video they had made, incorporating photos taken by Bob. Because he had been rushing to finish in time, Bob had downloaded some photos from actual restaurant home pages and included them as well, although he didn't mention this to either Beth or to the class. In their presentation, the two discussed their original four-point marketing strategy. This was set up within an interactive menu, just like one they had found on a Web site they had seen while doing their research.

Using their developing skills in computer programming, Charlie and Chris created their own free music sharing project, demonstrating its use in class with a mini-concert.

Marc and Mari decided to look into the way a few media giants have been gobbling pieces of the communications industry. They started their research early and were well underway when—because of personal problems that came up three weeks before the end of the semester—Marc disappeared. The day before their presentation, Mari was still unable to contact him. Panicked, she spruced up the outline he had given her using Microsoft PowerPoint™ and did her best to flesh out some of the ideas for the talk she would have to give by herself. Not surprising for a senior in Media and Communications, Mari was energetic and convincing. Only later did she learn that Marc's outline was not his own—unless something becomes your own when you buy it over the Internet. The professor routinely checks all written materials with anti-plagiarism software. When she discovered that the outline was not original, she flunked both Marc and Mari.

This chapter explores a number of ethical issues surrounding the increasingly interwoven worlds of education, cyberspace, and business. We begin with an exploration of the ways in which the Internet may be changing our views of academic honesty and plagiarism. Then, in a section on distance education, we look at the impact of computers and the Internet on educational opportunities and experiences—the "digital divide"—and the ways in which the commercial and educational worlds complement and conflict with each other. We end by leaving the virtual university and returning to face-to-face education, where surfing the Net in class—and students' use of the Internet to make their presence felt outside the classroom—leads to discussions of appropriate use and abuse of the Internet.

ACADEMIC HONESTY IN CYBERSPACE

A postmodern perspective of plagiarism and intellectual property suggests that one cannot own ideas or words. All we can do is honor and recompense the encoding of those ideas, the use of those words, in the certainty that such honor and compensation are negotiated in contexts of time and place, class and power, within social and economic considerations. Whether ideas or words could be owned surely has not changed—only the contexts and with them the negotiations....[1]

—Lise Buranen and Alice M. Roy

Information wants to be free; plagiarism saves time.

—Anonymous

In the first decade of the 21st Century, technology/education/business partnerships sometimes converge around what educator Jeanne Wilson has called a "new twist on a perennial problem," that is, plagiarism. In the mid-1970s, a dozen states around the country adopted new laws aimed at shutting down "term paper mills"—businesses that hawked research papers. Although there is little evidence of any sustained attempt to enforce those laws, they represent a kind of consensus about at least one form of academic dishonesty—buying someone else's work and passing it off as one's own for academic credit or a degree.

On the Internet today, this form of dishonesty can be served with even more sophistication. NoCheaters.com, for example, invites "honest students" to download an "example of a good term paper or research study" from its inventory of more than 20,000 "pre-written models" on "every academic subject imaginable." Students who need to produce a paper for which there is no model available can still purchase "models rich with information, ideas" and current sources, properly cited, by choosing the "custom" option. "Honest students," it seems, do not actually submit someone else's paper; at most they might use one to "get ideas."

But the Internet has also made possible another kind of business: one that enables faculty members to identify papers that have been copied or purchased. Glatt Plagiarism Services Inc. offers software programs to help deter and detect plagiarism. With the help of experts in pattern recognition and information technology, Plagiarism.org (now called Turnitin.com) developed a Web-based detection service that electronically scans student papers for plagiarism. According to Wilson, "The process

---

[1] Buranen, Lise and Alice M. Roy, eds. *Perspectives on Plagiarism and Intellectual Property in a Postmodern World* (Albany, NY: State University of New York Press, 1999) p. xviii.

creates an 'electronic fingerprint' for each paper and uses key words to search millions of Internet documents. The result is a color-coded report identifying any sources and underlining identical language...[that] highlights properly quoted and cited material as well as undocumented borrowing."[2]

QUESTIONS

1. Is there anything wrong with selling "models" of good research papers? Is that any different than making "model student papers" available in a school library? Is there any difference between seeking help on a paper from a friend who is also a student or from a relative who is a teacher or lawyer, for example? Seeking help from a tutor at the College Writing Center or an online service like **noCheaters.com**? What values are at stake in each case?

2. The Center for Academic Integrity, affiliated with the Kenan Ethics Program at Duke University, is a consortium of 200 colleges and universities established in 1992 to identify and affirm the values of academic integrity and to promote their achievement in practice. Visit them at **http://www.academicintegrity.org**. What guidelines for affirming the values of academic integrity do you find?

3. Go to your own school's homepage. Can you find any policies or guidelines on academic honesty? What are they? If not available online, where can you find them?

Lise Buranen, who teaches Composition and English as a Second Language [ESL], argues that plagiarism is a complex, cross-cultural issue. This selection begins with an excerpt in which Buranen talks of trying to track down what may be an FOAF story—friend of a friend—about culturally diverse approaches to what Americans call plagiarism.

"But I Wasn't Cheating": Plagiarism and Cross Cultural Mythology[3]

Lise Buranen

No one I talked to had heard directly from an Asian student that his copying from the text was a form of respect for the received wisdom of his ancestors or from the Middle-Eastern student that her family was only trying to help her gradu-

[2] Wilson, Jeanne, "Hi-Tech Plagiarism—New twist on a Perennial Problem," in *Acumen: A Quarterly Newsletter for Faculty,* 1:3, distributed by Follett Higher Education Group.

[3] Lise Buranen, "'But I Wasn't Cheating': Plagiarism and Cross Cultural Mythology," in Buranen, Lise and Alice M. Roy, eds. *Perspectives on Plagiarism and Intellectual Property in a Postmodern World* (Albany, NY: State University of New York Press, 1999), p. 63.

ate, but many seemed to have a "friend of a friend" who had.

To further investigate the issue, in addition to holding informal discussions with colleagues on the subject, I asked students in one ESL class to write short essays about what they had been taught by their parents and teachers in their own country about copying or using other people's words or ideas...about their own definitions of plagiarism, their experiences with it, and their attitudes toward it....

The results of my inquiries surprised me....[A majority of the respondents to a question about attitudes toward plagiarism] were almost unanimous in their belief that there was no basic difference between what they had been taught in their home country and in this country—on this issue, it seems, they are in agreement with...assumptions that plagiarism was unequivocally bad and wrong, and that people who engage in it are to be either censured or pitied. This was true regardless of the student's country of origin, and at least twenty different countries on five continents were represented....

[But Buranen also heard from a colleague in the English Department who is originally from China. His colleague had worked as a translator before coming to the U. S. for his doctorate in English:]

I described to him what I had heard about Asians' belief that the use of other sources is a sign of respect for the received wisdom and the knowledge of others, and he agreed that that characterization made sense: being able to quote or cite the work of "the masters" is a way of demonstrating one's own learning or accomplishment. One need not formally document such references in footnotes and bibliographies, because the assumption is that any knowledgeable reader or audience knows the source. Thus, since the "acknowledgement" of the source is the very use of it, listing them in a bibliography is at best redundant and at worst an insult to a reader's intelligence. My colleague sees a distinction between the Western "scientific model" of discourse often used in this country, in which the emphasis is on proving a position by giving a great deal of documented evidence, as opposed to a more subtle kind of persuasion used by the Chinese, perhaps best described as philosophical or even literary rather than scientific. But there is still a "moral issue" at stake in both cultures, despite the differences in emphasis, because, he feels, the assumptions that underlie the use of that received wisdom are not so different from ours. One still credits one's sources, but what is different is the form in which the "credit" is given, whether explicit or implied. According to my colleague, however, this tradition has been changing over the past twenty or thirty years, and the Chinese are moving to a more Westernized method of citation and bibliography, in part because of the global shrinkage taking place.

What may be a more likely explanation for these students' "plagiarizing" in the first place is our propensity for insisting on a rigid and often uninformed kind of grammatical correctness, our lack of tolerance for the kinds of errors native speakers simply do not make, even though such "errors" (misplaced articles and prepositions, novel syntax, missed idioms) do not necessarily interfere with our comprehension of the writer's message and meaning. At worst, there may even be an element of self-righteousness and indignation at someone's ruining "our" language. Or it may be that such myths originated with well-intentioned ESL teachers (we are notoriously well-intentioned) to protect their/our students from prosecution for unknowingly breaking the rules....

Because our classrooms are becoming more and more multicultural...and because of changes in pedagogy that emphasize greater collaboration among students and possibly tutors and that often employ portfolios as a means of evaluation, questions about plagiarism have become not only more numerous but more immediate and more complex. It seems that we have always oversimplified to all students, not just ESL students, what is meant by plagiarism, and thus we have misrepresented it, if unintentionally, even while we ourselves engage in perfectly legitimate writing behaviors that undertaken by students would be denounced as plagiarism....

QUESTIONS

1. Is it always unethical to claim another's work as your own? Use the utilitarian and deontological models to explain your answer. What is the ethical distinction between handing in a paper that consists of all copied material, mostly copied material, or including only a few "cut and pasted" paragraphs in a paper that is mostly your own work?

2. Faculty members do not always cite the sources for their lecture material or give written credit for the information they use in handouts or other course materials. They often borrow materials, ideas, and exam questions from colleagues, handbooks, and journal articles without telling their students. Are any of these actions unethical? How do they compare to a student's failure to cite her sources in a paper?

3. Some students explain cheating by claiming the system is unfair, the assignments unclear, and the teacher inept. Are these excuses that carry ethical weight—or are they empty? Why/why not?

4. How would you feel if your teacher asked you to submit your papers to **Turnitin.com** for a check?

In the next reading, Stuart P. Green, Professor of Law at Louisiana State University, looks at what he calls the "norm of attribution" and the idea of plagiarism as theft. As you read it, ask yourself: What is stolen by the plagiarist?

Plagiarism, Norms, and the Limits of Theft Law[4]

Stuart P. Green

In September 1990, the poet Neal Bowers published a poem in the journal *Poetry,* entitled "Tenth-Year Elegy." It began like this:

> *Careless man, my father, always leaving me at rest-stops, coffee shops, some wide spot in the road. I come out, rubbing my hands on my pants or levitating two foam cups of coffee, and can't find him anywhere, those banged-up fenders gone.*

A year later, a man named David Sumner published a poem in the *Mankato Poetry Review,* entitled "Someone Forgotten." Sumner's poem began like this:

> *He is too heavy and careless, my father, always leaving me at rest-stops, coffee shops, some wide spot in the road. I come out, rubbing my hands on my pants or levitating two foam cups of coffee, and I can't find him anywhere, that beat-up Ford gone.*

Sumner, of course, had copied Bowers's poem—line for line, practically word for word—and published it under his own name (actually, his own pseudonym), with a different title. In a fascinating and eloquent memoir, entitled *Words for the Taking,* Bowers describes his reaction to discovering Sumner's "crime" and his quest for retribution. "I was convinced," Bowers says, that "something had to be done to rectify my...situation, though I wasn't sure what that something was. I spent languid afternoons at home, when I should have been writing poems, fantasizing about how my thief would react if he opened his door and found me there, with accusations and evidence."

Like many writers on plagiarism, Bowers characterizes the "offense" that has been committed in the language of criminal law. Again and again, plagiarists are referred to as "thieves" or "criminals," and plagiarism as a "crime," "stealing," "robbery," "piracy," or "larceny." Even some dictionaries define plagiarism as "literary theft"—a definition that is consistent with the term's etymological origin, the Latin word *plagium* (which, at Roman law, referred to the stealing of a slave or child).

Yet, despite such talk, the fact is that no plagiarist has ever been prosecuted for theft....

Plagiarism has been variously defined as the act of "steal[ing] and pass[ing] off (the ideas or words of another) as one's own," "us[ing] (another's created

Plagiarism is upsetting because it is personal.
—Debora Halbert

---

[4] Stuart P. Green, "Plagiarism, Norms, and the Limits of Theft Law: Some Observations on the Use of Criminal Sanctions in Enforcing Intellectual Property Rights," 54 *Hastings Law Journal* 167 (2002).

production) without crediting the source," or "present[ing] as new and original an idea or product derived from an existing source...."

In minor cases, plagiarism can involve the copying of even a small number of words or ideas without citation to their real author. In the most serious cases, a significant portion of an entire work (a poem, story, article, or book) is presented, without attribution, as if it were the plagiarist's own.

The concept of plagiarism is embedded within the context of a complex set of social norms. To see how this set of norms functions, we begin with the proposition that people generally value the esteem of others, particularly their peers. Among the ways one can earn the esteem of one's peers is by being recognized for one's originality, creativity, insight, knowledge, and technical skill. This is particularly so among writers, artists, and scholars, who, in addition to achieving satisfaction through the creative act itself, usually wish to see those acts recognized by others.

This desire for esteem produces a norm that I shall refer to as the "norm of attribution." According to this norm, words and ideas may be copied if and only if the copier attributes them to their originator or author. This norm leads to a form of social cooperation with obvious benefits. It maximizes the author's chances of achieving esteem by providing, at relatively low cost to author, copier, and society generally, opportunities for both wide dissemination of, and credit for, the author's words and ideas,

without which there would be fewer incentives to create new work....

For most people within the relevant community, the attribution norm becomes internalized. Such people view attribution as being, or closely akin to being, a moral obligation, rather like showing respect to one's elders. People who have internalized the norm of attribution would regard credit earned for someone else's work as illegitimate. Indeed, such people can achieve satisfaction only if they know that the work they are being recognized for is in fact their own.

The problem is potential cheaters—those who fail to internalize the norm....

...[F]ew, if any, artists or writers or scholars always achieve originality. None of us wholly invents the stories we tell, the metaphors we use, or the arguments we espouse. We all work within a cultural tradition, and, to some degree, we all absorb those cultural traditions by copying....Many influences are unconscious. An idea, phrase, argument, melody, or insight read or heard long ago can lodge in the unconscious. Writers with an unusually retentive mind, such as those with a photographic memory, are particularly at risk of failing to attribute.

Moreover, if one were to attempt to attribute each and every source of one's ideas, one's work would likely suffer. Excessive concern with one's sources can thwart the creative process and lead to pedantry.... Indeed, it may at times seem pointless to use new language to describe a fact or phenomenon that has become part of our common culture....

Notwithstanding these complications, however, it seems obvious that there is a legitimate distinction to be made between mere influence, unconscious imitation, and inadvertent failure to attribute (on the one hand), and extensive copying that is intended to convey the impression that the copier is the original author (on the other). However forgiving we may be of the student who, as a result of sloppy note taking, neglects to put quotation marks around a sentence copied from one of his sources, most of us would not hesitate to condemn David Sumner, the plagiarist who submitted Neal Bowers's poems under his own name....

...If theft requires intent, and plagiarism derives much of its meaning from theft law, it seems to follow that plagiarism should also require intent. At the same time, I would modify this requirement to say that the element of intent can be satisfied by "deliberate indifference" to the obligation to attribute. That is, if the reason a person was unaware that he was copying or failing to attribute is that he was deliberately indifferent to the requirements of attribution, he should be viewed as having committed plagiarism.

Consider the recent cases involving the noted historian...Doris Kearns Goodwin...accused of copying up to fifty improperly attributed passages from the work of Lynne McTaggart, in her book *The Fitzgeralds and the Kennedys*....

[I]t seems hard to imagine how a writer could have included as many as fifty improperly attributed passages in a single book without being deliberately indifferent to the rules of attribution. Accordingly, we might say...[that] Goodwin possessed the "knowledge" necessary to commit plagiarism because [she was]..."aware of a high probability" that [her] sources had been inadequately acknowledged.

...[W]e need to consider those circumstances in which a person accused of plagiarism argues that he was unaware of the requirement of attribution itself. For example, I recently sat on a university disciplinary committee before which the respondent, a foreign graduate student, argued that he was unaware of the obligation to use footnotes and quotation marks. This kind of mistake is analogous to what the criminal law refers to as a "mistake (or ignorance) of the law."...According to the common law maxim *ignorantia legis neminem excusat* (ignorance of the law excuses no one), a defendant who was either unaware of the existence of a statute proscribing her conduct or who mistakenly concluded that the relevant statute did not reach her conduct has no defense, except in certain narrow circumstances....

An analogous rule should apply in the context of plagiarism. A writer who fails to give credit to his sources as a result of ignorance or mistake about the rules of attribution should be regarded as having no defense. Allowing a plagiarist to argue that he was unfamiliar with the rules of attribution themselves would seem to encourage ignorance of such rules and lead to confusion and uncertainty in the community generally, just as ignorance of the law is said to do in the broader context. On the other hand, a writer who fails to credit his sources as a result of a reasonable mistake of fact about the provenance of such words should not be regarded as a plagiarist. Indeed, to treat such cases as plagiarism might well create a chilling effect, by causing would-be writers to be hyper-cautious and pedantic in their scholarly practices, or worse, refrain from producing creative works altogether.

[Green cites studies and anecdotal evidence that the incidence of plagiarism—from copying phrases without attribution to buying entire term papers—is on the rise, and suggests why this should be so.]

...One reason is simply that copying is easier than ever to do, owing to widespread access to computer technologies (including, of course, the Internet and "cut and paste" features of word processing programs). Amazing as it seems, there are said to be more than six hundred Internet businesses specifically designed for students who are looking for sources to copy. Somewhat more difficult to document are apparently changing attitudes about what constitutes academic and authorial integrity. Of particular interest here is the effect of attitudes towards the misappropriation of intellectual property. Many students apparently believe that because a text appears on the Internet, it is somehow in the "public domain," and therefore need not be attributed. Moreover...the fact that many people believe there is nothing wrong with pirating computer software or MP3 files may make them less inclined to believe that plagiarism itself is morally wrong.

[Green suggests the idea that there are gradations of plagiarizing.]

How might the Internet be leading to more plagiarism?

...There is, of course, a significant normative difference between passing off as one's own an entire short story, poem, or scholarly article, and failing to attribute an occasional phrase or sentence in an otherwise original book. Copying another's words verbatim, moreover, may be more objectionable than merely paraphrasing them....[P]lagiarism involving best-selling historians and novelists, for example, is more likely to elicit attention than plagiarism committed by unknowns.

The identity of the community within which the plagiarism occurs is also significant. The scientific community, for example, tends to have little tolerance for those who plagiarize, as can be seen in the case of Yale researcher Vijay Soman, who was forced to resign after it was discovered that he had plagiarized a mere sixty words in a medical paper. Historians who plagiarize also tend to be dealt with harshly. Doris Kearns Goodwin has been vilified by her peers and in the media, forced to withdraw as a Pulitzer Prize judge, dismissed from her regular stint on PBS's *News Hour With Jim Lehrer*, disinvited from various college speaking engagements, and subject to pressure that she be removed from the Harvard Board of Overseers....

The dynamics of journalism also differ from the sciences. Multiple journalists cover the same stories, often on a short deadline, relying on a limited number of similar sources. Originality just isn't that important. Under the circumstances, it is almost inevitable (and perhaps even forgivable) that some journalists engage in unattributed duplication of words and ideas.

QUESTIONS

1. What ethical analysis would lend support to the idea of sanctioning some forms of plagiarism more severely than others?

2. Use stakeholder analysis to compare and contrast the ethics of each of the following from utilitarian and deontological perspectives: (a) A rock star who publishes a book under his own name, without crediting the ghostwriter; (b) a politician who gives a speech in which she quotes from her own previous talks or writings, without mentioning that the content is not new; (c) a student who submits a paper written—but freely shared—by a fraternity brother who graduated two years ago.

3. Green argues that the norm of attribution is reinforced by what he calls an "informal reputational stigma." In other words, people don't want to plagiarize because they don't want to be called a plagiarist. In what other ways does society deal with this form of cheating?

4. Elsewhere in the article from which this reading is taken, Green concludes that plagiarism involves the kind of theft that could potentially be prosecuted under criminal laws. Articulate the similarities and differences between the theft of something like money and the theft of original expression that is plagiarism. Does a plagiarist deserve criminal punishment the way an embezzler would?

5. Consider the various stakeholders in the Sumner-Bowers scenario with which Green opens this article. Exactly what harms does plagiarism cause, and who are its victims? Would it make any difference if Sumner had been: (a) A junior faculty member seeking tenure? (b) A promising college student seeking admission to graduate school? (c) A high-school dropout who is a single parent, struggling to support her family and dreaming of being a poet?

6. In Spring 2003, a well-known, prize-winning investigative reporter for the New York Times was found to have allowed an article to be published under his byline which mainly consisted of facts and quotes gathered by one of his young assistants. Is this the kind of product that Green might view as "almost inevitable" in journalism? What can you find about this incident? Was the reporter's behavior within acceptable limits of journalistic ethics?

7. Green suggests several reasons why students cheat. Do you agree with his explanations for why plagiarizing is so prevalent in schools? Can you think of any additional reasons? How might educators effectively reverse this tide?

As we learned in chapter 1, intellectual property laws are designed to balance the interests of the public and the creators of original work. Authors and inventors gain the exclusive rights to make use of their work for a limited period of time, after which it becomes available to the public. But, as the next reading suggests, it is not always easy to identify the person or persons who should be credited as author or inventor. Rochelle Dreyfuss, an expert in intellectual property, believes that copyright and patent law should be rewritten to create a new category of "collaborative work." In the following selection she explores some of the ethical and practical conflicts created by collaborative research.

Collaborative Research: Conflicts on Authorship, Ownership, and Accountability[5]

Rochelle Cooper Dreyfuss

The artist, starving in a garret; the dedicated scientist, experimenting in a garage; the reclusive professor, burning midnight oil in the office—these are becoming endangered species. The creative industries have evolved: collaborative production is replacing individual effort. Works of the new order are exemplified by the likes of NewStand, the television news magazine produced by teaming the cable station CNN with Time Magazine; by Rent, a play created by Jonathan Larson with the help of the dramaturg, Lynn Thomson; by "distance learning" initiatives at many universities, and most especially, by the multi-authored articles now common in scientific journals.

The reasons for this evolution are manifold. In large part, it is a consequence of intellectual limitations. In many fields—biotechnology is one example—the intensity of specialization makes it nearly impossible for any one researcher to know enough to work alone; interdisciplinary investigation is essential if the frontiers of knowledge are to be pushed forward. The globalization of the marketplace has also had an influence, for in that environment, multinational input is needed to produce goods that appeal across a broad range of cultures. Advances in the tools of creativity account for yet another part of the change. Most obviously, the growth of the Internet has made long distance collaborations much easier. More subtly, the Web, when coupled with advances in scanning and digitizing technologies, has created new artistic forms, such as chain novels and chain art—what might be called sequential collaboration. One author puts a story on a Web site, intending that others will add new plotlines and characters; an artist uploads an image, expecting it to be repeatedly downloaded, manipulated, and uploaded. There is also an economic factor. As the costs of making even marginal advances surge, firms

---

[5] Reprinted from Rochelle C. Dreyfuss, "Collaborative Research: Conflicts on Authorship, Ownership, and Accountability," 53 *Van.L.Rev.* 116 (2000).

find that hiring needed expertise on a permanent basis is not as cost effective as entering into transient associations. In academia, where the push toward collaboration is especially notable, the rise in costs has been accompanied by a steady decline in public financing, leading both faculty members and university administrators to search hard for new sources of support. In fields where theory and application converge, these have become easy to find, and they have led to close relationships between commercial entities and faculty working in such disciplines as medicine, chemistry, and computer science. Finally, intellectual property law has, in recent years, expanded to cover an array of creative efforts that were previously largely ignored or considered ineligible for protection. With that move, there is work that once appeared to be individually developed, which must now be viewed as multi-authored.

[Next Dreyfuss uses two disputes between scientists to illustrate the "uncertainty problem." In a typical business transaction, parties can anticipate recurring problems such as delays or fluctuating prices and allocate risks accordingly. But, she says, "Unpredictability is an inherent feature of innovation." Researchers cannot be certain that their work will pay off, nor predict what information or products will result or whose contributions will be most important. So, there is no basis for fair allocation of rights.]

[Robert Gallo of the National Cancer Institute and Luc Montagnier of the Pasteur Institute in France] did little more than exchange virus samples—not an uncommon form of collaboration in science. In this instance, however, their work led to the identification of the AIDS virus, opening the door to the development of a diagnostic test and a vaccine. The parties had not anticipated this outcome—indeed, the jointness of their discovery may have been the result of inadvertent cross contamination. But however the problem arose, the resulting dispute over credit and patent rights drew in their institutions as well as other scientists. The controversy took a long time to resolve. During the time it was pending, research was delayed and goodwill between important organizations was compromised....

[M]atters are further complicated by the fact that collaborators in the creative sector are often working with different metrics. For example, many academic collaborators consider early publication to be the central concern. Their commercial partners may feel differently. They may see publication as compromising patent rights, disclosing trade secrets, or creating evidence that could be used against them in tort cases....

[Next, Dreyfuss looks at ways that institutions connected to inventors have tried to anticipate and prevent some of the problems created by collaborative research. Professional journals have tightened the rules for identifying the "authors" of published studies to assure that everyone named as an author can vouch for the work. Universities are more concerned with financial issues.]

[D]eclines in public funding have turned universities inward, to the exploitation of innovations made on campus and with university resources.... [Most new university policies] have been in the direction of increasing university control. As to patents, many universities now require faculty (as a condition of employment) and students (as a condition to enrollment) to assign all rights to inventions made with substantial university resources. In exchange, the schools agree to take administrative control (applying for patents, negotiating licensing agreements) and to share royalties with the inventors (and in some cases, with the departments in which the work took place). It is also becoming more common for universities to claim ownership in raw materials, and to use that control to assure access....

[What do you think: Is it ethical for universities to claim ownership of materials created by faculty and students? Should inventions that can be patented, such as genetically altered mice or wheat, be considered similar to a computer program or distance-learning course outline that can be copyrighted?]

Similar developments are occurring with respect to copyrights. At one time, universities largely ignored copyrights, probably because scholarship rarely paid off in a financial way. The output of computer science departments led to a change in outlook and the advent of the Internet, which allows universities to package and distribute teaching materials as "distance learning," further enhances their interest. Accordingly, as universities revise their policies on patents, they now also consider copyrights. A few treat copyrights just like patents: they consider the faculty (or student) author as

the legal author. However, they then require an assignment of rights in any work made with substantial university resources. In exchange, the university agrees to handle administrative matters and to share royalties with the creators.

Some institutions are...setting up separate, for-profit entities (for example, for distance learning materials) and then hiring their faculty and students as the employees of these entities [so that schools can claim copyright of work produced for these entities].

Nonpecuniary matters have received some attention as well, especially in regard to graduate students, the most vulnerable of all academicians. Thus, some schools now require appropriate acknowledgment of students' intellectual contributions. The American Association of University Professors has, for example, included the following in its Statement on Professional Ethics:

> [Professors] respect the confidential nature of the relationship between professor and student. They avoid any exploitation, harassment, or discriminatory treatment of students. They acknowledge significant academic or scholarly assistance from them.

Finally, a special word should be said about graduate students. Although this is largely speculation, it may be that one reason there are now so many disputes about authorship is that important changes have occurred in the mentoring relationship. Thus, while there has always been something of a tradition to ignore student input into faculty research, that tradition was once accompanied by the equally strong custom of advisors placing their graduate students in jobs. When job markets in academia shrank, that sense of responsibility for students' careers declined. But, unfortunately, the tradition of failing to acknowledge student input survived. Since students now need to find positions on their own, they need to receive formal credit for their work. Academics and administrators should therefore be particularly scrupulous about remembering student input when patent applications are filed and papers are published; courts should be equally careful to consider whether students have been treated appropriately....

QUESTIONS

1. Some have suggested that the scientific community should develop new categories of authorship to acknowledge diverse contributions to the finished product, much as a movie credits the actors, director, best boy, etc. What do you see as the pros and cons of this idea? Which problems of collaborative work would it solve? Which would be left unsolved?

2. Research universities generally have policies on fair treatment of student researchers. Find out what guidelines your school uses. Do they apply to both academic research and faculty use of students in commercial enterprises? Do they address university ownership of inventions generated entirely by students? Do they seem fair to all parties?

3. Some universities have rules against full-time faculty holding second jobs; many require faculty who do grant-supported research to pay a portion of their grants to the college as "overhead costs." If Ivy League University writes such rules into its contract with a well-known and well-paid professor, should that professor be able to sell her course notes to a new, for-profit "online university?" Is it ethical for Ivy League University to restrict its faculty from earning additional money? Is it ethical for the professor to sell her notes? For the online school to attempt to buy them?

Plagiarism, Copyright, and Authorship

One of the privileges of a copyright owner is the right to allow—or not allow—others to reproduce one's work and to charge for such permission ("license") if she chooses. However, as we learned in chapter 1, the fair use doctrine allows limited use of copyrighted work even without permission. "Fair use," as it is known, allows a teacher to copy an article out of the morning newspaper to distribute to his class, or a scholar to make a single copy of an article for her own use. The following reading addresses an increasingly common situation: faculty Web sites. The article from which it is excerpted is based on a presentation at Temple University given by the author, Jane Ginsburg, Professor of Literary and Artistic Property Law at Columbia University School of Law.

Stolen Content: Avoiding Trouble on the Internet[6]

Jane C. Ginsburg

Consider the following scenario:

Professor Donna Prima, of the Basilica College English Department, teaches a course in popular culture. Her reading list includes magazines, articles, excerpts from books, film clips, recorded music, and cartoons. She has made all of the "readings" available through her Web site. It has not occurred to her to request permission from the authors or publishers to do so. Because Professor Donna Prima believes fervently in academic freedom and open communication, she has not restricted access to her course Web page to students enrolled in the course, or even to those enrolled at Basilica College. Because Professor Prima is Web-adept (or has hired student teaching assistants who are Web-adept), her course Web page has lots of bells and whistles. It includes a cartoon of the week, scanned from sources such as the *New Yorker* and the Sunday comics, and a song of the week downloaded from a variety of sites (not all of them authorized)....The Web page also has a chatroom that allows students and others to comment on the classes and the "readings." Sometimes participants post excerpts from other works as part of the online discussions. Not surprisingly, Professor Prima's Web page has developed quite a following in and outside Basilica College; the Web page's counter shows thousands of "hits" at the site. Basilica College Dean Willard Worried has become concerned that Professor Prima's site may pose copyright problems. He wonders what, short of shutting the site down (which would spark tremendous resentment), he can do to minimize the risk of liability to the college.

Dean Worried is right, at least in part, to feel uneasy. While some of Professor Prima's postings may well be permissible under a reasonable interpretation of the fair use doctrine, other features of her Web site compel an interpretation so aggressive as to be unconvincing. To evaluate this site, we need to analyze both its content and its audience. When we discuss content, we must distinguish the posted "readings" from the cartoon and song of the week, as well as from material that the chatroom participants post.

First, the "reading list": Professor Prima has taken the college "course pack" a step or two further. Rather than create a printed anthology by photocopying excerpts from books and other sources, she has put everything on her

---

[6] Jane C. Ginsburg, "Stolen Content: Avoiding Trouble on the Internet," *ACADEME* Jan-Feb 2001, p.49.

Web site, making it available for end-user downloading (and possible printing out). If Professor Prima had given a course-pack order to Kinko's or a similar off-campus copy shop, it would be clear… that the shop would need to obtain permission from the authors or other copyright owners in order to engage in the photocopying.…

But, Professor Prima might object, what she is doing is not like taking Kinko's operations in house, since she has not become photocopy central for Basilica College. What she does, she would argue, is more like putting books on library reserve, anticipating that students will individually photocopy the reading assignments. This argument assumes, of course, that end-user students photocopying would be fair use. But what may be fair in isolation becomes more troublesome when it is done cumulatively. In the context of Web sites, moreover, there is the matter of posting a copy on the Web site, from which students make more copies. In the context of library reserve, the library has lawfully acquired the copy or copies it puts on reserve. But Professor Prima assembled her Web "reading list" by making unauthorized copies—copies that are not for private research but for further dissemination, indeed, for dissemination beyond her course and even her college.

ACCESS AND PURPOSE

This fact brings us to another problem: the scope of access to Professor Prima's Web page. Claims of educational fair use become substantially attenuated if access to the Web site is not limited to students enrolled in the course for which the readings have been posted. Unrestricted access in effect competes with sales or licensing of the works for all purposes; moreover, it is not necessary to the pedagogical purposes of the particular course.…Since the fair use doctrine inquires into the necessity for making a copy, unnecessary copying or dissemination is a strike against the activity.

The need to rely on duplication is another way in which a Web page may differ from photocopies and course-pack anthologies. If the works on Professor Prima's reading list are already available on freely accessible Web sites, she may not need to copy them onto hers. She can simply link from her site to the Web page with the work.…

[For some] kinds of work, however, Web availability may be deceptive. That is, the work may be downloadable, but not necessarily with the author's or the copyright owner's permission [see chapter 1].…So it is not safe for Professor Prima to conclude "if it's out there, it can be in here, on my Web page."…

Under *NAPSTER*, [T]he song-of-the-week soundtrack is a dubious addition to her Web site.

Another reason the song of the week and, by the same token, the cartoon of the week are questionable accouterments to the Web site, is their slim relation to the pedagogical purpose of the site. Works on the reading list at least are subject to scrutiny and analysis in class, in the chatroom, and perhaps in student papers. The song and cartoon of the week seem to be purely decorative. They may make the Web site more appealing or amusing, but they are not the stuff of scholarly inquiry (unless Professor Prima modifies her page to direct discussions toward the weekly additions). The courts have frequently emphasized that the fair use doctrine excuses "productive" or "transformative" copying in which subsequent authors build from the copied material to create something new. But copying simply to add "zest" to a work, to make it more popular by appropriating some of the first author's appeal, is not what fair use is about. So the zestful song and cartoon of the week seem to be features Professor Prima would do better without.

INSTITUTIONAL LIABILITY

So far, we have been addressing whether Professor Prima may be a copyright infringer. What about her employer, Basilica College? Under normal principles, called *respondeat superior* in lawyers' Latin, the employer is liable for the wrongful acts committed by its employees in furtherance of their employment....

Since the end of 1998, however, universities can breathe a little easier, at least with respect to professorial copyright infringement by way of Web sites that the university hosts....[Under the Digital Millennium Copyright Act of 1998] universities that comply with the requirements of the Online Services Provider Liability Limitation Act will benefit from a significant reduction in liability. These requirements include obligations to post contact information for sending notices of alleged copyright infringements to the university, and, once proper notice is received, to disable access to the allegedly infringing content that resides on the university's server. (The process is called "notice-and-take-down.") That means, for example, that if the copyright owners of [the song of the week] allege that Professor Prima's posting of the sound recording to her Web site is infringing, Basilica College will not be liable for damages if it takes the work down, or blocks access to the site.

But the Online Service Provider Liability Limitation Act does not insulate universities for all postings made by their personnel....Suppose, for example, that among the materials posted to Professor Prima's Web site is the screenplay of the classic aquatic horror movie, *It Came from the Titanic*. If the screenplay is recommended or required reading for her course, and if she posted it without authorization (and if that posting is infringing), then Basilica College will be fully liable in damages to the screenplay's author for the professor's unauthorized posting. [This would also be true] if she posts the screenplay this year without assigning it, but had in the past three years included the screenplay on the required or recommended reading list....The purpose of the prohibition is clear: to avoid the competition that availability of the book on the course Web page would pose to sale of the work (or licensing of photocopies or downloads) to enrolled students.

PERMISSION

So what can Donna Prima or Willard Worried do to avoid liability to the copyright owners of the works Donna

Prima wants to post? First she can (and should) ask permission to post the material....[C]opyright owners, particularly authors, might be willing to allow a colleague to post a work in progress for discussion by enrolled students, but would deny permission to make unrestricted disclosure of the work. Thus, despite Donna Prima's desire to keep her Web page open to the world, she may need to modify it to password protect or otherwise limit access to some of the materials on it. What if the copyright owner is willing to allow posting but wants to be paid? If the posting would exceed fair use limits, even for a restricted site, then a license should be acquired, or the posting forgone. For many materials, permission and licenses can be secured through the Copyright Clearance Center....

For copyright permissions see http://www.copyright.com

QUESTIONS

1. Assume that Donna Prima taught at a school whose dean was less vigilant. If no one at her school questions her, is it ethical for her to continue to create her Web site without permission?

2. Assume a newly hired professor spends his summer preparing a set of PowerPoint™ presentations to accompany his class lectures. Is it ethical for a student to take copious notes of the lectures and share them with classmates? Sell them to classmates? Sell them to a company called "BetterNotes" to be copied and re-sold? How would your analysis differ if the professor linked an in-class presentation prepared on Microsoft PowerPoint™ to his own Web site? Posted them on a Web site created especially for his class?

3. Suppose that the professor does not get tenure—or leaves for a better job. Would it be ethical for the university to demand he leave his notes behind for the teacher who replaces him? To retain the Web site with its links to his computer presentation? To take the presentation and sell it as a "course outline" for a profit?

DISTANCE LEARNING

As more people seek higher education and costs continue to increase, some educators are investigating the "free market model of virtual education"[7] to solve the problem of shrinking resources. Yet, some would argue, technology is more than an efficient new

---

[7] Moran, Rachel F. See excerpt from her article, "Diversity, Distance and the Delivery of Higher Education," later in this chapter.

tool for educators; it can change the very meaning of learning and education. In the readings that follow, we explore a range of perspectives on the 21st-century version of distance learning.

Perseus Unbound[8]

Sven Birkerts

To arrive at the edge of the world's knowledge, seek out the most complex and sophisticated minds, put them in a room together and have them ask each other the questions they are asking themselves.
http://www.edge.org

Like it or not, interactive video technologies have muscled their way into the formerly textbound precincts of education....

[M]ore than any other development in recent memory, these interactive technologies throw into relief the fundamental questions about knowledge and learning. Not only what are its ends, but what are its means? And how might the means be changing the ends.

From the threshold, I think, we need to distinguish between kinds of knowledge and kinds of study. Pertinent here is German philosopher Wilhelm Dilthey's distinction between the natural sciences (*Naturwissenschaften*), which seek to explain physical events by subsuming them under causal laws, and the so-called sciences of culture (*Geisteswissenschaften*), which can only understand events in terms of the intentions and meanings that individuals attach to them.

To the former, it would seem, belong the areas of study more hospitable to the new video and computer procedures. Expanded databases and interactive programs can be viewed as tools, pure and simple. They give access to more information, foster cross-referentiality, and by

reducing time and labor allow for greater focus on the essentials of a problem. Indeed, any discipline where knowledge is sought for its application rather than for itself could only profit from the implementation of these technologies. To the natural sciences one might add the fields of language study and law.

But there is a danger with these sexy new options—and the rapture with which believers speak warrants the adjective—that we simply assume that their uses and potentials extend across the educational spectrum into realms where different kinds of knowledge, and hence learning, are at issue....

In the humanities, knowledge is a means, yes, but it is a means less to instrumental application than to something more nebulous: understanding. We study history or literature or classics in order to comprehend and refine a narrative, or a set of narratives about what the human world used to be like, about how the world came to be as it is, and about what we have been—and are—like as psychological or spiritual creatures. The data—the facts, connections, the texts themselves—matter insofar as they help us to deepen and extend that narrative. In these disci-

---

[8] From, Birkerts, Sven, *The Gutenberg Elegies: The Fate of Reading in an Electronic Age* (New York, NY: Farrar, Straus and Giroux, 1998).

plines the process of study may be as vital to the understanding as are the materials studied....

[I]t is easy to imagine that in the near future a whole range of innovative electronic-based learning packages will be available and, in many places, in use. These will surely include the manifold variations on the electronic book. Special new software texts are already being developed to bring us into the world of, say, Shakespeare, not only glossing the literature, but bathing the user in multimedia supplements. The would-be historian will step into an environment rich in choices, be they visual detailing, explanatory graphs, or suggested connections and sideroads. And so on. Moreover, once the price is right, who will be the curmudgeons who would deny their students access to the state-of-the-art?

Being a curmudgeon is a dirty job, but somebody has to do it. Someone has to hoist the warning flags and raise some issues that the fast-track proselytizers might overlook. Here are a few reservations worth pondering:

1. Knowledge, certainly in the humanities, is not a straightforward matter of access, of conquest via the ingestion of data. Part of any essential understanding of the world is that it is opaque, obdurate. To me, Wittgenstein's famous axiom, "The world is everything that is the case," translates into a recognition of otherness. The past is as much about the disappearance of things through time as it is about recovery of traces and the reconstruction of vistas. Say what you will about books, they not only mark the backward trail, but they also encode this sense of obstacle, of otherness....Old-style textual research may feel like an unnecessarily slow burrowing, but it is itself an instruction: it confirms that time is a force as implacable as gravity.

Yet the multimedia packages would master this gravity. For opacity they substitute transparency, promote the illusion of access. All that has been said, known, and done will yield to the dance of the fingertips on the terminal keys. Space becomes hyperspace, and time, hypertime....One gathers the data of otherness, but through a medium which seems to level the feel—the truth—of that otherness....And if our media restructure our perceptions, as McLuhan and others have argued, then we may start producing generations who know a great deal of "information" about the past but who have no purchase on pastness itself....

2. Humanistic knowledge ultimately seeks to fashion a comprehensible narrative. It is, in other words about the creation and expansion of meaningful contexts. Interactive media technologies are, at least in one sense, anticontextual. They open the field to new widths, constantly expanding relevance and reference, and they equip their user with a powerful grazing tool. One moves at great rates across subject terrains, crossing borders that were once closely guarded. The multimedia approach tends ineluctably to multidisciplinarianism. The positive effect, of course, is the creation of new levels of connection and integration; more and more variables are brought into the equation. But the danger should be

obvious: The horizon, the limit that gave definition to the parts of the narrative, will disappear. The equation itself will become nonsensical through the accumulation of variables. The context will widen until it becomes, in effect, everything....The technology may be able to handle it, but will the user? Will our narratives—historical, literary, classical—be able to withstand the data explosion? If they cannot, then what will be the new face of understanding? Or will the knowledge of the world become, perforce, a map as large and intricate as the world itself?

3. We might question, too, whether there is not in learning as in physical science a principle of energy conservation. Does a gain in one area depend upon a loss in another? My guess would be that every lateral attainment is purchased with a sacrifice of depth. The student may, through a program on Shakespeare, learn an immense amount about Elizabethan politics, the construction of the Globe theater, the origins of certain plays in the writing of Plutarch, the etymology of key terms and so on, but will this dazzled student find the concentration, the will to live with the often burred and prickly language of the plays themselves? The play's the thing—but will it be? Wouldn't the sustained exposure to a souped-up cognitive collage not begin to affect the attention span, the ability if not the willingness to sit with one text for extended periods, butting up against its cruxes, trying to excavate meaning from the original rhythms and syntax? The gurus of interaction love to say that the student learns best by doing, but let's not forget that reading is also a kind of doing.

4. As a final reservation, what about the long-term cognitive effects of these new processes of data absorption? Isn't it possible that more may be less, and that the neural networks have one speed for taking in—a speed that can be increased—and quite another rate for retention? Again, it may be that our technologies will exceed us. They will make it not only possible but irresistible to consume data at what must strike people of the book as very high rates. But what then? What will happen as our neural systems, evolved through millennia to certain capacities, modify themselves to hold ever-expanding loads? Will we simply become smarter, able to hold and process more? Or do we have to reckon with some other gain/loss formula? One possible cognitive response—call it the "S.A.T. cram-course model"—might be an expansion of the short-term memory banks and a correlative atrophying of the long-term memory....

But here our technology may well assume a new role. Once it dawns on us, as it must, that our software will hold all the information we need at ready access, we may very well let it. That is, we may choose to become the technicians of our auxiliary brains, mastering not the information but the retrieval and referencing functions. At a certain point, then, we could become the evolutionary opposites of our forebears, who, lacking external technology, committed everything to memory. If this were to happen, what would be the status of knowing, of being educated? The leader of the electronic tribe would not be the person who knew most, but the one who could execute the broadest range of technical functions. What, I hesitate to ask, would become of the already antiquated notion of wisdom?

QUESTIONS

1. What differences does Birkerts see between the sciences and the humanities ("culture")? Which of the two is most like computer sciences? Communications? Business studies?

2. What does he see as the benefits of Internet learning? What are his fears?

3. In March 2003, the U.S. Department of Education approved an online Teacher's College to make it easier for current and prospective teachers to earn degrees. The federal government granted $10 million to fund the program, run through the Western Governors (Virtual) University. What might Birkerts think of this program? Can you make an ethical argument in favor/against it?

In the next reading, Arthur Levine, President of Teacher's College, Columbia University, predicts that American universities will soon be transformed by "Five Great Forces": The rise of an information economy, changing demographics, new technologies, privatization in higher education, and the convergence of knowledge producers. His remarks are taken from testimony he gave to the Web-based Education Commission on behalf of Teacher's College in September 2000.

The Remaking of the American University[9]

Arthur Levine

...One could argue that the most profound change in American higher education is the demographics. The majority of enrollment growth in the 1980s and 90s were students over the age of 25, women, working adults, and part-time attendees. Sixteen percent of today's college students meet the traditional stereotype—attending full time, being 18 to 22 years of age, and living on campus.

For the new majority of students, higher education is not as central to their lives as it was for previous generations of students...As a consequence, older, part-time, and working students, especially

---

[9] http://www.hpcnet.org/upload/attachments/The_Remaking_of_the_American_University_145442_000921083425.doc

those with children, often said in a national study that I conducted that they wanted a very different type of relationship with their college than students have historically had. They preferred relationships like those they already had with their bank, the electric company, and the grocery....They are looking for just four things from their colleges—convenience, service, quality, and low cost....They are prime candidates for institutions like the University of Phoenix, now the largest private university in the U.S. with regional accreditation and traded on NASDAQ. It offers limited majors, few electives, and instruction by part-time faculty, convenient hours for students, great customer service, and a premium placed on frequent evaluation and high quality instruction in nearby locations—in the suburbs and the business districts of our cities. They are also excellent candidates for distance learning programs that are available in their home or at the office at any hour.....

We are also living in a time in which virtual reality is no longer the stuff of science fiction....Couldn't we recreate fifth-century Athens, the Washington D.C. of Abraham Lincoln, or the Russian Revolution? What will this mean for traditional pedagogy? How will a stand-up lecture, a talking head describing the age of Pericles, compare with actually being there?

...The bottom line is that the new technology has the capacity to revolutionize higher education. It poses challenges to much that we consider fundamental in university life, including textbooks, faculty lectures, and even the very idea of a physical campus.

For the first time in U.S. history, the profit-making sector sees education as an investment opportunity. Increasingly viewed as poorly run, low in productivity, very high in cost and [not yet able] to effectively make use of technology, the 250 billion dollar annual higher education industry is being seen by the now cash-rich, for-profit sector as the next health care industry—another business ripe for takeover, remaking, and, of course, producing big fat profits. At least once a week, I am visited by a television, telephone, cable, software, hardware, venture capital, or start up company that wishes to enter the education market.

Higher education is an appealing industry for a variety of reasons. Not only is it perceived as weak and slow to change, but also it generates an enormous amount of cash and its market is increasing and growing global....And on top of all of this, the higher education industry is subsidized by the states and federal government through their financial aid programs. It's a terrific package.

Despite the rapid growth of the techno-instrumentalist model of education, there is a good deal of unease about its place in our society. This makes predictions about the future of distance education problematic, as it seems to be expanding and contracting at the same time. The United States Army now offers free online degree programs—complete with laptops and wireless access to libraries—to its recruits through eArmyU. Of the 15.7 million Americans enrolled in college, the Distance Education and Training Council estimated in June 2003 that 4 million had taken one or more distance-courses in the previous year. (DETC is an accrediting agency recognized by the U.S. Department of Education and the Council on Higher Education Accreditation.)[10] Yet, by the time this book goes to press, prominent distance-learning programs at Cornell, Temple University, New York University, and the University of Maryland have either folded or been drastically scaled back.

The following summary of conclusions by educators provides some insight into our ambivalence about cyberlearning. In 1999, the Higher Education Policy Institute, a Washington think tank, undertook a review of the then-current research on distance education for two national teacher unions.

What the Research Shows[11]

- There are large volumes of written material on distance learning, but a paucity of good, original research dedicated to explaining or predicting the phenomena related to it.
- Most studies conclude that distance learning compares favorably with classroom-based instruction and enjoys high student satisfaction.
- Much of the research does not control for extraneous variables and therefore cannot show cause and effect.
- Most of the studies do not use randomly selected subjects. When self-selected subjects are used, there is a risk that the technology is not the real factor in academic achievement.
- The validity and reliability of the instruments used to measure student outcomes and attitudes are questionable.
- Many of the studies do not adequately control for "reactive effects"—the feelings and attitudes of students and faculty, such as the "John Henry Effect" (When control groups or their teachers feel threatened or challenged by being in competition with a new program or approach, they may outdo themselves and perform well beyond what normally would be expected.)
- The research has tended to emphasize student outcomes for individual courses, rather than for a total academic program.
- The research does not take into account individual differences among students.

---

[10] Stephanie Armour, "Classrooms Filled with Returning Adults," *USA Today,* June 13, 2003.

[11] Phipps, Ronald and Jamie Merisotis, "Sharpening the Focus on Distance Education: What the Research Does and Does Not Show," *On Campus,* May/June 1999, p.10.

- There is no adequate explanation as to why the dropout rates for distance learners are higher than the dropout rates for students in traditional classrooms.
- It does not take into consideration how the different learning styles of students relate to the use of particular technologies.
- There is no theoretical or conceptual framework for the research.

Six months after the report, then-President Bill Clinton appointed a national commission on Web-based Education. Headed by Senator Bob Kerrey, the group consisted of a high school teacher, professors and college administrators, politicians, and members of the tech-business community, including John Gage, Director of Science for Sun Microsystems; Alan Arkatov, Chair and Founder of OnlineLearning.net; and Susan R. Collins, Senior Vice President and General Manager of bigchalk.com. Although the Commission is now expired, its full report is still available through a link to the South Dakota School of Mines and Technology, Rapid City, South Dakota. The following is an excerpt from the December 2000 report:

Breaching Canyon Walls: Bringing the World to Isolated Reservations[12]

Just as the Internet was opening up the world, the members of the Havasupai Indian reservation in Arizona felt the walls closing in on them.

Living at the basin of the Grand Canyon, the Supai are isolated on all sides by high canyon walls that make even radio communications impossible. Cable, fiber, and ISDN Internet access, common in densely populated areas, are prohibitive luxuries for this remote reservation.

In short, the "Information Age" gives the Supai reason to feel even more isolated. No group among them has suffered more from this isolation than the Supai children. It was bad enough that these children were left out of the revolution in Web-based education. Even worse, they faced a cut-off in critical Head Start services, triggered by changes in the federal program. Head Start now requires teachers in every state to obtain an associate degree in early childhood development or a related field by 2003 and certification by 2005, or face disqualification from the program. While meeting these requirements is a challenge for many Head Start programs, they absolutely threaten to wall-off geographically remote Indian reservations such as the Supai's.

Fortunately, the Supai decided to take destiny into their hands. They used satellite technology to vault the canyon walls, to open their isolated community, and save their Head Start program.

They did this by turning to Northern Arizona University, an institution experi-

---

[12] Report of the Web-based Education Commission (http://www.hpcnet.org/Webcommission/. Breaching.doc).

enced in using the Internet and video-conferencing to broadcast higher education classes to isolated communities. Using a federal grant to install satellite dishes, the Supai contracted with StarBand Communications for six satellite dishes: one in the Head Start office; another at the Indian Child Welfare Act office; two at the school; one at the tribal court; and another at the tourist lodge. Now the Supai are working with the university to have an early childhood education program beamed into the community.

A similar story is unfolding in New Mexico, where only 13 percent of Head Start teachers have their associates degree. In this state, the Southwestern Indian Polytechnic Institute (SIPI) has stepped forward to help train Native American Head Start teachers online.

SIPI began with a response to requests from tribal leaders, developing a 70-hour associates degree program in early child-hood education that can be delivered by satellite to remote tribal sites in New Mexico.

Early in 2000, SIPI began satellite broadcasts of a two-credit introductory course in child development to the Head Start staff located at the Santa Clara Pueblo....

The early childhood education degree program, which will be transferable to four-year institutions in the state, began in January 2001 with an enrollment of 60 student-employees of a tribal Head Start Program.

Harlan McKostao, producer of the national call-in radio program "Native America Calling," sees in these efforts the beginning of a greater opportunity for the reservation to link to the wider world. Connecting tribal schools, colleges, and community centers, McKostao says, is critical because "if you get the school online, you get the whole community."

QUESTIONS

1. What are the implications of each of the findings of the Higher Educational Policy Institute study?

2. The "study" undertaken by the federal government relied heavily on testimony on actual experiences with distance learning, such as that described above. Find and read the report of the Web-based Education Commission at **http://www.hpcnet.org/webcommission**. What were its major findings? What rec-ommendations did the Commission make?

3. Compare and contrast the study done by the federal government with the report of the Higher Educational Policy Institute. What might account for differences in the two?

4. To what extent have Dr. Levine's predictions about higher education come true?

5. What ethical arguments can you make for or against the expansion of distance learning programs by traditional colleges and universities?

6. By May 2003, the Center for Education Reform was trumpeting a revolution: Some 50 cyber-schools for grades K–12 were chartered in twelve states. In Pennsylvania alone, more than 5,100 students were enrolled in eight cyber-charter schools. What benefits/harms do you see in cyber-education for elementary school? High school? Should all children be able to opt for online schools as an alternative to brick-and-mortar public education? Should their parents have that choice?

7. Langdon Winner, a professor of political science at Rensselaer Polytechnic Institute has created a prototype for a device that could do away with traditional colleges and teachers, the A.P.M. (Automated Professor Machine.) Go to Winner's home page at **http://www. rpi.edu/~winner/apm1.html** to find out what the A.P.M. is all about. What do you think Winner would say about the reports on Distance Learning?

Rachel F. Moran, a University of California (Boalt Hall) law professor, warns that we are headed for a new divide in higher education. "At first glance, the affirmative action debate seems to be wholly about race. Only incidentally does the controversy focus on higher education. In reality, this debate is integrally connected to efforts to transform the delivery of educational services and redefine the terms of access to higher education," she writes in the next selection. Soon, only the privileged will be able to enjoy the benefits of residential college experience; the rest will be rendered bystanders, learning at ever-greater distances from the campus, according to Ms. Moran.

Diversity, Distance, and the Delivery of Higher Education[13]
Rachel F. Moran

The debate over affirmative action in colleges and universities has focused on race as the critical issue. Certainly, the fate of race-conscious admissions programs rests heavily on society's commitment to correcting past injustice. Yet, the controversy over affirmative action also reflects shifting conceptions of higher education.

In *Regents of the University of California v. Bakke*, Justice Lewis Powell treated racial diversity as part of a pedagogical process in which students draw on their experiences to learn from each other. He characterized this vigorous exchange of ideas as key to creating the environment of "speculation, experiment, and creation"

---

[13] Moran, Rachel F., "Diversity, Distance and the Delivery of Higher Education," 59 *Ohio St.L.J.* 775 (1998).

at the heart of higher learning. Today, new technologies are being touted as a way to deliver education without face-to-face contact. The virtual university fundamentally reconceives the pedagogical process in ways that implicate not only the affirmative action debate but also the structure of post-secondary education.

In the field of higher education, the reconsideration of affirmative action is integrally connected not only to notions of race but also to images of the university's place in a democratic society. With the rise of new technologies, the very concept of the university is being revisited. Today, educational entrepreneurs tout the benefits of the virtual university, a university without walls that exists largely in cyberspace.

[As you read the next section, ask yourself: What changes does Moran see in the meaning of education? Does her description match your own experience?]

This new way of learning depends less on face-to-face interaction and more on the transfer of information. It unsettles the ties between personal identity, residential education, and the learning process. The futuristic focus on a "brave new world" of higher education and the tendency to forget our history when eliminating affirmative action are not coincidental events but are related in significant ways. New technologies permit substantial amounts of information to be transferred at relatively low cost to a large number of individuals. As a result, the information society seems to be egalitarian: Everyone can log on and participate in the flow of ideas. Yet, logging on is a practice generally undertaken alone, often in the privacy of one's home. The sender and the receiver need not know one another. Each can remain anonymous or even present a wholly false identity. The impersonality of information transfer reduces the salience of personal qualities, like race, that are historically situated. Knowledge is treated as objective and factual, rather than intersubjective and cultural. For this reason, the idea that race or other personal characteristics could be relevant to finding shared truths through the robust exchange of ideas becomes hard to fathom. In all of these ways, then, the debate over affirmative action can be understood as the first battle over the meaning of residential education itself....

In its early years, the desegregation movement focused on colleges and universities because the benefits of those privileged spaces could not be widely duplicated. Today, however, new technologies are being offered as a way to minimize barriers to access to higher education, use free market ideology to make educational markets efficient, and enable individuals to transcend their personal circumstances to participate in a universal learning process. By profoundly altering ideas about the rationing of educational services, this transformation has obscured corrective justice arguments. By reconstructing images of how people learn, the shift also has undercut pedagogical claims based on the benefits of face-to-face interactions with peers from a range of backgrounds....

Recently, a consortium of governors in Western states decided to cooperate in creating a virtual university for their residents. The governors hoped that this "Virtual U" would provide a low-cost means of meeting the burgeoning demand for higher education. With limited tax revenues to build new campuses, a university located primarily in cyberspace appeared to be one of the few ways to keep the promise of widespread access to post-secondary education alive....

The Western governors' initiative illustrates some of the changes in the notion of "public education" that new technologies engender. This movement tends to commodify information, treating it as a product to be packaged and sold. A free market ideology converts citizens into consumers, and government into a service provider. Efficiency becomes the most important objective in transactions between the State and its citizens. Ideally, government should streamline itself to look as much like a business as possible and should be forced to compete with private providers of educational services. Because all citizens will be better off with a largely unimpeded educational market, cumbersome regulations designed to promote fairness or equity are misguided and meddlesome. In this deregulatory regime, affirmative action is little more than a form of price fixing or price discrimination, an unwarranted interference in the marketplace that merely promotes inefficient outcomes.

The emphasis on efficiency necessarily reduces the weight given to the equity concerns that are central to a corrective justice rationale. Yet, the altered notion of public space further marginalizes racial concerns. The virtual university is lauded precisely because it transcends barriers of time and space and is not narrowly bound to a particular geographic location. The corrective justice model was rooted in battles over access to privileged physical space, but education in cyberspace pooh-poohs the relevance of bricks and mortar. New technologies divorce education from a particular place with all of its "local color." As a result, the virtual university obscures the relevance of residential education marked by racial segregation. In the disembodied world of cyberspace, intellectual exchange seems unimpeded by the legacy of discrimination inscribed in racially identifiable colleges and universities. The principal identity of the disembodied learner in cyberspace derives from being a consumer of information, a commodity packaged and sold like other products. The consumer's convenience is paramount: Why should students have to go to the trouble of assembling at a particular time and place to hear a lecture? Why not let them log on at their leisure in the privacy and comfort of their own homes? The information, after all, is just the same, however it is transmitted. It does not change because students sit in a classroom together. Moreover, the mastery of information can easily be measured through competency tests that are standardized, quantifiable, and efficient to administer. Why should learners be measured on any other criteria, particularly non-quantifiable and intangible traits, in a world of information transfer? Why should classroom attendance and participation really matter at all, even if they could be part of a virtual university experience?

What this consumer-oriented approach ignores is that learning is not the passive receipt of information, but active participation in the construction of knowledge. As Powell pointed out in *Bakke*, students must react critically to information, seeing it through the prism of their own values and experiences. Moreover, they must have the opportunity to contrast their own reactions with those of their peers. Otherwise, students are likely to succumb to parochialism and insularity, however many facts they may memorize. Information is just a set of random observations until it is put into a framework of values and priorities. This framework for knowledge may be hard to develop in isolation....

Advertising that touts cyberspace as raceless reveals another facet of the ideology of technological transformation: New technologies are presumed to be great equalizers because everyone will have free-ranging access to information...[however s]o far, studies indicate that those left by the wayside of the information highway are disproportionately non-white....As states face declining revenues and growing demand for affordable higher education, residential education is increasingly being depicted as a luxury for the few. For the rest, "distance learning" will be the realistic alternative.

The "distance" in distance learning should not be understood in purely physical terms. In addition to being far away from the teacher, the student is removed from other pupils both physi-cally and socially. This social distance creates dangers of insularity when lessons are discussed face-to-face with friends and family rather than with students from different walks of life. There is also a distance from the site where the production of information occurs. Somewhere, a fortunate few hear the "real" lecture in the luxury of a residential setting. These elites shape the production of knowledge through face-to-face interaction, while the masses of students are bystanders in cyberspace. Even interactive technologies are not likely to rectify completely this marginalization of the distance learner.... [H]aving a conversation with a professor in a classroom or office is probably more effective than sending an e-mail missive as one of a number of faceless pupils. The debate over affirmative action is arguably the "first wave" in the battle over growing stratification in higher education. If residential education is a luxury for the privileged few, it must be rationed....Already, changes [making University of California admissions policies "color-blind"] are having this effect: There are increasing concerns about the fate of ethnic studies, student-run journals devoted to black and Latino issues, and student-supported programs to assist disadvantaged communities. Yet, these are dilemmas only for those who expect to shape their education in a residential setting. For those who expect to learn only at a distance, these lost opportunities to participate in the construction of knowledge are unrecognized because everyone has the same chance to log on at Virtual U.

Students in colleges and universities are being educated for citizenship, not just careers. They are expected to use the privilege of higher education to better society not only through productive jobs but also thoughtful participation in their communities. Powell's opinion in Bakke makes clear that diversity in higher education is key to understanding one's place in society and developing a sense of personal obligation in a country still deeply divided by race. Without vigorous exchange anchored in the concrete reality of individual identities, students can come to confuse the accretion of facts with knowledge. They may mistakenly take comfort in objective certainties when, in reality, we all must struggle constantly to find provisional, collective truths. Passive consumers of information can wrongly equate the receipt of encyclopedic amounts of information with wisdom, when, in fact, this hard-won combination of knowledge, experience, and character can be neither bought nor sold....

QUESTIONS

1. Recall the ethical theories described in chapter 1: utilitarianism and deontology.

(a) What are some of the utilities that distance learning offers its primary stakeholders? Disutilities (harms)? **(b)** Deontologists would focus on rights and duties, on fundamental principles such as justice. How does this ethical analysis uncover the themes of Moran's article?

2. According to Moran, how is technology in higher education problematic from the perspective of diversity? From the perspective of equality?

Bridging the Divide: MIT'S Open CourseWare Project

On April 4, 2001, the Massachusetts Institute of Technology (MIT) announced its OpenCourseWare project (OCW), estimated to cost from $7.5 to $10 million a year. Faculty at universities across the country had been using the Web for their own students for years. Some make standard course materials available online; others hold Web-conferences for their classes. There are even colleges that require a Web site for every class. But, as MIT pointed out, OCW was something new. MIT committed itself to the first institution-wide effort to provide course materials "free and open to the world." As its website explains, MIT OCW is not intended to be a substitute for an MIT education—the cornerstone of which is the "interaction between faculty and students." No degrees are offered, it is not a form of distance education. Instead, it "provides the content that supports an education."

Questions

1. Go to MIT's homepage and explore the OpenCourseWare project, especially the FAQs. As you read it, ask: Does this effort address any concerns that Moran raises? Does it exacerbate any? Does it create other ethical issues? Check out the courseware for any course similar to one you are taking this semester. Compare to the materials you are using. Ask yourself: How might MIT OCW enhance your educational experience? Would reading the online materials on your own be a good substitute for taking the course?

2. Check out **www.Free.Ed.net**, created in 1998 to provide free, online educational materials for a vast panoply of subject matter—from welding to computer programming. By 2002, **Free.Ed. net** claimed that almost 900,000 pages of materials had been viewed by more than 400,000 learners. Compare and contrast the goals/content of **Free.Ed.net** with MIT's OpenCourseWare project.

3. Frustrated by the rising costs of subscriptions to prestigious scientific and professional journals that publish research, a group of noted scientists decided to create an online journal to make scientific research findings available to the public for free. Instead of charging for subscriptions to the Public Library of Science, the journal charges scientists to publish their papers. PLoS posted its first issue in October 2003. What benefits do you see to this enterprise? Are there any ways in which it might threaten the academic-science mission of universities?

http://www.
publiclibraryofscience.org

BUSINESS & EDUCATION IN CYBERSPACE: A HEALTHY PARTNERSHIP?

Until relatively recently, there was a clear demarcation in American society between business, with its eye ever focused on the bottom line, and the non-profit enterprise we call education. But in a myriad of ways—some positive, some troubling—the worlds of business and education have become increasingly intertwined.

While educators acknowledge that the Internet has opened new opportunities for education, it is the commercial world that has done the most to promote online education. Global Education Network, or GEN, a private for-profit company, began selling college courses over the Internet in February 2001. Another venture, UNext.com, sells online business courses to companies such as AOL-Time Warner, Morgan Stanley, and Merrill Lynch, and is working on doing the same throughout the world. Indeed, the *New York Times* reported in October 2002 that commercial education companies owned roughly

THE DIGITAL DIVIDE

For more on the digital divide see *IT & Society: A Web Journal Studying How Technology Affects Society* at http://www. Tandsociety.org

JUST THE FACTS

The National Commission on Web-based Education

41.5 percent of American households had Internet access by 2000, but only 38.9 percent of rural households did; broadband penetration is greater in central cities (12.2 percent) than in rural areas (7.3 percent).

Between December 1998 and August 2000, the gap in Internet access between African-American households and the national average grew from 15 percent to 18 percent; for Hispanic households, the gap grew from 14 percent to 18 percent.

About a third of the U.S. population uses the Internet at home; only 18.9 percent of African-Americans and 16.1 percent of Hispanics do. Wealthy school classroom access almost doubles that of poor schools.

Schools with the highest percentage of students in poverty average 16 students per computer, while the national average is 9 to one.

58 percent of all postsecondary students own their own computer. This figure varies from a high of 79 percent of students at private universities, to 34 percent of those attending private two-year institutions, and 39.6 percent of those attending public two-year institutions. Currently, 55 percent of Hispanic- and Native-Americans and 46 percent of African-American undergraduates, are enrolled in community colleges.

In e-testimony to the Commission, the United Negro College Fund (UNCF) reported that only 15 percent of students attending member institutions had their own computers. Nationally, there is one computer for every 2.6 students in higher education institutions, but UNCF colleges have only one for every 6 students.

Seventy-four percent of faculty nationally own their own computers, as compared with only half of UNCF faculty. Less than half of UNCF faculty have college-owned computers at their desks.

The number of network servers at UNCF colleges per 1,000 students is approximately half that of all colleges and universities nationally. Seventy-five percent of these servers, hubs, routers, and printers are obsolete or nearly obsolete and need replacement.

QUESTIONS

1. Consider each of the gaps identified above as part of the digital divide. What are the implications of each? Who should bear responsibility for diminishing the gaps?

2. Since 1996, the federal government has offered discounts to public and private schools and libraries on the costs of telecommunications services, Internet access, and internal networks through the E-rate program. Can you think of other venues for learning that might benefit from similar discounts?

3. By the end of 2002, Mississippi became the first state to put a computer in every public school classroom. Find out about computer access in schools in your home state.

4. In February 2002 a study funded by the Ford Foundation[14] reported that while differences were narrowing, there were still significant digital divides between high- and low-income households, racial groups, Northern and Southern states, and rural and urban households. According to the analysis, 80% of those earning more than $75,000 a year used the Internet at home, compared to only 25% of people living in households with less than $15,000 a year. With increasing access to the Internet in schools and libraries, how critical is home usage? Does the disparity in home usage create an ethical responsibility on anyone's part? Whose?

5. A University of Maryland sociologist re-analyzed the same data used for *A Nation Online* and concluded that it will take nearly two decades for poor households to close the computer and Internet gap with more affluent households.[15] What are the policy and ethical implications of this controversy?

6. In 1993, Mitchel Resnik of MIT established the first computer clubhouse where boys and girls from the ages of 8 to 18 could learn high-level computer skills, creating their own computer games instead of merely playing them. Today, thanks to hardware, software, and services donated by the high-tech industry, there is an international network of clubhouses stretching from Ireland to the Philippines. Still, there is a global digital divide. Find out what you can about what each of the following is doing about it: the U.S. government, the telecommunications industry, American schools and universities, the United Nations.

[14] *A Nation Online: How Americans are Expanding Their Use of the Internet* (2002). The full report is available at http:www.ntia.doc.gov/nitahome/dn/.
[15] Steve P. Martin, "Is the Digital Divide Really Closing? A Critique of Inequality Measurement in *A Nation Online.*" 1 *IT & Society* 1 (2003).

three percent of the cyber-education market—then estimated at 50,000 students earning their B.A. or M.A. degrees entirely online. Textbook companies have developed software, which is marketed to universities, to make it easy to offer Internet courses. As colleges, universities, and K–12 schools struggle to keep down the costs of education and keep up with changing technology at a time when public monies are scarce, techno-business has stepped in to help. In the 1980s, Whittle Communications packaged Channel One programming consisting of short videotapes carrying ten minutes of current events and two minutes of commercials geared to teenaged audiences—for fast food, candy, deodorants. Channel One was marketed to schools throughout the country. Many accepted the free television sets, satellite receivers, and other equipment offered in exchange for a promise to show the entire daily newscast on all television sets on at least 90% of the days school was in session and Channel One transmitted. By 2000, 25 percent of the schools in the U.S. were showing Channel One.

But this was only one piece of the new relationships being forged between business and education. Several hundred school districts signed exclusive contracts with soft drink companies to sell their beverages in schools. A McGraw-Hill math textbook published in 1995 was among the first to name many consumer products, including Sony video games and Nike sneakers, in its problems. Zap Me, a California company, offers schools free computers with screens that include continuously flashing ads. Information provided by students can be tracked and passed on to advertisers. Campus Pipeline, a start-up company funded in part by Sun Microsystems and Dell, creates college homepages at no cost to the school. Pipeline makes its money by billing the companies whose ads appear on the college sites and on commissions earned from student online purchases.

Consider **notHarvard.com**. In May 1999, a new dot-com company based in Austin, Texas, and financed by venture capitalists, investment bankers, and Internet angels posted its Web site, **http://www.notHarvard.com**. It advertised the sale of Web-based technology to companies that wanted to offer free online courses to their users as a marketing tool. A disclaimer at the bottom of the site read:

> **notHarvard.com** by definition is NOT Harvard and is in no way associated with Harvard University. In no way does our name intend to convey any association with Harvard University. In fact, it is the intent of notHarvard.com—by using the word NOT—not to be associated with Harvard University.

In notHarvard.com's first year, it created online branded universities—including Barnes & Noble University, Jobs University, CodeWarriorU, and Web Street University—and enrolled more than 200,000 students. The company's basic business proposition, according to CEO Judith Bitterli, is that "buyers want to learn and they will embrace free online courses from trusted brands. eLearning can be a strategic sales and marketing weapon that drives stickiness and leads to additive revenue streams."[16] The brick-and-mortar Harvard University, unconvinced by the newcomer's disclaimer, brought suit against the company for infringing on its trademark. Shortly thereafter, notHarvard.com changed its name to Powered.com. What, if any, ethical problems are raised by notHarvard.com?

The author of the next reading points to some of the troubling consequences of new partnerships between the commercial market and tax-exempt, non-profit institutions of higher learning. This excerpt begins with Minow asking why we should worry about the blurring of lines between profit and non-profit.

Partners, Not Rivals[17]

Martha Minow

As the non-profit/profit line blurs as non-profits turn to profit-making activities and relationships with for-profit entities, three problems should worry us. First, non-profits that undertake their own efforts in profit-generating activity should beware of the high failure rate of for-profit start-ups. Up to 70 percent of all business start-ups fail in the first eight years. Many that have initial success are difficult to sustain. These serious risks can jeopardize a non-profit's reputation, assets, and even its existence.

Second, for-profit activities and affiliations entered into by non-profits can produce serious conflicts of interest and conflicts of mission that raise direct ethical problems and long-term dangers to each mission....Sponsorship by a corporate actor can undermine the credibility of nongovernmental organizations (NGOs), especially where the corporate sector decides to sponsor the organization in order to overcome a bad public image involving the precise issues handled by the NGO. Close ties can jeopardize not only the appearance but also the reality of self-determination by the non-profit, especially if the two entities pursue joint decision making and management of shared activities.

Thus, conflicting interests reveal potentially conflicting missions. Increasingly, corporate managers restrict charitable giving except where justifiable in preserving or increasing shareholder value. When corporate charitable giving is accounted for in strictly public relations or research and development terms, the result may, but also may not, advance the mission of the recipient groups. A for-profit enterprise that puts social service first can lose both customers and investors and, ultimately, its

---

[16] Cisneros, Oscar S. "NotHarvard.com Sues Harvard," *Wired News* (www.wired.com/news/print/0,1294,3/883,00.htm).

[17] Minow, Martha, "Partners, Not Rivals? Redrawing the Lines Between Public and Private, Non-Profit and Profit, Secular and Religious," 80 *B.U.L.Rev.* 1061 (2000).

What role should business play in global educational reform? See http://www.worldbank.org/education/globaleducationreform

very existence....A for-profit health care, social service, or education agency can turn away those most in need because of [the]bottom line....

When the non-profit undertakes its own profit-making activity or licensing agreement with a for-profit, it may scare away charitable contributions and government aid. Public and private grant-makers and donors grow reluctant to give to an enterprise that makes money for shareholders and managers. If non-profits license their name on a product, help with its marketing, and avoid paying taxes on proceeds, this kind of boundary-blurring may jeopardize the legal and political basis, as well as the philanthropic base, for non-profit enterprises.

A technical legal problem also arises. The tax-exempt status of the non-profit depends upon compliance with the tax laws, including the requirement to pay taxes on income generated for a purpose unrelated to the charitable mission.... Non-profits can run afoul of the complexities and jeopardize their tax-exempt status....[S]mall for-profit businesses charge that the growing profit-making activities of non-profits involve unfair competition. Because the non-profits enjoy tax-exempt status and receive tax-deductible gifts from private donors, small businesses, backed by the Small Business Administration, seek to eliminate any tax exemption for profit-making activity by non-profits. Charges of unfair competition neglect how the community and public service missions of non-profits often involve them in providing services in situations where competitive markets have failed....Moreover, unlike for-profit enterprises, non-profits do not have access to venture capital and equity investment. These defenses fade, however, the more the distinctive identity of non-profits blurs through partnerships and other affiliations with for-profit entities.

Blurring the borders between profit and non-profit organizations could undermine legal and political support for the non-profit sector and eliminate its distinctiveness. Loss of the non-profits would weaken civil society and democracy. In the words of one scholar, "The non-profit sector acts as a counterpoise against excessive displays of power emanating from the public or private sectors." Non-profits involve people in civic activity and service to others and thereby teach skills of self-government and inculcate habits of tolerance and civility. Impairment of the non-profit sector could exacerbate declining civic and political engagement. Loss of civic and public activities disproportionately hurts poor and working class people. Non-profits provide an array of collective goods and services that neither the market nor government addresses because non-profits proceed with distinct missions and a willingness to take certain kinds of risks that the other sectors bypass.

Higher education, university presses and public broadcasting each enable a pursuit of knowledge and culture that purely private markets cannot sustain.... If forced to compete with for-profit enterprises or required to become self-sustaining, non-profits can falter, just as for-profit enterprises jeopardize their duties to shareholders and consumers if they pursue charitable purposes instead of their primary mission. Yes, collaborations between profit and non-profit activities can produce benefits for each, but only if the clarity of each mission and the certainty of each accountability mechanism remain intact.

QUESTIONS

1. According to Minow, what is wrong with the blurring of the lines between profit and non-profit?

2. Should education always be a non-profit enterprise?

3. Check out some of the e-learning sites such as **http://www.CodeWarriorU.Com**, or **htttp://www.smartplanet.com**. What do they have in common? How do they differ? How would you evaluate the value of these services?

4. In 2002, **HungryMindsUniversity. com** boasted that it offered 17,000 online courses from top universities like UC Berkeley, UCLA, and NYU. A year later, those who visited the Web site were told that it was "no longer active" and were urged to visit **http://www.Wiley. com**. Find out what happened to Hungry Minds University.

5. What are the advantages/disadvantages to commercial arrangements that aid education? Compare Channel One to Zap Me, and the exclusive contracts that companies like Pepsi Cola or Coca Cola have entered into with various schools, to the Web-based services of Campus Pipeline. Are there similarities? Significant differences? How would you evaluate the ethical decisions made by various parties to each contract?

6. Many colleges use their own Web sites to recruit students. Others use Web portals, or online "Yellow Pages", that provide recruitment services to colleges. But a college risks losing federal funding if it finances its Web portal services by agreeing to tuition share or referral fees. Is there anything unethical about colleges outsourcing their recruitment to private companies?

Responsible Netizens

The Center for Safe and Responsible Internet Use, a nonprofit organization, provides research, development, and educational outreach related to information technology ethics for young people. Its director, Nancy Willard, has written extensively about the safe and responsible use of the Internet. In "Capturing the 'Eyeballs' and 'E-Wallets' of Captive Kids in School: Dot.com Invades Dot.edu," Willard argues that "[s]chools have an obligation to protect the welfare of their students and ensure the integrity of the learning environment. Allowing dot.com companies to engage in online profiling and targeted marketing of students is exploitation and a violation of public trust."[18] Among the practices that she warns against are: sites that purport to provide educational materials that turn out to be highly entertaining-biased promotional materials, and ads—especially animated ones—in locations where they are likely to distract students.

Educated in both law and psychology, Willard analyzes sites and services by asking: How does the intended use meet an identified educational need? What information will be collected directly or indirectly from students as they use the site? What is the purpose of the collection of information? Does the site have any banner ads? How intrusive and distracting are they? Are the ads for youth consumer items or for educational products or services? Is advertising a vehicle to support delivery of the educational resource, or has the educational resource been established for the purpose of advertising, brand, or corporate promotion?

How does your college's home page stack up under Willard's analysis? That of the high school you or your children attended?

ANOTHER GLANCE AT THE INTERNET: STUDENT USE AND MISUSE

As computers become the modern-day "pen and pencil" tools of education, students and educators alike must grapple with the possibility that ethical behavior sometimes means limitations on their use. Computer labs, "smart" classrooms linked to the Internet, and laptop communities present wonderful learning opportunities: Students of finance can watch the daily fluctuations of the stock market in real time, communications majors can discuss and analyze CNN and MSN headlines, those studying history can visit a simulated scene. Yet students can also spend class time using their laptops to watch a film, catch up on e-mail, make purchases, play games, or pass notes. Are any of those classroom uses unethical? Would it be fair for professors to ban laptops in class to prevent such uses? For other reasons? What ethical argument can you make that professors have an obligation to monitor the use of computers in the classroom?

---

[18] http://responsiblenetizen.org/onlinedocs/documents/eyeballs.html.

In an article focused on the use of the Internet in K–12 schools,[19] Nancy Willard argues that school districts establish Internet services for a reason: to enhance the delivery of education. That limited purpose creates an obligation on the part of those in charge to oversee student use of computers. She lists her concerns:

1. Prevention of learning displacement: When young people are using technology, including the Internet, for activities that are merely entertainment, valuable time and resources are wasted.

2. Appropriate use of taxpayer resources: Taxpayers are supporting the costs of technology in schools because of the promise that technology will assist students in achieving challenging academic standards....

3. Preparation for workplace use: The purpose of education is to prepare students for success in life and work in the twenty-first century....Schools have a responsibility to help educate young people how to self-monitor when they are using a limited-purpose system, so that these behaviors may be ingrained by the time the students reach the workplace.

4. Prevention of problems with misuse and addiction: There are growing concerns with online addiction—people who spend hours and hours of time in essentially worthless activities. When schools force their students to think about their online activities in the context of the value of that activity to their education and self-improvement, schools are assisting students in gaining critically important self-monitoring skills that may assist in preventing online addiction.

http://responsiblenetizen .org

QUESTIONS

1. To what extent do similar or analogous concerns arise in the university setting? In business?

2. If school Internet usage were to be limited to "educational purposes," which of the following would be banned?

- Buying products
- Lobbying
- Career development activities for students
- Professional development and communication activities for school employees
- Independent Web research
- Independent research or communication through mailing lists and newsgroups
- Personal communication via e-mail

---

[19] Nancy Willard, "Legal and Ethical Issues Related to the Use of the Internet in K–12 Schools," 2000 *B.Y.U. Educ. & L. J.* 225 (2000)

3. How ethical would it be for a public school to take each of the following actions? For a college or university? A business or government agency?

- Restricting use to specific class or business-related activities
- Engaging students/employees in dialogue about the purpose and quality of their online activities
- Requiring students/employees to keep a log of their online activities, purpose, and time
- Giving priority to students/employees requiring access for class/business activities
- Monitoring student online use
- Monitoring teacher/staff/employee online use
- Prohibiting participation in group discussions unrelated to education/business

4. How aggressive should colleges be in trying to stop conduct that violates copyright laws? In spring 2003 the University of Florida estimated that almost 40 percent of dorm residents downloaded music illegally. In response, the school introduced ICARUS (Integrated Control Application for Restricting User Services), a software program that scans their network and bounces students using peer-to-peer software to download music. What arguments can you make in favor of ICARUS? Against it?

In chapter 3, we explored some of the parameters of free speech over the Internet. Think back to that chapter as you consider some of the specific ways that free speech concerns sometimes conflict with other ethical considerations when students go online. In one instance, for example, an 11th-grader chatting with another student over AOL named several classmates he considered "stupid." Then he wrote, "If we eliminated all of the stupid people and the crazy people and the short people we would all be a lot better off....We kill off chickens and cows so that we can eat them and survive, it's the same thing." Near the end, the student wrote, "I don't really think that they should be killed, but they are quite annoying." Another student gave a transcript of the chat to a chaperone on a school-sponsored trip. The chaperone reportedly was so disturbed by it that he handed it over to the headmaster of the school. This small, select private school in Philadelphia made local news headlines when it expelled the student, calling his private online conversation "completely antithetical" to the school's "most basic values."[20]

---

[20] *S.L., a minor, v. Friends Central School*, 2000 W.L. 352367 (E.D. Pa.)

Role Play: Guidelines for Internet Use

A series of scenarios—all based on actual cases—follow. Divide the class into various groups, each representing a local school board well aware of these and similar events related to student use of the Internet. Each board's responsibility is to create a set of guidelines for the school district to best promote ethical behavior on the part of all involved. A variation on this role play calls for only one school board and assigns other students to role-play witnesses representing various community stakeholders, such as parents, students, teachers, school administrators, and police.

- Abbe, an 11th-grade honor student, used the school computer to create a parody Web site in which she depicted the assistant principal in a variety of mocked-up pictures, including a Viagra ad and a sexual encounter with TV cartoon character Marge Simpson; a second site accused the principal of committing a crime and falsely implied that she might be guilty of a serious crime.

- Bobbi, a marginal student at Local H.S., posted a copy of the inflammatory Web site created by Littleton, Colorado, killer Eric Harris on the Internet. When the FBI investigated and ordered Bobbi to close the site, Bobbi repeatedly moved duplicates of the hate-diatribe to other sites.

- Chris created **http://www.Schoolrumors.com**, a site that invited students to post comments about other students, teachers, and schools. After 67,000 hits and many disparaging remarks, the principal at Chris' school ordered the site shut down.

- Danni, a college freshman, logged onto an Internet chat room and posted a threat to bomb a local high school, signing it, "the phantom." The threat was a hoax.

- Whiz-kid Edie created a Web site from a home computer, giving detailed explanations for hacking into the school's computers.

- Jack Flaherty, an 18-year-old senior, was kicked off the high school volleyball team, barred from attending school events, and suspending from using school computers after posting taunting messages on a private message board devoted to high school volleyball. All but one of the messages was posted from home; some included mild profanity; none were threatening.

Go online and find news reports about the above or similar cases. Compare the action taken in the real case with the recommendations of your group or class.

CHAPTER PROBLEMS

1. Assume a teacher creates an interactive virtual Web site where students can view comments made by previous visitors or add their own comments. Some students add musical accompaniments and short video clips of previously televised news broadcasts. Is it ethical for anyone to claim authorship of this space?

2. Suppose a college adopts a new rule requiring every student to have use of a laptop computer. Some newly-admitted students cannot afford to purchase a computer. Analyze the policy from deontological and utilitarian perspectives. Does it matter whether the college is a public or private institution? Whether the students knew about the rule when they chose to attend?

3. Some of the most popular online games involve "historical games" like Civilization II, the Age of Empires, and Side Meier's Civil War Collection. Fans praise these games for giving players a chance to "experience" another time and place, to live another person's life. One problem, however, is that most of these virtual games offer juiced up versions of history that depart from historians' understanding of what "really happened." Do you see any ethical problems with such games?

4. In March 2000, Michael Saylor, a 35-year-old software billionaire announced he would spend $100 million to create a giant free Web site to provide access to the "10,000 greatest minds of our time" via online lectures and interviews. His goal was free education—including degrees—for everyone. He hoped that the promise of leaving a legacy to the world would be enough to induce the "great minds" to offer their thoughts free of charge. Unfortunately, with the bursting of the technology-bubble on Wall Street and other events, Saylor's proposal is still "on hold." What do you see as the benefits and possible harms of his proposal?

5. Compare Saylor's idea to LearnNow, a for-profit network of charter schools founded by Gene Wade. Wade, a 31-year-old Harvard Law/Wharton MBA grad, is trying to help people like himself—poor, minority students who "are treated as if there's a correlation between their zip codes and their IQ's." His schools emphasize training for the future by offering youngsters classes in computer programming languages. LearnNow schools also offer computer courses to parents at night. In 2001, LearnNow was acquired by Edison Schools, a for-profit corporation that runs more than one hundred schools throughout the country. Do you see any problems with a school district turning over its schools to a company like LearnNow or Edison Schools? Find out how Edison is doing in Philadelphia, where management of 20 of the city's worst-performing public schools was turned over to Edison Schools in 2002.

6. The Alliance for Childhood has called for a moratorium on the further introduction of computers in early childhood and elementary education. Visit their Web site at **http://www.alllianceforchildhood.net/**. Who are they? What are their objections to computers in early childhood education? Which of their concerns might be allayed by visiting the Web site at **http://www.superkids.com** and scanning its reviews of software?

7. Che Café Collective, a student group at the University of California at San Diego, provides a venue for bands, serves vegan food, tends an organic garden, and is involved in left-wing political causes. When the group listed a link to a Columbian rebel organization on its Web site, a visitor "from the east coast" contacted the University. Fearing the link violates both the PATRIOT Act and the University's policy on acceptable use of computer resources, the school ordered the Collective to remove the link. The Collective refused. Find out how this controversy has been resolved. Did the Collective act ethically? Did the University?

8. Increasingly, educators are using the Internet to share classroom information with parents—posting homework assignments and course grades, for example. Some even post assignments and test grades, to allow parents to check out student claims that "everyone did badly on the midterm."

Are there any ethical problems with online gradebooks? Can you identify the harms/benefits attached to student/parent/teacher emailing?

9. In December 2000, Congress adopted the Children's Internet Protection Act. In return for federal reimbursement for the costs of connecting to the Internet (called "e-rate funds"), schools, and libraries throughout the nation are required to install technology to protect minors from online adult materials. Although more than 100 companies sell monitoring and filtering products that restrict Internet use, not all are the same. Some business plans include tracking students' Web wanderings and selling the data to market research firms. One company's software includes advertising to students on every screen. What factors should schools take into account before selecting software? Should companies that want to gather data from students have to disclose their plans to parents and obtain their consent, as scholarly researchers gathering data from students are required to do? Who should impose such requirements? Laws? Schools? If no one requires such disclosure and consent, does that mean it is ethical to bypass it?

CHAPTER 6

Democracy, the Market, and Cyberspace

Life in cyberspace seems to be shaping up exactly like Thomas Jefferson would have wanted: founded on the primacy of individual liberty and a commitment to pluralism, diversity and community.

—Mitch Kapor, founder of LOTUS (1993)

In case after case, the move to computerize and digitize means that many preexisting cultural forms have suddenly gone liquid, losing their former shape as they are retailored for computerized expression. As new patterns solidify, both useful artifacts and the texture of human relations that surrounds them are often much different from what existed previously. This process amounts to a vast, ongoing experiment whose long term ramifications no one fully comprehends.

—Langdon Winner (1997)[1]

If they were already in the dark side, they would probably not come here.

—Andrew Robinson, trainer at Tiger Team, a free after-school program that teaches teens ethical hacking (2003)[2]

ETHICS CASE: WHO'S IN CHARGE? HACKING AND CRACKING

It is the year 2003, and computer hacking has taken new twists. Kevin Mitnick—once labeled "the most wanted computer criminal in U.S. history" for stealing software and altering data at the University of Southern California, Nokia, and Sun Microsystems, among others—is starting a business that protects companies against computer attacks. This after five years in federal prison and three years' probation, during which he was barred from using computers or the Internet.

---

[1] Langdon Winner, "Cyberlibertarian Myths and the Prospects for Community," 27:3 *Computers and Society* 14 (1997).

[2] Julie Flaherty, "Enlisting the Young as White-Hat Hackers," *New York Times*, May 29, 2003, Late Ed., Sect.G, p.5, Col.1

His expertise is needed. A computer security firm based in London estimates there were some 20,000 successful hacker incidents worldwide in January, alone. Costs to business are estimated to be in the millions of dollars, although analysts have difficulty tracking losses since most businesses would prefer not to make them public. One technology consultant is quoted as saying, "If people found out how astoundingly large this problem is, they'd be shocked."

During the spring, French and American authorities together investigated a hacker suspected of breaking into and defacing some 2,000 Web sites in France, Britain, Australia, and the U.S. During the U.S. war against Iraq he concentrated on government offices and military sites, including the U.S. Navy, leaving messages in favor of the Palestinians or against U.S. military policy. The chief suspect: a 17-year-old French high school student who belongs to no political group and appears to be operating alone. Those who know him well say all he cares about is improving his technical skills.

In a seemingly unrelated incident, more than a thousand computers around the world are hijacked and secretly loaded with software that directs them to send pornographic Web sites and fliers soliciting porn-customers to thousands more computers. The program does no apparent harm to the computers and is downloaded so quickly that only the most sophisticated users are ever likely to know their machines have been hijacked. By creating a ring of high-speed computers, the hackers are able to send porn from just one machine at a time, making it particularly difficult to trace. Whoever is behind the scheme—some say it's the Russian mafia—is making money on every customer who signs up for sexually explicit materials and is probably capable of skimming credit card numbers.

This chapter revisits themes already touched upon in this book, weaving them around a new set of questions at the intersection of democracy, the market, and technology.

We begin with some assumptions: that both freedom and democracy are good things, that the worldwide movement toward more democratic governance is to be applauded and nurtured, and that the Internet can and should be a force supporting the growth of democracy. But the boundaries between cyberspace and the material world are porous; their locations and meanings are contested. The stakeholders in this global power struggle are many and varied: governments; individuals whose Internet use varies from net-shopping to hacking; international institutions like the WTO; cyberactivists; mom-and-pop dot.coms; citizens everywhere around the globe; and Microsoft, possibly the most powerful corporation in history.

Today, most people enter cyberspace through a Microsoft Window. In a world where access to cyberspace may be a prerequisite to participation in the democratic community or in the global economy, a single market player, Microsoft, is capable of wielding power in a way that has never been possible before. Across business sectors, across nations, the techno-titan has such pivotal influence that the U.S. government spent more than five years and millions of dollars trying to hold it accountable in a massive antitrust suit.

It was not always that way. Computer insiders—geeks and hackers—had been playing with what would become the Internet for decades prior to 1981 when Bill Gates co-founded Microsoft. They had their own ideas, their own ways of working, their own obsessions. This chapter starts by introducing an approach to programming that dates to the beginning of the information society: open source software. The competition between Linux, an operating system whose source-code is freely available to all, and Microsoft Windows allows us to consider how law, code, norms, and the marketplace vie for control of cyberspace.

Our focus in this chapter is on big-picture ethical concerns: Should government try harder to regulate cyberspace—through law? If so, which government(s)? Although the Internet originated in the U.S. and is currently dominated by Americans, cyberspace is global, inviting us to consider the role of international law or multinational norm-setting.

Finally we ask how cyberspace might affect real-world governance. Readings on democracy and the Internet highlight some of the critical faultlines that are appearing where political challenges meet the information revolution.

OPEN SOURCE SOFTWARE

Given enough eyeballs, all bugs are shallow.

—Variously attributed to Linus Torvalds and Eric S. Raymond

Although Windows is the dominant computer operating system in the world today, it is not the only one. Apple Computer Company runs on a wholly separate system—MAC-OS—and IBM, once considered the giant in the computer world, created OS/2 Warp. Those systems have something in common with Windows: They are proprietary. In effect, their creators "own" the source code that a computer reads and translates into "operating code" that in turn runs the computer hardware. And the source code is kept secret, closed to the outside world unless licensed by its owners.

Ordinary users who buy a computer with a pre-installed operating system have no way of reading the closed code that runs their machine. Even software developers who want to create an application to run on Windows or MAC-OS know very little about the source code. While they can negotiate with Microsoft or Apple to gain access to some of the code, more often, programmers follow the "black box" model. This enables them to use Application Program Interfaces written for various computer languages to get things done without seeing the source code. Instead, the OS-provider tells the programmer only as much as she needs to know to accomplish a task (e.g., writing a file to a disk). Then the programmer provides the information, and the computer's OS performs the task without the programmer ever really knowing how it is done.

But there is another kind of operating system, one whose code is not secret. As the author of the next reading explains,

> [A]nyone may download Linux for free. [What] distinguishes Linux from the dominant commercial software model epitomized by Microsoft's products is first and foremost its openness: in the same way scientific researchers allow all others in their fields to examine and use their findings, to be tested and developed further, hackers who take part in the Linux project permit all others to use, test, and develop their programs. In research, this is known as the scientific ethic. In the field of computer programming, it is called the open-source model ("source code" being a program's DNA, its form in the language used by programmers to develop it; without the source code, a person can use a program but is unable to develop it in new directions). (Pekka Himanen)

The Linux Operating System grew from a kernel planted by a 22-year-old Finnish hacker, Linus Torvalds, who posted his ideas for a computer operating system to an electronic bulletin board in 1991. In the following excerpt, we can see the development of the Internet as a chapter in the history of computer hackerism.

The Hacker's Ethic[3]
Pekka Himanen

The Network Working Group, a cluster of hackers culled from a talented group of university students...operated on the open-source model: anyone was allowed to contribute ideas, which were then developed collectively. The source codes of all solutions were published from the very beginning, so that others could use, test, and develop them....

[T]he Internet does not have any central directorate that guides its development; rather, its technology is still developed by an open community of hackers. This community discusses ideas, which become "standards" only if the larger Internet community thinks they are good and starts to use them. Sometimes these hacker ideas have taken

---

[3] Himanen, Pekka, *The Hacker's Ethic,* New York: Random House, 2001.

the Net in totally unanticipated directions, such as when Ray Tomlinson introduced e-mail in 1972. (He chose the @ symbol we still use in e-mail addresses.) Reflecting on this development, [Janet] Abbate notes that "there seems to have been no corporate participation in the design of the Internet....[I]t was designed informally and with little fanfare, by a self-selected group of experts.... "

[The mass breakthrough of the Internet and the Web] would not have been possible, of course, without the creation of that other remarkable invention of our time, the personal computer. Its ideational history goes back to the first MIT hackers who pioneered interactive computing. In their time, the computer field was still dominated by IBM's model of batch-processed mainframe computers, in which programmers did not have direct access to the computer but had to receive permission to pass their programs

on to a special operator. It could take days to receive the results. In contrast to this method, the MIT hacker favored interactive computing on minicomputers, in which the programmer could write his program directly into the computer, see the results, and immediately make desirable corrections....It meant a freeing up of direct exchange between individuals.

In 1976, using the information shared freely within the [Homebrew Computer Club in the Bay Area, Steve Wozniak] built, at the age of twenty-five, the first personal computer for the use of people without engineering degrees, the Apple I....In accord with the hacker ethic, Woz openly distributed blueprints of his computer to others, and published bits of his program. His hacker-created computer inspired the larger personal-computer revolution, the consequences of which are everywhere around us....

The Cathedral and the Bazaar by Eric S. Raymond is an evolving view of hacker history. http://catb.org/nesr/writings/cathedral-bazaar/

Questions

1. Does open source software encourage hacking? Is that a good thing?

2. Richard Stallman, a self-styled computer hacker, came up with the idea of a "copyleft" license. To perpetuate "free" software, Stallman grants a "copyleft" license that requires users to promise not to assert copyright to protect any improvements or changes they make, to distribute any changes subject to the same copyleft

license, and to make the entire source code for those changes publicly available. What ethical issues arise as we compare "copyleft" with the more common licenses granted by large software companies? Visit the homepage of the Free Software Foundation, **http://www.gnu.org**. What are its current concerns? What kinds of open-sourceware are available? How useful are they to the average person?

We win the political struggle against state control so as to re-entrench control in the name of the market.

—Lawrence Lessig, "The Future of Ideas"

Microsoft: The Power of the Market

http://www.microsoft.com

Microsoft offered its first operating system—MS DOS—in 1981. Four years later, it introduced Windows. In less than a decade, Microsoft captured more than 90% of the worldwide market for Intel-compatible PC operating systems. It held tightly to its "dominant, persistent and increasing share of the market"—so tightly that the U.S. Department of Justice, state attorneys general, and the European Union invoked antitrust laws to loosen Microsoft's control.[4] Eventually, U.S. courts concluded that Microsoft had used various means—unfair pricing policies and licensing agreements; pre-installation of applications like its own browser, Internet Explorer—to illegally acquire and maintain monopoly power.

The major federal antitrust suit against Microsoft ended in November 2002 with a court-approved settlement. Under the terms of that agreement, Microsoft was forced to change its business practices. The monopolizing tactics it used to drive out Netscape were to end. Microsoft could no longer enter exclusive deals that would hurt competitors. It agreed to offer uniform contract terms to its major customers, original equipment manufacturers like IBM PC, Compaq, and Dell. And, importantly, the company could no longer refuse to release some technical data to software developers working on applications that would run on Windows.

QUESTIONS

1. Microsoft's legal problems were not over. In December 2002, a federal judge ordered the firm to include Sun Microsystems' Java programming language in its Windows operating system amidst an ongoing billion-dollar lawsuit filed against it by Sun. As this book goes to press, Massachusetts is still pressing for stiffer penalties in its antitrust action, and European officials are pressing for penal-ties in their antitrust investigation into Microsoft. Find out how these controversies have been resolved.

2. Is it unethical to limit competition? One of the antitrust charges made against Microsoft was that it had used its monopoly power in the operating system marketplace to prevent the successful development of competing systems. Yet

---

[4] In 1999, the federal government estimated its costs at over $7 million. By 2002, Microsoft would agree to pay some $25 million to cover the costs of state antitrust litigation.

Linux—10,000 lines of code and used by fewer than a dozen people in 1991—has grown to more than 1.5 million lines, with an estimated seven million users. Animators like Dreamworks SKG and Pixar Animation—which have long used a proprietary version of UNIX—have been switching to Linux. Most recently, Walt Disney decided to switch from UNIX to Linux for their animation work. Doesn't this mean that Linux is already a major competitor to Windows? If so, is the heavy hand of the law needed to reign in Microsoft's growth?

3. In 1995, IBM spent tens of millions of dollars to attract independent software vendors to develop applications for its new OS/2 Warp operating system and to attempt to reverse-engineer or "clone" part of the Windows code. But IBM won no more than 10% of the market, even though OS/2 ran close to 2,500 applications at its peak. IBM essentially gave up trying to compete with MS Windows and instead, targeted a small market niche, mainly banks interested in particular applications that run on OS/2 Warp. In recent years, IBM has begun to incorporate Linux into some of its products. Go to IBM's Web site at **http://www.ibm.com** to find out what operating systems it currently offers in its computers. Are other major companies offering alternatives to MS Windows?

4. In what has become a complex legal dispute, various companies have claimed ownership of Linux. In March 2003, SCO Group brought a $1 billion lawsuit against IBM, charging IBM with illegally incorporating Unix code into Linux, and warning large corporate users of Linux that they, too, were in violation of copyrights. SCO's claims to the Unix code rest on a 1995 licensing agreement with Novell. But Novell disagrees and in November 2003, Novell tried to register its copyright to the Unix code with the U.S. Patent and Trademark Office—a move denounced by SCO as fraudulent. Throughout the dispute, Linus Torvalds insisted that he was the original creator of some of the disputed code. Follow developments in the disputes between SCO Group, Novell, IBM, and Torvalds. Do any of the players appear to have acted unethically?

5. Under the court decree and its own 2001 "shared source initiative," Microsoft allows researchers, industry partners, and governments to view and sometimes even modify the company's source code. Compare this shared source initiative to that of Mitch Kapor, the software industry pioneer best known as the developer of the Lotus 1-2-3 spreadsheet. In October 2002, Kapor used $5 million of his own money to found the Open Source Applications Foundation, a nonprofit, to create software applications with underlying codes to be freely shared with the public. His first project was Chandler, a "personal information manager that combines email and calendar functions with file sharing tools." Kapor hoped to make it available as a free download by the end of 2003 and to market it to small

The mission of the Open Source Development Labs is to be the "center of gravity" for Linux. http://www.osdl.org

organizations. Open Source Applications will be free to those who make variations available to others for free; those who want to use it to produce proprietary, commercial products of their own will have to pay a fee. What do you think of this idea? Find out what has happened to Chandler and the Open Source Applications Foundation.

6. Bruce Perens, a largely self-taught computer programmer, developed hardware and software tools for Pixar and later worked for Hewlett-Packard. Perens left HP in 2002 to launch Sincere Choice, promoting a "fair, competitive market" for both proprietary and Open Source software. Believing that governments would see huge cost savings by buying only software that operates well with other programs, Perens argues that software companies should be required to supply software with open technical standards and file formats that can be used by outside developers without having to pay royalties. **(a)** Find out what is going on with Sincere Choice. With whom does it compete: Gnu? Kapor's Open Source Foundation? Microsoft? **(b)** To what extent have governments—federal, state, or local—in the U.S. adopted Perens' ideas? Do any use Linux or other open source software?

7. Microsoft's dominance of the software that runs PCs and computer networks does not extend to smaller computer-driven devices like cell phones and hand-held computers. In April 2003, Microsoft changed its policies to allow its industry partners—including chipmakers and East Asian electronics companies like Mitsubishi and Samsung—to modify and redistribute the underlying programming code used in small devices such as cell phones and hand-held computers. Why do you think Microsoft made this policy change? Is there anything unethical about it?

8. What might be some of the ethical values underpinning the free market? Does threatening to break apart a huge corporation like Microsoft amount to punishing a company for being too successful, for being too good at operating within the free market value system? What ethical argument can you make against Microsoft's behavior as it grew to become a techno-titan?

New Platforms for Communication: WiFi

Wireless communications networks known as "WiFi"—for wireless fidelity—or "802.11b" might well be the PC revolution of the twenty-first century. The terms apply to a set of technical standards developed by the nonprofit Institute of Electrical and Electronics Engineers (IEEE) that facilitate high-speed wireless transfer of data. By defining requirements for interoperability, 802.11b makes it possible for anyone to design a device to communicate with anyone else's.

WiFi is facilitating a new kind of Internet access. This is how it works: Users usually access the Internet using a modem or an Ethernet card that fits into their computer. WiFi is basically a wireless (radio) version of Ethernet. Users replace their Ethernet controllers (which require a cable connection) with a card that performs the same function wirelessly. The service provider needs to install a series of "access points"—each providing a roughly 300-foot-radius service area or "hotspot"—in places where they want to provide signals. Although WiFi cards are more expensive than Ethernet cards, they have the huge advantage of being portable and untethered.

And, just as Linux and other open source software pose a challenge to proprietary software, WiFi threatens the power of the media giants that control the telephone and cable networks on which most computer users depend, holding out the promise of real competition in the future. Today, as Gray McCord, an engineer who has worked in the computer field for decades, noted, "the big boys are stumbling all over themselves to get into the act of making money from WiFi. Intel, for example, has joined with a consortium of companies to push their Centrino WiFi products. Verizon, SBC, and other Baby Bells are announcing and deploying hotspots and related services. The truth is that very few are making money from WiFi services, and a killer business model has not yet emerged."

By 2003, players around the world—local governments, dozens of organizations, and entrepreneurs—had created "hotspots" where laptop owners with a WiFi card could tap into wireless Internet services—some free, others for fees as high as $10 per day—to check e-mail at airports. Their motivation varies enormously. Four volunteers who put together the San Francisco Bay plan to provide free wireless service around the city's convention district hope it will help the tourism industry. Eric Engstrom reportedly walked away from a lucrative position at Microsoft to start Wildseed because he thinks the cutting edge of software development "has got to be the phone."[5] Starbucks allows customers to sign up for wireless service on the spot, hoping they'll stay to sip more lattes. Pubs—dubbed the coffee shops of England by WiFi entrepreneur George Polk—are the first stage of a planned nationwide network in the U.K. In Paris, the first hotspots are along a bus route between two train stations—a prototype for a planned network that will span the Metro system, allowing commuters to send e-mail and browse the Web.

---

[5] Steve Lohr, "Untethering From Clunky PC Box, Silicon Valley Hikes Wireless Frontier," *N.Y.Times*, April 7, 2003, Bus. 1.

QUESTIONS

1. One glitch in the WiFi system is that the system is not as secure as the telephone/cable system. Once plugged in, any computer equipped with the right wireless card within a roughly 300-foot radius of one of the small radio transmitters ("access points") that emit WiFi signals can sometimes pick up and use the signal—without necessarily paying a fee to the person or company paying for it. How ethical is such free-riding from a utilitarian perspective? Be sure to consider the long-term consequences to the various stakeholders.

2. The most common layer of security that can be placed on the connection is called Wireless Equivalency Protocol (WEP). WEP encrypts the data between the user and the access point. You have to have the same "key" on both ends to make it work. But the encryption is relatively simple to break with readily available software tools and a WiFi card. And since you have to manually give each user the key, there is always the possibility of it falling into the wrong hands. While all WiFi systems support WEP, not all systems actually use it. Is it ethical to set up a system without WEP? What can you find out about another emerging standard, WPA?

3. Wireless phone companies like Sprint PCS offer location-based services that allow users to track hand-held computers and adjust what the computers are doing to suit the circumstances. For example, by comparing information stored in an electronic database with the user's actual loca-tion, a handheld computer might remind its user of appointments. So, for example, if you're walking in front of a clothing store and your phone service knows you are there, it can send you an ad from that specific store as you walk by. Scientists are working on WiFi systems that would work on similar principles. What might be the benefits/harms of such tracking?

4. Cellphones compete for the same radio spectrum that the U.S. military uses. Some people have voiced concern that if WiFi is stored in millions of portable computers, it might further crowd communications, despite the fact that WiFi operates on a relatively small, unregulated frequency band that does not interfere with the military. **(a)** Presume for a moment that the military opposition to WiFi is legitimate. How should we as a society weigh these military concerns against the commercial and social benefits of a flourishing WiFi? **(b)** Now presume that the military opposition is not based on a legitimate concern. What ethical and social issues arise when a military arrogates technology or resources to the exclusion of a flourishing civilian WiFi market?

5. Many people pay their $40/month for a cable modem connection and then put a WiFi AP on it and share the connection with their friends. This can be especially prevalent in apartment complexes and other high density areas. Some of those "free" services that exist in cities are actually built on the same premise: that someone along the line has a broadband link which becomes "shared." How ethical is this practice?

6. WiFi is getting faster. While most WiFi today is 802.11b, (11Mbit) there are already newer versions at 54Mbit speed. Some people are chucking their wired phones and just using wireless PCs. If WiFi becomes truly ubiquitous, what will the impact be on other information access technologies, especially when the speed gets to the point where WiFi can carry video, voice, etc? Will people get rid of their dedicated phone and cable links and just use WiFi? What might this do to the wireless phone providers like Sprint PCS and T-Mobile and to the Baby Bells and cable companies? Should government try to prevent this from happening?

7. Another alternative platform for communication is the electrical power grid that already criss-crosses the nation. The Federal Communications Commission (FCC), among others, is on record as supportive of the idea of using that power grid to provide Internet access. What are the relative advantages/disadvantages of wireless vs. wired transmission?

GOVERNING IN CYBERSPACE

> *We, the representatives of the peoples of the world, assembled in Geneva from 10–12 December 2003 for the first phase of the World Summit on the Information Society, declare our common desire and commitment to build a people-centered, inclusive and development-oriented Information Society, where everyone can create, access, utilize and share information and knowledge, enabling individuals, communities and peoples to achieve their full potential in promoting their sustainable development and improving their quality of life, premised on the purposes and principles of the Charter of the United Nations and respecting fully and upholding the Universal Declaration of Human Rights.*
>
> *Communication is a fundamental social process, a basic human need and the foundation of all social organization. It is central to the Information Society. Everyone, everywhere should have the opportunity to participate and no one should be excluded from the benefits the Information Society offers.*
>
> —Declaration of Principles, WSIS, 12 December 2003

Throughout this text, we have invited you to engage in the important debate as to whether—and how—virtual life should be regulated, from the copying of music to the display of pornographic images. When the Internet began in the 1970s, it was closely linked to the academic and scientific community and used by relatively few people. Regulation at that time, when permissible uses were limited to "research and education," would have had slight impact on our overall economy. By 1994, however, some

2 million users worldwide had discovered the Net, which was opened to commercial use for the first time. Today, with 20 million people accessing the Internet using more than 2 million host computers, regulation clearly has broad economic implications.

As you read the articles in this section, try to identify concepts that have surfaced in earlier chapters and think how they relate to how cyberspace might be governed to enable fair global business.

From Trademark to Domain Name

> [W]ithout a single agreed-upon and continuously updated file, which maps IP numbers such as 216.33.139.78 onto domain names such as http://james-boyle. com, there is no such thing as "the" Internet. If your site is removed from this file, it will, for all practical purposes, cease to exist for the rest of the world.
>
> —James Boyle[6]

A person's address on the Internet is referred to as a domain name. In the early days of the Internet, a domain name seemed nothing more than a technical requirement for communication on the Net, a way of making sure that every computer on the Internet is uniquely identifiable. By the mid-1990s, as the pace of e-commerce quickened, the economic value of a cyber-address had become clear, and "cybersquatting" entered our vocabulary to describe the practice of registering another company name as your domain name so you could sell it back to them for a fat fee. The ethics, and even the legality, of cybersquatting were open to question. What was wrong with being the first to recognize the value of "travel.com"—even if you didn't own a travel agency? Or, better yet, registering **http://www.DeltaAirlines.com** or **http://www. niemanmarcus.com**, as one enterprising individual did? Would registering familiar company names as domain names violate American trademark law? Even if you are a European citizen? Or does Delta Airlines presumptively own the cyberversion of its address even before it acts to register it? Suppose you added a pejorative—trying to register **http://www.Walmartcanadasucks.com**, for example. Would that be ethical? Should you be punished for being ahead of the curve, for coming up with a new way to profit?

Today, the power to decide who gets which address on the Internet appears to rest with an organization called ICANN, which controls the creation of top-level domain names such as .com, .org, and .net. As Boyle and others have explained, the power to control domain names has spillover effects; ICANN can also make policy about the available world of Internet addresses as well as trademarks and domain names and can decide whether to add new top-level domain names such as <.union>. ICANN's current status was preceded by a power struggle. The following chronology outlines part of the history.

---

[6] James Boyle, "A Nondelegation Doctrine for the Digital Age?" 50 *Duke L.J.* 5 (2000).

INTERNET DOMAIN NAMES: CHRONOLOGY OF CONTROL

1983   A U.S. government agency, the National Science Foundation, creates InterNIC to oversee development of Internet architecture and registration of network groups.

1983   Telecommunications and info-tech companies form the Internet Society (ISOC) to oversee administration of the Internet.

1993-98   InterNIC joins Network Solutions Inc., a private company, to form NSI to register domain names on a first come, first served basis. NSI checks for duplicate domain names but does not investigate registered trademarks.

1998   Several groups, including the World Intellectual Property Organization (WIPO), form an International Ad Hoc Committee (IHAC) to champion internationalization of Internet government, declaring, "The Domain Name System is an international resource," and creating a committee to assign second-level domain names in accordance with "fair use."

1998   Another group, **http://www.gtld-mou.org**, tries to take control, declaring the Internet's top-level domains system to be a "public resource subject to the public trust," and advocates "global distribution of registrations." Eighty organizations sign on.

1998   Broad coalition from Internet business, technology, and academic communities forms a private, non-profit corporation, the Internet Corporation for Assigned Names and Numbers (ICANN).

1999   U.S. government gives oversight of Internet infrastructure to ICANN to manage domain names, allocate Internet Protocol Address spaces, and assign protocol parameters; ICANN adopts Uniform Domain Name Dispute Resolution Policy. To fulfill its mandate to introduce competition, ICANN allows some 100 companies to sell Internet addresses to the public.

1999   U.S. Congress passes Anticybersquatting Consumer Protection Act (ACPA), which outlaws cybersquatting (acting with a "bad faith intent to profit" from ownership of a domain name).

2003   U.S. Department of Commerce extends ICANN's authority until September 2006.

2003   International Telecommunications Union, a UN agency, convenes World Summit on Information Society (WSIS). WSIS calls for UN working group to examine Internet governance and possible need for more international oversight of semi-formal administrative bodies like ICANN.

Conflicts over trademark and cybersquatting are starting points for the broader questions of how best to regulate the Internet and resolve cyber-disputes. David Johnson and David Post argue that cyberspace requires a system of rules quite distinct from the laws that regulate physical, geographically-defined territories. It challenges the law's traditional reliance on territorial borders. Cyberspace, they say, is a "space" bounded by screens and passwords rather than physical markers. Using trademarks as an example, Johnson and Post illustrate how "taking Cyberspace seriously" as a unique place can lead to the development of both clear rules for online transactions and effective legal institutions.

Law and Borders—The Rise of Law in Cyberspace[7]

David R. Johnson and David Post

We take for granted a world in which geographical borders—lines separating physical spaces—are of primary importance in determining legal rights and responsibilities....Territorial borders, generally speaking, delineate areas within which different sets of legal rules apply....

[T]rademark law—schemes for the protection of the associations between words or images and particular commercial enterprises—is distinctly based on geographical separations. Trademark rights typically arise within a given country, usually on the basis of a mark on physical goods or in connection with the provision of services in specific locations within that country. Different countries have different trademark laws....There is no global registration scheme; protection of a particularly famous mark on a global basis requires registration in each country....

ABSENCE OF TERRITORIAL BORDERS IN CYBERSPACE

Cyberspace radically undermines the relationship between legally significant (online) phenomena and physical location. The rise of the global computer network is destroying the link between geographical location and: (1) the power of local governments to assert control over online behavior; (2) the effects of online behavior on individuals or things; (3) the legitimacy of a local sovereign's efforts to regulate global phenomena; and (4) the ability of physical location to give notice of which sets of rules apply....

Cyberspace has no territorially based boundaries....[E]]fforts to control the flow of electronic information across physical borders—to map local regulation and physical boundaries onto Cyberspace—are likely to prove futile, at least in countries that hope to participate in global commerce....Individual electrons can easily, and without any realistic prospect of detection, "enter" any sovereign's territory. The volume of electronic communications crossing territorial boundaries is just too great in relation to the resources available to government authorities. United States Customs offi-

---

[7] "Symposium, Surveying Law and Borders," 48 *Stan. L.Rev.* 1367 (1996).

cials have generally given up. They assert jurisdiction only over the physical goods that cross the geographic borders they guard and claim no right to force declarations of the value of materials transmitted by modem....

Nor are the effects of online activities tied to geographically proximate locations. Information available on the World Wide Web is available simultaneously to anyone with a connection to the global network....

[Finally, no particular country can claim that its laws rightfully control a particular claim] "[b]ecause events on the Net occur everywhere but nowhere in particular, are engaged in by online personae who are both "real"...and "intangible" (not necessarily or traceably tied to any particular person in the physical sense), and concern "things" (messages, databases, standing relationships) that are not necessarily separated from one another by any physical boundaries....

[Next, the authors return to the trademark example:]

Consider the placement of a "traditional" trademark on the face of a World Wide Web page. This page can be accessed instantly from any location connected to the Net. It is not clear that any given country's trademark authorities possess, or should possess, jurisdiction over such placements. Otherwise, any use of a trademark on the Net would be subject simultaneously to the jurisdiction of every country. Should a Web page advertising a local business in Illinois be deemed to infringe a trademark in Brazil just because the page can be accessed freely from Brazil? Large U.S. companies

may be upset by the appearance on the Web of names and symbols that overlap with their valid U.S.-registered trademarks. But these same names and symbols could also be validly registered by another party in Mexico whose "infringing" marks are now, suddenly, accessible from within the United States....

[The authors then argue that the "more legally significant...border for the 'law space' of the Net consists of the screens and passwords that separate the tangible from the virtual world...."]

A NEW BOUNDARY FOR CYBERSPACE

Treating Cyberspace as a separate "space" to which distinct laws apply should come naturally. There is a "placeness" to Cyberspace because the messages accessed there are persistent and accessible to many people. Furthermore, because entry into this world of stored online communications occurs through a screen and (usually) a password boundary, you know when you are "there." No one accidentally strays across the border into Cyberspace....[T]he line that separates online transactions from our dealings in the real world is just as distinct as the physical boundaries between our territorial governments—perhaps more so.

Crossing into Cyberspace is a meaningful act that would make application of a distinct "law of Cyberspace" fair to those who pass over the electronic boundary....

THE TRADEMARK EXAMPLE

There is nothing more fundamental, legally, than a name or identity....The domain name system, and other online uses of names and symbols tied to reputations and virtual locations, exist operationally only on the Net. These names can, of course, be printed on paper or embodied in physical form and shipped across geographic borders. But such physical uses should be distinguished from electronic use...[which is like] distribution to all jurisdictions simultaneously. Recall that the non-country-specific domain names like ".com" and ".edu" lead to the establishment of online addresses on a global basis. And through such widespread use, the global domain names gained proprietary value. In this context, assertion by any local jurisdiction of the right to set the rules applicable to the "domain name space" is an illegitimate extra-territorial power grab.

Conceiving of the Net as a separate place for purposes of legal analysis will have great simplifying effects. For example, a global registration system for all domain names and reputationally significant names and symbols used on the Net would become possible. Such a Net-based regime could take account of the special claims of owners of strong global marks (as used on physical goods) and "grandfather" these owners' rights to the use of their strong marks in the newly opened online territory. But a Net-based global registration system could also fully account for the true nature of the Net by treating the use of marks on Web pages as a global phenomena, by assessing the likelihood of confusion and dilution in the online context, and by harmonizing any rules with applicable engineering criteria, such as optimizing the overall size

of the domain name space.

A distinct set of rules applicable to trademarks in Cyberspace would greatly simplify matters by providing a basis to resist the inconsistent and conflicting assertions of geographically local prerogatives. If one country objects to the use of a mark on the Web that conflicts with a locally registered mark, the rebuttal would be that the mark has not been used inside the country at all, but only on the Web. If a company wants to know where to register its use of a symbol on the Net, or to check for conflicting prior uses of its mark, the answer will be obvious and cost effective: the designated registration authority for the relevant portion of the Net itself....

[Next, the authors ask who will set the rules and how will they be enforced.]

WILL RESPONSIBLE SELF-REGULATORY STRUCTURES EMERGE ON THE NET?

We believe the Net can develop its own effective legal institutions....

Experience suggests that the community of online users and service providers is up to the task of developing a self-governance system. [For example, the current domain name system evolved from decisions made by engineers and the practices of Internet service providers.]...

Every system operator who dispenses a password imposes at least some requirements as conditions of continuing access, including paying bills on time or remaining a member of a group entitled to access (for example, students at a university). System operators (sysops) have an extremely powerful enforcement tool at their disposal to enforce such rules—banishment. Moreover, communities of users have marshaled plenty of enforcement weapons to induce wrongdoers to comply with local conventions, such as rules against flaming, shunning, mailbombs, [and more]. And both sysops and users have begun explicitly to recognize that formulating and enforcing such rules should be a matter for principled discussion, not an act of will by whoever has control of the power switch.

While many of these new rules and customs apply only to specific, local areas of the global network, some standards apply through technical protocols on a nearly universal basis. And widespread agreement already exists about core principles of "netiquette" in mailing lists and discussion groups—although, admittedly, new users have a slow learning curve and the Net offers little formal "public education" regarding applicable norms. Moreover, dispute resolution mechanisms suited to this new environment also seem certain to prosper. Cyberspace is anything but anarchic; its distinct rule sets are becoming more robust every day....

Questions

1. How would you analyze the ethics of each of the following scenarios from a utilitarian perspective? A deontological one? How would a cyberlibertarian view each?

- Internet Dimensions registered the domain name **http://www.barbiesplaypen.com** and used it for a porn site.

- A company selling high-end stereo equipment under the registered trademark "Cello" was upset when the owner of AudioOnLine (seller of vintage audio equipment) registered the domain name **http://www.cello.com**. The owner did so only because there was no other musical-instrument name available. In the end, AudioOnLine offered to sell its Web address to any of ten companies for $5,000.

- In 1993, Joshua Quitters, a journalist, sent several letters to McDonald's Company, warning them to register for a Web site before they lost big money. The company ignored him until Quitters registered the domain name **http://www.ronaldmcdonald.com** for himself. Quitters refused to give it up until McDonald's agreed to donate a substantial sum of money to a public school in New York.

While Post and Johnson offer the vision of a body of cyberspace law to govern the jurisdiction of cyberspace, others suggest that law alone is not sufficient. As you read the next article, compare it to both Post and Johnson and the discussion in chapter 1 of

Lawrence Lessig's theory that market, law, norms, and architecture (code) are four mechanisms for controlling human behavior.

Governing the Internet[8]

James Boyle

The United Nations convened a World Summit on the Information Society in 2003. See http://www.itu.int/wsis/geneva to learn how it is addressing Boyle's concerns.

Because the network is global, national regulation merely invites relocation to another node in another jurisdiction. Because the network is distributed, with no central point to shut down or censor, it is very hard to grant partial access; the tap is either off or on full. Because the content is intangible, nonrivalrous, and infinitely reproducible, it is hard to police.

Many lay people, and a few legal scholars, have an implicit Austinian vision of law—roughly speaking, a command backed by threats, coming from a political superior who acknowledges no other superior, aimed at a geographically-defined population that renders the sovereign habitual obedience…. [I]t is hard to imagine a model of law better designed to fail at regulating the Internet. The clumsy fingers of the Leviathan cannot hold back the liquid flows of information; the sword's swing arrives too late; the parties have already relocated to another jurisdiction, hidden themselves with cryptography or "anonymous remailers," or simply vanished into the digital murk. Seeing these characteristics, many have concluded that the Internet will simply be impossible to police; states will wither away as their regulatory powers are undercut and their tax flows disappear into private currencies and anonymous international

transactions, hidden behind the walls of asymmetric cryptography….

But a number of scholars have argued that this assessment counts out the possibility of regulation too quickly, though the form of that regulation may not be the familiar command and control mechanism….

My own work has argued that regulation of the Internet will increasingly rely on a three-fold strategy—privatization, "propertization," and the use of technological controls. For the world of the global network, the effective form of regulation is likely to be built into architecture, designed around property-right claims, and both promulgated and enforced by quasi-private organizations.

PRIVATIZATION:

First, unable to respond at Internet speed, and limited by pesky constitutional constraints, the state can use private surrogates to achieve its goals…. [similar to the use of the V-chip rating system for television.]

PROPERTIZATION:

Second, the attempt to extend and then protect intellectual property rights online will drive much of the regulatory agenda and produce many of the technical methods of enforcement. Legal and technical features developed to prevent

---

[8] James Boyle, "A Nondelegation Doctrine for the Digital Age?" 50 *Duke L.J.* 5 (2000).

the next Napster, such as pervasive digital IDs, can be turned to the purpose of collecting sales tax or preventing Internet gambling. At the same time, contentious political issues—such as the allocation of domain names, or access to corporate information on pollution—can be restated as "intellectual property issues…."

TECHNOLOGICAL CONTROLS:

Third, governance of the Internet, as Lessig so presciently points out, will depend upon hardwired technological controls. Rather than have the sovereign strike your head from your shoulders after you violate copyright (but only if you can be found, and your jurisdiction is agreeable), it is better by far to design the system so as to hardwire in the desired regulatory features. Digital texts and music could be encoded to a particular person. Detection devices could be built into players, so that you cannot play my music. Unique identifiers could be built into computer chips, so that your computer would broadcast a universal ID with an associated set of legal characteristics as you roamed the Net: over eighteen years old, solvent up to a $3000 credit limit, lives in a jurisdiction that prohibits marijuana, certain levels of obscenity and online gambling, etc.…

"[P]ublic" regulation of the Internet will increasingly be done through "private" specialized groups, whose decisions are couched in terms of technical standards and/or as neutral resolutions of property-right conflicts. The point is, of course, that ICANN fits precisely within these parameters. ICANN is a nonprofit corporation, formed in a backhanded, semi-demi-unofficial way by a bewildering blur of government agencies, deriving its power from some kind of claim to control (if not ownership) of the root file, the "A" server, and the domain name system. Its policy leverage comes from the power of network effects. If you want to play on the Internet, you have to play ICANN's game.…

QUESTIONS

1. Since the U.S. started the Internet, the U.S. should determine how the Internet is governed. Is this an ethical statement? If not the U.S., who?

2. Find out what actions have been taken by the International Telecommunications Union since the World Summit on Information Society meeting in Geneva in December 2003 by checking **http://www.itu.int/home/index.html**.

3. Network Solutions (NSI), once "the" organization for registering domain names, is now only one of several registrars accredited by ICANN. Visit its Web site at **http://www.nsi.com** to find out what additional services currently are offered by NSI.

4. Visit ICANN's Web site at **http://www.icann.com**.

(a) Find out how it views its current role.

(b) Follow the links to one of the "accredited" registrars for domain names and compare its procedures and costs to those of NSI.

5. Critics of ICANN complain that the organization is neither as democratic nor as representative as it should be. Find out what changes were called for in the 2003 Memorandum of Agreement between ICANN and the U.S. Find out if any of those reforms have taken place and how critics have responded.

6. The domain server Verisign is the monopoly clearinghouse that directs Internet users to .com and .net addresses. In September 2003, Verisign began a new service, Site Finder. Users who misspell a .com or .net Internet address are redirected by Site Finder to sites supported by advertising. Internet Software Consortium (ISC), a nonprofit company that distributes the software used by service provides to direct their network traffic, was outraged. Within days of Verisign's launching of the Site Finder service, ISC offered a free patch that would counteract Site Finder. What ethical concerns arise when a quasi-official organization like Verisign decides to offer a service like Site Finder? Find out what has happened to Verisign's Site Finder service.

In the next reading, Viktor Mayer-Schonberger characterizes the dispute between those who want to regulate everything on the Internet and cyberlibertarians such as John Perry Barlow as a "battle of absolutes" that neither will win.

Impeach the Internet![9]

Viktor Mayer-Schonberger

...[W]e started off with this dream of a society in cyberspace, not bogged down by complex rules and laws, but in peaceful understanding of each other. And in the end we find that all communities form laws, attempting to regulate behavior. So while the Internet might win over the Law in the short term, in the long run it cannot escape regulation....

In comes a third scenario, the synthesizing outcome of the conflict between the Law and the Internet: Let us just assume that cyberspace is what it is—an extension of our real lives. And thus, the rules that make us tick in real life we will have to follow in cyberspace as well. Ostensibly, with this approach we reach for pragmatism and do the obvious: Cyberspace would be bound by rules, but nations—acutely aware of the pitfalls of regulatory activism à la [American laws passed to protect children from internet pornography]—would vow to abstain from regulating the Internet through purely national legislation. And instead of excessive law-making activity, we

---

[9] Viktor Mayer-Schonberger, "Impeach the Internet!" 46 *Loyola L.Rev.* 569 (2000).

would enforce existing rules and keep amending the ones that just do not work in virtuality. This is, at least in principle, the European Union's approach: pragmatic, careful, and deliberate....

And over time we would move ahead towards a model of rules for cyberspace devised and—I may add—enforced by its own citizens—a self-rule of the virtual realm....

...Real and virtual communities differ, however, in enforcement; being expelled from a community in medieval times was akin to death, and in small communities today it still carries with it weight and social disgrace. But in a global network, being expelled from one of the many "virtual" communities will not be as harmful—there are many others to join. Economists refer to this as the problem of "transactional cost."

A global virtual community, if it exists at all, will thus have to grapple with both the design of laws the community members will accept and such laws' effective enforcement. And in the end, if everything works in accordance with our plans, we will have a pragmatic set of legal rules for cyberspace; rules that have proven their validity in real life and laws that have been accepted by the community....

[W]hat I fear: We will have the laws on our books, but they will be useless. In cyberspace the true source of most of the rules is architecture. Let me explain: The Internet is a communicative network. What kind of information we may exchange and how it is exchanged is predetermined by technology....Whoever decides [the software protocols] decides the way we interact in cyberspace.

But who is deciding these structural issues? Which legislative body drafted the rules of Web browsing? Where can I vote for my representative to this rule-making body? And finally: If I do not agree with the decisions made and feel that they violate some larger, more fundamental principle, a liberty or a right of mine, which institution will hear my case, render judgment, and possibly enforce a ruling changing these communicative standards?

As a lawyer and a political scientist, I find it deeply troubling that the most vital issue of all in cyberspace, its governance, who passes the rules and who enforces them, is left in large part to the whims of an undoubtedly smart, but still just human being up there in Redmond, Washington. If the legislatures in the world want to keep a real say in issues that truly matter in cyberspace, they should think less about which laws to pass or whether the Internet needs special regulations and much more about how we can democratize the technical standard and protocol-setting process. How can we involve our polity in the decisions made by the software engineers at Microsoft, Intel, AOL, and maybe a handful of other companies, which together hold much of the decision-making power for our networked future?

In cyberspace the law as we know it may not be the conflict resolution mechanism of choice anymore. What we may instead have to do is to open up our conception of legal thinking, to extend it towards the underlying architecture of information infrastructures, and to refocus our attention on the democratization of rule design.

QUESTIONS

1. What does Mayer-Schonberger mean by a "democratization of rule design"? How might that be achieved?

2. Is it reasonable to expect Microsoft to allow others to tell it how to design its software for the Internet? To impose limits on Linux?

3. Compare Mayer-Schonberger's perspective to earlier readings by Johnson & Post and by James Boyle.

THE DIGITAL DIVIDE

What is the International Telecommunication Union doing to assist developing countries in harnessing the Internet to reduce the social divide and promote universal access to the Information Society? http://www.itu.int/ITU-D/e-strategy/.

As you move through the next readings, ask yourself what relationship you see between Internet governance and the digital divide.

In chapter 1, we introduced cybertarians—those who argue against government regulation and in favor of self-regulation of cyberspace. According to Amy Bomse, author of the next reading, their arguments rest on several grounds. Some digital libertarians, like David Post and David Johnson, rely on "descriptive arguments that focus primarily on the nature of the Internet, its intangibility, and the absence of geographic boundaries in virtual space." Others point to two precepts that "build on the belief that state regulation of the Internet is either infeasible or illegitimate: distaste for government and faith in market regulation." In the following passage, Bomse opens with a view of Internet history that challenges that put forward by cybertarians. The Internet traces its roots to the Advanced Research Project Agency (ARPA), a program created by the Eisenhower administration in the 1950s to coordinate military research and development. ARPA-funded projects at MIT and elsewhere linked their computers to create a government-funded collaborative research network, presumably safe from attack because it could re-route information through various nodes.

The Dependence of Cyberspace[10]

Amy Lynne Bomse

Internet history is a problem for digital libertarians. The claim that cyberspace is a stranger to government intervention founders on the actual history of the medium and the role the United States government played in establishing the Internet....In fact, while the NSF was developing the Internet as a non-commercial communications network, commercial enterprises, particularly banks, developed their own electronic data interchanges, which spawned credit card processing systems and then ATMs. When the Internet was opened to com-

---

[10] Amy Lynn Bomse, "Note, the Dependence of Cyberspace," 50 *Duke L.J.* 1717 (2001).

merce in the 1990s, mainstream corporations (including the largest player in the computer industry, Microsoft) were unprepared. "[T]hey had spent the previous decade investing in proprietary commercial on-line services like Prodigy, and yet suddenly here was this superior system they neither controlled nor understood." In the 1960s, AT&T predicted that a packet-switched network could not work and turned down the request from scientists to help build the Internet. These egg-on-your-face stories conflict with, and thus are omitted from, the story of the Internet as a triumph of private entrepreneurialism.

...Ironically, as the nature of the Internet shifted toward both greater controllability, with the arrival of encryption and identification tools, and greater significance in people's lives (thus creating more potential need and demand for regulation), the rhetoric around the Internet became more militantly libertarian. At the same time, it should be noted that despite the high-tech lobby's insistence that the Internet should not be subject to regulation, it has not been shy about lobbying Congress for desired legislation, such as increases in visas for foreign-born high-tech workers and indemnity from Y2K liability.

...[M]ost of the original programmers and users of the Internet probably subscribe to some version of antigovernment suspicion. But in the transition from an idiosyncratic domain of a cyber-intelligentsia to a highly commercialized mainstream medium, libertarianism shifted quietly from its countercultural roots to a free-market philosophy....

[In the next section, Bomse explores what she calls the "spillover conundrum". Cybertarians want cyberspace left to its own devices, to create its own rules. They don't want real-world governmental power to "spill-over" into cyberspace, where it might restrict the freedoms of people who are not represented by a particular nation. This might happen, for example, if the U.S. banned online gambling. The impact would extend from American citizens to those who live in Monte Carlo, where the government thrives on a legal gaming industry. At the same time, Bomse contends, cybertarians tend to ignore the spillover harms that occur in the real world as a result of online activity, such as invasions of privacy, consumer fraud, and the social costs of addictive gambling.]

[In theory] a self-ordered Internet would be responsive to the unique nature of the medium, because it would arise organically at the hands of Internet users, those "who care most deeply about this new digital trade in ideas, information and services." Users and systems operators would create rules through "principled discussions" and "a collective conversation about online participants' core values." Most importantly, a self-ordered Internet would be more democratic because its laws would be selected and endorsed by those who are subject to them. The consent of the governed, however, requires that the effects of online behavior stay within the boundaries of cyberspace. In other words, the self-regulation model of cyberspace requires a conception of cyberspace divorced from the real world.

The dilemma of spillover is a question about where cyberspace "is," where we are when we are "there," and, ultimately, who we are when we are "there."…

Who are we in cyberspace? In a classic New Yorker cartoon, a dog sits grinning at a computer terminal and the caption reads, "In cyberspace, no one knows you're a dog." The joke captures what is uniquely liberating about going online, the opportunity to be someone else, or to be multiple someone elses.…

The libertarian vision of cyberspace in fact requires that spillover not be considered a problem, because spillover, conceived of broadly as the interrelation between the physical and digital worlds, defeats the escapist fantasy. The desire to escape the messiness of real life, which on the Internet seems possible, is at the heart of the libertarian hope. But… spillover undercuts the cyberspace escapist dream.

The belief that cyberspace produces an absence of material conditions (geography, gender, and race, to list just a few) is implicit in the oft-repeated claim that cyberspace is "everywhere and nowhere." There is a sense in which "everywhere and nowhere" is an accurate description of one's experience in cyberspace. But the statement also tells us something about the privileged social position of the speaker. Cyberspace, in fact, is not everywhere. According to a Department of Commerce study, less than one in ten households with incomes under $20,000 has Internet access (compared to 60% of households earning $75,000 or more). In the United States, the so- called "digital divide" can be measured along income, racial, and educational lines, as well as between urban and rural populations. There is also an enormous international gap in access to new communications media. In South Asia, one person in 10,000 uses the Internet. Countries like Pakistan and Yemen have fewer than two telephone lines per hundred citizens. And the World Bank estimates that developing countries will require $60 billion to develop their telecommunications networks.…Social inequalities in the offline world shape the Internet while, at the same time, the Internet may intensify already existing social divisions.

[Next, Bomse argues that "the claim that cyberspace is 'everywhere but nowhere,' a utopian dream of human equality, turns out to mask political realities."]

A more chilling example is offered in an essay by Margaret Chon. She describes a discussion in a "gender and cyberspace" class about Jake Baker, the University of Michigan student who was arrested for sending e-mail messages describing sexual fantasies of rape and torture. A female student shares how her initial reaction ("that the government never should have brought the case against Baker") changed after a personal experience: she was nearly raped after her car broke down. It turned out that the American Automobile Association was posting the locations of stranded motorists on its website, making it easy for anyone to find them. Chon's story is not just about direct spillover. The story also is about the different ways in which the Internet will affect different members of society in their online and offline interactions....The primary subject of Chon's essay is the Internet's expansion of the market for mail-order brides from the Philippines. Women forced by poverty to sell themselves into slavery offer an important counterpoint to the digital libertarian faith in easy exit. Both examples offered by Chon point to the fact that the electronic space of the computer screen and the flesh-and-bone space of the users is a two-way street. As much as real-world conditions impact the Internet, the Internet is also itself a real-world condition....

The Internet does not exist apart from the world in which it was created and in which its users, and those who are not yet its users, reside. Claims of dematerialism are not just descriptively false, they are normative statements motivated by a particular political goal: the triumph of private, market-based decisionmaking. While one can sympathize with and even share in a fantasy of escape, via cyberspace travel, from the tediously fractious and difficult human condition, this fantasy is not a useful premise on which to base public policy. With growing political and economic realities such as the recent AOL-Time Warner merger, it is essential to acknowledge that power structures already exist in cyberspace. Acknowledging that politics is inevitable allows us to shift the discussion to the question of what style of politics is preferable. While there is certainly room for freedom from government intervention in some areas, and a need for protection of property in others, neither of these goals is currently at risk in the same way as the public aspect of the Internet. For this reason, it is critical that policymakers and other students of the Internet carefully consider the broader implications of the argument for privatization.

QUESTIONS

1. Restate the author's critique of cybertarians in your own words.

2. The International Telecommunications Union estimated that only 1 percent of people in the world's poorest countries were connected to the Internet in 2003. The 450,000 residents of Luxembourg have more Internet capacity than Africa's 760 million people. How does the digital divide fit into Bomse's argument?

3. According to Bomse, "While there is certainly room for freedom from government intervention in some areas, and a need for protection of property in others, neither of these goals is currently at risk in the same way as the public aspect of the Internet." What does she mean here? In what sense is the public aspect of the Internet at risk? Think of issues raised in chapter 1 and other parts of this book to enlarge your answer.

In the following reading, Reed Hundt, former chairman of the FCC and lecturer at Yale Law School and Yale School of Management, explains his vision of the relationship of law, code, and the market in controlling the Internet. Hundt would agree with Bomse that cybertarians tend to overlook the digital divide. He writes that "the champions of freeness do not normally address the costs involved in connecting children, the poor and rural people to the Net. By contrast, believers in pro-active government focus on developing reasonably efficient subsidies that stimulate competitors to offer Net access to everyone."

The Future of the Net[11]

Reed Hundt

...Code is a particularly complex and insidious product. Monopolists—such as the Bell companies, whose networks serve about 85% of America's on-line consumers, or Microsoft, which controls the personal computer's operating system gateway to the Net—may use software code and law to control cyberspace. However, their power is at bottom no more or less than market power. Where they have that, the essential question is whether we use regulations to try to limit their influence over the future of the Net or instead use regulations to erode that market power by introducing competition....

The central political idea of the American government in the 1990s about the Internet was this: spending and regulation should be employed to make the Net widespread and cheap. The "information highway," as the concept of distance communication was called before we recognized it was the Internet, was supposed to connect everyone in the world to everyone else. It would thereby permit an exchange of information that would stimulate global economic development and the spread of democracy.

...The governmental assumption was that, if access was widespread and cheap, the broad new audience of users would attract a rapidly multiplying number of Internet content providers. The ability of users to come together from all over the country and the world has encouraged providers to generate niche content that would be unappealing to a traditional mass media audience. So a progressive magazine called commondreams.org has materialized on the Net, whereas it would not be able to attract a print-on-paper audience due to distribution and marketing costs. A broad base of e-consumers has stimulated **slashdot. com** to change consumer reporting. Day traders catalyzed the creation of thestreet.com and **motleyfool.com**, which in turn have contributed to stability in individual investor confidence that has mitigated the severity of the recession. Despite Hollywood's initiatives against file sharing (also known as music "downloading"), never in history has so

---

[11] Reed Hundt, Book Review, "The Future of the Net—Comments on Lawrence Lessig's *Code and Other Laws of Cyberspace* and *The Future of Ideas*," 68 *Brook.L.Rev.* 289 (2002) (book review).

much new content been created so quickly. As a billion people join the world of Net users in this decade, no end is in sight for content creation.

Consistent with the policy of making the Internet the new mass medium, government should, over time, phase out subsidies of voice telephony and instead provide the funds necessary to make Internet access a universal service. For example, under the e-rate [program, classroom Internet access rose from] 6% in 1996 to about 84% today. [The E-rate program] built a constituency for openness: children....

...[T]he information sector is not just any industry, but the part of our economy that makes democracy possible. A regulatory approach to assuring openness—versus a structural approach—means that government must constantly monitor the software and the pricing of the companies that mediate between government and the voters. The history of broadcast regulation indicates that in such a relationship, the industry inevitably gains the upper hand over the lawmakers....

There are three key steps that the government must take to secure the future of the Net. First, the FCC should flood the market with cheap or even free spectrum....In a competitive market, it is highly likely that all will adopt the lingua franca of open code. Competition is a good method of assuring open code; proprietary codes are more likely to survive in non-competitive markets.

Second, the United States should insist on the globalization of the competitive paradigm for building the Net....

Third, government should set comprehensive, inclusive social goals for the Internet. For example, broadband should be universally affordable. Health care, education and politics (especially voting) should be delivered fairly and efficiently over the Net. On a global level, the Net can be a tool in promoting democracy, stimulating economic development in poor countries and attacking the ignorance and hatred that may spawn terrorism. To pursue these social goals, competition among providers seeking reasonable government subsidies is the ideal approach....

QUESTIONS

1. Hundt was chair of the FCC from 1993 to 1997, during the Clinton administration. What can you find out about the views of the current chair? Are they more or less consistent with your view of the appropriate role for a U.S. agency trying to regulate the Internet?

2. To what extent are Hundt's recommendations realistic? Have any been carried out?

3. In June 2003 the FCC voted to loosen up a decades-old regulation that prevented one entity from owning too large a share of traditional news media. Its decision rested, in part, on the argument that the Internet ensured ample diversity of views. But a report by the National Center for Digital Government at Harvard cast doubt on that rationale. "Relying on links and search engines, most people are directed to a few very successful sites; the rest remain invisible to the majority of users," according to Matthew Hindman and Kenneth Neil Cukier, "[resulting in] greater media concentration online than in the offline world." They give an example: Two thirds of all hyperlinks to sites on "gun control" direct users to the ten most popular sites—despite the fact that there are more than 13,000 Web pages on gun control. Why does this matter? How might it be changed?

4. Find out about the cybertarian perspective on the digital divide. Do they deny that it exists? If not, do they hold out for a market-based solution? Explain.

Alfred C. Yen, Professor of Law at Boston College Law School, challenges the cybertarian use of the "wild west" metaphor with its connotation of "cyberspace as a 'place' whose natural characteristics guarantee freedom and opportunity...different from real space...[where] government should generally refrain from regulating." In the next reading, Yen cautions against unchallenged acceptance of that view: "[T]he operating image of the Western Frontier metaphor is one where the virtuous prevail and evil is wiped out. Unfortunately, the West was not such a place. Genocide, racism, and personal exploitation in the name of progress comprise a significant portion of Western Frontier history, but popular culture has cemented a romanticized version of the West that ignores or discounts this reality." He proposes we find a new metaphor for cyberspace.

Western Frontier or Feudal Society?[12]

Alfred C. Yen

...The feudal state sprouted from a series of agreements between a king and his followers. The king, who claimed all of the country's land for himself, divided his land into parcels known as "fiefs" and granted them to his most loyal followers. In return, these "tenants-in-chief" swore their loyalty to the king and promised to provide military service, money, prayer, or civil service....[These vassals to the king] could in turn subdivide their lands and become lords to vassals of their own...through multiple layers of "mesne lords" who simultane-

---

[12] Alfred C. Yen, "Western Frontier or Feudal Society? Metaphors and Perceptions of Cyberspace," 17 *Berkeley Tech. L.J.* 1207 (2002). ©2002 Alfred C. Yen.

ously acted as vassals to their superiors and lords to their inferiors....

The feudal character of cyberspace emerges from the hierarchical privatization of its government associated with the granting of Internet domains. In particular, ICANN is a private entity that controls a most precious commodity—cyberspace "land" in the form of domain names. Like a feudal king, ICANN grants "cyberfiefs" to those who promise to pay money and abide by ICANN's rules in exchange for Internet domains. Recipients of cyberfiefs need only comply with minimal technical standards such as TCP/IP [Internet Protocols] before making their cyberfiefs operational. ICANN distributes these cyberfiefs in a manner reminiscent of the methods used by feudal kings...[dividing] the available "cyberland" into [Top Level Domains or] TLDs such as .com, .edu, and .org. It then delegates the management of TLDs to TLD managers like VeriSign Global Registry Services. TLD managers then deal with various Internet domain name registrars, who in turn deal with the general public. This pattern of distribution makes TLD managers' status analogous to [medieval, feudal] tenants-in-chief and domain name registrars' status analogous to mesne lords, and it effectively creates a class of "cyberlords" that includes TLD managers, registrars, ISPs, businesses, and others who obtain and exploit significant interests in "cyberland."

The hierarchical distribution of cyberfiefs means that, as in feudal society, every interest in cyberland is held from a superior computer operator who func-

tions as lord over vassal or serf....[T]he Internet has become too unwieldy for any attempt to manage all aspects of its operation. New cyberlords therefore face very few restrictions on how they operate their computers. Cyberlords can post whatever content they like on their computers, permit or refuse communications from particular individuals and domains, limit the number of users their computers serve, or observe the behavior of users....

Ordinary individuals generally get Internet access by purchasing service from a commercial Internet Service Provider ("ISP") or employers who act as ISPs. The typical ISP is a cyberlord who sells access to the Internet...[and] takes complete control of the user's existence in cyberspace as soon as she logs on.

If the ISP chooses to do nothing, the user can employ whatever software she desires to experience cyberspace as she sees fit. She can view movie trailers, read about history, send e-mail, or "chat" with her friends. However, the ISP has the power and authority to alter this experience in whatever way it desires....Like city planners, they can create meeting places, facilitate travel through cyberspace, and control the size of crowds...keep their users from visiting certain parts of cyberspace, censor what they say and read, review their e-mail, monitor their behavior, and enforce codes of conduct. Moreover, an ISP can enforce its will because it controls the user's ability to enter cyberspace. An ISP can "sentence" users who defy its rules by denying access to certain materials, logging them off for specified amounts of

http://icann.com directs users to active websites related to ICANN.

time, deleting files kept on the ISP's server, or even terminating the user's account completely. Moreover, it can do these things arbitrarily without providing notice, a hearing, or any other form of due process. In "real space," the power to behave this way rests with the state. In cyberspace, however, it belongs to the cyberlord.

Why does Yen call ISPs "cyberlords"?

Almost every cyberlord exercises the same power as ISPs by dictating the experience of those who connect to his computer. In some cases, the appearance of the virtual state is clear because the cyberlord creates a virtual community that comes with a governing "constitution." In other cases, the appearance of

state power seems nonexistent because the site offers users a limited experience such as pure text or technical connection to the Internet's backbone. However, it is still the cyberlord's choice, and not her inability, to offer the limited experience. The private power to shape and control the user's experience still remains.

The hierarchical organization of domain names and computers gives the Internet a distinctly feudal form of government. Cyberlords exercise the power of states as an incident of private property....[and] this power resides in the hands of numerous cyberlords. The Internet's government, like that of a feudal society, is highly fragmented.

QUESTIONS

1. Yen goes on to say that "each of a cyberlords' users represents an opportunity to sell or advertise something." This gives ISPs and other Web site cyberlords incentive to attract and retain as many users as they can "while connecting their users' 'cyberlives' to profits whenever possible." How does this play out in cyberspace? Is there anything unethical about it?

2. In theory, at least, the author claims that the economic incentive "does not, however, mean that cyberlords routinely abuse their cyberserfs. Just like their medieval counterparts, cyberlords have to limit the exploitation of their cyberserfs because overexploitation will drive cyberserfs to join the cybermanors of his competitors." Assume you are a

cyberserf. How easy would it be for you to join a new cybermanor?

3. Yen has a reason for invoking the Feudal Society metaphor.

[It] challenges the Western Frontier metaphor by diverting attention from romanticized images of the West to the darker ones of feudal Europe. Like America's Western Frontier, medieval Europe had abundant land that governments found difficult to control. However, these conditions did not give rise to a happy European version of the Western Frontier experience. Instead, Europe endured three centuries of feudal rule that declined only as the evolving modern state expanded its regulation of otherwise private feudal arrangements. The Feudal Society metaphor contradicts the idea that plentiful land and minimal government regulation ensure widespread freedom and prosperity. Indeed, the metaphor implies that such conditions support the fragmentation of political authority and the private exercise of political power. By doing so, the metaphor draws attention to the many instances where, as in medieval Europe, weak states created political vacuums ultimately filled by powerful individuals and clans who governed for private gain.

Using Yen's metaphor, Bomse might say that cybertarians think they live in the wild west when they reside in a feudal world. Can you come up with a new metaphor for cyberspace that expresses your vision of what it should be?

4. Like the metaphor of the wild west, the idea of cyberspace as a "place" is both widespread and contested. Consider the following:

No one is "in" cyberspace. The Internet is merely a simple computer protocol, a piece of code that permits computer users to transmit data between their computers using existing communications networks.... [R]egardless of the form that the data takes, it is data and not people traveling. Data have been traveling on wires and through the airwaves for centuries at the behest of humans, but no one believes the television, the telegraph, or the telephone are "places" within which people travel....

...[P]erhaps when we access the Internet it seems so much like we are in a different physical space that we accept cyberspace as a "real" or physical place....[But] most users of the Internet surely do not experience it as anything remotely resembling a physical place. What's really different about the Internet is interconnection...With a click of the mouse we can see information offered on billions of web pages by millions of people and companies from all over the world...[and] move from a page in Switzerland to one in Swaziland merely by following a link. Perhaps it is this automatic connection to pages that come from distant lands that makes us feel as though we are traveling through cyberspace.[13]

(a) Cyberspace as space and cyberspace as the wild, wild west are two of the most powerful metaphors of our time. What does it matter if neither is a perfect fit with reality?

(b) If cyberspace is not a place, then no one really "enters" a Web site. If no one enters a Web site, no one can fill the space and deprive its owner of it. And spammers who mass mail to AOL or Juno customers should not be considered trespassers. Does that logic make sense? Is it any more or less ethical to intrude on someone's computer by spamming than it is to trespass on someone's lakeside property?

---

[13] Mark A. Lemley, "Place and Cyberspace," 91 *Cal.L.Rev.* 521 (2003).

DEMOCRACY AND THE INTERNET

I'm very optimistic about the role of human beings in the Information Age, because this is an era where people—their knowledge, and their ability to put that knowledge to work—will be more important than ever before....[T]he Information Age is enabling people who were previously forced to pursue a single means of wealth creation—those, for example, who lived in remote areas had no option but to work on the land—to choose from a far wider range of work. Technology such as the PC; the Internet and cheap telecommunications have brought amazing mobility to the factors of production.

—Bill Gates (1999)

Freedom of the press is guaranteed only to those who own it.

—A.J. Liebling (1975)

One of the defining characteristics of the Internet is that it is a net. It is a vast web of connections, potentially revolutionizing any societal goal for which quick, cheap communication is useful. To the extent that we are struggling for improved democratic decision-making in most nations and for better ways to reach agreements for peace, economic prosperity, and environmental purity globally, the Internet seems to hold out tremendous promise. Ideally, citizens in a democracy are well-informed. They have access to information and analysis that affects the polity; they have access to public exchange where issues of importance can be hashed out. In other words, people in a democracy live in an open information climate, and they have the tools they need for forming and expressing opinions. Many believe that information technology is exactly what we need to enhance such a climate, to ensure that open debate flourishes. In the U.S., we have moved from a time 200 years ago when there were hundreds of small presses and every town had a public commons to what many see as a tightly restricted arena for human interaction. Today, a handful of huge companies control what Benjamin Barber has called "the infotainment telesector," offering a relatively limited menu of news that often blends too well with advertisements and entertainment and too often cuts up issues into "sound bytes" or submerges them completely beneath "human interest" and scandal. This is a world where too many of us do not get the chance to meet face-to-face for discussion of important public issues because our traditional public forums have changed. Our inner-city parks are dangerous; we go to privately owned malls where we—separately—shop. Into this scene, the Internet has been recently dropped, and we wonder what it might mean for civic involvement.

In chapter 2, we read an excerpt from John McChesney's 1997 interview with David Brin.[14] Here we look at another part of that interview in which the two talk about alienation in the postmodern world. As you read it, consider the implications of their comments for democracy.

Alienation

John McChesney: One of the things that struck me, one of the ironies about this period of the 20th century, is that as we've moved into more isolated lives, because of the automobile and our commutes and so on, and we travel sealed in steel, back and forth, and we go to our suburban homes, and often there's a fairly anonymous neighborhood there, but that lifestyle has demanded other kinds of electronic conveniences: Cellular phones in the car because we're in the car so much, using the Internet for shopping at home, and perhaps that will increase in a few years—so as we've become more private in a way, and more isolated, we've become also more accessible to those who want to know more about our lives.

David Brin: Well, Clifford Stoll and Howard Rheingold have taken the opposite tacks on this. Howard Rheingold says that in our private homes, we may not know our neighbors, but we will expand into a virtual community of our own interests. We're not becoming a nation of lotus-eaters; the one-third who sit around watching TV, back a hundred years, that one-third used to sit around watching the fire. And the TV is more enlightening than the fire.

But there was also a third making chamber music or poetry together. Well, guess what, these people are on the Web, making friendships 10,000 miles away; they have a million hobbies, you know these Civil War reenactment societies, and now the snowboarders aren't harassing the skiers anymore; they're jumping out of airplanes. So we have a vigorous, vigorous society that's not decadent at all. And Howard is right that the extended virtual communities will for some of us just be an enhancement of what it is to be a human being.

But Clifford Stoll is right too. When he talks about Silicon Snake Oil, he talks about getting glued to electronic media for others can be another addiction. Ever since the invention of beer in Sumeria 6,000 years ago, each generation of humans has had to fight a new addiction. And being trapped inside an electronic world, trapped inside a little house, not knowing your neighbors, not attending a July Fourth barbecue in your neighborhood, not participating in a little local political action, not participating in your elementary school—this is fairly sad, it's pathetic....

---

[14] Excerpts from *The Transparent Society,* June 6, 1997, HotSeat Interview (http://hotwired. Lycos.com/packet/hotseat/97/22/trasncript4a.html).

QUESTIONS

1. What connections do you see between the observations of McChesney, Brin, and those of

Robert D. Putnam:

Will the Internet in practice turn out to be a niftier telephone or a niftier television? In other words, will the Internet become predominantly a means of active, social communication or a means of passive, private entertainment? Will computer-mediated communication "crowd out" face-to-face ties? It is, in this domain especially, much too early to know. Very preliminary evidence suggests, hopefully, that time on the Internet may displace time in front of the tube: one survey in 1999 found that among Internet users, 42 percent said they watched less TV as a result, compared with only 19 percent who said they read fewer magazines and 16 percent who said they read fewer newspapers. On the other hand, an early experimental study found that extensive Internet usage seemed to cause greater social isolation and even depression. Amid these scattered straws in the wind, a final caution: The commercial incentives that currently govern Internet development seem destined to emphasize individualized entertainment and commerce rather than community engagement. If more community-friendly technology is to be developed, the incentive may need to come from outside the marketplace.[15]

2. There are now newsfilters that enable individuals to customize their access to news. Is there anything potentially disturbing about this technology?

CYBER-ACTIVISM

In 1990, the military government in Myanmar (formerly Burma) refused to recognize the results of democratic elections. Activists around the world protested the regime's ongoing pattern of human rights abuse and hoped to emulate the success of the movement that helped end apartheid in South Africa. Across the U.S., they lobbied for "Burma laws." The Massachusetts version was a selective-purchases statute—one that required the state to create a blacklist of persons and companies with business connections to Burma. Neither the legislature nor any government agency was allowed to buy goods or services from anyone on that restricted list.

USA*ENGAGE, a coalition of business groups, sued to challenge the constitutionality of the Massachusetts law. In November 1999, as the Free Burma Coalition was getting ready to join environmentalists, union members, and other activists in the

---

[15] Putnam, Robert D., *Bowling Alone: The Collapse and Revival of American Community*, New York: Simon & Schuster, 2000, p. 179.

"Battle in Seattle" against the WTO (World Trade Organization), the Supreme Court agreed to decide the Burma-law case.

In the end, the sanction laws were overturned, and activists needed to adopt new strategies. But, as the next reading describes, they had a powerful tool for doing so: the Internet.

Massachusetts, Burma, and the World Trade Organization: A Commentary on Blacklisting, Federalism, and Internet Advocacy in the Global Trading Era[16]

Peter L. Fitzgerald

The new communication technologies embodied in the Internet are fueling the globalization of the world economy. The marketing hyperbole associated with the "global village" is now common-place, as exemplified by IBM's long-running "Solutions for a Small Planet" advertising campaign. From meditating Tibetan Monks spiritually communicating about the possibility of collaborating over computer networks, ecologists lost in the rain forests of Brazil using a laptop to find their way...or a small Texas company using the Internet to win a contract supplying parts to a Japanese multinational...the message is one of individual empowerment in a marketplace that transcends national boundaries....

Ironically, the same tools that create these worldwide opportunities for businesses are also revitalizing an old strain of anti-corporate and anti-colonial sentiment while providing the ability to present these concerns in new ways. For example, as Naomi Klein wrote in her book, *No Logo: Taking Aim at the Brand Bullies*:

More and more...we in the West have been catching glimpses of another kind of global village, where the economic divide is widening and cultural choices narrowing.

This is a village where some multinationals, far from leveling the global playing field with jobs and technology for all, are in the process of mining the planet's poorest back country for unimaginable profits. This is the village where Bill Gates lives, amassing a fortune of $55 billion while a third of his workforce is classified as temporary workers....On the outskirts of Manila, for instance, I met a seventeen-year-old girl who assembles CD-ROM drives for IBM. I told her I was impressed that someone so young could do such high-tech work. "We make computers," she told me, "but we don't know how to operate computers." Ours...is not such a small planet after all.

While pervasive distrust of corporate power and regulatory institutions in the global marketplace is a common and familiar theme, the extensive use of the Internet to mobilize and communicate

---

[16] 34 *Cornell Int'l L.J.* 1 (2001).

the protesters' positions on the "contested terrain of very public choices" is entirely new. The Burma example illustrates how the power of the Internet gives these popular concerns new currency in the marketplace, consequently requiring adjustments in how governmental institutions respond to the issues.

MASSACHUSETTS BURMA LAW AND INTERNET ADVOCACY

[The] Burma laws are just one in a series of state and local sanctions measures that followed the anti-apartheid [in South Africa] movement....[S]tate and local governments across the United States have passed various measures expressing opposition to Castro's government in Cuba, ethnic strife and human rights violations in Nigeria, the Chinese occupation of Tibet, Indonesia's actions in East Timor, and the Swiss banks' handling of Nazi loot and property from the victims of the Holocaust. Proponents consider these measures "tools for democracy" because they are often intended to promote democratic reforms in the target country and because they reflect a local government response to grassroots concerns about conditions or actions in other countries.

The proliferation of state and local sanctions...prompted the opponents of these measures to become increasingly organized and active, establishing industry groups such as USA*ENGAGE, to lobby against sanctions in the name of free trade.

[Next, Fitzgerald explains how advocacy groups have used technology:]

All the parties have embraced technology to great effect. In the case of Burma,

the organizations opposing the [military regime, SLORC] mounted an extensive online campaign to coordinate their efforts through e-mail, the online BurmaNet, and similar Internet sites. On the other side, USA*ENGAGE, with more than 600 major businesses as members, used its Web site and e-mail lists to coordinate support for the suit by its parent organization, the National Foreign Trade Council, against the Massachusetts Burma law. The Free Burma campaign directed against Pepsi illustrated the growing importance and impact of technology on these issues over the past decade. The campaign progressed from an unheralded grassroots boycott to a catalyst for passage of state and local selective purchasing laws around the country.

Pepsi opened a bottling plant in Rangoon in late 1991 as a joint venture with a prominent business figure associated with the [government.] Burmese dissidents immediately denounced Pepsi's new plant as providing tax monies and support for the military junta. At roughly the same time, Pepsi, like other companies, was trying to capture the youth market by expanding its presence at schools and universities. Students at Carleton University in Ottawa, Canada, the location of one of Pepsi's earliest exclusive vending deals, became concerned about the company's business in Burma and distributed a flyer in early 1993 detailing the situation in Burma and linking Pepsi's joint venture to the SLORC and that government's abuse of human rights. Students posted the flyer to various Usenet newsgroups. This flyer prompted increased interest at other universities where Pepsi was the "official" soft-drink, and a special newsgroup was created to discuss the situation in Burma. Students also established the BurmaNet e-mail newsletter.

These tools played a significant role in spreading the emerging Pepsi boycott campaign and distributing campus "info pak" action kits to several hundred groups around the world by late 1995. These kits contained background information on Burma and Pepsi's involvement, as well as stickers parodying Pepsi's slogans as "Pepsi: The Choice of a New Genocide." The kits urged students to "[p]ressure schools to terminate food or beverage contracts selling PepsiCo products until it leaves Burma." Additionally, the Free Burma Coalition was one of the first activist groups to take full advantage of the World Wide Web when it established its Web site in 1995 with the support of the Soros Foundation and the Open Society Institute. This site later became the basis for the current BurmaNet Web site. The use of these various tools prompted Mike Jendrzejczk, the Washington Director of Human Rights Watch/Asia, to comment, "Cyberspace spawned the movement to restore human rights to Burma."

Proponents of reform in Burma used Internet communications to proceed simultaneously on a variety of fronts: uniting and spreading the campus boycott, seeking sanctions legislation at the federal and state level, and prompting and supporting shareholder action against Pepsi. The Internet made it possible for a relatively small number of activists to have a greater impact in part because electronic communications bypass the editing that occurs in the traditional media and the filtering that naturally occurs when relying upon third parties such as international nongovernmental organizations. With the Internet, those concerned with a particular issue can avoid the sporadic coverage afforded by other media; supply almost daily reports, commentary, and analysis to their supporters; and maintain an effective and relatively inexpensive means of coordinating responsive action. As Simon Billenness declared, the Burma effort was "one of the first cybercampaigns....If something happens in Rangoon, I'm going to know about it the next day by reading my e-mail....The Internet has proved to be an invaluable tool for organization."

By 1996, the campus boycott had gained sufficient momentum that Harvard rejected a $1 million vending contract with Pepsi, after students raised concerns regarding Pepsi's dealings with Burma. ...Later that year, the campaign picked up further momentum when the Third World First organization, with chapters on forty percent of university campuses in the United Kingdom, made the Pepsi boycott a major issue...and with Pepsi being sold in over 800 student unions at the time, the company faced a rapidly growing international boycott. This increasing pressure, at least in part, led to Pepsi's announcement in late April 1996 that it was selling its interest in the Burmese bottling plant. But the story and the Pepsi protests were not finished.

While the student protests were growing in the mid-1990s, substantial support was also building through the Internet for various national "Burma laws." ...[I]t was the combination of the campus boycott, legislation, and the third prong of the campaign—shareholder resolutions—that finally pushed Pepsi to terminate its business relationships with Burma.

Interestingly, much of the Burma campaign against Pepsi went largely unnoticed by the traditional media....

Moreover, the use of the Internet and e-mail is integral to the broader protests against the machinery of international trade generally, as illustrated by the "Battle in Seattle" against the WTO in November 1999 and the demonstrations against the World Bank and IMF in Washington, D.C. in April 2000. A large number of groups with incredibly diverse agendas were involved in those protests and have used the Internet to continue their efforts. These groups range from self-proclaimed anarchist groups, such as the Direct Action Network...to consumer groups, such as Public Citizen; environmental groups; labor unions; groups opposing foreign "sweatshop" labor... think tanks; and international financial reformers....

Some tactics associated with these protests, such as "organized coincidences," "culture jamming," "cyberjamming," or outright vandalism, may have surprised many who were unaware of the rising anti-corporate movement. However, these tactics nevertheless reflect a culture of "direct action" that has been fostered by and spread over the Internet in the 1990s through nonviolent movements, such as Critical Mass and Reclaim the Streets, as well as more militant groups who question whether property damage should even be considered "violence."...

INTERNATIONAL LEGAL DIMENSION

The WTO Director-General, Mike Moore, initially took the lead in responding to the concerns over globalization brought to the fore by the Seattle demonstrators. Even as the protestors were gathering, he initiated a series of steps aimed at better educating the general public about the role and operation of the WTO and making the operation of the WTO more transparent. Beginning with a strong speech to the nongovernmental organizations assembled at the opening of the Seattle Ministerial Conference, Moore hit several concerns head on:

[L]et's be clear about what the WTO does not do. The WTO is not a world government, a global policeman, or an agent for corporate interests. It has no authority to tell countries what trade policies—or any other policies—they should adopt. It does not overrule national laws. It does not force countries to kill turtles or lower wages or employ children in factories. Put simply the WTO is not a supranational government—and no one has any intention of making it one. Our decisions must be made by our Member States, agreements ratified by Parliaments and every two years Ministers meet to supervise our work. There's a bit of a contradiction with people outside saying we are not democratic, when inside over 120 Ministers all elected by the people or appointed

by elected Presidents, decide what we will do....

The real question we should ask ourselves is whether globalization is best left unfettered—dominated by the strongest and most powerful, the rule of the jungle—or managed by an agreed system of international rules, ratified by sovereign governments.

Recognizing that Internet-based tools work both ways, the WTO [made] changes to its Web site.

QUESTIONS

1. The writer notes that the traditional media did not pay much attention to the Burma Pepsi boycott. Why do you think that was so? And why, on the other hand, do you think the press did give plenty of exposure to the anti-WTO protests in Seattle?

2. After the Supreme Court decision, the Free Burma Coalition was forced to re-think its strategy for influencing the political scene in Burma. What can you find out about current efforts from online news or advocacy sites?

3. Many of the protesters who took to the streets to protest free trade and glob-alization in 2000 were disturbed by the way technology has transformed the global economy. Enhanced delivery tracking capacities and "just in time" inventory control allow even small companies with a Web site to compete globally. The Internet makes it possible to contract out information-based services—accounting, legal, recordkeeping—from anywhere, allowing large firms to downsize their core workforce and supplement with part-time or temporary workers. How should the disruptions in workers' lives be addressed: Nationally? Internationally? By law? Some other way? How might employees use the Internet to protect themselves?

4. In April 2000, the same coalition that protested in Seattle took to the streets in Washington, D.C., to confront members of the International Monetary Fund (IMF). Since then, protests against the WTO have continued. Both the WTO and the IMF have expressed concern about their public images. Compare the Web presence of the two organizations, **http://www.wto.org** and **http://www.imf.org**. Does either seem designed to promote transparency? Are they accessible to the public? How do they address concerns about trade and environmentalism? Find out about more recent conflicts over globalization, such as the November 2003 meeting of the Free Trade Area of the Americas (FTAA) in Miami, Florida.

> ## Smart Mobs
>
> Howard Rheingold, a founder of *Hotwired,* the first commercial webzine with a virtual community, has long been associated with the virtual community known as "The Well." Rheingold coined the term "Smart Mobs" to describe groups of people who don't know each other but use technology to act collectively. In 2001, he visited a collective of some five hundred Finns who "flock and blog, socialize and collaborate in geographic and virtual places simultaneously."[17] Aula has sponsored concerts, dinners, and conferences, along with its online presence.

Questions

1. Check out the Aula collective at **http://www.aula.cc/**. What collective action has it taken in recent months? Is this a virtual community—or something else?

2. Locate another Smart Mob and compare its recruitment strategy to that of Aula. Does one strategy seem more ethical than the other? Which would you expect to be more effective?

Writing in 2000, the author of the next reading described China on the verge of entering the global economy through the WTO. At the time, he raised the possibility that the Internet would bring instability to the governing regime.

The Dot.Com(munist) Revolution: Will the Internet Bring Democracy to China?[18]

S. David Cooper

There is a new revolution beginning to stir in the last great country still enamored with the communist ideal. China is one of the world's largest countries by land mass and its largest country by population, and it has waded into the deep, unknown waters of the Internet. China's leaders are taking a huge risk. In a country that could claim virtually any information as a "state secret," the greatest tool ever invented for the promotion of free speech seems like a disaster waiting to happen. Some may think that China has signed a deal with the devil—sold its soul for the financial rewards promised by the Internet. If a free market society is

---

[17] Howard Rheingold, "Helsinki's Aula," *The Feature,* July 17, 2002. http://www.thefeature.com/article.jsp?pageid=15435 (visited July 19, 2003).

[18] 18 *U.C.L.A. Pac.Basin L.J.* 98 (2000).

the devil and communism is China's soul, then they may be right.

China's economy has been described as a three-in-one economy. First, more than 80% of China's people live in an 18th century agrarian society. In many rural villages, especially in the west, roads are mere trails traveled by mule-drawn carts and commerce is done in open-air markets. Other than the obvious political changes, life in these areas has changed little in the past few centuries. Second, China also has a large 20th century industrial society. These industries are reminiscent of ones found in Detroit, Pittsburgh and other "blue-collar" towns. Third, China has only a very small 21st century advanced technology industry. It is on the advanced technology sector that China has placed its hopes for its economic future. A major part of that sector is the Internet.

Although only 14% of Chinese have even heard of the Internet, the number of Internet subscribers in China is exploding. In October, 1997 there were a reported 620,000 Internet subscribers.... Since each Internet account is shared by as many as 10 to 20 people, it is difficult to determine the exact number of Internet users in China, but as of January 2000, there were 35.6 million Chinese e-mail accounts. The number of users is expected to grow to over 100 million by 2003 [a mere 8% of the population.]...Four years ago, China opened its first wang ba, or Internet bar. Now wang bas have sprung up all across the country from Beijing to Shanghai to even the rural outreaches of Tibet.

Acceptance of the technology does not come without problems however. By opening up its communication systems, China has in a sense opened up Pandora's box....

DISSENT FROM WITHOUT

Previously, all news was filtered through the Ministry of Information in Beijing. With a connection to the world outside China, however, its citizens can receive news not permitted by the Ministry of Information. The Internet is "fast fraying the Government's monopoly on information."...China News Digest is a volunteer organization based out of Maryland that bills itself as "The CyberSpace Info Center for Chinese and Friends Worldwide." It reported that traffic to its Web site doubled from 2,000 hits per day to 4,000 hits per day when it ran a package of pictures and commentary marking the anniversary of the Tiananmen Square "unrest." Not surprisingly, the Chinese government blocked access to the site within days. VIP Reference is an electronic newsletter sent out by Chinese democracy advocates in Washington. VIP "sends out reports on dissident activities, essays and reprinted articles on human rights and other issues" to more than 250,000 e-mail addresses in China. It also has a daily news edition that goes to 25,000 Chinese e-mail addresses.

DISSENT FROM WITHIN

The Internet magazine, Tunnel, which is mainly written in China, uses the Internet to e-mail its newsletter to a Silicon Valley address. The newsletter/magazine is then e-mailed back into China to thousands of addresses. This practice makes it difficult if not impossible to track down its authors. Newsletters like these, along with online discussion groups, have been an important link between political activists....Supporters of the banned spiritual group Falun Gong have already used the Internet to organize demonstrations and protests, and in January 2000, a group of disgruntled farmers in a small Chinese village used the Internet to expose a corrupt local Communist Party chief. Because of these problems, Party officials are faced with the near-impossible task of controlling which information is available in China. They have attempted to do this with technology and with regulations.

TECHNOLOGY

Just a couple of years ago when the Chinese Internet was in the planning stage, many of China's leaders supported a domestic version of the Internet that would be "walled-off" from the international Web. This "Intranet" idea was apparently abandoned when it became obvious that this technology would not stop the flow of information into the country. Instead, China has relied on filter programs and blocking technology. International links must go through the Ministry of Post and Telecommunications. There, software searches out sites with certain words or phrases and prevents them from passing further.... Strangely, these blocking techniques are either of variable quality or unevenly applied. At one point, the *New York Times* was blocked, but access to the *Washington Post*, *Playboy* and many X-rated sites were not. Blocking is also inefficient, as some sites, such as VIP

Reference, are mailed from a different American address every day to avoid government attempts to block. Moreover, even though the Web site of the group Human Rights in China is blocked, it still receives dozens of hits from within China per week. China News Digest, also blocked, receives hundreds.

REGULATIONS

Beginning in 1996, China has passed a series of regulations aimed at controlling the use of the Internet. In that year, Premier Li Peng announced a ban on transmission of state secrets, information harmful to state security, and pornography over international computer links. It is also a crime to defame government agencies or to promote separatist movements....There are laws against "hacking" and [bans on using] the Internet to "split the country" (this is the Chinese terminology used to describe the independence movement in Taiwan as well as the supporters of the Dali Lama)....Internet users are required to register with the police. Security agencies have formed special units to fight the spread of dissident information, and all people who use encryption software to protect the privacy of their e-mails are required to register with the government.

[Since t]hese laws apply to both the individual users and the content providers...[m]ost Chinese sites, including its most popular, Sina.com, screen chat room discussions and limit their political news to copies of the official state media. [Internet Service Providers and intra-network systems] do "not hesitate to shut down chat groups where politically sensitive ideas [are] exchanged."...

QUESTIONS

1. Imagine you are a dissident in China. You want to collect accurate news and information, discuss it with others, and act on it. Does the Internet make this process more or less effective? More or less safe?

2. Imagine you are a Chinese government official. How does the advent of the Internet as an engine of domestic protest affect your efforts to maintain the status quo? Is it possible to eliminate the Internet factor? What ethical arguments would surface on either side if the Chinese dissident debated the Chinese official on the question of cyber-censorship?

3. Visit an English translation of Chinese news (try **http://www.cnd.org** or **http://english.peopledaily.com.cn/home.html**). How does it compare to typical American newspapers? To online news services such as **http://www.cnn.com** or **http://www.wired.com**?

4. As this book goes to press, China and Saudi Arabia have perhaps the most restrictive Internet access policies in the world. The Saudi government spent two years building an infrastructure that routes all Internet traffic through a government-controlled "Internet Service Unit". Using software created in San Jose, California, the Saudis block Web pages related to pornography, alcohol, gambling, bombs, and drugs and those insulting to the Islamic religion or Saudi law. According to a study released by the Berkman Center at Harvard University in spring 2002, censored sites included rollingstone.com, women.org, and religioustolerance.org. The Chinese government completely blocked access to some 19,000 Web sites deemed threatening—including major sites on Tibet and Taiwan—and temporarily blocked **Google.com** in 2002. Find out if the Saudis and Chinese have maintained their tight control over the Internet. What, if anything, has changed since 2002?

5. The international war on terrorism has prompted some nations to increase their vigilance over Internet communications. In November 2003, for example, Singapore adopted tough new laws that allow authorities to take action against cyber-terrorists before they strike. Find out if these or similar laws elsewhere have been invoked to thwart terrorism. What impact would you expect such laws to have on dissent?

6. Jonathan L. Zittrain, a director of the Berkman Center, warns that Microsoft is working on "trusted" PCs that will "employ digital gatekeepers that act like the bouncers outside a nightclub, ensuring that only software that looks or behaves a certain way is allowed in. The result will be more reliable computing—and more control over the machine by the manufacturer or operating systems maker, which essentially gives the bouncer her guest list." What dangers do trusted PCs pose to Americans? To those who live in China or Saudi Arabia?

7. Go online and find other examples of political dissent and information-sharing in countries around the world. Some places to start: **http://www.safeweb.com**, **http://www.amnesty.org** or **http://www.indexoncensorship.org**.

Cyber-Activism Assignment

Create a class e-zine or blog. Working with a teammate, choose a current issue being debated in Congress, your state, your university, or your neighborhood—such as energy policy, free trade, health care, or education reform. Then use any search engine to locate the Web site of an advocacy group that is interested in your issue. Once you have found an appropriate group, explore their Web site to learn what actions/activities they are involved in to influence public policy on the issue you have identified.

(a) Post a story on your issue on the e-zine. Include a discussion of one or more advocacy groups (who they are, what they hope to achieve and how). Take a position of your own and include recommendations for actions that can/should be taken to further your position.

(b) Alternatively, find another way to become a cyber-activist and document how you have used the Internet to try to influence policy on your issue.

Computer scientist Philip E. Agre's homepage links to ideas for "designing effective action alerts on the Internet." http://polaris.gseis.ucla.edu/pagre

In 1992, Ross Perot, an undeclared candidate for the U.S. presidency, caused a stir when he proposed an electronic town hall. Opponents feared that "video democracy" might undermine the real thing. Little more than a decade later, in another election campaign, issues of technology and democracy once again caught the attention of traditional media. In his lead-in, National Public Radio host Robert Siegel told viewers that Democratic presidential-candidate Howard Dean set a four-day online fund-raising goal at $250,000—an amount equal to a Republican goal for an invitation-only luncheon featuring Vice President Dick Cheney. Peter Overby takes it from there:

Internet Campaign[19]

Peter Overby, Reporting:

Lunch with Vice President Cheney cost $2,000 a plate, the legal maximum for a presidential campaign donation. Cheney wound up raising $300,000. This afternoon, the Dean campaign was $87,000 ahead of that....Every half-hour today, Dean Webmaster Nico Mele has been reading new totals to Internet coordinator Mathew Gross. Gross posts them as updates on their campaign's Web log, or blog.

---

[19] *All Things Considered*, NPR, July 28, 2003 (transcript available from npr@newsbank.com).

Mr. Gross: Dean team vs. Bush-Cheney update: 6,004 Americans contributed 313, 995. OK, it's up on the blog.

P.O.: The blog amounts to a constant conversation between campaign headquarters and Dean loyalists. Last week, the campaign used the blog to test this fund-raising challenge. Gross posted a message about it and then watched the responses roll in….This is Dean's second Internet fund-raising extravaganza in less than a month. Internet money made him the top Democratic fund-raiser for the quarter ending June 30th, also the major candidate least dependent on wealthy donors. That catches the attention of Carol Darr…[who] notes that almost half of Dean's dollars come in contributions of $200 or less.

Ms. Carol Darr (Director, Institute for Politics, Democracy and the Internet, George Washington University): If you look at somebody, for example, like Bush or Edwards or Graham or Gephardt or Kerry or Lieberman, you know, somewhere around 75 to 80 percent of their money is coming from people who make a hundred thousand dollars or more. And what you have is for the first time, the Internet allows a practical way to change that, and that is a sea change in American presidential politics.

P.O.: But the blog may turn out to be as important as the money. Until now, campaign Web sites usually have let you do two things, volunteer or give money. Significantly, blog central is right outside the door of campaign manager Joe Trippi at the campaign headquarters in Burlington, Vermont. Trippi said last week it's a perfect match: people have come to trust the Internet, activists want to take the initiative and Dean is willing to surrender the usual political top-down management.

Mr. Joe Trippi (Dean Campaign Manager): Do not get in the way of that. Let go of the will, let those people have control of the campaign in their neighborhoods.

P.O.: The campaign doesn't let go of everything. A sign at blog central says "You have the right to remain on message." But Mathew Gross, the head blogger, keeps in touch with an astonishing number of independent Dean groups.

Mr. Gross: Music for Dean, One Father for Dean, Progressive Christians for Dean, Republicans for Dean, Rock for Dean, Students for Dean…the list goes on and on.

P.O.: The other main blogger is Zepher Teachout. She's been busy setting up software so the independent groups can talk to each other.

Ms. Teachout (Dean Campaign Blogger): Like the Georgia group has learned how to be polite and effective in introducing themselves to the Democratic Party. The San Francisco group has done an incredible job with flyering at farmers' markets. And so we're trying to build tools so that the independent groups can communicate best practices with each other.

P.O.: Another independent but coordinated Web site is called Dean Defense Forces. Its subscribers monitor media coverage and can blister journalists with what one participant called nastygrams. Then there are the meetups, monthly

http://www. followthemoney.org was set up to track political contributions in the electronic age.

meetings organized by an outside company. Meetup.com says Dean has 66,000 people signed up, far more than any other candidate. Last week, Nico Mele, the Webmaster, was clicking on photos of recent Dean meetups.

Mr. Mele: Atlanta, Georgia. Daytona Beach, Florida, right? Austin, Texas. This, like, Americans across the country meeting in small groups with people in their communities and trying to figure out how they're going to make Howard Dean the next president of the United States.

P.O.: A task that, if they succeed by doing what they've been doing, could remake American politics more radically than any reform bill passed by Congress. Peter Overby, NPR News, Washington. (Copyright NPR® 2003. Any unauthorized duplication is strictly prohibited.)

In chapter 2 we explored some of the threats to privacy posed by the Internet. In the last reading we return to that idea. The author makes the case that information technology's great promise—to form new links between people and to marshal these connections to promote democratic community—will not be realized unless we create standards to protect personal privacy.

Privacy and Democracy in Cyberspace[20]

Paul M. Schwartz

DEMOCRATIC DELIBERATION

Cyberspace has the potential to emerge as an essential focal point for communal activities and political participation. This development would help counter several negative trends in the United States. Voter turnout is declining; membership in many kinds of traditional voluntary associations is sinking; and a sense of shared community is frayed. Information technology in general and the Internet in particular have the potential to reverse these trends by forming new links between people and marshalling these connections to increase collaboration in democratic life.

Elements of this provocative vision are already being realized. For example, the Internet is being used to modernize the historical and constitutional right of petition. In June 1995, Senator Patrick Leahy became the first Congressperson to bring an Internet-generated petition onto the Senate floor. This document consisted of 1,500 pages listing the names of citizens who had indicated their opposition to a Bill then under debate. In addition, neighborhoods throughout the United States are setting up virtual community bulletin boards. These and other networking ideas are intended to improve dissemination of

---

[20] 52 *Vand.L.Rev.* 1609 (1999).

information about and discussion of community issues such as zoning, new ordinances, and city government.

[Next, Schwartz describes the core beliefs of those who call themselves civic republicans:]

In their view, the good society is a self-governing one based on deliberative democracy. In place of liberalism's emphasis on the individual, civic republicans seek an ongoing social project of authorship of a country's fundamental political values by its people. In searching for ways to construct strong democracy, this group emphasizes common participatory activities, reciprocal respect, and the need for consensus about political issues.

From the civic republican perspective, the true promise of the Internet will not be as a place for electronic commerce, but as a forum for deliberative democracy. Cyberspace appears as the answer to their search for a new hospitable space. It satisfies Benjamin Barber's wish for shared areas "where we can govern ourselves in common without surrendering our plural natures." Cyberspace can provide a space for "civic forums," where, to cite Frank Michaelman's general formulation, "the critical and corrective rigors of actual democratic discourses" can occur. Or, to return to Barber, cyberspace offers the promise to fulfill his call for a "free space in which democratic attitudes are cultivated and democratic behavior is conditioned." Such deliberative democracy will not occur in cyberspace unless certain preconditions are in place. [These include] access to the Internet…[and] information privacy.

In the absence of strong rules for information privacy, Americans will hesitate to engage in cyberspace activities—

including those that are most likely to promote democratic self-rule. Current polls already indicate an aversion on the part of some people to engage even in basic commercial activities on the Internet. Yet, deliberative democracy requires more than shoppers; it demands speakers and listeners. But who will speak or listen when this behavior leaves finely-grained data trails in a fashion that is difficult to understand or anticipate? Put differently, when widespread and secret surveillance becomes the norm, the act of speaking or listening takes on a different social meaning.

[T]he role of town crier in cyberspace is often secretly assigned—a person can take on this role, whether or not she seeks it or knows afterwards that she has been given it. Already one leading computer handbook, the Internet Bible, concludes its description of the low level of privacy in cyberspace with the warning, "Think about the newsgroups you review or join—they say a lot about you."

[Yet] deliberative democracy…demands that access to these data be guaranteed in many circumstances. Such information disclosure is needed for public accountability; democratic community relies on a critical assessment of public persons and events. To return to the town crier metaphor, the release of at least some personal information about speakers at the public square is needed under some circumstances.…

INDIVIDUAL SELF-DETERMINATION

Beyond democratic deliberation, information use in cyberspace poses an important threat to a second value necessary for life in a democracy.…The health of a democratic society depends both on the group-oriented process of democratic deliberation and the functioning of each person's capacity for self-governance.

[W]ithout the right kind of privacy rules, the potential of cyberspace for promoting self-governance will be lost. The fashion in which society and law insulate certain acts and places from data collection affects the process of development of identity. The need is to insulate an individual's reflective facilities from certain forms of manipulation and coercion. Privacy rules for cyberspace must set aside areas of limited access to personal data in order to allow individuals, alone and in association with others, to deliberate about how to live their lives.

[D]emocracy requires more than group deliberation at a town square located either in Real Space or in cyberspace. It requires individuals with an underlying capacity to form and act on their notions of the good in deciding how to live their lives....Communal life requires something beyond isolated decision making—self-governance takes place in individuals who are not located on discrete behavioral islands, but are tied to others and necessarily open to influence through outside persuasion.

Social life's give-and-take is not merely compatible with individual autonomy, but an essential factor in it because life is lived among others. Prior and ongoing commitments make a difference in the choices we make and in the hierarchy of our goals....

QUESTIONS

1. According to Schwartz, what is needed for a deliberative democracy? How might cyberspace enhance or diminish the possibility of democracy?

2. What connections does Schwartz identify between Internet privacy and democracy?

CHAPTER PROBLEMS

1. The Internet Security Foundation is dedicated to educating the public about information security. Consultants to its Tiger Team project sharpen the skills of young hackers by working together to analyze system security risks lawfully and ethically. Participants are bound by an honor code that insists they not create mischief outside their labs. Is this a good idea? What are the benefits and risk of such a program?

2. In the summer of 2003, SoBig.F wormed its way onto computers around the world until anti-hackers identified it and distributed a "patch" to cure the virus. At the peak of the epidemic, messages generated by SoBig.F accounted for 73 percent of global email. The outbreak stirred new interest in "trusted computers" that would be unable to run any software without a specific cryptographic signature. Several months later, Microsoft announced another effort: A $5 million antivirus reward program to encourage people to identify the "sabateurs of cyberspace"—those who release viruses on the Internet. Do either of these approaches seem consistent with the common metaphors for cyberspace? Identify the harms/benefits of each approach. Can you think of any better solutions to the virus problem?

3. Michael Robertson, founder of MP3.com, also started Lindows.com. His goal: to create an operating system that will run programs designed for MS Windows on the Linux operating system. Find out how Microsoft has responded to this latest competition. What do computer experts say about Lindows these days?

4. PCs have built-in excess capacity, not unlike the human brain. A number of years ago, someone learned to harness this power by plugging into thousands of individual PCs and re-directing their processing power to other uses. This led to distributed-computer networks such as United Devices and Entropia, which began by recruiting individuals willing to allow their excess computing power to be used for good causes such as AIDS research. In the spring of 2001, United Devices made news headlines when it decided to become profitable by re-selling some of the collected computer power to profit-making businesses. Is it ethical for them to do so without the consent of those who signed up? Should they reimburse every individual, or is it enough to reward only those computer owners who provide the most processing power? Should such practices be regulated by the U.S. government? In some other way? Check out a peer-to-peer site such as **http://www.ud.com** or **http://www.entropia.com** to learn their current policies. Do they satisfy your ethical concerns?

5. Calls for electoral reform in the U.S. rose after the close presidential election of 2000. Some have suggested that one way to enhance voter turnout is to allow electronic voting.

(a) Can you identify problems and benefits associated with electronic voting? Find out about the logistics of online voting through **http://www.election.com** or a similar site.

(b) In early 2003, voters in a suburb of Geneva, Switzerland, were given the option of casting their ballots on the Internet. Find out how well the experiment worked.

(c) Technology may lead the way to anti-democratic developments. Florida was the first state to create, computerize, and purge lists of allegedly "ineligible" voters. Prior to the 2000 election, more than 94,000 voters—disproportionately black or Hispanic—were removed from Florida's central voting files. Is this a reason to oppose computerizing our democracy?

For information on pro-
posals for voting the
Internet, phone and
mail see: http://lorne.
cranor.org/voting/
hotlist.html

6. Diebold Election Systems makes voting machines. The company became the center of controversy in 2003 when opponents of electronic voting systems posted 15,000 Diebold e-mail messages and internal memos, including discussions of bugs in company software and warnings that its network is vulnerable to hackers. Students at the Swarthmore Coalition for the Digital Commons were warned to take down the documents. An anticensorship organization, Freenet, then used a peer-to-peer service similar to Kazaa and Napster to post the documents.

(a) What ethical arguments can you make in favor of posting the memos?

(b) Against such postings?

(c) Find out what has happened to the Diebold controversy and what impact, if any, it has had on the movement in favor of electronic voting.

(d) Find out about pending legislation that would require electronic voting machines to provide voters with a paper receipt of their vote. What arguments can you make for and against such a law?

7. Noah Zatz has called for sidewalks in cyberspace, arguing that it is not only public forums such as parks and malls but "the places in between" that enable ordinary citizens to engage one another in ways essential to a free democratic culture. He compares the material world, in which we face bottlenecks and blockades as we travel from place to place—a pamphleteer we pass by on our way to the airport, a newsstand next to the subway that can't be avoided—to the geography of cyberspace, where distance, adjacency, and fixity take on new meanings. Cyberdistance, he argues, is both contingent and compressible.

After a first journey to a new site, a simple "bookmark" makes your second visit just a step across the street. Except that there is no street to cross. The lack of direction and continuity in cyberspace means that there are no fixed places that lie between any other two, nor is the environment of one place affected much by any other. There are no neighbors in cyberspace and, there-fore, no blockades, no loud noise bothering you from the disco next door, and no neighbor's tree dropping fruit on your side of the fence.[21]

Would any of the following help to create cyberwalks?

(a) open, electronic message boards

(b) repeal of all anti-spam laws

(c) modification of software so that "speakers" seeking access to users could flash an icon on a user's screen, similar to the ads that appear when a person logs onto **http://www.juno.com** or **http://www.netzero.com**

Which of these suggestions would enhance democracy? Is the idea of free-speech-in-public-places too American to impose on the world?

8. India's $10-billion software and services industry continued to grow, even during the technology slowdown in the U.S. in the early part of the 21st century. In part, this is because of outsourcing. More than half of the world's top 500 companies outsource work to India.

Microsoft opened its first offices in India in 1987. Today, its software development center in Hyderaband is the only Microsoft facility outside the U.S.

In recent years, Indian software companies have increasingly opted for Linux, setting up development centers to make Linux-based software. In 2002, Microsoft chair Bill Gates announced a three-year, $400 million initiative in India, including partnering with Indian states to create ten information technology centers, investing $100 million in the company's Hyderaband center, and spending $20 million to train teachers and students on computers and software at government-run schools. Is this simple philanthropy—or smart business? What ethical concerns does the situation in India raise?

9. (a) A new form of computer mischief emerged in 2000 when hackers remotely commandeered hundreds of personal computers connected to the Internet and used them to deluge **http://www.Amazon.com**, **http://www.Yahoo.com**, and **http://www.eBay.com** with hostile data that bogged down the sites. Are these "distributed denial of service" pranks unethical? Should they be stopped? If so, how? By voluntarily re-designing Internet browsers to better guard against them or by a law requiring such safeguards?

---

[21] Noah D. Zatz, "Sidewalks in Cyberspace: Making Space for Public Forums in the Electronic Environment,"12 *Harv.J.L.& Tech.* 149 (1998).

(b) In June 2001, the press reported that the new edition of Windows, scheduled for release that fall, would make it easier to pull off a distributed denial of service. Would it be ethical for Microsoft to ignore the problem? Should the law require the company to address it?

10. According to a UN report issued in November 2003, most of the world's nations have their own Web sites. Only 18 countries, many in Africa, were completely offline. In the U.S., even state and local governments are making increased use of the Internet to provide government services. Find out what services are offered online by your own local officials. What harms and benefits can you see from this increasing use of the Internet by governments?

Index

A

access control, 147
accountability vs. privacy, 66
ad-free-ads, 164
affirmative action, 207
airports, face recognition
    software, 62
alienation, 257–258
all-purpose ID cards, 62
AlterNet, 61–62
AML vendors, 63
anonymity, 104
        Internet, 68–69
        right to read anonymously,
        105–107
anti-spam measures, 154
AOL and online consumer
    privacy, 73
Article 1, Section 8. *See*
    intellectual property law
authorship, 193
avatars, 146

B

Barlow, John Perry, 17–18, 21, 90
Bertin, Joan, 108
biometric identifiers in ID cards,
    63
biometrics, errors in, 64
biometrics technology, 62

Birkerts, Sven, 198
Brin, David interview, 66–70
broadcast media, 19
Buranen, Lise, 182
Burma laws, 260–261

C

Cannon, Graham, 109
categorical imperatives, 33
CEOs of defense companies,
    earnings, 64–65
Children, kidnapping, 63
Chillingeffects.org, 98
China and the Internet, 264, 267
        dissent, 265
        regulations, 266
Chon, Margaret, 118
click-wrap license, 165–166
code
        and copyright law, 6 8
        as intellectual property,
        4–9
Cohen, Julie E., 105
Communication, limited and
    protected, 52
computer ethics, ten
    commandments of, 23
Congress
        Courtney Love, 15–17
        Michael Eisner, 10–13
consumer profiling, 72–73

content filtering, 110–112
    discussion boards,
       116–117
    international examples,
       122
cookies, limiting, 68
copyright law
    and code, 6–8
    digital
    enforcing in the digital
       age, 18–19
    management in
       cyberspace, 105–107
    plagiarism, 193
    timeline, 5
corporate cybersmearing, 96–98.
    See also cybersmearing
cost of hacker attacks, 226
counterterrorism, security vs.
    privacy, 54–56
cryptography, 20–21
cyber-activism, 258–259, 268
    international legal
       dimension, 262–263
    Massachusetts Burma law
       and Internet advocacy,
       260–261
Cyberangels.org, 127
cybercrime, eBay.com, 75–76
cyberethics
    Napster, 24–29
    plagiarism, 184
    sharing or cheating,
       179

    stolen content online,
       194–197
cyber-harassment, 121–124
cyberhoaxes, 99–103
cyberlaw, 34–37
cybernorms
    netiquette, 131–133
cybersmearing, 90–91, 95,
    102–103
    corporate, 96–98
cyberspace, 9
cyberspeech
    Encyclopedia of Jihad,
       92–94
    freedom of expression,
       90–91
    libel, 87–89
    netiquette, 131–133

D

defense against peeping Toms,
    66
defense companies, CEO earn-
    ings, 64–65
democracy and the Internet, 256
    alienation, 257–258
deontological ethics, music file
    sharing, 29–32
Diamond, Joe, 110
digital copyrights, 18
digital divide, 212
digital media, copyrights, 10–13
digitized property, protecting,
    17–18

direct-to-consumer sales
(pharmaceuticals), 139–144
discussion boards, content
control, 116–117
distance learning, 197–199
business and education
partnership, 211–214
concerns, 200
consumer convenience,
208
educational delivery
methods, 206–207
Havasupai Indian
reservation, 204
non-profit/for-profit
partnerships, 215–217
OpenCourseWare project
(OCW), 210–211
racelessness, 209
recent research, 203
remaking of the
American university,
201–202, 205
domain names, 236–237
dot-cons, 156
Dreyfuss, Rochelle Cooper, 190

E
eBay
content filtering, 122
cybercrime, 75–76
e-commerce
ad-free-ads, 164
click-wrap license,
165–166

direct-to-consumer sales,
139
e-mediation, 171–174
ethics, 137–138
fraud, 156–158
pharmaceuticals,
140–144
privacy concerns, 72–73
spam, 153–155
tobacco sales, 159–162
trust, 145–150
UCITA, 165–170
varying laws, 163
word of mouse, 151–152
economy of verbs, 21
editors, 109
education. *See* e-learning
Eisner, Michael, 10–13
e-learning, 179
academic honesty, 181
business and education
partnership, 211–217
collaborative research,
190–193
distance learning,
197–211
guidelines for Internet
use, 221
plagiarism, 182–188
sharing or cheating, 180
stolen Web content,
195–197
student use/misuse of
Internet, 218–219

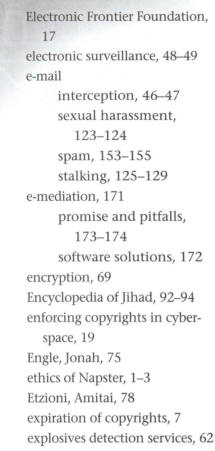

Electronic Frontier Foundation, 17
electronic surveillance, 48–49
e-mail
    interception, 46–47
    sexual harassment, 123–124
    spam, 153–155
    stalking, 125–129
e-mediation, 171
    promise and pitfalls, 173–174
    software solutions, 172
encryption, 69
Encyclopedia of Jihad, 92–94
enforcing copyrights in cyber-space, 19
Engle, Jonah, 75
ethics of Napster, 1–3
Etzioni, Amitai, 78
expiration of copyrights, 7
explosives detection services, 62

F

face recognition software, 62–64
fair use, 8
Feder, Barnaby, 99
Federal Trade Commission (FTC), 157
file sharing (music industry), 28–29
filters, 107–110

GLAAD, 111
governmental control, 113
PICS, 112
self-regulation, 109
use of spreading, 112
fog of war(quotes), 55–56
fraud, 156
    avoiding, 157
    FTC, 157
    international modem dialing, 158
freedom of expression, 90–91
    Encyclopedia of Jihad, 92–94
freedom of speech, 89
    child protection, 114
    cyber stalking, 125–129
    cyberspace, 115
    filters, 108–112
    interactive online forums, 115
    racism, 118–121
    Role-playing scenarios, 130
    sexual harassment, 123–124
    spam, 153
FTC (Federal Trade Commission), 157
future of Internet regulation, 244–245
future of the net, 250–251

G

genetic testing, 44–45
GIA (Government Information Awareness), 71
Ginsburg, Jane C., 194
GLAAD, content filters, 111
Global Business Dialogue on E-Commerce, 12
government
    cyberspeech regulation, 91
    Internet filtering, 113
governmental privacy breaches, 55

H

hacker's ethic, 22, 228
hackers of open source software, 229
hate speech, 121
    auction site filtering, 122
Heffner, Jason, 111
Himanen, Pekka, 228
Hit Man, 93
hoaxes, 100–101
Hole, 15–17

I

ID cards
    all-purpose, 62
    biometric identifiers, 63
identity
    online trust, 146
    transparency, 147
information technology. *See* IT
infotainment telesector (the), 256
institutional liability, 196
intangible property, 7
intellectual property
    code, 4–9
    collaborative research, 190–193
    law, 3–9
    Napster, 1–3
    payment for, 20
    propertization, 242
    redefining, 21
international modem dialing, 158
Internet
    absence of material conditions, 248
    accessing, 227
    anonymity, 68–69
    as feudal society, 253–254
    bringing democracy to China, 264–267
    cyber-activism, 258–263
    cybernorms, 132
    democracy, 256–258
    dependence on, 246–249
    e-commerce, 137–138
    future of, 250–251
    guidelines for use, 221

individual self-
determination,
271–272
law, 238–241
Privatization, 242
regulation, 235–237
self-regulation, 240
student use/misuse,
218–219
technological controls,
243
Western Frontier
metaphor, 252
interoperability, 233
IT (information technology), 43
privacy, 43–47

J – K – L

Kant, Immanuel, 30
kidnapping children, 63

law
borders in cyberspace,
238–241
cybercrime enforcement,
75–76
electronic surveillance,
49
future of the Internet,
244–245
lawsuits (music file sharing), 28
online drug sales, 143
online tobacco sales, 160

plagiarism, 185–188
varying between states,
163
Lee, Rebecca K., 125
legislation (anti-spam), 153
Lessig, Lawrence, 4–9
Levine, Arthur, 201
libel (BIG case study), 87–89
Library Bill of Rights, 114
limiting cookies, 68
Linux, 228
lookup organizations, 67
Love, Courtney, 15–17
lurkers, 127
Lyndersen, Kari, 61–62

M

Major, April Mara, 131
managing copyrights in cyber-
space, 105–107
Martin, David, 64
Mayer-Schonberger, Viktor, 244
McGuire, Breffini, 63
medical information, 78–80
MIB (Medical Information
Bureau), 79
Michael A. Smyth v. The
Pillsbury Company, 46–47
microchips (subdermal), 63
Microsoft, 230
dominance, 232
evolution, 231
Microsoftsucks.com, 98
Mill, John Stuart, 24

Minow, Martha, 215
morality of music file sharing, 33
Moran, Rachel F., 206
music file sharing,
    moral issues, 33
    industry perspective,
      10–13

N

Napster, 1–3, 24–25
    cyberlaw, 35–37
    deontological ethics,
      29–32
    indie musicians, 28–29
    industry perspective,
      10–13
    recording industry
      response, 27
    royalty dispute, 26
national identity cards, 60
netiquette, 131–133
    private conference
      operators, 117
Nissenbaum, Helen, 145
notHarvard.com, 214

O

O'Brien, Christine Neylon, 96
OCW (OpenCourseWare
    project), 210–211
online conferences, 115–117
open source software, 227
    hackers, 229
    interoperability, 233
    Linux, 228

OpenCourseWare project
    (OCW), 210–211

P

PATRIOT II, 55–56
payment for virtual product,
    19–20
peeping Toms, defense against,
    66
Pelco, Inc., 62
personal autonomy, 50–51
pharmaceuticals, 141
PICS, 112–113
piracy. *See* music file sharing
Pirates of Encryption, 11
plagiarism, 193
    cultural aspects of, 183
    theft law, 185–188
plagiarism.org, 181
Post, David, 34–37
privacy, 43, 74, 104. *See also*
  anonymity
    counterterrorism con-
      cerns, 54–56
    David Brin interview,
      66–70
    and democracy in
      cyberspace, 270
    eBay privacy policy, 76
    electronic surveillance,
      48–49
    e-mail interception,
      46–47
    functions of, 50–53

genetic testing, 44–45

medical information, 78–79

national identity cards, 60

online consumers, 72–73

opposition to reform, 80

personal information online, 77

surveillance, 85

TIA, 58, 59

vs. accountability, 66

privacy paradox, 80

privacyalliance.org, 74

PrivacyExchange.org, 74

private information

publishing, 68–70

selling, 67

private sector in war on terror, 61–62

privatization, 242

Prodigy content control, 116–117

propertization, 242

property (intangible), 7

protected communication, 52

protecting

digitized property, 17–18

intellectual property, 3–9

pseudoanonymity, 69

publishing of private informa-tion, 68–70

R

racism, 118

assimilation, 120

hate speech, 121

passing, 119

racelessness of distance learning, 209

Reder, Margo E. K., 96

reforming privacy regulations, 80

regulation (Internet), 235

China, 266

cookies, 68

domain names, 236–237

future concerns, 244–245

law and borders, 238–241

self-regulation, 240

technological controls, 243

S

Safire, William, 60

security

cost of hackers, 226

counterterrorism and privacy, 54–56

cryptography, 20–21

cyber-stalking, 127

filters. *See* filters

fraud, 157

trust (e-commerce), 148

WiFi systems, 234

self-evaluation, 52

self-regulation

free speech, 109

of the net, 240

selling private information, 67

sexual harassment, 123–124

shrink-wrap license, 165

smart mobs, 264

Smolla, Rodney A., 92

Sobel, David L., 104

software

e-mediation, 172

face recognition, 64

face recognition software, 62

filtering. *See* filters

Microsoft, 232

open source, 227–229, 233

plagiarism detection, 181

shrink-wrap license, 165

spam, 153

anti-spam measures, 154

management of, 155

spillover, 248

spy technology, 77

stalking, 121

e-mail, 125–129

Steinhardt, Barry, 112

subdermal microchips, 63

surveillance, 48

law, 49

relationship to privacy, 85

technology, 63–64

T

tele-medicine, 141

ten commandments of computer ethics, 23

territorial borders, 238–241

terrorism, 93

Terrorism Information Awareness (TIA), 57–59

The USA PATRIOT Act, Impact on AML Vendors and the Market, 63

TIA (Terrorism Information Awareness), 57–59

timeline of copyright law, 5

tobacco commerce, 159

FCTC, 162

marketing, 160

national/state regulation, 161

trademarks, 236

trust (online), 150

access control, 147

e-commerce, 145–146

surveillance, 148

transparency of identity, 147

vulnerability, 149

U

UCITA (Uniform Computer Information Transaction Act), 165

opposition to, 167–169

re-drafting, 170

Ulrich, Lars, 26
United for a Fair Economy, 64
USA PATRIOT Act, 55–56
USA*ENGAGE, 258
utilitarianism, 23, 24

V

values in cyberspace, 9
vendors (AML), 63
Viisage, 62
virtual anonymity, 107
virtual universities, 208
Visionis, 62
Volokh, Eugene, 115

W – X – Y – Z

W.T.O cyberhoax, 99–101
war on terror, 61–62

Web cramming, 158
Web sites
    cyberhoaxes, 99–101
    stolen content, 194–197
WEP (Wireless Equivalency
    Protocol), 234
WiFi systems, 234
Wireless Equivalency Protocol
    (WEP), 234
word of mouse, 151–152
works for hire, 17

Yahoo!, content filtering, 122